Why Forage?

HUNTERS AND GATHERERS IN
THE TWENTY-FIRST CENTURY

Edited by Brian F. Codding and Karen L. Kramer

D1231199

SCHOOL FOR ADVANCED RESEARCH PRESS • SANTA FE

UNIVERSITY OF NEW MEXICO PRESS • ALBUQUERQUE

Library of Congress Cataloging-in-Publication Data
Names: Codding, Brian F., editor. | Kramer,
Karen, editor.
Title: Why forage? : hunters and gatherers in the
twenty-first century / edited by Brian F. Codding
and Karen L. Kramer.
Description: Santa Fe : School for Advanced
Research Press ; Albuquerque : University of
New Mexico Press, 2016. | Series: School for
Advanced Research Advanced Seminar Series |
Includes bibliographical references and index.
Identifiers: LCCN 2015050549 (print) | LCCN
2016014134 (ebook) | ISBN 9780826356963
(paperback) | ISBN 9780826356970 (electronic)
Subjects: LCSH: Hunting and gathering
societies. | Subsistence farming. | Subsistence
hunting. | Economic anthropology. | BISAC:
SOCIAL SCIENCE / Anthropology / General.
Classification: LCC GN388 .W58 2016 (print) |
LCC GN388 (ebook) | DDC 306.3/64—dc23
LC record available at http://lccn.loc.gov
/2015050549

Cover photograph: *Pumé foragers* by
Russell D. Greaves

FIGURES

TABLES

First and foremost, we are grateful for the hunter-gatherers who have opened their lives to us. We greatly appreciate having been able to spend many years living, working, weighing, measuring, and observing in their camps and communities. Their patience, and often humor, in answering endless questions and sharing many details of their lives has been remarkable. More lasting than the data that we have collected, their gifts of friendship, generosity, and wisdom have taught us about the many ways to look at the world.

Thanks to all of the seminar participants and chapter contributors for their dedication to this project. This book could not have come together without their tireless efforts. We very much appreciate the opportunity provided by the School for Advanced Research for us to convene in Santa Fe and discuss this pressing issue that is close to all of the participants who have spent years working to understand hunter-gatherer adaptations. We thank two anonymous reviewers for their thoughtful comments on each chapter. The manuscript greatly benefitted from the editorial assistance of Sarah Soliz and others at SAR Press; their attention to detail was critical to its completion. Special thanks to Ellyse Simmons for her diligent work on figure I.1.

Hunters and Gatherers in the Twenty-First Century

KAREN L. KRAMER AND BRIAN F. CODDING

Introduction

Prior to the onset of the Holocene about twelve thousand years ago, humans shared the globe only with other hunter-gatherers and made their living exclusively by collecting wild resources.[1] With domestication, some foragers transitioned to agriculture and pastoralism. But this transition was not inevitable. Many hunter-gatherers continued to forage, while others pursued a mixed economy combining wild resources with the low-level use of domesticated plants and animals. By the 1960s hunter-gatherers were estimated to represent 1 percent of the world's population (Lee and Devore 1968). Due to rapid population growth, habitat transformation, and globalization, that percentage is far smaller today. But one thing is certain: hunter-gatherers are still here.

Foraging persists in the contemporary world as a viable economic strategy in remote regions as well as within the bounds of developed nation-states. This fact frames the central question we address in this book: given the economic alternatives available in the twenty-first century, why do some choose to maintain their hunting and gathering lifeways? Rather than viewing the decline in hunting and gathering as conclusive, the contributors to this book examine the decisions made by modern-day foragers to sustain a predominantly hunting and gathering way of life. In this introductory chapter, we briefly discuss the history of hunter-gatherer research, present the current status of some hunter-gatherer populations, and outline the main findings discussed in this book (figure I.1).

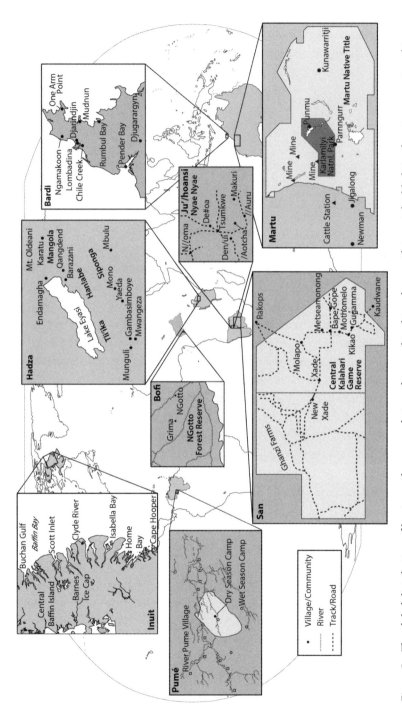

Figure I.1. The global distribution of hunter-gatherer populations discussed in this volume with inserts highlighting locations mentioned in each chapter. Map by the authors, compiled by Ellyse Simmons.

Hunter-Gatherer Studies

The study of hunter-gatherers is thoroughly treated in a number of recent and classic publications (Bettinger 1991; Binford 2001; Ingold et al. 1988; Kelly 2013; Lee and Daly 2005; Lee and Devore 1968; Panter-Brick et al. 2001; Schrire 1984; Winterhalder and Smith 1981). Here we focus on those historic aspects that have shaped contemporary views of foraging economies and were instrumental in launching our seminar and book on twenty-first-century hunter-gatherers.

As European explorers, naturalists, and colonizers began traveling the world, they returned with stories, artifacts, and descriptions of other cultures. Hunter-gatherers entered the public's imagination as people who were living in either a Rousseauean heaven or a Hobbesian hell. Scholarly interest in hunter-gatherers, however, languished. Until the late 1800s, antiquarians were interested in Egyptian, Greek, Roman, and Chinese history—the visible archaeological and spectacular artistic human achievements. But as anthropology distinguished itself as a discipline in the latter part of the nineteenth century, ethnographic depictions became more probing and detailed, emphasizing the cultural uniqueness of different societies (Boas 1888a; Roth 1899; Smyth 1878). This particularistic view shifted again in the late nineteenth and early twentieth centuries with the resurgence of evolutionary thinking, which placed an emphasis on the relationship between environments and cultural variation (Kroeber 1939; Steward 1936, 1938; White 1959). While links between environmental, biological, and cultural variation remained largely descriptive through the mid-twentieth century, as anthropologists working in different parts of the world began to compare ethnographic notes, researchers recognized that more exacting field methods and quantitative analyses were needed to make meaningful cross-cultural comparisons.

The watershed "Man the Hunter" conference in 1966 brought together anthropologists working with foragers in Africa, Australia, South and North America, and the Arctic and Subarctic (Lee and Devore 1968). When researchers compared their empirical observations from different regions of the world, it was clear that hunter-gatherers lived in very different environments and that no one group encapsulated all of this variation. Their appreciation of this diversity raised questions about the degree to which women worked, how much time hunter-gatherers spent in subsistence activities, and assumptions about the importance of meat. These questions invigorated the synthetic study of hunter-gatherers, eventually giving rise to the ethnoarchaeologically and ecologically oriented research of the 1970s and 1980s (Binford 1977, 1984, 2001; Binford and

O'Connell 1984; Gould 1967, 1968, 1978, 1981; Lee 1979, 1984; O'Connell 1987, 1995; Oswalt 1973; Yellen 1977). Inspired by new theoretical (e.g., MacArthur 1972; MacArthur and Pianka 1966) and methodological (e.g., Altmann 1974) work in biology, these research programs brought ethology, behavioral observation, and systematic demographic and biological methods to the study of human foragers (Altman 1987; Hames and Vickers 1982; Hawkes et al. 1982; Howell 1979; Kaplan and Hill 1992; O'Connell and Hawkes 1981, 1984; E. Smith 1991; Smith and Winterhalder 1992; Winterhalder and Smith 1981).

Alongside these developments in hunter-gatherer research, new hominin fossils were being discovered in Africa, Asia, and Europe (Klein 2009). In order to understand variability in the hominin fossil record and the origins of our species, researchers turned to contemporary foragers to shed light on past hunter-gatherer adaptations (Harding and Teleki 1981; Isaac 1978; Lovejoy 1981). Living hunter-gatherers again came to be seen as relics of the past, models who could breathe life into the fossil record. Scholarly interest in hunter-gatherers grew because "they represent an ancient stage of human culture—a living snapshot of human life in its oldest, more primitive state" (Bettinger 1991:1). The further people lived from what was considered a "pristine" setting, the less useful they were for explaining past hunter-gatherer adaptations. The problems inherent in this line of thinking and in defining what is a pristine or true hunter-gatherer are obvious. The inevitable end point of this perspective is to conclude that "the very subject matter of . . . investigation is disappearing" (Burch 1994:442). One of our incentives for convening a group of researchers at the School for Advanced Research (SAR) was to counter this misconception about hunter-gatherers and hunter-gatherer studies and to discuss the state of foraging in the twenty-first century.

COMMON MISCONCEPTIONS ABOUT HUNTER-GATHERERS

Several commonly held academic and popular suppositions about foragers reflect this focus on the "untouched" hunter-gatherer. First, modern hunter-gatherers are frequently cast as a direct analogy to people living in the past, often millions of years ago, without attention to those attributes that have likely persisted, changed, or are environmentally sensitive or plastic (Hill et al. 2014; Marlowe 2010). Because hunter-gatherers live closer to the energetic, technological, demographic, and social conditions of the past than do people living in most agricultural and urban settings, they allow us to observe how humans spend their time, make a living, grow up, reproduce, and die under these conditions. But they are not relics of the past. This distinction is a subtle but important one that Binford (1977, 1984, 1985, 1988) and others (e.g., Schrire 1984) have explicitly and forcefully made. Some modern traits have a deep ancestry, while others are the outcome of more recent changes. For example, many derived human life history traits—such as early weaning, short birth intervals, multiple overlapping young, improved juvenile survival, and long life-span—have been evolving over the last several million years. Consequently, life history traits observed in contemporary foragers may not adequately reflect the selective pressures that produced derived behaviors such as food sharing, cooperative breeding, pooled energy budgets, non-kin cooperation, pair-bonding, and male parental investment (Kramer and Otárolla-Castillo 2015). Other density-dependent behaviors, such as broad-spectrum foraging adaptations (Flannery 1969; Morgan 2015; Stiner 2001), may not emerge until more modern demographic pressures arise.

Skepticism that the present is a direct analogy of the past leads to our second point that a characterization of hunter-gatherers as isolated from the forces of change obscures what hunter-gatherers are best at—flexibility. Hunting and gathering is successful because it incorporates many dietary and social options, not because it excludes them. Hunter-gatherers have been making decisions about whether to diversify and replace traditional resources and strategies for as long as they can be identified in the archaeological record. Throughout the Pleistocene, foragers adopted novel technologies, intensified their resource base, and moved into an ever-increasing number of environments (Klein 2009). Sometimes they added new resources or strategies to their diet, and sometimes they replaced previously traditional foods and technologies. Since the advent of domestication approximately eleven thousand years ago, hunter-gatherers knew of and had contact with neighboring food producers. Likewise, the ethnographic record indicates that foragers often live in close proximity to and interact with food producers without themselves becoming food producers (B. Smith 2001). Thus, hunter-gatherers have always made decisions about what to change and retain in their lives.

Third, the ideal of a pure hunter-gatherer, uncontaminated by outside influences, is at odds with the archaeological and ethnographic records. Contemporary foragers, like those in the past, live in an ecologically but also a socially dynamic world. Long-distance exchange networks have been identified archaeologically by the Upper Paleolithic in parts of Europe and Asia and by the

Middle Stone Age in Africa (Shea 2011:T2). This research often focuses on non-food items, but we also have evidence that different food economies have been interacting for a long time. Transitions from the first use of cultigens visible in the archaeological record to systems reliant on domesticates often occurred across several thousands of years (Piperno and Pearsall 1998; Richerson et al. 2001; B. Smith 2001; Winterhalder and Kennett 2006). By at least eleven thousand years ago, foragers shared regions of the world with people pursuing very different subsistence strategies. Moreover, we have archaeological evidence of hunter-gatherers persisting long after agricultural societies began to expand (Bollongino et al. 2013; Jochim 1998). Exchanges between hunter-gatherers and non-hunter-gatherers are also well documented in the historical record. Best-known cases include the Ituri and Philippine foragers and farmers (Bailey and Aunger 1989; Hart and Hart 1986; Headland and Bailey 1991; Peterson 1978). While the origins of domestication literature often emphasizes an inevitable transition from foraging to agriculture following access to cultigens, what is interesting about relationships between farmers and foragers is that they are often long term and stable (Lupo, chapter 6). In other words, foragers do not necessarily become farmers because of their interactions. Archaeological and historical evidence suggests that many aspects of a hunting and gathering lifeway are worth conserving, and transitioning to another mode of subsistence can be uncertain.

While modern hunter-gatherers often are portrayed as Stone Age people, especially by nonspecialists who may be unfamiliar with contemporary debates, this portrayal obfuscates what is really interesting about them: hunters and gatherers have always lived on a transitional landscape, adapting to new social and environmental conditions, interacting with and being influenced by other groups and new ideas, and making decisions about what is worth retaining from and changing about their subsistence economy and social organization. Hunting and gathering has been a successful strategy throughout human history because it incorporates a broad array of food acquisition strategies and social behaviors. Modern foragers are part of this continuum, making economic and lifestyle decisions as they are exposed to novel situations. This opens the door to a more dynamic study of hunter-gatherers in the twenty-first century.

Hunter-Gatherers in the Twenty-First Century

As they have always been, hunter-gatherer lifeways today are highly variable and adaptable. Some rely more heavily on traditional technologies, subsistence practices, and social networks, while others have incorporated novel technologies, foraging strategies, and social interactions. Regardless of the level of change in their daily lives, however, all twenty-first-century hunter-gatherers now live within nation-states. Some groups have been encouraged or forced into permanent settlements by governments, nongovernmental organizations (NGOs), or missionaries. Others live in countries that provide economic, health-related, or educational subsidies. Still others are virtually unrecognized by national or regional governments and have no interaction with health-care providers, educational systems, or the market economy.

Although they may have economic autonomy, many hunter-gatherers do not have a political or legal voice within their governing state. In some cases nations or NGOs, intentionally or not, have facilitated the integration of hunter-gatherers into regional and national economies and the wage labor market. In many cases, hunter-gatherers have no legal or exclusive rights to land, and their territories have been opened to multinational corporations and tourists. Intrusion by outsiders may lead to conflicts of interest between foraging populations and national governments, which enforce policies that restrict access to land, resources, or cultural practices.

Although these contemporary parameters have altered the conditions under which hunters and gatherers find themselves today, they do not keep us from learning about subsistence decisions and their social implications in these populations. Indeed, current conditions pose a number of intriguing questions. For example, the persistence of wild food subsistence in combination with non-foraged elements provides valuable information and presents a kind of natural experiment about how foragers make decisions. The contributors to this volume evaluate how individuals within traditional foraging populations respond to these impacts, which may be predominantly economic, social, regulatory, or some combination thereof, depending on the specific case.

WHO AND WHAT THIS BOOK IS ABOUT

Although we do not pursue typological issues in this volume, we do need to clarify who this book is about since all human societies have an ancestry in hunting and gathering and many economies today incorporate some elements of foraging. Most agriculturalists and horticulturalists, for example, also collect wild resources. Some well-known examples include the Yanomamo, Tsimane, and Machiguenga peoples. Indeed, foraging has recently increased in popularity even among urban elites (e.g., Cook 2013; Pollan 2007). Our intention is to focus on groups who were historically hunter-gatherers, who today rely on wild resources to sustain their livelihoods, and with whom researchers are currently working.

The seminar convened experts working with hunting and gathering populations in diverse locations (figure I.1) to attempt to understand how hunter-gatherers adapt in a transitional world and why some choose to remain foragers. Some of the seminar's participants have lived and worked with hunter-gatherers for much of their long careers and were instrumental in shaping the field by bringing a scientific perspective to hunter-gatherer research. Others built on this pioneering approach by expanding the analytic and comparative methods used, the kinds of questions asked, and the range of groups studied. All authors have in common a focus on human behavior. Most were trained in ecological and evolutionary approaches to human behavior, and emphasize quantitative methods, hypothesis testing, and the analysis of individual decision making. In working and living with modern hunter-gatherers, one cannot avoid the effects of institutional and market forces. Rather than emphasizing change as cultural degradation, or ignoring it altogether, each contributor examines the interactions between external forces and the internal decision making of hunter-gatherer groups.

The groups included in this book live in diverse social, economic, and ecological landscapes. All were traditionally full-time hunter-gatherers. Today, many of their calories still come from hunting and gathering, while the groups vary in how much they are involved with state programs and are impacted by market integration. Not surprisingly, these differences tend to correlate with whether a group lives in a developed or developing nation and how exposed they are to governmental, NGO, and anthropological influences. On one end of global and market influences are the Pumé, who live independently with no medical or economic support and negligible governmental or market contact. The Bardi, Inuit, Martu, and Namibian San are on the opposite end of this continuum and rely on state programs that operate in indigenous communities and, to varying degrees, provide wage labor jobs. The Botswana San, Bofi, and

Hadza live at an intermediate level of global integration, engaging with some forms of labor and trade but limited to no support from government entities. Despite differences in the availability of health care, new technologies, and financial subsidies, hunting and gathering remains at the core of each group's subsistence and social life.

BOOK ORGANIZATION AND QUESTIONS

Why do some people around the world maintain a hunting and gathering lifestyle? Does the fact that most people today subsist in other ways suggest that other economies offer better alternatives to foraging? Through a series of detailed case studies, this volume examines what economic and social elements hunter-gatherers retain and what they adopt in today's rapidly changing global environment. In short, what are the costs and benefits of different foraging decisions in a transitional world?

In addressing this question, we asked authors to write lengthier ethnographic background sections than normally appear in academic journals so that the book can serve as a compendium of the current conditions of modern hunter-gatherers. Because text space is limited, however, attributes that can be quantified are summarized in two extensive tables at the end of the book. One table summarizes social organization and demographic variables (Kramer et al., appendix A), and the other economy and subsistence variables (Greaves et al., appendix B). These are intended to be useable by readers for cross-cultural comparisons.

Some commonly thought-of hunter-gatherers are missing from this volume, in part due to the unavailability of researchers to attend the conference and in part because of the limitations of book length. We have tried to compensate for this by including as many modern hunter-gatherers as possible in the economic table at the end of the book (Greaves et al., appendix B). We apologize in advance for any oversights.

General Themes: Benefits of Foraging, Costs of Not Foraging

Given the economic alternatives, why forage? From this central question, several themes emerged during the seminar. We focus on two of these: the economic benefits of foraging and the social costs of not foraging. While much has changed for many contemporary hunter-gatherers, these case studies reveal the resilience of their diet and medicinal knowledge and, most of all, their sharing relationships and social organization.

All the chapters explore reasons for maintaining traditional subsistence and social practices and the degrees to which these are maintained. The foci of individual chapters, however, vary. Some are overviews or retrospectives (Blurton Jones, chapter 5; Hitchcock and Sapignoli, chapter 4; Lee, chapter 3; Wenzel, chapter 2) and reflect on the long history of research and intellectual debates in the Arctic and Africa. Other chapters (Bliege Bird et al., chapter 9; Codding et al., chapter 8; Coxworth, chapter 7; Kramer and Greaves, chapter 1; Lupo, chapter 6) analyze specific decisions made by foragers today.

Many factors contribute to changes in hunter-gatherer lives and affect decisions about what traditional practices to retain and what novel element to adopt. These may include new technologies, health services, external monetary support, environmental access and productivity, political subjugation, and the influences of regional, national, and global institutions. Not all of these factors are discussed in every chapter. Here we preview the two common themes of the economic and social costs and benefits of maintaining a foraging way of life that are discussed in each chapter (for a quantified summary of these variables, see Kramer et al., appendix A).

ECONOMIC DIMENSIONS

Detailed analyses of the trade-offs between different economic opportunities show that the benefits of foraging often outweigh the alternatives. In chapter 1, Kramer and Greaves discuss how the Pumé, like many other South American foragers, have had access to bitter manioc for hundreds of years, yet they have not become increasingly reliant on food production. An analysis of the nutritional and energetic trade-offs between collecting roots and cultivating manioc shows that the wild resources are equally if not more efficient. In addition, bitter manioc is compatible with the mobility and seasonal scheduling requirements of the pursuit of wild foods. For these combined reasons, the Pumé favor wild resources over the domesticated alternatives. Rather than replacing wild foods, small-scale manioc cultivation extends the viability of a primarily hunting and gathering economy.

This pattern is repeated across Africa. Among San speakers in Namibia, even after fifty years of oftentimes forced sedentarization, 99 percent of individuals still depend on foraged foods, with 54 percent relying on bush foods as a primary or co-primary food source (Lee, chapter 3). Similarly, foraging is integral to the economic and social lives of San in Botswana (Hitchcock and Sapignoli, chapter 4). The Hadza likewise maintain a hunting and gathering economy even where agriculture is possible, in part due to the benefits foraging provides relative to farming (Blurton Jones, chapter 5). In the Central African Republic, forest foragers actively adopt new technologies to increase their foraging efficiency in an increasingly depleted environment (Lupo, chapter 6).

In the western Australian desert, Martu can pursue a number of economic alternatives that include foraging, wage labor within the community, or the production and sale of paintings for the expanding Aboriginal art market. When the costs and benefits of each are compared, the results suggest that foraging may be one of the best options available to individuals (Codding et al., chapter 8), particularly within a heavily modified anthropogenic landscape that facilitates the hunting of reliable resources (Bliege Bird et al., chapter 9).

While some aspects of living in a modern nation-state may limit hunting and gathering options, a number of cases included in this book show that new technologies enhance foraging in a globalized setting. For example, when the Inuit opted to centralize in government-sponsored communities in order to have access to medical care, seal hunting became more difficult because hunting grounds were too far away for them to successfully make the round trip with dog sled teams (Wenzel, chapter 2). The Inuit then adopted snowmobiles, which facilitate long-distance travel. Because snowmobiles run on gas and not seal meat, however, individuals are required to engage further with the market economy to fund the costs of fuel and maintenance.

Similarly, in Australia Bardi have adopted boats and Martu Land Cruisers to access fishing and foraging grounds, respectively (Codding et al., chapter 8; Coxworth, chapter 7). In Africa, the Botswana San now use horses to travel to remote hunting grounds (Hitchcock and Sapignoli, chapter 4). In these cases, traditional foragers have chosen to adopt new technologies as a way to continue foraging as a viable economic alternative in an altered landscape.

SOCIAL DIMENSIONS

While the literature is replete with examples of innovations in subsistence and technological practices among hunter-gatherers historically, much less is known about the social effects of these transitions. It became clear during the seminar's discussions that not only the economic benefits of continuing to forage but also the social costs of not foraging are significant. This commonality emerged as the most salient across all groups. Despite other changes, what appears critical to contemporary hunter-gatherers is the preservation of their sharing and cooperative relationships that allow them to maintain their identities. Although governments and NGOs may enact policies incentivizing the use of cash, traditional sharing relationships persist. In the struggle to preserve social autonomy, social relations become a durable good.

In the case of the Inuit (Wenzel, chapter 2), what has remained constant through the technological shift from dog sleds to snowmobiles is the role of women. In the past, women manufactured much of the traditional technology that enabled men to hunt with sleds. Now it is women who have the wage labor jobs that generate the cash needed for the purchase and upkeep of snowmobiles.

Martu use Land Cruisers as a means of continuing traditional hunting practices, attending rituals, and fulfilling social obligations. Vehicles allow Martu people to reside in permanent, government-sponsored settlements and still access traditional foraging grounds, typically up to an hour's drive away. While traditional patterns of residential mobility would have brought individuals together for ritual aggregations (such as initiations) and social obligations (such as funerals), vehicles now permit them to cross vast distances in a few days, such that men and women maintain their extensive social and ritual networks across western Australia and beyond, despite living in isolated pockets (Bliege Bird et al., chapter 9; Codding et al., chapter 8).

Among the Pumé, critical inputs of wild tubers during the wet season have important social implications stemming from the subsistence value of women's contributions to the diet and their political equality with men. The retention of wild plant and animal foods also reifies several group cohesion mechanisms, including bilocal residence patterns and a commitment to ritual activities, that enhance resource sharing and activity coordination in a depauperate terrestrial environment where protein returns have a high seasonal and daily variance (Kramer and Greaves, chapter 1).

Although initially cast as a normative explanation, Woodburn's (1982) distinction between immediate and delayed-return economies is a common theme in several chapters, although not always with the same results. While some foraging groups store food, Woodburn suggests that foraging economies are largely focused on immediate returns that are shared widely with others. New modes of subsistence—such as pastoralism, agriculture, or wage labor, in which returns are delayed or are stored (i.e., in a herd, granary, or bank)—remove one from the many social obligations that function to maintain networks of interdependence, shared risks, and rewards. The maintenance of social networks, for example, appears to help explain the persistence of foraging among the Botswanan San (Hitchcock and Sapignoli, chapter 4). Among the Hadza, foraged foods are shared widely, and sharing ethics are closely tied to Hadza identity (Blurton Jones, chapter 5). The shift from hunting and gathering to farming or herding can entail forfeiting social connections in times of hardship, the loss of accumulated social capital, or exclusion from one's social network. In this context, the social costs of not foraging are too high and to stop foraging would mean, in essence, that one is no longer Hadza.

Among the Bofi we see similar social implications of delayed- versus immediate-return foods. The Bofi have long-term relationships with neighboring horticultural populations (Lupo, chapter 6). While alternative economic opportunities concentrated on the bushmeat trade could earn higher returns, participation would force Bofi individuals to break ties with their neighbors.

In contrast, the social cost of incorporating bitter manioc cultivation is negligible among the Pumé. Even though bitter manioc is a delayed-return resource, because its sharing distribution is similar to that of wild roots, it does not disrupt the traditional system of exchange obligations. Rather, manioc an additional resource within the existing redistribution network (Kramer and Greaves, chapter 1).

Navigating novel leadership roles also impacts the social costs of not foraging. Among many mobile hunter-gatherers, individuals may be reluctant to become leaders (Bird and Bliege Bird 2010; Wiessner 2009). Those who do assert leadership typically are knocked down or ostracized (Lee, chapter 3). In some hunting and gathering societies, such as the Martu, foraging may be incentivized because status is linked to the prestige of acquiring and distributing wild resources (Bliege Bird et al., chapter 9). In other cases, novel leadership roles emerge through the incorporation of new economic pursuits, as among the Bardi (Coxworth, chapter 7).

Conclusions

What becomes clear throughout these chapters is that hunter-gatherers continue to forage because the economic benefits of doing so are high relative to the local alternatives. But perhaps more importantly, they continue to forage because the social costs of not foraging are prohibitive. Across the twenty-first-century hunting and gathering societies we discuss in this book, the social networks built through foraging and sharing appear to be more highly valued than the potential marginal gains from shifting to a new means of subsistence. These societies are integrated within local and global economies and reliant on state subsidies to varying degrees. Despite these differences, hunting and gathering continues to be a viable and vibrant way of life. Given the nuanced ways in which foraging populations adapt to changing conditions in an ever globalizing world, as revealed by the case studies in this book, we should expect that hunting and gathering will remain a viable way of life well into the future.

Acknowledgments

Editing this book was a true collaborative effort, and the question of editorship was left unresolved until moments before we put the first draft into the mail. We followed Gray and Anderson's (2010) example and decided the order of editorship with a coin toss. Thanks to Leslie Knapp and Richard Paine for administering the toss.

Note

1. Throughout the text, the terms *hunter-gatherer* and *forager* are used interchangeably to refer to the mode of subsistence. Ethnographic and linguistic terms for specific hunter-gatherer populations are defined within each chapter.

CHAPTER ONE

Diversify or Replace

What Happens to Wild Foods When Cultigens Are Introduced into Hunter-Gatherer Diets?

KAREN L. KRAMER AND RUSSELL D. GREAVES

Introduction

Much of our success as a species derives from our ability to adapt hunting and gathering to diverse ecologies and integrate a wide range of food resources into our diet. Throughout their history, foragers have been making strategic decisions about whether to incorporate new resources, technologies, and strategies, which maintains both the strength and resilience of hunter-gatherer lifeways. Despite recognition that hunting and gathering includes broad-spectrum subsistence options, scholars commonly assume that the incorporation of domesticates leads to greater reliance on food production (Bellwood 2005; Diamond and Bellwood 2003; Richerson et al. 2001; Zeder and Smith 2009). In this chapter we consider instead how the adoption of some horticulture supports the continued viability of, and primary reliance on, hunting and gathering. While the decisions facing foragers have been theoretically and empirically addressed, few paired nutritional and return rate data are available to demonstrate the replacement or complementary value of wild versus domesticated foods.

This volume addresses the question of why hunter-gatherers continue to forage given the economic alternatives of living in the contemporary world. For Pumé foragers living on the llanos of Venezuela, the answer seems clear (figure 1.1). Although the Pumé cultivate small quantities of manioc, this broadens their subsistence base at little cost to other hunting and gathering activities and without compromising their social relations and political autonomy. Rather than indicating the erosion of a foraging way of life, some cultivation extends the social and economic security of hunting and gathering.

Figure 1.1. A savanna Pumé couple hunting small game and collecting wild tubers during the wet season. Photograph by Russell Greaves.

MIXED FORAGER ECONOMIES

Both the archaeological record and historic ethnographic examples indicate that foragers have often lived in close proximity to, and interacted with, food producers (B. Smith 2001). As evidenced in the archaeological record, prior to widespread intensive farming many forager populations have combined cultivated foods with a primary reliance on wild plant gathering, hunting, and fishing (Harris 1989; Piperno and Pearsall 1998; Richerson et al. 2001; B. Smith 2001; Wills 1995; Winterhalder and Kennett 2006). Scholars hypothesize that cultivated crops are adopted not only for economic reasons, but for many other demographic or social reasons as well (Bowles 2011). The persistence of mixed strategies over long periods of time suggests that the integration of some cultigens within a hunter-gatherer economy can be a long-term and stable strategy that supports foraging options rather than replacing wild foods.

Mixed foraging economies may develop primarily through one of two processes (table 1.1). One pathway is trade and exchange between foragers and

Table 1.1. Modern hunter-gatherer societies that combine wild resource use with some cultivars or domesticated animals.

	Environment	Cultigens	References
AFRICA			
Hadza	Savanna	Exchange	Blurton Jones et al. 2002; Marlowe 2010
Kalahari foragers	Savanna	Adoption/shift back to foraging	Hitchcock and Ebert 1984; Lee 1979; Silberbauer 1965a; Wilmsen 1989
Mbuti, Efe, Aka	Forest	Exchange	Bailey and Aunger 1989; Hart and Hart 1986
Mikea	Woodland	Adoption	Stiles 1991; Tucker 2006
ASIA			
Agta	Forest	Exchange	Headland and Bailey 1991; Peterson 1978
Batak (Malaysia)	Forest	Adoption/exchange	Endicott 1979
Batak (Philippines)	Forest	Adoption/exchange	Eder 1978, 1988
Mlabri	Forest	Exchange	Oota et al. 2005; Pookajorn 1992
Semang	Forest	Exchange	Gomes 1982; Rambo 1985
SOUTH AMERICA			
Hiwi	Savanna	Adoption	Hurtado and Hill 1990; Metzger and Morey 1983
Hoti	Forest	Adoption	Coppens 1983; Zent and Zent 2007
Nukak	Forest	Adoption	Milton 1984; Politis 2007
Pumé	Savanna	Adoption	Gragson 1989; Greaves 1997a, 1997b
Sirionó	Forest	Adoption	Holmberg 1950; Stearman 1989

farmers. The association of Ituri forest foragers with agriculturalists and the bartering of meat for rice among the Agta are well-known examples of mixed economies being established through regular, long-term economic interactions between foragers and farmers. Access to nonforaged foods, including market foods, may occur either directly through food exchanges or indirectly through labor exchanges. Another pathway to a mixed economy is adoption. Hunter-gatherers may add nonforaged foods, such as rice, maize, or domesticated animals, into their diets (Bailey and Aunger 1989; Tucker 2006) but continue to include significant inputs of wild resources.

Mixed hunter-gatherer economies are evident in many parts of the world both historically and prehistorically. Hunter-gatherers who lived in temperate and equatorial zones almost certainly were knowledgeable of, and had contact with, food producers. Numerous archaeological examples show that since the advent of domestication, small-scale cultigen use was incorporated into forging economies well before reliance on cultivation was established (Harris 1989; Piperno and Pearsall 1998; B. Smith 2001; Wills 1995; Winterhalder and Kennett 2006). While some foragers eventually transitioned to agriculture, many did not or continued to combine foraging with low-level use of cultigens. The observed persistence of hunting and gathering despite long periods of association with small amounts of cultivated food challenges the view that domesticates will inevitably replace wild foods. Most contemporary hunter-gatherers include some horticulture, animal husbandry, or periodic wage labor in their subsistence repertoire. This variety provides an opportunity to examine economic tradeoffs among twenty-first-century hunters and gatherers and has implications for understanding how hunter-gatherers made decisions when faced with new options in the past (Greaves and Kramer 2014).

MAKING FORAGING DECISIONS

Recent research has addressed several important aspects of the economic decisions and tradeoffs involved when foragers adopt domesticates (Tucker 2006; Winterhalder and Kennett 2006, 2009; among others). From a forager's perspective, resources vary in their nutritional values, which are weighted by the time and effort expended to obtain a given food and the opportunity cost of pursuing one resource relative to another activity. While a cultigen might add diversity to a hunter-gatherer diet and minimize risk by broadening the subsistence base, the labor investments required to grow crops (clearing, planting, weeding) create a delay between production and consumption compared to foraged foods. Because delayed returns can represent lower immediate utility, economic choices may vary depending on current (future discounting of potential payoffs) or future (funding lower current returns with labor invested in future harvests) needs.

Although scholars widely recognize that foragers may combine some use of domesticates or market opportunities with a predominantly hunting and gathering subsistence pattern, little empirical evidence exists for the relative return values of wild versus domesticated resources (but see Politis 1996; D. Thomas 2008; Tucker 2006). Pumé foragers of the Venezuelan neotropical savannas primarily rely on wild resources (<90 percent of their diet) but seasonally cultivate small amounts of manioc. This combination of wild and cultivated tubers is recorded in the earliest European documents of the region (AGI 1776, 1786, 1787, 1788). If the continued prevalence of foraging is a strategic decision by savanna Pumé, can it be understood in relation to energy expenditure and return rates?

We address this question by first reviewing key characteristics of wild and domesticated tubers. We then compare the relative value of roots used by the Pumé through an analysis of their nutritional composition, labor investment, and food returns. We use these data to test several predictions about the conditions under which hunter-gatherers might retain a predominantly foraging diet, and our results indicate that cultivated roots provide no clear nutritional or labor-related advantage. In addition, the evidence does not suggest that wild roots are an inferior resource. This finding may explain why a number of South American tropical foragers incorporate manioc into their diets as a fallback food without it replacing their reliance on wild foods. Historical records indicate that this combination has been a long-term, stable strategy and does not suggest a transition to an agrarian way of life. We then compare tropical hunter-gatherers and discuss why trade for food may be more prominent among some African and Asian foragers, while adoption is more common among South American foragers as a mechanism for introducing nonforaged food into a foraging economy. Based on our results, we outline some conditions that affect whether hunter-gatherers adopt or trade for nonforaged foods.

ROOT FOODS

Underground plant storage organs (collectively referred to as roots or tubers throughout) are important plant resources for many hunter-gatherers. They are exploited across diverse climates and habitats (Bailey and Headland 1991; Hurtado and Hill 1987; Marlowe and Berbesque 2009; Yasuoka 2009a) and feature in evolutionary debates about hominin dietary shifts, expansion into novel environments, food-sharing practices, and division of labor (Laden and Wrangham 2005; Marean 1997; O'Connell et al. 1999).

Wild tubers have several key attributes that make them particularly attractive hunter-gatherer foods. Roots are generally high in carbohydrates and starch and can be harvested across a greater proportion of the year than many fruits and seeds, especially in more seasonally extreme environments. Data from Africa (Tucker and Young 2005; Yasuoka 2006a), Australia (O'Connell and Hawkes 1981), Asia (Eder 1978; Endicott and Bellwood 1991), and the Americas (Hurtado and Hill 1987; Kelly 2013:table 3-4) indicate that return rates for roots average approximately 1,000–3,000 kcal per hour. While return rates can be higher for resources such as honey or meat, roots are more frequently included as daily dietary items because of their greater predictability. Because hunter-gatherers know the locations of patches and can monitor resource conditions prior to foraging trips, search time is negligible and daily variance in return rates is much lower than for hunted or fished resources (Greaves 1997a; Tucker 2006). Wild roots are critical food sources for smoothing daily consumption requirements when downturns occur in the availability of protein and fat resources (Hildebrand 2003; Malaisse and Parent 1985; Rusak et al. 2011).

If hunter-gatherers incorporate cultivated foods into their diets, then certain crops should be more appealing than others. Manioc is a cultivated tuber, originally domesticated in northern South America. It has a long seasonal availability, is less vulnerable to pest loss than many seed crops, is available in large package sizes, can be stored underground with no investment in structural facilities, and has similar harvesting requirements to wild roots (Wilson and Dufour 2006). Bitter manioc is more widely cultivated than sweet manioc because it grows well in poor tropical soils and is thought to be more pest resistant (Cock 1982; Wilson and Dufour 2006).

In addition to the Pumé, whom we report on here, most mobile tropical South American hunter-gatherers, including the Nukak, Hoti, Sirionó, and

Hiwi, incorporate some manioc cultivation into their primary reliance on wild foods (see table 1.1). Does the inclusion of manioc into South American hunter-gatherer diets represent a transition to horticulture or the addition of a complementary resource that maintains their foraging economy? If cultivated foods are more nutritious or offer labor savings in search or handling costs (or have a market value), then we would expect hunter-gatherers to use them to replace wild foods. Alternatively, if cultivated foods do not offer these advantages, then hunters and gatherers may either ignore them or add them into the diet as complementary or fallback foods.

While few paired nutritional and return rate data are available to evaluate the replacement or complementary values of wild versus domesticated foods, these data are important to further understand the complexity of foraging decisions. Because manioc is available in dense packages, it may be harvestable in quantities that make return rates comparable to or greater than those for wild tubers. However, investments in clearing, weeding, and other garden labor may lower overall returns for manioc relative to wild roots. Distances traveled to manioc and wild root patches may vary, as may processing costs. While the processing required to reduce the cyanogen content in bitter manioc has been well documented (Lancaster et al. 1982), some wild roots also require processing to remove toxins. Potential toxicity and poor nutritional content are two of the reasons researchers give for why wild roots drop out of diets after the incorporation of cultigens (Eder 1978; Headland 1987); however, quantitative data supporting this expectation are lacking.

Nutritional studies of wild roots habitually used by foragers come primarily from Africa and Australia (Cane 1987; Miller et al. 1993; Schoeninger et al. 2001; Yasuoka 2006a) and occasionally include individual species from other regions. Much less is known about toxicity levels and the nutritional content of South American wild roots. Additionally, unlike for maize and Old World cultigens, the nutritional return-to-labor investment required to produce bitter manioc versus wild roots is unknown. To fill this gap, we test the prediction that wild roots remain an important food resource because their return rates and nutritional quality do not significantly vary from those of cultivated roots. Using data from Pumé, we evaluate this expectation by comparing the nutritional value of, time investments in, and energy gained from wild roots and manioc.

Savanna Pumé Foragers

The savanna Pumé are indigenous to the llanos (low plains or savannas) of west-central Venezuela. They are a subset of the larger Pumé ethnic and linguistic group, most of whom are semisedentary horticulturalists living along major tributaries of the Orinoco River drainage. In contrast, the savanna Pumé are mobile foragers living in the grasslands between the major rivers. The Pumé recognize these distinctions in mobility and subsistence and use the terms *savanna dwelling* and *river dwelling* to reference these differences. An estimated eight hundred savanna Pumé live in approximately fifteen disbursed mobile communities of about seventy people each.

HISTORY OF RESEARCH

Archaeological and historic evidence indicates that hunting and gathering Pumé were living in the region when it was first visited by Europeans (AGI 1776, 1786, 1787, 1788). Early ethnographic studies focused primarily on the river Pumé (Leeds 1961, 1964; Petrullo 1939) and the larger, more accessible semisedentary horticultural villages. The first quantitative research among the savanna Pumé was Gragson's (1989) study in the 1980s. Greaves (1997a, 2006) has worked in the savanna Pumé community of Doró Aná since the early 1990s (Hilton and Greaves 2004). In 2005 we began a new demographic and economic project to expand research into several additional hunter-gatherer communities (Kramer and Greaves 2007). Since 2010, the bureaucratic standstill in Venezuela and political instability related to the FARC (Fuerzas Armadas Revolucionarias de Colombia) near the Colombian border have made work in the region increasingly difficult. The following describes the savanna foragers when we visited them between 1990 and 2009.

ENVIRONMENT AND SUBSISTENCE

The llanos make up an extensive hyperseasonal savanna with approximately 85 percent of the annual precipitation falling from June to November. This extreme rainfall variation alters the available flora and fauna during each season and affects many aspects of Pumé subsistence, mobility, residential patterns, and demography. During the six-month dry season, subsistence is centered on

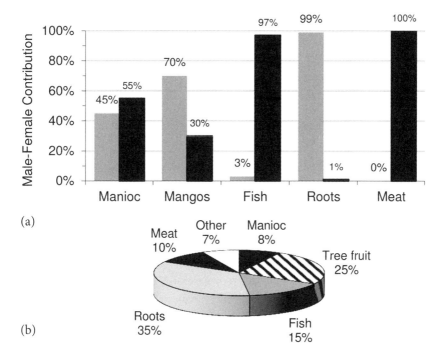

(a)

(b)

Figure 1.2. The Pumé subsistence base: (a) annual contribution of food by weight; (b) division of labor showing proportional male (black bars) and female (gray bars) contributions to principal food categories by weight.

a range of aquatic resources, feral mangos, and small amounts of wild tubers (figure 1.2). Food is relatively abundant during this season. Although the mean fishing returns per trip are similar to wet season hunting returns (returns for fishing and hunting average about 2.2 kg/man/trip), more men fish on any particular day and some men fish every day. Fishing is a relatively low-skill foraging activity and most boys have return rates equivalent to adult men.

When the llanos flood during the wet season, fish are difficult to locate, and the subsistence base shifts to small body–sized terrestrial game (primarily armadillos and teiid lizards ranging from <0.1 to 1.5 kg), wild tubers, and small inputs from manioc cultivation (<10 percent of the diet). The llanos have a low diversity and density of terrestrial fauna, and the wet season is associated with low calorie and protein returns. Both male- and female-contributed foods are critical to the diet, and carbohydrate and protein foods are widely shared across households (Kramer and Greaves 2011). Women's food contributions of roots, feral mangos, and a few other plants foods are crucially important to the savanna Pumé diet in both seasons.

MOBILITY

The savanna Pumé move their residential camps five to six times throughout the year in response to variation in subsistence and water availability (Greaves 1997b; Kramer and Greaves 2011). During the six-month dry season, clusters of related nuclear families live in ephemeral brush shelters located adjacent to streams and lagoons. Camps may move several times during this season to maintain proximity to drinking water. When the llanos flood during the wet season, camps are relocated to higher ground and extended families aggregate into more substantial thatch houses (Gragson 1989; Greaves 1997b, 2006; Mitrani 1988). Although the Pumé are generally central-place foragers, small groups of individuals may leave residential camps and establish temporary camps for a few days up to a couple of weeks for focused subsistence activities or raw material exploitation. Short-term fishing camps are particularly common during the dry season. Temporary camps may include the kin of either spouse or unrelated individuals who have close subsistence or labor relationships. Membership in these temporary camps has few regular associations, except that husbands and wives always accompany each other.

RESIDENTIAL PATTERNS

Based on their cultural norms, the Pumé were originally identified as matrilocal (Leeds 1964; Mitrani 1988; Petrullo 1939), although Mitrani (1988) recognized some ambiguity. Petrullo (1939) mistakenly wrote that a moiety system existed in Pumé kinship. However, longitudinal observational data give quite a different picture. Our analysis of individual residential behavior documented over a twenty-five-year period shows a clear predominance of natalocality, in which both spouses maintain lifelong affiliations with their natal community (Kramer and Greaves 2011). Natalocality is similar to multilocality, which characterizes many hunter-gatherer postmarriage residence patterns (Alvarez 2004; Marlowe 2004), in that it maximizes bilateral kin affiliations (Kramer and Greaves 2011). The Hadza, for example, maintain bilateral kin affiliations by continually altering the composition of short-term camps (Marlowe 2006, 2010). The Pumé likewise maintain a broad base of bilateral kin but through a different residential pattern. For ecological and labor reasons, the Pumé move as a group during seasonal relocations and maintain relatively large residential camps. Marriages tend to be endogamous, and 66 percent of first marriages and 57 percent of second marriages are among individuals of the same community. While camp composition remains quite stable, memberships within any particular household and the spatial associations between houses are reshuffled during residential moves and the formation of temporary logistic camps. At a deeper temporal scale, kin associations are re-sorted through group fissioning and geographic relocation.

PUMÉ ECONOMIC AUTONOMY

While the Pumé are aware of and have had both positive and negative interactions with neighboring ethnic groups, they have almost no contact with the labor market or regional economics and politics. No savanna community has a school, health clinic, electricity, well, or store. None can be reached by a permanent road. The savanna Pumé are monolingual, and only a few adults in our study communities ($n = 2$) understand some Spanish. No savanna Pumé child or adult in our sample has attended school or is literate.

The savanna Pumé have access to a few nonlocal goods (cloth, machetes, cooking pots) through trade with the river Pumé, who live along the major rivers that are the transportation routes into the region. This trade network likely has been in place for as long as the Pumé have lived in the area. Small family groups travel between the river and savanna and exchange goods primarily during the dry season, when travel is easy. Tools and clothing are well worn by the time they reach the savanna interior, where they are exchanged for raw materials such as arrowcane, fiber, resin, weaving materials, and finished arrows. The Pumé do not use currency or exchange food items. On the rare occasion when a man might work for a rancher, he is paid with rice or pasta, which is the only input of market foods into the Pumé diet.

In the late twentieth century, Venezuelan nationals moved into the savanna Pumé area to raise cattle on small family ranches. This influx is problematic for the Pumé, who do not speak Spanish and have no political representation or legal rights to land and water. Although the river Pumé who live in the more accessible villages are occasionally contacted, government officials and health workers very rarely travel into the savanna interior. We have never known a representative of a nongovernmental organization to visit the area.

HEALTH AND DEMOGRAPHY

In the past, vaccination teams sporadically visited the savanna interior, and some older individuals have been immunized. These visits have not occurred for some time, however, and very few children ($n = 3$) in the study communities have been inoculated in the last fifteen years. Except when we visit, no health care or intervention is provided to the savanna Pumé. Food is most abundant during the dry season and disease exposure is minimal compared to the wet season. Nutritional stress, extreme in some years, is most pronounced during the wet season (Kramer et al. 2009). This period also brings the highest exposure to epidemiological challenges, especially arthropod-borne diseases.

Pumé girls marry at a young age, and 95 percent of girls marry by the age of fifteen. Although marriages are usually arranged by parents, young women are not obliged to accept these matches and control when and whom they marry as well as when to initiate coital relations. Average age at first birth is 15.5, with 90 percent of Pumé women having their first-born child between the ages of 15 and 19 (Kramer 2008; Kramer et al. 2009).

The extreme seasonal variation on the llanos has pronounced effects on fertility and mortality. Although nutritionally stressed for part of the year, the Pumé have enough food during the dry season to support conception and pregnancy. Both cohort and period measures of completed fertility show that women ($n = 48$) on average have 7.4 live births over their reproductive careers (Kramer and Greaves 2007). However, child mortality is high ($n = 61$ women, surviving completed fertility = 4.2, period rate). Young children are especially challenged to survive their first several wet seasons, when food availability and the quality of mother's milk decline and disease exposure increases. Of children born over the last twenty years, 35 percent do not survive infancy and an estimated 45 percent do not survive to reproductive age (Kramer and Greaves 2007).

SOCIAL ORGANIZATION AND LEADERSHIP

The Pumé have a strong sense of group identity. When asked, they state that being Pumé means speaking Pumé and practicing their traditional all-night dances (*tohé*). They are genetically (Layrisse et al. 1961, 1964; Salzano and Callegari-Jacques 1988) and linguistically distinct (Mosonyi 1975; Mosony et al. 2000; Obregón Muñoz 1981) from the surrounding neighboring Guahiboan peoples. Pumé is usually classed as a language isolate, although it may have affinities to extinct Esmeralda and Otomaco languages of the llanos. Conflicts with at least two segments of the Guahiboan population (the Chiricoa to the south and Hiwi to the west) were common into the 1960s.

Despite a strong group identity, Pumé communities themselves are autonomous. The political influence of men is associated with their reputations as elegant storytellers and demonstrated abilities in subsistence or important cultural activities such as healing or dance leadership. One ascribed male political role (*capitán*), which has been misinterpreted in the literature as designating community leadership, is designed primarily to negotiate interactions with outsiders. Among river Pumé, a capitán may hold greater influence. Among the savanna Pumé, however, this role does not carry decision-making authority. Within each camp, most issues are mooted through group discussions and consensus. Women's status is equivalent with men's. Women in their thirties and older frequently participate in and have powerful influences during mixed-sex group discussions of social and subsistence decisions. Some of the literature suggests that a single shaman is present in each Pumé camp (Bernasias 1948; Leeds 1960). However, this interpretation oversimplifies the complex social dynamics associated with dance leadership, which rotates among males, and with individual capabilities for healing and resolving social tensions through calculated possession in these public performances (Greaves 1997a).

In addition to the stability of camp membership and natalocal residence, several other behaviors underscore Pumé social cohesion. The Pumé extensively share both men's and women's foods across households, use kinship terminology rather than names when addressing and referring to each other, and frequently attend all-night (sundown to sunup) tohé dances (37 percent of all nights that we have been in residence) in which every member of the community participates. These behaviors reify group solidarity as a key feature of Pumé social organization and subsistence security in this harsh environment. In the discussion section at the end of this chapter, we link the results of our analysis to these aspects of Pumé social life.

The Economic and Social Value of Wild versus Domesticated Roots

The Pumé collect wild tubers, corms, bulbs, and roots in large quantities, and these foods constitute approximately 25 percent of their total annual diet, comparable to that of other savanna foragers (Hurtado and Hill 1987; Kramer and Greaves 2011; Marlowe and Berbesque 2009). During root-gathering trips, women travel to predetermined patches and spend the majority of their foraging-trip time digging and harvesting roots. The most common roots (*Dracontium margaretae*) are relatively small (mean = 20 g), but they are located in dense patches and usually are only a few centimeters belowground. Unlike foods pursued by men, root patch locations are known, and root collection requires minimal search time. Women monitor the locations and conditions of wild roots as part of their normal travel during other foraging activities. Also unlike male-acquired foods, return rates are directly proportional to the time spent collecting roots, and all root-foraging trips result in food returns (Greaves 1997a).

The savanna Pumé are knowledgeable about the range of crops planted by the river Pumé, but bitter manioc is the only plant they successfully cultivate, in part because the lowland savanna soils are extremely poor for agriculture (Elizalde et al. 2007). Their garden locations and sizes are limited to the relatively small patches of forest not flooded during the wet season, and they use swidden areas for two to three years before leaving them fallow. Pumé cut new gardens in the dry season and allow them to dry, then burn them prior to the rainy season. They also utilize these burned patches as sources of firewood.

Manioc is consumed only during part of the wet season. Consumption varies from year to year depending on the availability of other higher quality resources and may constitute 5–10 percent of the annual diet. The relatively low importance of manioc in the Pumé diet is evidenced by the small size of gardens and of harvested roots and their lack of specialized technology (i.e., no griddle or *sebucán*) for processing manioc, compared to more committed manioc horticulturalists and agriculturalists.

Wild root collection is almost exclusively a female activity. Mixed-age groups of related and unrelated females often forage together in wild root patches. While patch locations are known and fairly stable, no one has priority access or owns them. In contrast, gardens are cultivated by husband-wife couples. Men mostly cut and burn trees and brush to prepare new gardens, while both men and women plant, weed, and harvest. Related individuals without gardens may help weed, plant, and harvest manioc, but they rarely assist with the initial clearing of a swidden plot. Plots are owned only in the sense that the couple identified with a particular garden loosely controls activity within it, and those who contribute labor have some access to the harvest. During any particular year, many households (approximately 45 percent) have no gardens under cultivation. Individuals without gardens, mostly younger couples, widows, or widowers, receive manioc primarily through sharing rather than as payment for labor. Despite these social differences in the production of wild and domesticated roots, the redistribution of their returns is notably similar.

Woodburn (1982) suggests a distinction between how delayed- and immediate-return foods are shared among the Hadza (Blurton Jones, chapter 5, this volume). Others have made the similar point that among some mixed-economy foragers (Gurven et al. 2004), horticulturalists, and agriculturalists, cultivated foods do not enter exchange and sharing networks or entail social obligations in the same way as wild foods. We do not find this to be the case with the Pumé. Rather, manioc is treated like any other food, which may correlate with its role in the Pumé diet as a fallback food (Greaves and Kramer 2014).

Wild tubers and domesticated roots have similar redistribution patterns in which both raw and cooked roots are shared among labor groups, families, and less related individuals regardless of whether they helped produce the resource. No household retains all of the manioc it harvests or processes without sharing some with multiple other hearths. Despite the demands of garden production, of planting, weeding, and harvesting—labor inputs needed to realize delayed returns—manioc remains a fluidly exchanged food and does not appear to occupy a separate realm of "ownership."

Families with gardens tend to be those who also are more productive as foragers. The production and sharing of manioc appears to be part of the extensive delayed reciprocity the Pumé practice, which we interpret as a rational economic strategy in this impoverished environment. Sharing cultigens, wild plant foods, fish, and even small terrestrial game (<1 kg) establishes mutual obligations against future stochastic failure of critical resources. We elaborate on this point in our discussion about why the Pumé and other foragers might incorporate domesticates when they are neither superior to wild foods nor evidence of economies transitioning to a greater reliance on cultivated foods.

RETURN RATES FOR WILD AND DOMESTICATED ROOTS

Greaves (1997a) recorded wild root and manioc trips over an eighteen-month period during two consecutive wet seasons. Manioc patch activities include weeding, most planting, and harvesting and are performed only during the wet season, which is the same period when wild root collection features most prominently in the savanna Pumé diet. While some wild root– and domestic root–related activities occur during the dry season, we limit our observations to the same season so that the analyses of wild and cultivated foods are comparable.

The return rate analyses include a total of 126 wild root and 153 garden trips (table 1.2).[1] All wild root trips result in some product being returned to camp; however, many garden trips produce no food harvest ($n = 79$), but involve weeding, planting, and other activities. Because a harvest can only be realized through the input of such labor, we included these zero-return trips to be able to compare the return rates of wild and cultivated resources.

Since these data are non-normally distributed, we conducted a permutation test as the best estimator of whether the two samples could be derived from the same distribution (Adams and Anthony 1996; Edgington and Onghena 2007; Manly 2006). For this analysis, return rates were aggregated by individual because foraging returns are expected to be optimized over the long term (Stephens and Krebs 1986). We would expect an individual rate, which estimates returns over many trips, to be a better estimate of average returns than a trip rate.[2]

Results of the permutation test indicate that wild root and manioc return rates do not significantly differ (wild root mean = 1.831 kg/h; bitter manioc mean = 2.459 kg/h; $p = 0.0737$; for conversion to kilocalories, see table 1.2). A number of alternative methods of evaluating return rate differences also were calculated (Greaves and Kramer 2014). All test results show that wild and domesticated root return rates are either not significantly different or are greater for wild roots.

Although much of the labor cost of producing a manioc crop is incorporated into the return rates, it is important to note that this estimate does not include dry-season investments in clearing and burning. Adding these labor costs would lower manioc return rates relative to wild roots. Post-harvest processing is also not included in the return rate calculation of either resource

Table I.2. Descriptive characteristics of Pumé wild root and manioc trips.

	Wild Roots[a]	Manioc
Individuals	21	19
Trips	126	153
Age	41.2 (1.52)	37.8 (1.15)
Trip distance (m)	5,647 (487)	1,090 (82)
Trip return rate (kg/h)	2.63 (0.12)	2.76 (0.37)
Trip time (h)[b]	4.67 (0.14)	2.11 (0.09)
Trip weight (kg)	12.19 (0.60)	4.23 (0.64)[c]
Trip return rate (kcal/h)[d]	2,449 (108)	2,608 (349)
Individual return rate (kg/h)	1.83 (0.22)	2.46 (0.37)

Note: Counts are given for the first two variables and means (se in parentheses) for the subsequent variables.
[a]Includes root-gathering trips targeting large roots (>5 cm), *Dracontium margaretae*, which is the primary root species collected at the same time of year that manioc is available for harvest.
[b]Time and distance record round trips from residential camps. Most manioc- and root-gathering trips are focused on collecting a single resource.
[c]For manioc trips for which there is a harvest, the average weight is 8.7 kg (1.10), $n = 74$.
[d]Edible calories returned per hour. Calorie counts are taken from the nutritional analysis of cooked large root and manioc specimens: 349/100 g dry matter for large roots and 352/100 g dry matter for manioc. Dry matter is approximately 0.267 of wet weight (field-recorded weight) in wild roots and bitter manioc. Return rate$_{wild roots}$ = [(kg of field weight × 0.267)3,490 kcal] ÷ trip time. Return rate$_{manioc}$ = [(kg of field weight × 0.267)3,520 kcal] ÷ trip time. The manioc return-rate average includes no-harvest trip times.

but differs between them. While some wild plant foods collected by the Pumé require leaching to remove toxins (Barreiro et al. 1984; Stergios Doe 1993), common wild roots are eaten after boiling without further processing. Post-harvest manioc processing involves a greater time commitment to remove the cyanogenic glucosides. First, bitter manioc is grated and the liquid expressed; then the grated root is sifted to oxidize it; then it is finally cooked. For an average savanna Pumé harvest return of manioc (8.7 kg, se = 1.10; $n = 74$ trips), this process minimally requires two hours.[3] Although the data reported here indicate no significant differences in the return rates for wild and domesticated roots, the addition of dry-season garden work and detoxification would lower the return-to-labor investment for manioc.

NUTRITIONAL ANALYSIS

While return rates are commonly used to compare the values of different foods, one critique of diet-breadth approaches has been that calories and weight do not account for the macronutrient composition of food, which is likely to be important in human foraging decisions. Consequently, we include macronutritional data for two species (six cooked samples) of commonly eaten Pumé roots and one sample of cultivated manioc.

Both wild roots and manioc generally have a high carbohydrate and starch content, are low in protein and lipids, and have minimal amounts of other nutrients (table 1.3). In cross-cultural comparison, the roots crucial to the Pumé diet have lower fiber content and higher nutritional value than those reported for the Hadza (Schoeninger et al. 2001), Aka (Yasuoka 2006a), and Australian Aboriginals (Miller et al. 1993).[4]

To evaluate whether the nutritional contents of wild roots and manioc are statistically different, we conducted a principal coordinates ordination analysis (PCoA) and the multivariate distance between specimens was measured along a gradient using the Canberra dissimilarity metric (Legendre and Legendre 1998; Otárola-Castillo 2010). The analysis shows that protein and lipid contents have

Table I.3. The nutritional composition of two common wild root species collected by Pumé foragers compared to bitter manioc. Values are for cooked specimens and give the percentage of field dry matter for lipids, crude protein, nonstructural carbohydrates, and calories per 100 g (left to right).

Latin Name (Common Name; Pumé Name)	n		Crude Protein	Lipid	Total Nonstructural Carbohydrate	Kcal/100 g Dry Food
			% Field Dry Matter			
Dracontium	4	Mean	2.25	0.425	85.6	355.0
margaretae		SD	0.25	0.29	1.11	3.54
(*changuango*; *jipái*)						
Manihot esculenta	1	Mean	1.1	0.5	87.5	359.0
(bitter manioc; *tambái*)						
Myrosma cannifolia	2	Mean	4.4	0.4	77.6	332.0
(*guapo*; *cokuí*)		SD	0.0	0.1	0.5	2.5

a significant gradient along the ordination ($r^2 = 0.8666$, $p = 0.0307$ and $r^2 = 0.9463$, $p = 0.0048$, respectively), but carbohydrate content and calories do not ($r^2 = 0.6418$, $p = 0.1392$ and $r^2 = 0.6264$, $p = 0.1467$, respectively). This result can be interpreted to mean that manioc has significantly less protein but more lipids than do wild roots. However, no difference is evident in either the carbohydrates or calories per unit weight.

In sum, the energetic costs and benefits of incorporating cultivated resources into a hunting and gathering diet include both the nutritional quality of and the labor invested in manioc versus wild roots. Evaluated as the amount, or calories, returned relative to the labor invested, manioc provides no clear nutritional or labor advantage. Manioc has similar caloric returns as wild roots and a slightly higher lipid content. Evidence also shows that wild roots are not an inferior resource and have a somewhat higher protein content. If clearing, burning, and detoxification are included as time costs, manioc would be a less efficient choice. This lack of clear advantage may explain the persistence of hunting and gathering despite generations of familiarity with and use of manioc.

Discussion: Why Should Hunter-Gatherers Cultivate Rather than Intensify Use of Wild Resources?

If manioc provides no clear advantage over wild roots, why invest *any* time and energy in swidden production? Although gardening is not a part of normal wild food–foraging activities, several properties of bitter manioc compared to other cultigens make it an attractive addition to the diet. The opportunity cost of allocating time to cultivation tasks is relatively low since these tasks do not conflict with foraging activities. Garden labor does not negatively impact the time men spend hunting or fishing or the time women spend foraging for wild roots. This point has been made, for example, with respect to the use of *Chenopodium*, a low-quality small-seed crop incorporated into the diets of hunter-gatherers in eastern North America (Gremillion 2004). Unlike other crops, such as maize, that require greater labor inputs and seasonally regulated support tasks (Kramer 2005), bitter manioc garden labor is much less demanding, distributed throughout the year, and timed around other temporally constrained foraging tasks. Pumé garden preparation, while calorically expensive work, occurs during the dry season, when food is relatively abundant and disease less prevalent (Kramer et al. 2009), thus minimizing competing energy demands. Unlike seed and fruit crops, manioc can be stored in the ground until needed with little loss in yield

(Cock 1982; Rival and McKey 2008), which avoids harvest labor bottlenecks and conflicts with other activities. Compared to other crops, manioc's vegetative propagation entails less garden preparation time and reduces the vulnerability of new plantings to rainfall. Bitter manioc is drought tolerant and pest resistant relative to many other crops, and it requires little tending and weeding. These are the principal reasons suggested for its successful adoption among Old World agriculturalists and foragers, despite its low nutritional content and toxins (Griffin 1984; Lancaster et al. 1982; Okigbo 1980; Terra 1964; Tucker 2006). Although bitter manioc takes more time to process than wild roots, it is more economical than many cereal crops (Cock 1982; Ember 1983). In sum, manioc is not highly nutritious (Cock 1982), but its adoption creates another kind of root patch with relatively low labor and opportunity costs.

Other aspects of manioc cultivation also complement a mobile forager's way of life. Because both wild root patches and gardens are known locations, foragers need little time to find either a patch or harvestable plants within a patch. Returns for both resources are predictable, and access is similar. The savanna Pumé do not manufacture specialized leaching or cooking implements to process manioc, and the same simple tools (i.e., digging sticks or machetes) are used to harvest both wild and domesticated roots. We point out these particulars of Pumé foraging because they are likely common to other hunter-gatherers who integrate some bitter manioc into their subsistence base.

While their investment in cultivation supplies additional calories during the wet season, the savanna Pumé could alternatively increase their foraging range for wild roots. But the fact that they use manioc during their peak reliance on wild roots suggests that increasing wild root productivity is not as beneficial an option as combining foraging with minimal cultivation. Intensifying root collection requires additional mobility and energetic costs during the season of greatest nutritional and epidemiological stress. Women lose approximately 8 percent of their body weight during the wet season (Kramer and Greaves 2007, 2010). Rather than expanding foraging ranges, the savanna Pumé promote plant productivity in nearby locations where roots are not otherwise available and, importantly, increase their dietary diversity during the lean season. Travel distances to gardens are lower than for wild tuber collection, and when asked, the Pumé say that they cultivate manioc because it provides additional food on days when they do not expend effort foraging for wild roots but that wild roots are more effective in fighting hunger.

STABLE MIXED-FORAGING ECONOMIES

A dependence on wild resources in combination with some manioc cultivation appears to be a stable subsistence strategy. Importantly, this strategy is not linked to an economic shift toward food intensification. Historical accounts indicate the Pumé have a long-established practice of minimal cultivation with a primary subsistence base of mobile hunting and gathering (Leeds 1961; Mitrani 1988). Manioc might best be characterized as a seasonal fallback food because it is incorporated into the diet situationally in response to the changing availability of wild foods or is left unharvested as a source of future calories (Greaves and Kramer 2014). Because the annual consumption of manioc varies with the availability of wild roots, rather than the other way around, it suggests that wild roots are the more valued food.

The Pumé's lack of engagement with the market economy further supports their retention of foraging. Since no venue exists to transform either surplus wild or domestic foods into cash, one product is not driven by the market to be valued more than another. Under these conditions, a mixed economy may be stable because it maintains diversified options responsive to environmental fluctuations, without a trajectory toward replacement of wild foods by a greater dependence on food production.

Novel Resources: Adopt or Trade?

We have made the case that the characteristics of bitter manioc, unlike maize or rice, which require more costly and rigidly scheduled time investments, make its adoption particularly compatible with hunting and gathering, without it replacing wild foods. Most South American foragers add some small-scale manioc cultivation to their primary reliance on wild foods (see table 1.1). It is striking that this combination usually occurs through adoption and that few cases of trade for food have been identified among South American rain forest–(Milton 1984) or savanna-dwelling foragers. Yet food trade between foragers and farmers has substantial time depth and stability in other parts of the world. Robust and long-term trade relations are most well documented among hunter-gatherers in the Congo Basin, the Philippines, and Southeast Asia (Bailey and Aunger 1989; Endicott and Bellwood 1991; Headland and Bailey 1991; Rai 1990). Hunter-gatherers in Africa and Asia became the center of the debate over whether foragers could subsist in tropical forest environments without exchange relationships with agriculturalists (Bailey and Headland 1991). Punan groups in Borneo have had trade relationships with agriculturalists for hundreds of years, but these relationships are unusual for not involving food (Brosius 1991; Hoffman 1986).

IMPLICATIONS FOR FUTURE HUNTER-GATHERER RESEARCH

We consider that a nonforaged resource can enter a hunter-gatherer economy either through adoption or trade and that it may either replace traditional foods or be incorporated to diversify the existing subsistence base. While these decisions are interrelated, for clarity we discuss them as distinct in order to outline the conditions that affect the decisions hunter-gatherers make as they encounter novel resources.

From a forager's perspective, the distinction between adopting a new resource and trading for it is that in the former case the forager pays the production cost, while in the latter, someone else does. However, trading for a good requires producing a surplus of some other resource (or alternatively, acquiring cash through wage labor). Conditions that affect whether foragers adopt or trade for nonforaged resources might include the scheduling costs and labor complementarity of wild and nonforaged goods, the potential to overproduce wild resources for exchange, land constraints, and a proximity to neighboring populations with surpluses and demands for wild resources (table 1.4).

Based on the Pumé analysis and other ethnographic examples, scheduling and labor complementarity appear to be important factors predicting whether a nonforaged food enters the hunter-gatherer diet through adoption. The successful and long-term adoption of manioc among the Pumé has occurred because it does not detract from or compete with foraging activities. In contrast, the Mikea are inconsistent in their commitment to maize cultivation because the scheduling demands of crop maintenance conflict with the collection of wild roots (Tucker 2006). Crops yields suffer because the immediate returns of spending time collecting roots outweigh the delayed returns of investing in tending gardens. As with Pumé, wild roots are the more valued resource. But unlike manioc, the labor, scheduling, and harvest requirements to successfully adopt maize do not complement traditional Mikea subsistence activities. Traditional people living in a range of savanna and rain-forest environments tend to incorporate crops with vegetative propagation while continuing to rely on wild

Table I.4. The conditions under which a nonforaged resource may enter a hunter-gatherer diet through adoption versus trade.

Adopt	Trade
Low opportunity cost.	Land constraints limit intensification of wild resources.
Scheduling and labor complement existing foraging strategies.	Exchange market exists.
No market value exists for foraged food or no other surplus items are available for exchange.	Market value of bush foods greater than market value of cultivated foods.
	Seasonal availability of bush and cultivated foods differs pronouncedly.
	Commodification of wild resources feasible.

resources (Barton et al. 2012), which suggests that manioc and wild roots have a particular compatibility.

In contrast, several foraging populations have developed trading relationships with neighboring farmers, including the Agta (Headland and Bailey 1991; Peterson 1978; Rai 1990), the Philipine Batak (Eder 1978), the Malaysian Batak (Endicott and Bellwood 1991), and Congo Basin foragers (Bailey and Aunger 1989; Hart and Hart 1986). In these rain-forest environments, foragers can overproduce forest goods, beyond what they need for subsistence needs, and use them in exchange for agricultural foods from farmers. In less seasonally abundant environments, low diversity and resource density may limit opportunities to overproduce for external exchange.

If new resources are adopted or traded for, then they may either be added to the subsistence base or replace wild resources. Both scenarios occur in modern foraging groups. If investment in a new food does not conflict with existing subsistence practices, we would expect traditional foods to be retained as long as their value is the same as or greater than that of the new food. This expectation appears to borne out by the Pumé, who experience no loss in diversity of wild foods while including some cultivation. The Mikea, in contrast, have experimented with maize cultivation, but their work has not resulted in stable diversification. Neither the Pumé nor the Mikea have changed their consumption of wild resources.

However, wild foods may be replaced if the returns from investments in gardening, labor exchange, or the procurement of select resources for trade (i.e., bushmeat, forest products) offer higher payoffs than wild resource options. In response to the availability of rice, for example, several southeast Asian foraging groups that historically depended on wild roots have reduced their dietary reliance on some varieties. The Agta, Phillipine Batak, and Malyaysian Batak live in forests with unusually high diversities of wild yams (*Dioscorea* spp.). All three groups continue to gather certain wild yams but have added some cultivation and obtain rice through exchanges of forest foods and products. The commodification of some wild resources that can be produced in excess of consumption needs (e.g., the Agta exchange of meat for rice) results in the neglect of some wild yam species with high procurement costs or particularly high toxin content.

Subsistence Choices and the Maintenance of Group Cohesion

Subsistence choices about whether and how to incorporate new resources affect a range of other hunter-gatherer behaviors. One commonality that emerged during the course of the SAR seminar, and which is discussed in the other chapters of this volume, is the social cost of not foraging and the lengths to which diverse groups of hunter-gatherers go to maintain group cohesion, identity, and social relationships. Here, we link the implications of retaining wild foods for Pumé sharing patterns, the social status of women, mobility, and cultural institutions associated with promoting group cohesion.

Foods acquired by women are often assumed to be shared less frequently or extensively than men's hunted foods (see discussions in Kelly 2013). However, female foods are shared among some foragers (Gurven et al. 2000; Gurven et al. 2002; Hames 1990), including the Pumé, who widely redistribute roots and other plant foods gathered by women. During the wet season, while game is present, animals are small bodied (lizards, armadillos) and available only in low densities. In comparison to low hunting returns (2.2 kg/man/trip), roots have much higher and more frequent returns (12 kg/woman/trip). Not enough game comes into camps to provide a reliable opportunity or currency for its common distribution. Thus, the sharing of roots gathered by women not only provides food but also functions to maintain reciprocal relationships during times when a provider is not foraging or returns are poor (Mauss 1924; O'Shea 1981). For the Pumé, only women's gathered foods are common and predictable enough wet season resources to serve both these functions. As previously discussed, the importance of women's contributions to the diet is reflected in their political equality with men.

Other aspects of Pumé mobility and ritual activity also highlight the importance of cooperation, pooling risk among camp members, and group cohesion. Despite the predictably poor hunting returns during the wet season, camp membership remains stable across both dry and wet seasons (Kramer and Greaves 2011). This raises the question of why the Pumé do not disaggregate into smaller social units during seasons of protein scarcity, as many foragers do (Kelly 2013; E. Smith 1985). Although smaller camps would reduce the density of consumers, they would also reduce the number of hunters. A critical number of men may be needed in each savanna community to offset the variance in male return rates, long search hours, and low individual success rates.

Alternatively, men could hunt more often. However, even among foragers with much higher male return rates such as the Aché, more frequent hunting results in weight loss (Hill and Hawkes 1983). The reliance on foods gathered by women in all seasons and relatively abundant male returns only during six months of the year suggest that camp stability reflects long-term calculations of economic interdependence (E. Smith 1985, 1991). Women's labor during the wet season and men's fishing during the dry season appear to maintain exchange relationships that have to withstand thin paybacks of game during the other six months that the Pumé characterize as "the season when we get thin and die."

The difficulty of making a living in a food-challenging environment is also reflected in the prevalence of community-wide dancing that reifies group membership and identity. During frequent all-night dances, individuals participate by singing and dancing, activities known to promote cooperation (Adams 2004; Wiltermuth and Heath 2009), as well as by telling stories and performing healing rites. Songs and stories typically reiterate kin relations and close ties among individuals (Wiessner 2014). Rarely does a camp member not attend these events. The Pumé are anomalous in both the frequency of and the effort committed to these social dances, which often are followed by bouts of foraging and hunting.

Conclusions

Hunting and gathering has been a successful adaptation because it incorporates a broad diversity of strategies, not because it excludes them. The persistence of foragers into the twenty-first century is evidence of their flexibility.

Hunter-gatherers today show an astute awareness of changing opportunities and often develop ways to take advantage of novel resources, technologies, or interactions with nonforaging neighbors. It is likely only anthropologists, not foragers themselves, who view the inclusion of these opportunities as incompatible with hunting and gathering.

In terms of the central question addressed in this book—why do hunter-gatherers continue to forage?—we make two points. First, for the Pumé the economic returns of foraging are equal to or higher than returns from the horticultural alternative. Second, because the redistribution of manioc is similar to that of wild roots, the social cost of incorporating bitter manioc cultivation is negligible. Rather than disrupting the traditional system of exchange obligations, manioc folds an additional fallback resource into the redistribution network.

One general prediction that can be made from our results is that hunter-gatherers adopt nonforaged resources when they offer comparable returns on investment and complement existing strategies. The Pumé case suggests two main reasons why some nonforaged foods are compatible with stable hunting and gathering economies. First, although wild foods often are characterized as being of lower value compared to cultigens, our analyses show that wild roots are equivalent to manioc nutritionally and have similar if not more efficient return rates. Because of these qualities, wild roots are unlikely to be replaced by manioc among the Pumé. Second, small-scale horticulture can extend the viability of a primarily hunting and gathering economy. Manioc is a predictable backup food that fills in gaps left by fluctuations in wild foods during particularly food-limited seasons. This seasonal incorporation of manioc, however, does not signal a directional shift away from hunting and gathering and toward greater reliance on food production (Greaves and Kramer 2014). In a changing world, whether it be in the past or present, the incorporation of novel resources or strategies can allow hunter-gatherers to continue their primary economic reliance on wild resources and maintain their autonomy.

Acknowledgments

We thank the Pumé of Doro Aná, who have patiently and enthusiastically supported our research and endeavored to teach us about the economic complexities of foraging. We are grateful to Nancy Conklin-Britain, director of the Nutritional Ecology Laboratory at Harvard University, and to Christi Butler and

Paula Lu for performing the nutritional analyses. We appreciate the statistical expertise of Erik Otárola-Castillo (Purdue University, Harvard University) and his assistance with the analysis. We wish to thank the National Science Foundation (DBS-9123875 and 0349963), the L. S. B. Leakey Foundation, and the Milton Fund for supporting this research.

Notes

1. We used two time-allocation sampling techniques to compile the return rates for wild roots and manioc (Alvard and Nolin 2002; Greaves 1997a). The first method records the time an individual departs from camp, any tools or gear taken, the return time to camp, and the weight of food items returned ($n = 97$ for wild roots and $n = 139$ for manioc). The second is a focal follow method during which the researcher accompanies the participant and collects start and stop times on all activities performed, records distances traveled, and weighs any food returns obtained during the trip ($n = 29$ for wild roots and $n = 14$ for manioc). A return rate is a common summary measure of the cost of a resource relative to its benefit and is calculated by dividing the time spent on a trip (leaving and returning to camp) by amount harvested. Since no statistical difference is evident in the return rates produced from these two methods (manioc trips: $p = 0.4722$ [mean $= 4.27$ kg/h, 2.60 kg/h; se $= 2.23$, 0.34 for focals and nonfocals, respectively]; root trips: $p = 0.7411$ [mean $= 2.56$ kg/h, 2.65 kg/h; se $= 0.26$, 0.13 for focals and nonfocal, respectively]), the two sampling strategies were combined to augment sample size.

    All raw specimens were collected by Pumé women during their normal foraging activities. Cooked samples were prepared by various Pumé households as part of regular processing, cooking, and consumption activities, which ensured that the foods analyzed were generated from normal dietary selection and processing. Each sample was ground through a hand-cranked meat grinder prior to weighing (a minimum of 40 g was collected for each sample), transferred to Nalgene sample bottles, mixed with 70 percent isopropyl alcohol, and covered with Parafilm prior to the lids being secured. Field weights were taken with an O-Haus model 1010–10 precision balance. Preserved samples were oven-dried at 40° C, then ground through a #20 (1 mm) mesh screen using a Wiley Mill electric grinder. Nutrient analyses were performed in the Nutritional Ecology Laboratory at Harvard University using standard laboratory procedures (Conklin-Brittain et al. 2006).

2. To aggregate by individual, the time he or she spends on nonharvest manioc trips is summed and added to the time spent on harvest trips. Some individuals ($n = 9$) never harvest manioc and only invest in other kinds of garden labor.

Their time was equally divided among individuals who did have harvest returns. This calculation seems reasonable since wild roots and manioc are widely shared across households.

3. An amount on the order of 8.7 kg is sufficient to feed, for example, two households of five people for two to three days. Processing time is shorter among groups who use specialized technology (i.e., sebucán or *tipití*; Carneiro 2000; Ember 1983:290; data from Hames, personal communication 2012).

4. Cross-culturally, the most important Venezuelan roots have a higher caloric value (324–349 kcal/100 g) than those used by other foragers. For the Hadza, wild tubers average roughly 300 kcal per 100 g (Schoeninger et al. 2001). Aka wild yams provide 120 kcal per 100 g (Yasuoka 2006a:table IV), and various Australian roots produce between 135 and 336 kcal per 100 g (Cane 1987: table VI; Miller et al. 1993). All values are in kcal per 100 g dry matter.

CHAPTER TWO

Inuit Culture

To Have and Have Not; or, Has Subsistence Become an Anachronism?

GEORGE W. WENZEL

Introduction

Inuit entered this century as one of the most written about, yet divergently understood, hunting cultures in anthropology. Through the last century, Inuit have been variously characterized as survivors of the world's harshest environment, as an example of the worst effects of acculturation, as a culture adapted to modernity while maintaining internal coherence, and, most recently, as the northern canary in the coal mine of global warming. In point of fact, it is possible to see all of these things in contemporary Inuit culture.

This contribution, however, will focus on Inuit living in a much more complex environment than any one of these descriptors accurately portrays. They live a subsistence culture, but to do so they must navigate an environment that in political, economic, and biophysical terms presents them with problems in combinations they have never previously encountered.

My overall thesis is that Canadian Inuit subsistence culture is the product of a range of adaptive responses to fifty years of varying, but increasingly intrusive, political, economic, and sociocultural policies, first from southern Canada and now from international bodies. This situation is one that many other hunter-gatherers have only recently experienced. So why do Inuit still forage? Essentially, Inuit have maintained a culture type, here understood as subsistence, that includes specific ideas and normative practices whose goal is collective social and material well-being (Sahlins 1972). In strictly economic terms, Inuit now practice a mixed, or hybrid (Codding et al., chapter 8, this volume), economic adaptation in which money and traditional foods are the currencies. This is no mean achievement given the increasingly constrained environment Inuit are

Figure 2.1. An Inuit man working on his snowmobile. With relocation into government-serviced communities, mechanization became essential to maintaining Inuit subsistence culture. Photograph by George Wenzel.

confronted by today. Their maintenance of this adaptation is the focus of my chapter.

Four interconnected issues affect the traditional food sector of the economy. The first is very basic—whether the production of traditional resources, heavily dependent as it is on money, is viable in an economic-political environment that is generally unfriendly to the consumptive use of wildlife. The second is what seems like a classic Malthusian problem—how to maintain a level of production of traditional foods sufficient to satisfy the nutritional and cultural needs of a geometrically growing population. The third is how money is distorting the social relations of production and consumption of Inuit subsistence culture. And the fourth is whether traditional economic activities will become, to use Polanyi's (1957) term, disconnected from Inuit subsistence culture (figure 2.1). These issues are by no means limited to Inuit or other First World hunter-gatherers (see Hitchcock and Sapignoli, chapter 4; Lee, chapter 3, this volume). What Inuit share with other foraging groups, and especially Australian Aborigines (Codding et al., chapter 8, this volume; Peterson 1991b), is increasing pressure from dominant, encapsulating societies to "rationalize" their indigenous economic activities and relations.

HISTORY OF RESEARCH

In 1994 Burch suggested that hunter-gatherer studies would soon be, if it was not already, confronted by a crisis in three dimensions: the practical, the methodological, and the conceptual. The first two, put most basically, concerned the disappearance of truly autonomous forager societies and whether a general model of hunter-gatherers could be developed from research on contemporary foragers (Burch 1994:442, 446). Regarding the third dimension, he asked, "[Does] a class of empirical referents for the concept hunter-gatherer society exist?" (1994:446).

Interestingly, several years before Burch's critique Balikci (1989) and Riches (1990) expressed not dissimilar concerns about the state of Inuit anthropology. Both their assessments, while following somewhat different paths, were remarkably coincident in that each saw research on Inuit as essentially thematically driven and atheoretical. Riches (1990:71) concluded that despite a voluminous literature that had made Inuit "one of the world's best known [peoples]," its main accomplishment was to reinforce the notion that Inuit have one of "the most precarious human adaptations on earth" (Lee 1968:40; Sahlins 1968:85).

While I disagree with parts of these assessments, the issues raised by Burch have not been well addressed in the North. Since the "classic era" of Eskimo ethnography (Birket-Smith 1929; Boas 1888; Jenness 1922; Rasmussen 1929), more or less from the 1950s onward, research about Inuit has lurched from the broadly general to the hyper-narrowly focused, perhaps excepting the work of Burch (1975), Damas (1963), and Heinrich (1963) on kinship and social organization. Inuit have been described as both quintessentially acculturated (see, for instance, Hughes 1965) and quintessentially adapted (Kemp 1971), whereas since the early 1990s dominant research themes have included land claims, cultural-political identity, food security and "the dietary transition," environmental contaminants, and vulnerability to climate change, often in various combinations.

A review of Inuit research, old or new, would be overly long, and I do not have the competence to range across the entire field of hunter-gatherer studies. Rather, I want to use Burch's comment about the "empirical referents" of the conceptual category of hunter-gatherer society to link present Inuit reality into our basal theme. His concern is still as relevant as when he wrote, not least because most hunter-gatherer peoples are even more enmeshed now with national, and increasingly international, entities than was the case twenty years ago. I also feel that this point is where Inuit research articulates most closely with the overall field of hunter-gatherer research.

THEMATIC FOCUS

Although I am using *Inuit* as shorthand for *Eskimo*, the data that will be presented here are drawn almost exclusively from Canada; therefore, *Inuit* is both accurate and appropriate. Moreover, many of these data come from research done in Nunavut, which was formerly the northern and eastern, and predominantly Inuit, part of the Northwest Territories. In particular, I rely on forty-three years of research on the ecology and economy of Inuit hunting in Clyde River, Baffin Island, a medium-size community in Nunavut's Qikiqtaaluk (formerly Baffin) Region.

While no single community can embody the current—much less historical—sociocultural, economic, and political dynamics of a culture that has members in two Canadian provinces (Quebec along with Newfoundland and Labrador) as well as in the Northwest Territories and Nunavut (which alone forms about 22 percent of Canada), it is also not atypical. Like the majority of Nunavut communities, Clyde River's location is the result of the government's social and economic policies. It retains a considerable dependence on traditional resources for high-quality food and has a rapidly growing population that includes a large youth component.

THE CULTURAL AND ENVIRONMENTAL SETTING

Not surprisingly, the Inuit environment of 2013 is considerably changed from when I arrived in Clyde River in 1971. The biggest changes relate to the fact that Nunavut did not exist forty years ago, when the total Inuit population of Canada was less than twenty-five thousand. Presently, it is approximately fifty thousand. The largest Inuit communities were Frobisher Bay (now Iqaluit, the capital of Nunavut), Pangnirtung, Rankin Inlet, Inuvik, and Tuktoyaktuk, with populations ranging between nine hundred and twelve hundred Inuit. At Frobisher, non-Natives outnumbered the Inuit.

In 1970 no land claim had been thought of, let alone finalized; today, four land claims extend across the areas traditionally occupied by Inuit, with the

Nunavut Land Claims Agreement (1993) covering about 22 percent of Canada (the others pertain to Nunavik/Northern Quebec, Nunatsiavut/Labrador, and the Inuvialuit Settlement Region of the Northwest Territories). In 1971 almost the entirety of the Inuit experience with non-Inuit was mediated through government administrators ("settlement managers"), the Hudson's Bay Company, and a very few nurses and teachers; Inuit rarely traveled "south," and almost always because they required serious medical attention. Today, Ottawa and Montreal each have one thousand or so Inuit residents, and Iqaluit, Nunavut's one city, has a population of over seven thousand people, of whom approximately fifty-five hundred are Inuit.

Additionally, the degree of contact that Clyde River, like all Nunavut communities, now has with the outside world was undreamed of forty years ago. Multiple flights arrive and depart each week, satellite telephone and television enter every home, most hunters (even on land) travel with a CB radio and use GPS, and fruits and vegetables can be bought in Grise Fiord, the northernmost town in Canada (lat 76°25′ N), albeit at prices about three times those of Montreal or Ottawa. At the same time, Inuit are now aware that decisions beyond southern Canada—in Washington, DC; Brussels; and Singapore—can have great effects, good and bad, on people's lives.

However, this macro view says very little about Inuit culture and adaptation, either as it was in 1971 or is now. To provide a more culture-centered perspective, I will use Clyde River as my "type" example of the small communities scattered from the Mackenzie Delta to Labrador, although in reality it is impossible to use one community to capture the diversity of a population spread across 4,000 km of tundra and coastline.

Clyde River (Inuktitut: Kangiqtugaapik; lat 70°28′26″ N, long 68°35′10″ W) is located on the east coast of Baffin Island and is fairly typical both in terms of the historical development and present conditions of two-thirds of the communities in Nunavut. The estimated population as of July 2013 was approximately 1,040 (excluding non-Inuit), an increase of 255 Inuit residents since the last official harvesting survey in 2000–2001 recorded a population of 785 (NWMB 2004) and an annual rate of growth of 2.7 percent. The settlement had its "origin" in the arrival of the Hudson's Bay Company in 1923, although the company discouraged Inuit from living near its post into the 1950s.[2] Aside from the Hudson's Bay Company, the only intrusions into Inuit life between 1923 and the early 1960s were an annual patrol by the Royal Canadian Mounted Police and an occasional missionary visit. Actual Inuit residence at Clyde only began in the early 1960s as the result of the Canadian government's policy to create centralized communities.

What is officially considered to be the Clyde area for administrative purposes extends along some 400 km of the Baffin Bay coastline, which is deeply indented by fiords and bays, while inland mountains, ice fields, and the Barnes Ice Cap dominate. Travel over land is limited to river valleys, whereas ocean travel is possible year round either by snowmobile over the winter landfast sea ice (usually from late November to mid-June) or motorized boat during the season of open water, weather permitting.

Until the 1960s, when the Canadian government decided to resettle Inuit in centralized communities (Damas 2002), almost all Clyde Inuit lived in seven or eight semisedentary, extended family winter villages with populations ranging from about a dozen to as many as forty individuals, the most distant of which was 200 km from Clyde River. Here, the main type of dwelling was the *qangmaq*, which was constructed of canvas over a wood frame and insulated with sod. Each "house" was occupied by a nuclear family. People used dog teams for winter transportation, although by the mid-1960s the snowmobile began to displace dog traction, and in summer people used outboard motor–equipped canvas and cedar "freighter canoes" obtained through trade with the Hudson's Bay Company.

Typically, Inuit located their winter villages near the mouths of fiords or bays to facilitate access to areas of dynamic sea ice with their high densities of ringed seals, the main winter food species (supplemented by polar bear and arctic char caught at inland lakes). Beginning around mid-May, people abandoned these winter communities in order to pursue summer season resources: migratory narwhal, anadromous arctic char, and caribou. Because of the periodicity and mobility of these species, summer was a time of frequent movement—to river narrows to fish, to small bays for narwhal, and inland in pursuit of caribou.

With centralization came health care, formal schooling, and relief services, and by 1970 just one extended family with some twenty members lived permanently apart from the government community (Aqviqtiuq closed in 1976). Clyde River itself was made up of some 225 Inuit, all of whom lived in prefabricated wooden houses and were served by the Hudson's Bay Company store, an Anglican mission, a school with three teachers for grades K–6, and a two-nurse health station. The main livelihood strategy, however, remained hunting and fishing. Because of the paucity of wage employment for Inuit (five positions), hunters sold sealskins, some polar bear hides, narwhal ivory, and petty handicrafts to make money to buy essentials (which were few) and to capitalize new technologies, like snowmobiles and outboard engines, needed for hunting. In the early 1970s, hunting households earned an average of about $2,500 annually from these income sources and had available about 880 g of wild food per person for daily sustenance (Wenzel et al. 2010; all prices in Canadian dollars).

This basic pattern of village life lasted until 1983, when the European Union imposed a permanent ban on the importation of seal products. With their main means of accessing money through traditional resource production closed, Inuit required wage employment, mainly through an expansion of local government service and seasonal house construction work for a growing population (Clyde River had reached nearly 450 resident Inuit), to finance food harvesting, although the spiraling cost of hunting equipment led to some contraction in the geography of harvesting activities. As Native educational and southern-skill levels grew, and especially because of the expansion of the local government service sector, Inuit participation in the wage sector expanded.

Presently, some ninety Inuit, about one-half of whom are women, hold full-time jobs, and another twenty-five to thirty-five work part time at seasonal or casual jobs. The annual per capita income is approximately $16,000, although about 60 percent of the adult labor force is either underemployed or unemployed. Hunting is still the main source for high-quality food (principally ringed seal, caribou, polar bear, arctic char, and narwhal), and it supplies roughly 265 g per person per day (Wenzel et al. 2010) but only 30–35 percent of the overall caloric intake. The rest comes from low-quality, carbohydrate-rich market foods. The number of households stands at about 170 (average size 5.1 persons), but another twenty-five to thirty-five nuclear families depend on "couch surfing" in the homes of extended family members, and this estimate of "houselessness" is low only because of the burst of public housing construction at Clyde between 2008 and 2011, which added twenty-five units.

In sum, Clyde Inuit are traditional-food secure, if only barely, and their extensive sharing of *niqituinnaq* (real food) within extended families generally allows everyone access to harvested foods. Access to money, however, is skewed heavily toward those with linguistic (English) and numerate skills, essentially dividing the community into haves and have-nots. Overall, the trajectory of the traditional food sector has been downward since the mid-1980s, and while this decline is partially due to near-geometric population growth, it also has social, as well as nutritional, implications for the cultural maintenance of subsistence traditions. I will elaborate upon this condition not only because of its effects among Inuit, but because it may have some relevance for hunter-gatherer groups facing similar conditions well beyond the North.

Inuit Subsistence: Economy or Culture?

The concerns that Burch articulated in 1992 about hunter-gatherers as a focus of research—and as a conceptual category—still have currency. And, as Peterson (1991b:14) has noted, one key issue is the authenticity of hunter-gatherers beyond their local realities.

Leaving aside questions about the relative purity of Inuit or any other hunter-gatherer society today or long ago (Headland and Reid 1989; Peterson 1991a, 1991b), one element of modernity more than any other is raised in rebuttal to claims by Inuit of a vibrant traditional culture. This is the very visible presence of money, or at least the proliferation of objects that populate most Inuit homes and the areas around them. Snowmobiles, televisions, washers and dryers, and computers are found in almost every Inuit house in Canada, and each was bought with money, usually large amounts. During the heyday of Inuit acculturation research (Graburn 1969; Honigmann and Honigmann 1965; Hughes 1965; Vallee 1962; see also Sahlins 1999; Wenzel 2001), the presence of missionaries and traders marked "culture change"; today, nothing says acculturation like a $15,000 snowmobile or a Nintendo console. In no small way, money has taken the place of the negative influences of Hughes's "Four Flags" era and monetization that of religious conversion.

It is easy to view money as the totality of Inuit livelihoods today, but life in Nunavut and across the Canadian North is expensive. The laptop is one way of characterizing how much Inuit culture has changed, but a better measure of modernity—certainly of its price—is the fact that in Clyde River a bullet can cost $4.00 and a liter of milk $5.50. Together, these objects and prices mean that we need to understand Inuit culture in terms of its present-day paradox: money is an essential resource within the contemporary subsistence system, and Inuit subsistence and Inuit culture are homologous.

In brief, Inuit now live a mixed-economy adaptation that incorporates two very different currencies. Money is obviously one and the most immediately and easily comprehensible. The other is traditional foods. While money is the standard within the economy of what to non-Inuit are the most visible and comprehensible aspects of Inuit life, niqituinnaq is the currency of sharing, or *ningiqtuq*. Put another way, money is the currency of the market and seal, caribou, and *maqtaaq* (whale skin) the currency of sociocultural life. Unfortunately, these two currencies, while they are both essential in and of themselves, are generally not in harmony.

This problem is not especially new. The conflict between "pure" subsistence and market-based influences was highlighted by Polanyi (1944) and has been the subject of various substantive analyses of "primitive/archaic" economies (Dalton 1961, 1962; Gemici 2008; Peterson 1991b; Polanyi 1957; Pryor 1977). Gemici (2008:18 [following from Polanyi 1944:251]) addresses the issue of integrative relations between "embedded" (i.e., reciprocal and redistributive) and "disembedded" (market) systems of economy and writes, "What defines an institutional arrangement is not a type of individual behavior but the characteristics of the 'structure.'" The critical thing, he adds, is not whether these forms can coexist, but which "arrangement is the one that has a central role in achieving integration" (2008:19).

The mixed economy practiced by Inuit today exemplifies the tension between the traditional resources economy, which is regulated through rules of kinship and strengthened by shared local residence, and the disembedded, market economy, in which Inuit must increasingly participate to acquire money. This tension is exacerbated by the reality that money, while essential to capitalize, operate, and maintain the equipment that harvesting requires, is tightly constrained by both the low availability of wage employment and the high cost of the things that can be purchased relative to the money that is available to individuals. Finally, money, in contrast to the cooperation that most harvesting activities necessitate, is almost always accessed through the "one man, one job" rule general to wage work.

This dynamic is made more complicated because engagement in regular wage employment is not cost free. While Inuit men with access to steady, reasonable wages are generally those with the best hunting equipment, for them time becomes a critical currency. Even the most ubiquitous Clyde hunting activity, centering on ringed seals, requires several hours of traveling and searching for, not to mention waiting at, breathing holes; as a result, an average winter seal hunt can last for six to ten hours. If, as Inuit say, the principal attribute one needs to be consistently successful as a hunter is patience, then the corollary is having the time to be patient. Men with regular wage positions have limited time for hunting, usually weekends, and men with time (a majority) are generally cash poor and thus also limited in their ability to hunt.

In spite of these obvious disharmonies, in Clyde River and most other

Nunavummiut communities the economy in its day-to-day functioning is regulated by cultural rather than market norms. While nearly half of all Clyde households are dependent on some form of social transfer payment, virtually everyone can access traditional foods and a place to sleep. Although money is a critical resource for the production of traditional foods, access to these foods is very much based in the functioning of a social economy (Damas 1972; Harder and Wenzel 2012; Wenzel et al. 2000). In other words, writes Lonner (1980:5), "a subsistence economy is a highly specialized mode of production and distribution of not only goods and services, but of social forms."[3]

Problems of Modernity and Subsistence

As much as the contemporary Inuit economy functions with a bias toward the maintenance of the traditional resource sector, money, if only because of its now essential role in harvesting, figures in the four issues that I will now discuss. Most obviously, money pervades nearly every aspect of harvesting, and because it is almost impossible to access in useful amounts through any traditional activity, it confronts Inuit with an immediate dilemma, namely how to best allocate time.

Possibly the biggest shock to Inuit with respect to traditional economic activities was the collapse of the sealskin trade in 1983. This collapse was precipitated by concerns in what was the European Economic Community (EEC) about seal hunting in Atlantic Canada. The EEC ban was written so that it effectively also banned Inuit-produced seal products, and despite political efforts by Inuit, the ban remains in place to this day.[4]

In brief, the sale of ringed-seal skins, which by the 1970s had all but disappeared from domestic use by Inuit, was sufficient to meet the monetary needs of Inuit for imported goods, while *natsiq* (ringed seal) remained the keystone traditional food. The money from these sales was particularly important because the Canadian government's policy of encouraging Inuit to immigrate into centralized communities (Damas 2002; Wenzel 2008a) presented them with the problem of maintaining access to their local resource base. At Clyde River, for instance, reaching seals' winter breathing holes took up to three times longer for dog team–equipped hunters than it had from indigenous winter villages (see Wenzel 1991:86).

Inuit responded by replacing dog teams with snowmobiles, taking advantage of their speed and so gaining more time for hunting. Whereas dogs were

Table 2.1. Clyde River traditional food production, 1980 and 1984.

Species	1980 (444)[a]			1984 (493)		
	Number Caught	Live Weight (kg)	Edible Weight (kg)	Number Caught	Live Weight (kg)	Edible Weight (kg)
Arctic char	4,368	15,288	11,793	5,404	18,914	14,591
Arctic hare	198	990	515	102	510	265
Bearded seal	38	10,374	2,584	25	6,825	1,700
Caribou	976	66,368	43,920	238	16,184	10,710
Cetacean	37	16,798	3,330	49	22,700	4,554
Duck	618	989	680	401	643	442
Goose	23	182	83	85	317	145
Polar bear	45	11,325	3,950	45	11,325	3,950
Ptarmigan	652	652	391	306	306	183
Ringed seal	3,905	175,725	70,290	2,189	98,505	39,402
Seabird	6	6	2.5	12	12	5
Walrus	1	682	460	none	none	none
All species[b]			137,998.5			75,947

Source: BRIA 1981, 1985.

[a]Numbers in parentheses represent the community population for that year.

[b]Total harvested edible biomass.

consumers of seal meat, snowmobiles ate money, though Inuit were able to capture sufficient seals so that they could absorb the expense associated with this technological change. They were helped by the fact that few imported goods were absolutely essential, and sealing, being a year-round activity, easily provided high-quality, culturally valued food and money to support the technology that facilitated hunting. As Kemp (1971) observed, the snowmobile, far from being a disruptive element, was the means by which Inuit could maintain hunting as a livelihood strategy and sustain traditional subsistence as a sociocultural adaptation.

Because seal harvesting and the sale of sealskins underpinned both the traditional food and monetary sectors of the Clyde economy, the collapse of the market for sealskins reverberated through the harvesting system (table 2.1). The effects were especially apparent with regard to the two most important mammalian food species: ringed seal (*Phoca hispida*) and barren-ground caribou (*Rangifer tarandus groenlandicus*). Harvests of both species declined steeply as their hunting requires considerable monetary investment, seals because they

Table 2.2. Per capita traditional food availability in Clyde River,
1980 and 1984.

	1980 (pop. 444)	1984 (pop. 493)
Total edible weight/year	137,998.5 kg	75,947 kg
Edible weight/person/year	311 kg	154 kg
Edible weight/person/day	852 g	422 g

are hunted frequently and caribou because of the distances involved in reaching them.

That sealing was affected is consistent with the EEC boycott action, and the marked decline in the harvest of ringed seals indicated that as much as 45 percent of that harvest had been market driven. However, the harvest of the main terrestrial food species, caribou, declined even more steeply—over 75 percent. Clyde Inuit explained that caribou were then located about 200 km from the community, and because sealskin prices had declined from twenty-one dollars in 1983 to less than two dollars in 1984, the cost of the fuel for distant hunting was prohibitive. The effect of this change in the harvest of these two species (table 2.2) was that the overall amount of traditional food available to Clyde Inuit was considerably less in 1984 than in any of the previous four years (BRIA 1981, 1982, 1983, 1984; Wenzel et al. 2010). Traditional food production at Clyde River was down 53 percent compared to the level in 1980, despite increases in the capture of narwhal (*Monodon monoceros*) and arctic char (*Salvelinus alpinus*) by 25 percent and 20 percent, respectively. Moreover, Clyde hunter productivity, which was about 2,490 kg in 1980, had fallen to 1,320 kg in 1984.

The sealing controversy's legacy was twofold. The most immediate result was the territorial government being confronted by the fact that hunters' sealskin revenues, as I have shown, were severely affected. The government's response was to devolve services directly to communities across the Northwest Territories, creating a municipal government stratum that took responsibility for activities formerly carried out by federal and territorial government personnel, most of whom were non-Inuit.

With growing populations and money scarcer than ever before for Inuit, settlements like Clyde River expanded their employment bases. Beginning in 1985, local employment steadily increased from some ten full-time positions to, by the early 2000s, more than fifty, with fully 80 percent of those employed either working directly for the municipality or holding Nunavut government positions earmarked for Clyde residents. Additionally, the local government also employed ten part-time workers.

This expansion of regularized employment, along with supplemental seasonal and casual work, meant that much more money was present in Clyde and similar communities than was ever the case before the loss of the sealskin market. But it also presented Inuit men, many of whom entered the wage economy with the explicit intent of being able to meet the increasing expenses associated with hunting, with a new problem: how to balance the opportunity costs associated with dividing their time between their employers' requirements and hunting. As one Clyde Inuk, who was one of the community's three full-time mechanics, succinctly put it, "I began working so I could support my snowmobile. I thought I would quit after a year, but then I needed a new boat. Now I only feel like hunting on the weekend" (Qillaq, personal communication 2001).

The other effect of the controversy in the mid-1980s was the Northwest Territories government's plan to develop tourism for suddenly cash-poor communities. While over time tourism has been a boon for southern entrepreneurs, the lack of a well-developed service infrastructure in most Nunavut communities has meant that very little money is derived from cruise ships or typical adventure tourism activities. The one exception has been sport hunting, especially polar bear trophy hunting, which in 2000 brought $1.3 million ($20,000 for each of the sixty-five hunts) into the twelve Nunavut communities that hosted trophy hunters (Wenzel 2008b:17).

While this revenue may appear minor when compared to the tens of millions spent by the government in nearly every community, the hunt is regulated such that monies are earned mainly by Inuit with strong traditional skills, including the ability to drive a dog team and read polar bear signs and the weather. The majority of such hunts are guided by a select group of hunters, most of whom have few other employment possibilities but who can earn $6,000 per trip and often guide two or three clients a season, thus earning sufficient funds to allow them to conduct extensive harvesting activities during the rest of the year.

These men are among the most active harvesters in their communities and invest on average about 55 percent of their sport hunt wages in new equipment. When the traditional food produced by six Clyde River polar bear guides was shadow priced at the cost of the hamburger meat sold in the community store ($10.02/kg), the return in ringed seal, caribou, or maqtaaq was $5.30 per kilogram for every guiding dollar spent on equipment (Wenzel 2008b:86).

Qillaq's opportunity-cost dilemma and the high intensity–high return situation of hunter-guides exemplify two aspects of how Inuit cope with the money component of the mixed economy. One is to basically become a week-end hunter, a high-risk strategy in that compressing harvesting activities into a very few days runs the danger of, for instance, the weather not cooperating when time and energy coincide. The other is to be dependent on an enterprise that has a fickle clientele and to which there is growing international opposition from wildlife conservation and anti-hunting groups (see Waters et al. 2009).

The circumstances surrounding Inuit engagement in wage labor are conten-tious; high-return seasonal employment underscores that even when Inuit are relatively secure with respect to the monetized component of the mixed econ-omy, traditional food production is not necessarily assured. The most recent harvest data gathered by the Nunavut Wildlife Management Board (NWMB 2004), spanning the years 1996 to 2001, show that traditional food production remains robust, but a closer examination reveals a steady decline both in rela-tion to harvesting in the early 1980s and to the present population. My (Wenzel et al. 2010) analysis of the data for Nunavut's Qikiqtaaluk Region demonstrates a widening gap between harvest production and Inuit population.

The Qikiqtaaluk Region is the most populous part of Nunavut. In 2001, the last year that comprehensive regional data on traditional food production were gathered, 12,540 Inuit were living in thirteen communities, including Iqaluit, the territory's capital and largest population center (3,327 Inuit in 2001). That year the harvest of all food species across the region amounted to 1,249,746 kg (99.6 kg/person/year). When calculated as the amount of production available per person daily, however, this volume translates into a less impressive 273 g. In comparison, annual production averaged for the four years (1980–1983; regional population) before the EEC sealskin boycott took effect was 2,174,000 kg (279 kg/ person/year) or a daily availability of 766 g per person.

The data clearly indicate a severe decline in traditional food security. Not only is the 2001 total harvest 44 percent less than the 1980–1983 annual average, it is 17 percent lower than in 1984, the year that the sealskin market collapsed, which led to a 25 percent decline in the regional harvest from the previous year. In fact, a virtually exact inverse relationship exists between the region's popula-tion growth (44 percent) from 1980 to 2001 and the decline in total harvest over these twenty years as the number of Qikiqtaalummiut increased from approxi-mately 7,000 to 12,500.

This twenty-year regional trend is mirrored at the community level. At Clyde River, the change in population—a 43 percent increase—is almost exactly that of the whole of the Qikiqtaaluk. The traditional food security situation is, however, much worse in terms of annual production and the daily amount available per person. In 1980 Clyde Inuit produced approximately 137,000 kg for a population of 444 people (843 g/person/day), whereas in 2001 production was only 66,907 kg for a village that had grown to 785 (233 g/person/day)—a reduction in total harvest volume of 51 percent but a 72 percent decline in the daily amount of harvested food available per person. Even more startling is that the decline in annual harvest volume and daily food availability is not the worst among Qikiqtaaluk communities.

The cause of this decline in harvest production has been the subject of a wide range of explanations. Scholars have variously proposed that it is the result of a "dietary transition" from traditional to market foods, that the collapse of the sealskin market discouraged hunters, that Inuit youth have too many distractions to learn to hunt, that intergenerational communication of traditional ecological knowledge is not occurring, and, most recently, that the effects of climate change have negatively impacted animal populations.

Given the extent of sociocultural change that Inuit have had to cope with over the last half century and the fact that change in the biophysical system is evident, at least some of these things can be presumed to be causative. They also are either hard to measure or are at present more model than reality. However, the relationship between money and harvesting is clear and not only in the terms already described.

The data from Clyde River show one of the most marked differences between food acquisition activities today and those of the early 1970s to mid-1980s: during what is the work week for job holders, amazingly few men travel out to hunt. In the past several years, even in the best weather, I have rarely been able to count more than ten or twelve snowmobiles heading out for sealing, which is quite different from the 1970s, when it was not uncommon on a calm winter day to meet or see at a distance twenty to twenty-five hunters searching for or waiting at breathing holes. In both the 1970s and in 2010–2011, those who might be considered highly active hunters went sealing, weather permitting, three or more times each week.

In the last two years, twenty-one Clyde men between the ages of twenty and fifty-four who are not job holders were interviewed about their winter and spring seal hunting. Among the information sought was the number of trips they made per week and the state of their equipment, as well as with whom they hunted cooperatively and shared food. Fourteen reported that they were limited to two to three sealing trips per month, unless they could travel as another hunter's passenger. The common explanation given for this low frequency was the poor condition of their equipment or insufficient funds for fuel and oil. Two others did report hunting more frequently (six and seven times in a month, respectively), but because of the age and condition of their snowmobiles, they limited their activity to an area relatively close to Clyde River. This self-imposed limit was so that in case of a breakdown they would be able either to walk back to the community (approximately 25 km) or hail hunters returning from more distant hunts.

The other five men were notable in that they were not engaged in wage employment and hunted at least three times a week. Four reported being able to do so because they had a spouse or daughters (one had both) with well-paying wage positions. The fifth was the younger sibling of the highest paid man in the community and had been designated by their grandfather to be the primary hunter in his generation of the extended family; his brother had been directed to support his hunting. Because of his salary, the older brother generally bought a new snowmobile each year, passing his "old" machine to his hunting brother.

Recent work with women at Clyde River suggests that the importance of close female kin as monetary contributors to men's hunting is not unique (Quintal 2012). Among the twenty-nine women in Quintal's sample, only ten (35 percent) said they were not making a monetary contribution to a male relative, whereas nineteen (65 percent) did so for one or more male relations (thirteen [45 percent] for their spouse only, two for their spouse and at least one other male kinsperson, and six for a nonspouse relation). According to Quintal, support could be as expansive as buying a new snowmobile or limited to the purchase of fuel or ammunition when needed.

Quintal's research is interesting in part because it provides a different view on Inuit women and subsistence. Generally women's economic activities beyond the domestic, such as skin clothing manufacture and food preparation, were seen as limited to the gathering of the few plant resources the Arctic offers. Giffen (1930) and Kjellstrom (1973) both describe the subsistence role of Inuit women as one that is complementary to, but clearly secondary to (but see Bodenhorn 1990), the activities of men. The work by Quintal strongly suggests, however, that at least in the near term, men's hunting and the security associated with traditional food resources are heavily dependent on women's work outside of the home. Her work also suggests the possibility of important changes occurring, if not immediately then in the future, in the social configuration of the Inuit subsistence system, in which women's contributions to the harvesting sphere are as important, if not the same, as those of men. It also gives new meaning to Briggs's (1974) provocative title, "Eskimo Women: Makers of Men."

If the present Inuit harvesting situation can be considered a Malthusian problem, then the resource that is in short supply is hunters, not animals. Not all hunters are equal; this was the case in 1971 and is the case today. But much of Inuit harvesting requires the cooperation of at least two men, and the present reality is that the monetary cost of traditional resource activities for individual hunters adversely affects food security.

Conclusions

Earlier I raised four issues. The last—whether the traditional economy will become "disembedded" from Inuit subsistence culture—has no definitive conclusion as it is dependent on how effectively Inuit adapt a scarce resource and an emerging set of socioeconomic relations into the subsistence system. The three elements affecting Inuit harvesting raise a very serious cultural question about whether recent economic conditions will transform subsistence products from a cultural good into a commodity to which access becomes completely dependent on market-related economic means. Ultimately, the question is whether Inuit subsistence is on a trajectory that will move it out of the realm of a social economy regulated by and embedded in cultural norms (Polanyi 1944) to become an activity determined by prevailing market forces (Peterson 1991b).

Hunting and harvesting, as such, are not central to this question. Rather, the matter may turn on the development of a socioculturally congruent framework that can sustain the traditional economy. Put another way, can sharing survive the twin stresses of a difficult-to-handle resource and a changed structural relationship that at least in part includes a shift in the relationship between genders?

"The continuing significance of kinship relations in the face of cash and commoditization is a measure of the extent to which supposed entailments of the market economy—secularization, technical rationality and individualism—have not been realized. Obligations to kin still appear to provide the context in which economic decisions are made and money used, and to take primacy over maximizing individual use and control of cash" (Peterson 1991a:82). Peterson's words about the weight of market economic forces on Australian Aboriginal culture (see Bliege Bird et al., chapter 9; Codding et al., chapter 8; Coxworth, chapter 7, this volume) seemed to me equally appropriate as a description of the robustness of Inuit subsistence culture. I also thought that in a near future, money would become better integrated into ningiqtuq, or at least have a less disruptive effect (Wenzel 2000; Wenzel and White 2000). Today, I am not less sanguine that Inuit will better adapt money to their cultural needs, but I did not anticipate in 1990, let alone 1984 or 1971, that the process would entail assessing social, and not simply economic, relations.

The twenty-first-century dilemma confronting Inuit is not the penetration of money per se or that money has become an essential resource for sustaining traditional food production and, thus, food security. Rather, it is that money as an aspect of subsistence may require a differently patterned arrangement of socioeconomic relationships in order to avoid the mixed economy becoming one in which subsistence is a quaint anachronism that, for the majority of Inuit, takes on a hypothetical rather than cultural meaning.

Notes

1. From July 2004 to July 2012 the population of Nunavut increased 12.9 percent (1.6 percent average annual growth). Approximately 51.0 percent of Nunavummiut are under the age of twenty-five (Nunavut Bureau of Statistics 2013).

2. See Wenzel 2008a, 2009 for an ethnohistorical account of the community's development since the late nineteenth century.

3. Structurally, Clyde Inuit and the great majority of Nunavummiut live in a subsistence culture, although the social dimensions and rules of economy differ between Inuit societies (see Damas 1972; Gombay 2010; Langdon 1984).

4. The ban on Inuit seal products was relaxed by the European Union in October 2015.

CHAPTER THREE

"In the bush the food is free"

The Ju/'hoansi of Tsumkwe in the Twenty-First Century

RICHARD B. LEE

Introduction

Since the development of serious ethnographic field research in the early twentieth century, the Ju/'hoansi of Namibia and Botswana have become one of
the best-documented hunter-gatherer populations in the world. While famous
for their traditional lifeways, directed economic and social change has greatly
altered their economic and social relations. But despite a history of having
development schemes, the cash economy, and bureaucratic overrule imposed
on them, foraging persists as an important economic and social force in
Ju/'hoan society today. In this chapter I examine the continuing importance of
foraging among the Ju/'hoansi and address both the question of why foraging
has persisted and the consequences of this persistence for Ju/'hoan society as a
whole (figure 3.1).

Background: Settlement at Tsumkwe

For the first six decades of the twentieth century, Tsumkwe was a modest water
hole supporting a small mobile population of Ju/'hoan hunter-gatherers, estimated at under thirty individuals (e.g., Muller 1912). Tsumkwe was situated in
the remote hinterland of the territory of South-West Africa, administered first
by Germany (1885–1915) and then by South Africa (1915–1990). In the years
1950–1959, the Marshall family pioneered fieldwork in the greater Nyae Nyae
area from their base at /Aotcha (/Gausha), 25 km south of Tsumkwe (refer to
figure I.1). The Marshalls documented in detail the foraging way of life of the
interior Ju/'hoansi, whom they labeled the !Kung Bushmen in accordance with

Figure 3.1. Ju/'hoansi women gathering wild foods south of Tsumkwe, Namibia, July 2010. Photograph by Richard Lee.

the naming convention prevalent at the time (J. Marshall 1980; L. Marshall 1960, 1976; Thomas 1959).

!Kung bands, consisting of twenty-five to fifty members, each occupied a *n!ore*, or territory, on a non-exclusive basis. Band members spent about half of each week hunting and gathering and moved four or five times a year with the seasons. They dispersed in the summer rainy season (October–March) and aggregated around a small number of permanent water holes during the winter dry season (April–October). Archaeological excavations have indicated that this pattern of life had considerable time depth, with links to Later Stone Age (LSA) lithic cultures extending for millennia.

Then, in December 1959, all this changed when Claude MacIntyre, a functionary in the Native Affairs Department of the apartheid-era South African administration, settled at Tsumkwe. The site was declared a government station, a borehole was dug to provide sufficient water supplies, and an all-weather gravel road was built connecting Nyae Nyae to the rest of the colony. A townsite was mapped out. At the time the estimated population of one thousand Nyae Nyae Ju/'hoansi was scattered around twenty-five water holes, over a territory of about 15,000–20,000 km² (L. Marshall 1976).

MacIntyre issued a general call to the Ju to abandon their home villages and come to live at Tsumkwe under the watchful eye of government. The government, in turn, would provide health services, schooling, and agricultural training, and a resident Dutch Reformed missionary would have the makings of a new flock of converts. The whole scheme would be sustained by weekly truck-loads of food, mostly bags of mealie meal, sugar, tea, and cooking oil.

Thus began a gigantic experiment in forced social change that to a degree has continued to the present day. Tsumkwe's history is a turbulent one. Through five-plus decades the Ju/'hoansi have experienced apartheid rule, a war of lib-eration, the transition to independence under a black government and its bureaucratic outreach, and immersion in the cold bath of the cash economy and capitalist relations of production. They have also been the recipients of several well-intentioned efforts by sympathetic outsiders to ameliorate the harsh condi-tions of overcrowding and social dysfunction faced by the people of Nyae Nyae.

An important monograph, *The Ju/'hoan San of Nyae Nyae and Namibian Independence* (2013), by Biesele and Hitchcock documents these developments and forms a necessary background to this chapter. My focus here is on the cur-rent status of the people of Tsumkwe and the surrounding district, particularly on the ways in which their subsistence needs are met. The roughly five hundred to eight hundred Ju/'hoan residents of Tsumkwe and the fifteen hundred to two thousand people of the outlying villages use a range of resources to meet their subsistence needs. How have the Ju faced the challenges of poverty, exclusion, partial loss of land base and culture, and the easy availability of alcohol? And how are these historical forces reflected in their relative reliance on hunting and gathering, farming and herding, and store-bought food acquired in the cash economy?

POLITICAL HISTORY

Biesele and Hitchcock (2013) have chronicled the ongoing struggles of the Nyae Nyae people to preserve their land base and way of life. The late John Mar-shall's five-part film *A Kalahari Family* (2005) covers much of the same ground, although the two works at times offer differing interpretations of the same events. Briefly, the history of Nyae Nyae, of both local and regional develop-ments, from 1950 to the present can be summarized as six historical moments:

The Years 1950–1959: The Last Years of Full-Time Hunting and Gathering. During the 1950s the Ju/'hoansi continued to subsist primarily by hunting and gather-ing. The border between South African–controlled South-West Africa and

British protectorate of Bechuanaland was virtually unmarked, and the people of the Dobe area and the Nyae Nyae area formed a single intermarrying population. During these years the Marshall family made major expeditions to Nyae Nyae, documenting the Ju/'hoan people's hunting and gathering way of life in research articles and monographs (L. Marshall 1960, 1969, 1976, 1999; Thomas 1959, 2006) and in film (J. Marshall 1980, 2005).

The Years 1959–1966: The Tsumkwe Settlement Experiment. In the first few years of the settlement, administrators spent their time gathering the San and adjusting them to town life. They issued numbered dog tags, possession of which entitled residents to food rations. However, the hinterland villages were never fully abandoned. Even the town residents retained ties to their old n!ores, and most made extended visits in seasons when water was abundant.

In the 1960s the apartheid land tenure system was formalized (favoring whites), and the Ju/'hoansi lost two-thirds of their land base (Marshall and Ritchie 1984). But the colonial government did preserve an area of 8,992 km², which was gazetted "Bushmanland," and their tenure was protected from encroachment by both other Africans and Europeans. On the British side of the border in 1963, DeVore and Lee (Lee and Devore 1976) initiated what was to become their long-term study of the "!Kung San" (Solway and Lee 1990).

The Years 1966–1979: The War for Namibia. Liberation movements were rising in neighboring African countries, including Angola, Mozambique, Zimbabwe, and South Africa. The white rulers of South-West Africa took steps to strengthen their grip on the colony in 1965 by erecting a 3 m fence along its entire eastern perimeter, cutting off the people of Nyae Nyae from contact with Dobe-area kin in Botswana. In 1966 the South-West African Peoples Organization (SWAPO) launched an armed struggle to achieve independence for the country they named "Namibia." South African counterinsurgency policies included organizing ethnic battalions of Namibian soldiers. Several hundred Ju/'hoan men were recruited as soldiers, as documented in John Marshall's (1980) classic film *N!ai: The Story of a !Kung Woman* (see also Lee and Hurlich 1982).

The Years 1979–1988: The Nyae Nyae Development Foundation of Namibia. As South African influence in Bushmanland waned, Marshall and Ritchie (1984) launched a bold initiative to support the Ju/'hoansi through apartheid's final years. They co-founded in 1981 an organization that later became the Nyae Nyae Development Foundation of Namibia (NNDFN), based in the capital, Windhoek, to support the Ju/'hoansi materially and foster the development of a grassroots organization to give the Ju people political voice and power. The Ju/wa Farmers Union (JFU) became an exercise in building representative democracy with elected leaders.

In the early 1980s, the JFU set out what was—for the times—a radical agenda and called for a return to the land. Hundreds of Ju longed to leave behind decades of crowded, alcohol-fueled living and reaffirm their connections to the land. The NNDFN strongly supported this movement and financed borehole drilling and the purchase of cattle on long-term credit. By 1987 ten groups totaling 342 people had moved; by 1992 some thirty groups numbering close to one thousand had moved to "outstations" (Biesele and Hitchcock 2013:70).

The Years 1988–1992: Namibian Independence. By 1988 South Africa—after serious military reverses—was finally persuaded by the international community to relinquish its hold on its South-West Africa colony. In United Nation–supervised elections, the liberation movement SWAPO won a decisive victory over the South African–supported party, the DTA, and formed the first democratically elected government based on one person, one vote. The Ju/'hoansi of Nyae Nyae solidly supported SWAPO. Only a month after the historic release from prison of Nelson Mandela in South Africa, Namibia celebrated its independence on March 21, 1990 (Biesele and Hitchcock 2013).

The Years 1991–2000: Which Way Nyae Nyae? At the 1991 National Land Conference that would set land-use and land-tenure policies for post-independence Namibia, the Ju/'hoan n!ore system of land tenure was recognized as a legitimate form within the new nation, a decision—later ratified by the new government—that gave a boost of credibility to San land rights throughout the country (Lee 2013a:195–196).

Despite this triumph, it soon became evident that there was a serious difference of opinion within the NNDFN about the direction of development of the Nyae Nyae region and people. Marshall strongly held that the Ju/'hoansi's future lay as farmers and herders. But other observers argued that the Nyae Nyae natural environment and wildlife constituted a prime asset that needed to be carefully managed. This latter goal was clearly not compatible with unrestricted livestock development. The Ju/'hoan people appeared divided on this issue, with some embracing the new life of husbandry and others holding to more traditional values.

Seeing the very limited agricultural potential of the region, the national government under SWAPO favored the wildlife option. Community-based natural resource management (CBNRM) was the new modality of local governance then sweeping Africa. CBNRM prioritized the conservation of indigenous plants and wildlife and gave the local populations a strong stake in managing these. This type of management represented a clear departure from colonial-era practices in which distant government bureaucrats often dictated land-use and wildlife policies with little or no local knowledge.

With the Namibian government and USAID through its LIFE (Living in a Finite Environment) program supporting the CBNRM option, the former Bushmanland, now regazetted as the Tsumkwe District East (refer to figure I.1), became the site of Namibia's very first CBNRM project in 1998. (Twenty-seven other community-based management projects throughout Namibia soon followed.)

The Nyae Nyae Farmers' Cooperative was reborn as the Nyae Nyae Conservancy and elected a leadership. Steps were taken to build a tourism industry, with several Ju villages becoming ecotourism destinations and the Tsumkwe Lodge opening its doors. In another initiative a large paddock was fenced off to raise eland and later Cape buffalo, and some fifteen hundred head of plains game, including hartebeest, wildebeest, kudu, and gemsbok, were introduced into the territory.

Another post-independence development was the setting up of a local government entity known as the Traditional Authority. Tsamkxau Toma, who had been a key member of the Marshall family's research village of /Aotcha (/Gausha in older spellings), was elected to the office of Traditional Authority along with a council composed of village notables. Known affectionately by his nickname, "Bobo," Tsamkxau evolved over the years into an able leader and a brilliant orator with the ability to articulate complex issues in elegant ways. Like his counterparts elsewhere in Namibia, however, he has been hampered by the serious lack of real power allowed local leaders under government statutes, which favor situating power largely at the regional and national levels.

Wildlife and Livestock: Coexistence or Conflict?

The people of Nyae Nyae entered the twenty-first century with a mixed subsistence base. Fortunately, the move to CBNRM did not entirely foreclose other development pathways for the Ju/'hoansi, and the legislation allowed for limited herding of cattle and goats and encouraged the planting of gardens.

Bow and arrow hunting for a range of game species continued to be permitted. While the fifteen hundred released animals, identified by their ear tags, were off limits, their offspring and untagged animals were all fair game. Commercial trophy hunting was added to the mix. The conservancy in cooperation with the Ministry of Environment and Tourism (MET) could issue licenses to commercial "white hunters" and allow them to hunt large game for trophies for clients, and these licenses became a significant source of income for Nyae Nyae. One elephant license cost a wealthy overseas client the substantial sum of USD$80,000, part of which was divided and distributed to conservancy members. Nyae Nyae Conservancy (NNC) payouts in recent years have averaged about NAD$300 per member, and the meat from elephant kills is also distributed, adding a major protein component to the diet.

However, the coexistence of even limited farming-herding with wildlife management also had serious drawbacks. Lions, protected as endangered game, increased in numbers and from the beginnings of the outstation movement were a serious threat to the cattle. The pro-livestock Ju/'hoansi labeled the lions "the dogs of Nature Conservation" for doing their part in the apartheid government's effort to thwart Ju/'hoan development. After independence the new government responded by assigning a full-time game warden to manage the reserve in consultation with local Ju/'hoan authorities and, when necessary, to cull lions and other predators (leopards, hyenas, and wild dogs) killing livestock.

A second and even more urgent matter was the dramatic increase in the elephant population of Nyae Nyae. Formerly seasonal migrants, an elephant population of eight hundred to one thousand became resident in the district, attracted by the year-round availability of water after some twenty-five boreholes were dug in the 1980s and 1990s. Elephants would routinely destroy borehole-pumping machinery and water storage tanks to get at the precious commodity. Starting in the 1980s and continuing to the present, people used more and more elaborate methods to protect the water from the elephants. At some water points the borehole machinery and water tanks were protected by what looked like the rings of concrete emplacements used in antitank warfare.

Gradually, the elephants learned to avoid these sites and seek water at other locations. Several water points were established with heavily protected, solar-driven borehole pumps to provide water for these elephants and other game.

Tsumkwe Today

Against this background, I present the results of social and economic surveys conducted in 2008, 2010, and 2011 and a follow-up study from July to August 2013. My goal was to take stock of the conditions of life for a wide range of Tsumkwe residents and visitors. One of my key questions was to what extent did foraging subsistence play a role in their overall adaptation to "modernity."

The town of Tsumkwe is located 300 km east of Grootfontein, the nearest large town, and 50 km west of the Botswana border. For a frontier outpost servicing a remote district of under three thousand people, the town has a surprising number of government and other institutional buildings, including a primary and secondary school, a police station and courthouse, a medical clinic, churches, and a broadcasting center. These are the most visible signs of "progress." The five hundred to eight hundred inhabitants of Tsumkwe live in a wide range of housing, and the lives they lead there are mostly invisible to the casual visitor. The housing ranges from standard South African "location"-style concrete-block row housing to informal clusters of mud-walled "Bantu" rondavels to traditional San "beehive"-shaped grass huts.

The town's Ju/'hoan inhabitants include "permanent" residents and a large segment of floaters whose primary homes are at one of the out-settlements and who come to Tsumkwe for stays varying from days to months. In the analysis I have divided them into Residents and Visitors, but in reality they form a continuum since most of the "residents" do claim n!ore links to and spend time at one of the remote settlements. Among several larger questions addressed by the surveys, a key one was to what degree were the Ju—like other indigenous people around the world—adhering to or disengaging from their traditional ways of life? By embracing modernity were some also repudiating their past? The answers to these questions and several others were surprising, and I present my findings in four key areas:

1. Subsistence strategies. The goal here was to get a good sense of the primary subsistence sources. What was the degree of reliance on wild, farmed, and store-bought food? How did meat from hunting figure into

subsistence, and, similarly, how did livestock husbandry and government rations contribute to the diet?

2. Degree of dependence on the cash economy. Money has entered the community by three different routes: wage labor for both inside and outside work; petty commodity production (artisanal production of crafts and collection of wild products as marketable commodities); and government transfer payments in the form of disability and old-age pensions.

3. Health issues. Although the survey did not include a demographic component as such (cf. Howell 2000, 2010), this chapter addresses several epidemiological issues. Researching in a country (Namibia) that has one of the world's highest rates of HIV infection, I was interested in how severely the Tsumkwe District had been affected by the AIDS pandemic. I also sought data on incidence rates of two other major diseases: malaria and tuberculosis. The survey provided some unexpected results.

4. Religious practices. For millennia the Ju/'hoansi have relied heavily on their indigenous healing practices in the treatment of diseases and trauma (Katz 1982; Katz et al. 1997; L. Marshall 1999). But after five decades of missionary efforts, to what extent had the Ju become converted to Christianity? Did this conversion mean that adherence to traditional forms of treatment and healing practices were on the wane?

Methods

My focus here is on the 2010 social survey, which was the most extensive and which contained just fewer than one hundred informants. The results of this survey are supplemented by findings from the other years. Two graduate assistants from the University of Toronto and I carried out the 2010 survey. Laura Meschino and Rhea Wallington were aided by local bilingual interpreters Leon Tsamkxau and Steve /Twi, while I conducted interviews in Ju/'hoansi. Questionnaires took forty-five to sixty minutes to administer. Overall, we collected ninety-eight interviews.

Tsumkwe is the capital of a sparsely populated district of 9,000 km². Approximately five hundred Ju live in Tsumkwe, and an additional nineteen hundred live in thirty widely scattered settlements. In our sampling we tried to get a good mix of Tsumkwe residents and visitors from the outlying villages. We

Table 3.I. A breakdown of 2010
Tsumkwe study participants by gender.

	Male	Female	Total
Resident	18	23	41
Visitor	25	32	57

tried to get a reasonable number of male and female informants. Table 3.1 shows the breakdown of informants by gender and residence.

Additionally, in July 2013 Lucah Rosenberg-Lee and I visited remote settlements to see if the subsistence mix differed from the town-based observations of 2010. Interviews took place at six widely dispersed villages 30–100 km distant from Tsumkwe. The six villages (refer to figure I.1) were Den/ui and /Gau!oma, 30 km to the west; N//oma School and N//oma village, 100 km to the northwest; //Aru, 85 km to the southeast; and //Au/oba, 25 km due north of Tsumkwe (distances approximate). In addition, we made brief observations at two other villages: Makuri, 30 km southeast of Tsumkwe, and De#oa, 15 km north of town.

Results

I present findings on the four key areas previously mentioned—subsistence strategies, the cash economy, health, and religious practices—as well as attitudes toward old and new ways of life.

SUBSISTENCE STRATEGIES: RELIANCE ON WILD, FARMED, OR STORE-BOUGHT FOOD

After fifty years of life settled on a government station, one would expect that a people's subsistence strategies would have shifted decisively from foraging for wild foods to reliance on farmed, store-bought, or government-handout foods. It was surprising that this was not the case (table 3.2).

Subsistence Strategies in Settlements. The results indicated the strong persistence in the Ju/'hoan food supply of gathered wild foods. One-third of all respondents (30/89) listed wild vegetable foods as *their most important single source of food.* The same number (30/89) listed store-bought food as their most important source, and just over half that number (18/89) stated that wild and store-bought

Table 3.2. Ju/'hoan informants' dependence on various food sources: wild, domestic, government, and commercial.

Food Source	Wild/ Foraged (%)	Farmed (%)	Herded (%)	Hunted (%)	Government Issued (%)	Store Bought (%)
Primary or co-primary source	54	7	4	1	0	54
Secondary	45	54	30	61	94	45
Percentage using source	99	61	34	62	94	99
Not using source at all	1	39	66	38	6	1

Note: *n* = 89; 9 informants were not ascertained on this question.

foods were equal in importance as primary sources. In other words, *over half of all those interviewed stated that wild food was of primary or co-primary importance in their diets*. Only a single informant said he did not eat gathered foods.

Some thirty-five different locations—including Tsumkwe itself—were listed by the informants as sites for gathering. Among the most widely collected wild foods were the abundant berries of the genus *Grewia*, collected by 50–90 percent of the respondents; the tasty potato-like roots of the genus *Vigna*, collected by 70 percent; and the fruits of the baobab tree, collected by 60 percent, which provide both a vitamin C–rich fruit and proteinaceous nutmeat. The mongongo nut and fruit, made famous by ecological research in the Dobe area of Botswana (Lee 1979), were gathered by 35 percent of the respondents.

Farming at 7 percent (6/89), livestock raising at 4 percent (4/89), and hunting at 1 percent (1/89) were distant third, fourth, and fifth choices. A large minority of informants (39 percent) had no access to farmed foods, while a two-thirds majority (66 percent) lacked access of any kind to livestock-sourced foods (milk or meat). Farming and livestock raising's low standing in the subsistence hierarchy is a reflection of the ecological limitations, referred to previously, seriously impacting crop and herd viability in a semidesert environment.

Although 62 percent of informants stated that they did eat *some* meat from hunting, 38 percent did not. We do not know why hunting ranked so low on the list of subsistence sources, but overall the number of men who are actively hunting has declined. The Australian Aboriginal Martu, for example, hunt regularly from vehicles with rifles, but neither are viable options for Ju/'hoansi (Bird et al., chapter 9; Codding et al., chapter 8, this volume). However, it is possible that at the more remote outstations, 30–100 km from Tsumkwe, the rates of returns from hunting would be higher.

Table 3.3. A rank ordering of the two most important food sources at eight remote Ju/'hoan villages.

Village	Distance[a]	Gathered	Hunted	Store Bought	Government Issued
/Gau!oma[b]	35 km W	1st			2nd
//Karu[b]	85 km SE	1st			2nd
//Kau/oba[b]	25 km N		2nd		1st
De/nui	30 km W	1st	2nd		
De#toa	15 km N	2nd		1st	
Makuri	30 km SE	2nd	1st		
N//oma School[b]	100 km NW	2nd			1st
N//oma Village	95 km NW	1st	2nd		

[a]Distance in km and direction from Tsumkwe.
[b]Villages with schools and school-feeding programs.

Subsistence Strategies in Remote Villages. One of my first impressions of these outer villages was of the abundance of wild food residues in kitchen middens behind each house. Mongongo nutshell casings were particularly plentiful at N//oma School and N//oma village. In //Au/oba village, we identified animal bones in the middens, including porcupine, springhare, warthog, and kudu. In each setting I asked village residents to rank their most important and their second most important subsistence source based on the quantity of food from each source.

One indication of subsistence diversity is the wide range of food sources people described, ranging from gathered to hunted to store-bought to government-supplied food (table 3.3). Nevertheless, the eight villages presented a clear hierarchy of food sources. Gathered food was primary in four villages and secondary in three others. Government-supplied food was primary in two villages and secondary in two others. Hunting showed surprising strength, being primary in one village and secondary in three others. Finally, at a single village the residents stated that store-bought food was the most important food source, while gathering was second in importance. These results indicate a high degree of dependence on *gathering*, first or second in importance in seven of eight locations, and considerably more important than store-bought food, which was primary in only one location. This finding corrected what was evidently an urban bias in the 2010 survey results.

The 2013 results yielded an additional significant finding: the increased importance given to *hunting* as a source of food. In one of eight villages it was actually quantitatively more important than gathering, and in three others it exceeded store-bought foods in importance.

I asked individual men in two of the villages whether or not they hunted. At Den/ui village eleven men between the ages of eighteen and fifty were interviewed about hunting. Seven acknowledged that they hunted and named the species of animals they killed. Three younger men eighteen to twenty-three years of age said they were still learning, while one thirty-year-old man lamented that though he tried hunting, he had not been successful. At N//oma village a group of women told us with evident pride that *all* the men in the village hunted.

In accounting for the continuing relevance of hunting and gathering after a full half century of directed social change, we must consider the role of the Nyae Nyae Conservancy. The NNC has fought to protect the land base and has provided a range of services to the community. Within the community it has championed the position that the livestock economy must be balanced against the importance of wild resources—game and plant based—in the lives of the people. The fact that wild plant foods and game are such important subsistence sources in the twenty-first century indicates that the preservation of the land by the conservancy is more than a symbolic exercise.

A second significant finding is the increased role in subsistence of *government-supplied food*, which was ranked first or second in importance in four of the eight outlying villages. A possible explanation for this finding is that the four villages that ranked government food as first or second all happened to be sites where village schools were located and where extensive feeding programs were offered to enrolled students and their caregivers. Another source of government food is the large distribution of elephant meat to Nyae Nyae Conservancy members during the commercial hunting season, estimated at 10,000–20,000 kg annually. In our travels around the villages we frequently saw strips of elephant meat hanging on drying racks.

DEGREE OF DEPENDENCE ON THE CASH ECONOMY

Despite the persistence of active foraging as a Ju subsistence strategy, half of the individuals in the 2010 survey sample did list store-bought foods as their primary or co-primary source of food. The cash to purchase the food was coming from three important sources: wage labor, government pensions, and petty commodity production.

Two-thirds of the respondents (65/98) listed *regular* sources of family cash income, thirty-two from wage work and twenty-five from pensions. Eight listed both wages and pensions as income sources. The remaining third had no regular source of cash income.

Income-generating jobs included government work, both inside (tribal authority councilors and clerks, health workers) and outside (game scouts, road workers, drivers). The Tsumkwe Country Lodge, the Nyae Nyae Conservancy (see following), local nongovernmental organizations (NGOs), and the general stores each employed one to three workers each.

Petty commodity production took two major forms: devil's-claw (*Harpagophytum procumbens*) grows abundantly in Nyae Nyae and is collected and sold by the bag to suppliers for the herbal remedies industry. It is considered to be a treatment for arthritis and is sold in health-food stores worldwide. Hundreds of 25 kg bags are shipped annually to a South African buyer, for example, and the harvester receives NAD$27 (about USD$3) per kilogram.

The primary source of petty commodity income, however, is craft production: beaded headbands, necklaces, and bracelets made primarily from ostrich eggshell beads. This work is almost exclusively an activity for women and compensates for the overall predominance of men in wage work. A majority of women reported at least sporadic income from craft production.

Women's beadwork is part of a very old tradition. The women of Nyae Nyae have been known for centuries for the production of ostrich eggshell beaded jewelry (OESB). Oral histories from both Ju/'hoan and riverine farming groups like the Kavango and Mbukushu document that Nyae Nyae and Dobe area Ju/'hoansi carried on for centuries a lively trade in which OESB objects were traded for pottery vessels, iron, and tobacco (Lee 2002). Currently, the artisanal OESB products are sold in gift shops and museums around the world.

The sheer volume of this production can be gauged from the fact that in Tsumkwe the production of crafts has far outstripped the local availability of raw materials. The bulk of the raw materials for bead making now comes from eggshells imported from commercial ostrich farms in South Africa. The conservancy craft shop receives regular shipments of crates of broken ostrich eggshells from the south and sells them at subsidized prices to female craft producers.

At dozens of households in Tsumkwe and beyond, Ju women can be seen sitting at their family hearths and making beads. They first shape the broken shards into bead-sized pieces, then drill them by hand and string them onto nylon fishing line. The long strings of rough beads are smoothed using technology—in the form of grooved shaping stones—very similar to that found in archaeological contexts. Ju craftswomen also widely use glass "seed beads" of many colors, imported from central Europe, to make jewelry, either in combination with ostrich eggshell beads or on their own. The Ju have used the medium of beaded headbands to create amazingly diverse and imaginative designs verging on abstract works of art, of which Shostak (1976) has written an interesting analysis.

In the 1980s and 1990s, the Dutch Reformed Church missionary purchased crafts during regular buying trips to outlying villages and encouraged the sellers to purchase useful household items (food, clothing, kitchenware) off his truck, rather than spending the proceeds on drinking binges in town.

With the advent of the NNC, craft production became a key priority. Overseas volunteers trained Ju women in business practices and in artisanal production, and those in the NNC gift shop worked hard to improve the quality of the work produced by the Ju women based on the principle that better quality would bring higher prices. Today, high-quality crafts with original designs are sold at the Tsumkwe craft shop for NAD$100–NAD$500 (USD$14–USD$70) and up. In museum shops in Europe and North America, the same items would sell for USD$30–USD$200. All conservancy production is fairly traded, and artisans receive 50 percent of the selling price.

Every month craft production generates several thousand US dollars of income for Tsumkwe Ju women collectively. But this figure may be disbursed to one hundred or more vendors. What is difficult to determine is the income earned monthly by individual women.

HEALTH ISSUES: MALARIA, TUBERCULOSIS, HIV/AIDS

Apart from the findings reported here, I have been involved, since the mid-1990s, in research and training on the social and cultural aspects of HIV/AIDs in Namibia. The research has focused on large urban centers and has been national in scope because Namibia is one of the five or six countries with the highest rates of HIV in Africa and, hence, the world. Whenever possible during the research, I extended my inquiries to the remote Tsumkwe district to get a sense of how the pandemic was affecting the community with which I had historic ties. The data from fieldwork done in the 1990s and early 2000s in collaboration with Ida Susser (Lee and Susser 2008; Susser 2009) indicated that, contrary to expectations of some observers, the Ju/'hoansi had an extremely low rate of HIV.

The 2010 survey reinforced these earlier findings: levels of HIV and AIDS infection remained low, in fact about 75–90 percent below the national rate of 15.3 percent (UNAIDS online 2010). The doctor who oversees health in Nyae Nyae recorded seventeen deaths from AIDS through 2003. For a base population averaging twenty-four hundred people, this mortality rate is considered very low.

The population of Nyae Nyae has not been as fortunate in relation to another major illness. Rates of tuberculosis are extremely high, and this disease constitutes by far the major health issue among the Ju/'hoansi. Of the ninety-eight subjects in the 2010 survey, no fewer than thirty (31 percent) reported that they were current or recovered TB patients, and seventy-eight (80 percent) had a member of their family or household with TB, current or past.

The Tsumkwe Clinic, a well-ordered government facility, has an active program of TB treatment. Under directly observed therapy (DOT), TB patients are required to appear daily to take their medication in the presence of the staff. In interviews, health workers were particularly concerned about multidrug-resistant (MDR) TB. Of the ninety-three patients at the clinic undergoing TB DOT, thirteen were MDR (14 percent). The medical staff were forced to resort to second- and third-tier drugs with more serious side effects and lower efficacies.

TB/HIV coinfection is extremely common in AIDS-endemic areas of Africa, often in the 50–75 percent range. And given the high rates of TB, one would expect the Tsumkwe coinfection rate to be high. But in another surprising finding, TB/HIV coinfection was quite rare. All diagnosed TB patients are automatically tested for HIV, but of the ninety-plus Ju/'hoan patients with TB, only four (5 percent) have tested positive for HIV. This last number is a solid confirmation of the general thesis that the rate of HIV among the Ju/'hoansi is, by regional comparison, remarkably low.

The third major African illness, malaria, has followed yet a different course from those of HIV and TB. Long a scourge of African populations, malaria has been shown by previous health surveys to have affected most of the Nyae Nyae and Dobe adults in the past. Happily, that incidence has been reduced almost to zero by a proactive and successful campaign of setting up women's sewing cooperatives and distributing anti-mosquito bed nets made from netting provided by the NGO Health Unlimited.

RELIGIOUS PRACTICES: INDIGENOUS OR MISSIONARY

Ju/'hoan traditional religious practices, centered on the healing or medicine dance, have been well documented. Women gathered around a sacred fire and sang and clapped in intricate patterns as men danced in a circle around them (Katz 1982; Katz et al. 1997; Lee 2013a:137–153; L. Marshall 1969, 1999). Healers—mostly men—would use the dance as a launch pad for entering trance states in which they would move from person to person, laying on hands and pulling out sickness. The Ju strongly believed that the healer's work was vital to maintaining a community's physical and spiritual health.

For many years missionaries made few inroads in the spiritual life of the Nyae Nyae people. But after 1980, religious practices began to change and small groups of Ju converted to Christianity. Today, traditional healing coexists in Tsumkwe with Christian churches, led by the Dutch Reformed Church and the evangelical sect Christ Love. Catholic and Seventh-day Adventist congregants are also present.

We asked informants whether they still participated in traditional healing ceremonies or went to Christian churches or participated in both traditional and Christian rituals. A large minority, 44 percent, attended church only, while only 9 percent exclusively participated in traditional healing. Thirty-eight percent participated in both church and traditional healing practices. Finally, 11 percent stated they were not involved with either the church or traditional healing. A sea change in religious beliefs and practices appears to be under way, with a steep decline in adherence to traditional healing and a corresponding rise in Christian church membership. We have some evidence, however, that people still use traditional herbal remedies made from local plants and administer them in various ways.

ATTITUDES TOWARD OLD AND NEW
WAYS OF LIFE: "DO YOU LIKE THE BUSH?"

Forty-five years ago at Dobe I conducted a survey of some 123 Ju/'hoan men between the ages of fifteen and seventy-five. The people in the Dobe area of Botswana in 1968–1969 were in the throes of a rapid transition from full-time hunting and gathering to a mixed economy of foraging, independent farming and herding, and work on Herero cattle posts. In order to get a sense of how people were processing the strains of this rapid transition, we posed in our questionnaire the seemingly simple question: "Do you like the bush?" (Ade a_re tsi?). The bush symbolized for the Ju/'hoansi their traditional life of hunting and gathering in contrast to a sedentary existence in cattle posts and towns with new foods, clothing, and gadgets like transistor radios.

Ju/'hoansi answered the question with great animation and strongly held opinions. The answers revealed a population sharply divided between a slight majority who still favored a traditional life of nomadic foraging in "the bush" and a large minority who favored settled life in villages. Fifty-one percent favored nomadic life in the bush, while 46 percent preferred settled village life; the rest (3 percent) liked both or were undecided. The pro–village living group mentioned thirst and hunger as minuses of bush living and a steady diet of milk, grains, and meat as pluses of settled life.

Fast-forward forty-two years to a similar survey conducted in 2010 in Tsumkwe. I asked the same question: "Do you like the bush?" But the answers were strikingly different. *In the 2010 survey, fully 97 percent of the subjects responded favorably; ninety-five of ninety-eight did like the bush and gave elaborate reasons why.* Two responded that they liked the town and the bush equally, and only one lone informant stated that he preferred living in town, where his children were employed (Lee 2013a).

The ambivalence expressed in 1968–1969 was gone, and respondents included many more positives about the joys of "bush living" and equal number of negatives about life in the town:

> "In the bush the food is free and plentiful compared to town."
> "I love the peace and quiet of the bush: the sounds of nature versus the
>   sounds of alcohol-fueled squabbles."
> "There is no alcohol or drinking in the bush."
> "The bush is part of our cultural tradition; it is who we are as a people."
> "Town life is stressful."
> "Town life is boring."

How are we to interpret this shift in attitudes toward the traditional Ju/'hoan life of foraging in small groups and its echoes in contemporary Ju adaptations? I see their pro-foraging values as a strong vote of confidence by the people themselves in favor of one large element of their tradition: the material bases of foraging life. The Ju/'hoansi of 2010 and 2013 have had two generations to let the reality sink in and are no longer infatuated with alternative ways of living.

And although they are not abandoning town life or technology, they are keeping access to country food as part of their ecological adaptation. Fortunately, the return to foraging as a major component of their daily lives has occurred while the traditional ecological knowledge (TEK) necessary for effective foraging is still being transmitted generation to generation and is part of the current body of knowledge of twenty- and thirty-year-old Ju/'hoansi. The 2013 research revealed a corresponding increase in hunting, which is clearest in the more remote villages.

The strongly favorable attitudes of Ju/'hoansi people toward their traditional way of life jibe with the continued importance of bush foods in their diet. Although medical examinations were not part of our research program, our overall impression was that the nutritional status of the population was relatively robust.

Discussion: The Ceiling and the Floor

While foraging has remained viable, it is useful to explore beyond ecology to some of the social consequences that the Ju/'hoansi—in common with the other groups discussed in this volume—have experienced as a result of rapid economic change. Sharing and egalitarianism are two of the core values long associated with basic hunter-gatherer lifeways (Gowdy 1998; Ingold 1999; Kelly 2013; Leacock 1982a; Lee and Daly 1999; Lee and DeVore 1968; Woodburn 1982), leaving aside for the moment the complex hunter-gatherers in areas like the Pacific Coast of North America.

How have the introduction of the cash economy and bureaucratic overrule by the colonial and postcolonial state affected these core values? In conceptualizing the sharing-focused and egalitarian way of life, I have found it useful to employ an analytical model based on the notion of a ceiling and a floor: a ceiling above which accumulation is considered unacceptable and a floor or social safety net below which people will not be allowed to fall. The ceiling and the floor are integrally linked and prevent both wealth *and* poverty from straying outside acceptable limits (Lee 1990).

But in the course of social evolution—during the invention of farming and herding, for example—the low accumulation regime is superseded. The ceiling must be lifted since livelihood comes to depend on ownership of property in the form of land and livestock and growing investments in permanent housing and facilities. So a new equilibrium needs to be established at a higher level of accumulation. We find evidence of similar processes when we observe the historic transition from simpler, egalitarian hunter-gatherers to more complex hunter-gatherers, such as the Indians of the Northwest Coast (Suttles 1990).

What happens to the floor in this evolutionary model? Initially, the social safety net is maintained. Widows and orphans are cared for, and no one is destitute. But as social evolution proceeds, as the ceiling rises with the emergence of social inequality, the floor begins to dissolve. Poverty coexists with wealth, and serfs and commoners, as well as chiefs and aristocrats, become part of the social formation (Lee 1990). The "invention" of debt and debt bondage in the first early states and empires appears to be a key turning point, sharply accelerating these trends that, in various forms, have continued to the present day (Graeber 2014; Piketty 2014).

Parallel to these fundamental changes in economics are corresponding developments in politics. Small-scale societies with groups in the twenty-five to fifty or fifty to one hundred range can function successfully without clear lines of authority and leadership. But as society increases in scale, encompassing hundreds and then thousands, maintaining order becomes a major challenge. Authority figures, often invested with supernatural legitimacy, come to the fore. Big men, chiefs, kings, emperors, and complex hierarchical organizations have come to characterize most of the world's societies. Power, once accumulated, is not easily relinquished.

With these evolutionary trajectories in mind, let us return to the Ju/'hoansi. After decades of directed social and economic change, the Ju of Tsumkwe are following these historical pathways—the lifting of ceilings and emergence of leadership—but are doing so on a much accelerated time scale. Nevertheless, at least so far, the Ju/'hoansi have resisted the trend toward inequality. Rather than abandoning cherished principles, the Ju/'hoansi of Tsumkwe have displayed a pragmatic streak, adopting new practices while still adhering to core values.

For example, a key component of those values was the Ju people's very low tolerance for property accumulation. Traditionally, anyone who appeared to be hoarding food or material goods was subjected to leveling devices in the form of merciless criticisms until they shared their food and redistributed surplus goods through the *hxaro* exchange network (Wiessner 1982). Today, given the availability of wage work and other income sources, virtually every household has accumulated at least some property in the form of livestock, clothing, furniture, household utensils, cell phones, and even appliances, where electricity is available. Some families maintain bank accounts.

Basic forms of reciprocity still prevail, but people tacitly recognize that a degree of property holding is acceptable and that not all items are in play through demand sharing. Most families keep a metal chest (or several) in which possessions are kept discretely out of sight. However, hxaro networks ensure that valuables still circulate and remain important markers of social relationships, including the beautifully designed and crafted beaded headbands, necklaces, and bracelets made by women. As noted, ostrich eggshell beadwork manufacture is thriving but is largely for sale to tourists.

Another way in which Ju/'hoansi level the subsistence playing field is by bridging the rural-urban divide. Townsfolk maintain ties to family in outlying villages, and rural people cultivate relations with relatives in Tsumkwe. Town dwellers commonly express craving for traditional bush foods, and villagers bring sacks of Grewia berries, *mangetti* (mongongo) nuts, wild oranges, or other bush products, now considered delicacies, when visiting family members in town. On the return trip they may be observed carrying bags of store-bought flour, mealie meal, or tea and sugar as gifts from town kin.

Left unanswered in the current research is the important question of the "floor." Has there been a significant loss of the social safety net in Ju/'hoan society of the twenty-first century? Elsewhere I (2013a:210–213) have addressed this question for groups on the Botswana side of the border. There we see good evidence for the continuing robust health and social cohesion of Dobe area villages, and our 2013 survey of remote villages on the Namibian side presents a similar picture. However, more research is needed in this area, especially for Ju heavily involved in alcohol consumption (see following).

In politics, traditional egalitarianism—once fiercely defended (cf. Lee 1969)—has been challenged by new bureaucratic forms of governance. This topic has been discussed in detail by Biesele and Hitchcock (2013). While some resentment of authority remains, most Ju have come to accept the necessity of allowing Ju leaders to emerge in dealings with the outside world. Tsamkxau "Bobo," the current chief of the Traditional Authority, has occupied senior positions with competence and compassion, as well as good humor. His younger brother Kau Moses was a popular representative to the regional council and parliament until his untimely death in 2012. It is worth noting that both are members of the family that was closest to and enjoyed, in the 1950s and 1960s, the patronage of the Marshall family: Laurence, Lorna, Elizabeth, and John.

One possible sign of the continuing Ju/'hoan mistrust of authority is the mixed reviews that were given to the work of the Nyae Nyae Conservancy. In our 2010 survey, a small majority spoke favorably about the work of the NNC in preserving the land and distributing benefits. But a significant minority expressed a litany of complaints about the conservancy. Some argued that the conservancy did nothing of value, while others acknowledged the benefits but alleged that these favored only a small minority of the membership.

Paradoxically, I took these criticisms to be a healthy sign. Harriet Rosenberg (2003) has written insightfully about the centrality of "complaint discourse," a dominant Ju/'hoan mode of speech between old and young, as well as between peers. Rosenberg interprets complaint as another effective "leveling device" that ensures care for the elderly and equitable interpersonal relationships. The NNC, by assuming a leadership role within the community, thus opens itself up to criticism by its very nature.

In spite of these criticisms the conservancy has played a critical role in sta-bilizing outer communities on the land. Key to a central theme of the pres-ent volume, the conservancy has worked hard to valorize the role of hunting and gathering in the ongoing life of the Ju/'hoansi, not simply as an economic expedient but as an anchor for social and cultural values as well. We do have one cause for concern, however: central government subsidies paid to local CBNRM conservancies, not just in Tsumkwe but throughout Namibia, were terminated in September 2014. Fortunately, the conservancy-support net-works in the capital were able to procure alternate funding from the European Union (EU), enabling the NNC to continue to fulfill its mandate, at least for the immediate future.

ANOTHER VIEW

Not all of the research on the Nyae Nyae people in the twenty-first century has produced an equally upbeat picture. Wiessner (1982) did pathbreaking work on traditional systems of hxaro exchange on the Botswana side of the border in the 1970s. After working in New Guinea for a number of years, she returned to the Kalahari in the mid-1990s and started intensive fieldwork on the Namibian side. In her important paper "Owners of the Future? Calories, Cash, Casualties and Self-Sufficiency in the Nyae Nyae between 1996 and 2003" (2003), she reports on nutritional and ecological research in the outstation community of Xamsa some 30 km east of Tsumkwe (as well as other locations).

The Xamsa community members had been part of the back-to-the-land movement of the 1980s and 1990s and had established themselves in their

Table 3.4. Findings from the
1996–1997 Xamsa study.

Source of Food	Percentage
Farming	1
Gathering	9
Government rations	37
Hunting	19
Store	34
TOTAL	100

Source: Wiessner 2003:151.

traditional n!ore with the aid of a borehole dug by the NNDFN. Wiessner's careful study of caloric intake over a seventeen-month period revealed that although food was adequate at some parts of the year, the community experienced a serious falloff when government vehicles failed to show up with food rations.

Wiessner describes a rural life with periodic food shortages and weight loss. She also documents the relative proportions of food sources for the village in the 1996–1997 period (Wiessner 2003:151). These data are summarized in table 3.4. Although Wiessner's data collection was framed differently from our 2010 survey (and hers was more thorough), some comparison and contrast are possible. Most striking is the difference between store-bought and foraged food. In the 1996–1997 Xamsa study, store-bought food was almost four times more important than gathered food. In the 2010 Tsumkwe study, the two were equal in importance (and both major). Also, government rations were the single most important source for Xamsa and only of secondary importance for the respondents in Tsumkwe. Although farming was very low in both studies, hunting provided a significant contribution in the Xamsa study.

In attempting to understand what accounts for the differences between the two studies, I will make several points. First, Wiessner's study was conducted in the run-up to and early years of the conservancy. Circumstances appear to have stabilized in the decade and a half since the Xamsa research. Government rations, the nondelivery of which caused real hardship for Xamsa residents in Wiessner's account, were in 2010 no longer the difference between well-being and deprivation. Second, the destruction of crops and water points by elephants, which caused such hardship in earlier years, had been brought under control by the second study. Third, pension payouts had almost doubled between 1997 and 2010, going from NAD\$250 to NAD\$450 per month and providing an additional cushion. Fourth, the overwhelmingly positive attitudes toward life in the bush in 2010 indicated that some of the ambivalence expressed during the Ju/wa Farmers' Union years had been resolved. One of the shortcomings of the 2010 study was the lack of any intensive scrutiny of rural villages. This gap was partially addressed by the research on the eight remote villages carried out in 2013, but further and more detailed research on these key issues is certainly warranted.

CAVEATS: ALCOHOL, MINING, AND LAND INVASIONS

The 2010 social survey had several other shortcomings and gaps not directly addressed in the 2013 follow-up. First was the underrepresentation of heavy alcohol consumers in the survey sample. Second was the looming possibility of mining development that could transform the region. And third was the problem of land invasions and illegal occupation by non-Ju/'hoan outsiders. These issues also need to be put into the picture.

On the first topic, we tried to get a representative cross section of the people of Tsumkwe: men and women, residents and visitors, employed and unemployed. But one significant element in the population—regular alcohol consumers—was underrepresented. Tsumkwe had at least forty *shebeens*, or informal drinking places, all of them run by non-Ju/'hoan entrepreneurs and serving home brew, bottled beer, and spirits. Shebeen-goers fell into two categories: The majority were visitors from outlying villages who came to town to shop, renew medications like TB treatments, collect pensions, and socialize. They spent time and money in the shebeens while waiting for transport back to their villages. The second component was a set of serious drinkers—dozens, perhaps hundreds, of Ju who lived in town and for whom the shebeen was the daily locus of social life.

Our interpreters were leery of taking us to interview at the shebeens because the respondents could be rowdy and incoherent even at nine or ten in the morning. One of our translators was himself a reformed drinker who was now deeply involved in his evangelical church. We also suspected that they wanted to show us their community in a more positive light. At our insistence they took us to several shebeens toward the end of the study, and we did interview confirmed heavy drinkers, including the lone informant who said he did not like the bush. With some difficulty and with interruptions by fellow drinkers, we did manage to get thirteen interviews from the shebeen-goers, both out-of town visitors and hard-core local drinkers.

The impact of alcohol on nutrition, family life, childrearing, and, of course, vulnerability to HIV infection has long been a major concern. We need to follow up on the heavy-drinking segment of the Nyae Nyae people to get a better sense of (1) how large it is and (2) whether it is growing, shrinking, or stable.

Another gap in the study concerns an external factor, the global commercial mining industry and its periodic local prospecting initiatives. Diamond hunters have made several attempts to find the next big "pipe," spending months in the Nyae Nyae area, but have found none at exploitable levels. The latest gamble is a major strike of coltan, the rare-earth mineral used in manufacturing circuit boards for computers and other electronic devices. If a coltan mine were developed it would seriously disrupt the delicate ecological and social equilibrium of the Nyae Nyae area. Although it might bring in short-term economic benefits to the area in terms of jobs, these benefits would be more than offset by the massive influx of outsiders and the real dangers of the spread of HIV.

But the most imminent (and serious) threat to the well-being of the people of Nyae Nyae is the illegal occupation of conservancy land by Herero pastoralists from the overcrowded /Gam area to the south. Repeated attempts by the Herero to invade and occupy land in the 1990s were successfully and nonviolently turned back by the Ju leadership, backed by state authority. But in 2009 Hereros cut the cordon and drove hundreds of head of cattle into the southern part of Nyae Nyae. The authorities responded by confiscating the cattle, but they allowed the Herero herders and their families to remain in Nyae Nyae, where they were able to exploit a loophole in the law.

As a registered municipality, Tsumkwe was legally not part of the conservancy. And although the Herero were banned from the rest of Nyae Nyae, they could squat in Tsumkwe town while their case worked its way through the courts. In its sixth year, over one hundred Herero continued to live in a cluster of compounds on the eastern edge of the Tsumkwe townsite. Claiming destitution, they were supported by government food shipments, and they supplemented their income by running shebeens and extracting precious cash resources from Ju/'hoan patrons.

Tsumkwe is situated in the Otjozondjupa region. The Herero governor of the region has declared that the Ju should drop their legal fight and give up the southern portion of Nyae Nyae to the Herero. This idea has been vigorously opposed by the NNC and Traditional Authority, backed by the Windhoek-based

Legal Assistance Center, which has defended minority rights throughout Namibia. With the sudden death of Kxau Moses Toma, the Ju/'hoan member of parliament and younger brother of Chief Tsamkxau "Bobo," in July 2012, the Nyae Nyae lost an effective advocate for their land and civil rights. The outcome hangs in the balance.

Conclusions

These very legitimate concerns notwithstanding, it is important not to lose sight of the larger significance of our overall findings. In relation to several important socioeconomic variables, the Ju/'hoansi of Tsumkwe appear to be making a reasonably successful transition to the cash economy and municipal life in a developing nation-state.

On conventional development economics indices, the Ju of Nyae Nyae would fall well below the poverty line. Yet such indices have no way of incorporating nonmarket or nonagricultural sources of food. These sources may well make the difference for the Ju/'hoansi between the observed genteel but survivable poverty and absolute destitution. This better level of nutrition combined with the high status of women and the area's relative isolation may also in part explain the very low incidence of HIV among the Ju/'hoansi. The rapid increase in HIV among the Ju long predicted by some observers has not materialized.

It is too early to ascertain what the shift in spiritual focus from the traditional healing dance and its underlying cosmology to a Christian ideology with its roots in Dutch Calvinism will mean for the well-documented Ju/'hoan core values of sharing and respect for personal autonomy. And the Herero land invasions still pose a threat to Ju/'hoan land and livelihoods. However, the strong persistence of foraging practices, the revalorization of "the bush," and the still very low rates of HIV in the population all give us grounds for cautious optimism for the future of the Ju/'hoansi.

Acknowledgments

My long-term fieldwork among the Ju/'hoansi began in 1963 with major research continuing in the 1970s, 1980s, and 1990s. I carried out fieldwork specific to this chapter at Tsumkwe, Namibia, and Dobe, Botswana, in 2003, 2007, 2008, 2010, 2011, and 2013. I wish to thank the following for their contributions to the research: Melissa Heckler, Phillip Kreniske, Taesun Moon, Bruce

Parcher, Ida Susser, Leon Tsamkau, and Steve /Twi, as well as University of Toronto students Lalitha Eswaran, Laura Meschino, Meghan Sandor, Mercy Southam, Steven Sovran, Adrienne Sweetman, and Rhea Wallington. A special thanks to Lucah Rosenberg-Lee and Rachel Yoes and a very special thank-you to Megan Biesele and Robert Hitchcock, who provided detailed feedback on parts of the chapter. Responsibility for any errors of fact or interpretation are my own. Earlier versions of this chapter were presented at the 2010 Annual Meeting of the American Anthropological Association, New Orleans, and as a commissioned report to the Nyae Nyae Conservancy Executive in 2011. Sections also appear in chapter 13 of *The Dobe Ju/'hoansi* (2013a:215–227). The 2013 fieldwork took place *after* the May 2013 workshop at SAR and in part addressed issues and questions generated by the workshop discussions. Thanks to the organizers of and participants in the SAR workshop for generating a useful research agenda, to be pursued in future fieldwork.

CHAPTER FOUR

Twenty-First-Century Hunting and Gathering among Western and Central Kalahari San

ROBERT K. HITCHCOCK AND MARIA SAPIGNOLI

Introduction

Hunting and gathering is often seen by the people who practice it and those who work with them as an innovative, flexible, and generally sustainable way of earning a living (see, for example, Anderson 2005; Myburgh 2014; Stoffle 2005:139; E. Thomas 2006; Valiente-Noailles 1993). The vast majority of foragers today live in transitional landscapes, ones that have undergone massive modifications as a result of the expansion of new technologies, transformations in land ownership and control, and the initiation of market-based exchange systems. Many nation-states have opted to encourage, or in some cases require, hunter-gatherers to settle down and to engage in agriculture, livestock production, and wage labor. In some cases, former foraging groups have become dependent on state support. Foragers, for their part, have frequently resisted these state actions. It is useful, therefore, to examine in some detail societies that have undergone these processes and that have opted to expand their foraging activities while at the same time seeking to restore or amplify their social, economic, political, and religious connections to the land and to each other.

Hunting and gathering has been a contentious topic among government officials and researchers working with San populations in western and central Botswana since the 1950s (Hitchcock 2001, 2002; Silberbauer 1965b:8, 14, 1972:282–294; Tanaka 1980:5, 9, 29–37; Tobias 1956:179–180, 1957:33; Wilmsen 1983:10–13). There is no question that the degree of dependence on hunting and gathering among Kalahari San in general has declined considerably over the past several decades (Biesele and Hitchcock 2013; Ikeya 1996; Imamura-Hayaki 1996; Maruyama 2003; Tanaka 1987:42–45; Wiessner 2003). It is interesting to note, however, that hunting and gathering has increased substantially among some San in the western and central Kalahari regions of Botswana in the twenty-first century. The questions that we will deal with in this chapter are (1) why has foraging continued to be such an important aspect of San culture, identity, and practice and (2) what factors are responsible for the resurgence of hunting and gathering in the twenty-first century?

In this chapter we address the ways in which the peoples of the western and central Kalahari Desert in Botswana have sought to continue hunting and gathering in spite of social, economic, legal, and environmental constraints. They have done so in a number of ways. First, many San continued to teach children about foraging even when they were not practicing it as a primary subsistence strategy. Second, San have diversified their subsistence options—incorporating agriculture, the care of domesticated animals, and wage labor—but many of them continued to rely on foraging as a buffering strategy. Third, many San resisted pressure to stop hunting and gathering and settle down, refusing to go to settlements established by the state. Fourth, they opted to organize themselves and to seek both local and international assistance and to make use of lawyers in efforts to retain their land and resource rights when the state threatened them with relocation from the lands where they had resided, sometimes for generations (Sapignoli 2012, 2015).

We explore the relationships among western and central Kalahari San, the state, nongovernmental organizations (NGOs), and other groups with particular reference to the following periods:

1. The years 1885–1958, the colonial period of the Bechuanaland Protectorate during which parts of western Botswana (the Ghanzi Ridge) were turned into cattle farms that were allocated to Afrikaners and English-speaking South Africans, the livestock industry was expanded, and the tenure system in the Ghanzi farms was converted from leasehold to freehold

2. The years 1958–1974, the period of the Bushman Survey (1958–1966) by George Silberbauer, the founding of the Central Kalahari Game Reserve (CKGR, 1961), and the work of Jirō Tanaka in the central Kalahari (December 1966–December 1974)

3. The years 1974–1997, the period in which the Remote Area Development Programme (formerly, the Bushman Development Program) was established, a land reform program in tribal grazing areas (1975–1982)

implemented, and the decisions by the government of Botswana to resettle residents of the CKGR outside of the reserve made

4. The years 1997–2004, the period of resettlement and the creation of Remote Area Dwellers Settlements outside the boundaries of the CKGR

5. The years 2004–2014, the period of the central Kalahari legal cases in the High Court, Republic of Botswana ([a] 2004–2006, [b] 2010–2011, [c] 2013), the post-CKGR legal case returns to the central Kalahari (2007), and the expansion of mining and tourism in the reserve

We consider a range of topics, including conflicts over land and resource use, the significance of external and internal factors affecting the San, and the resumption of hunting and gathering as a primary means of earning a living in an ecosystem from which people were essentially exiled by the state for a decade (1997–2007). We also examine the trade-offs among foraging, agropastoralism, wage labor, and dependence upon the state and discuss why some San and Bakgalagadi opted to leave the government-sponsored settlements and return to the bush where foraging is the main subsistence practice.

Drawing on interviews and observations obtained in 2011, 2012, and 2013, we examine the challenges and opportunities for those people who chose to return to the bush after being resettled in the late twentieth and early twenty-first centuries. Hunting and gathering, many of them said, was something that they *wanted* to do, though they had no illusions about how arduous a full-time or part-time foraging lifestyle was going to be. In spite of the difficulties, however, hunting and gathering today represents a crucial survival strategy for people in the central Kalahari (figure 4.1).

The San of Western and Central Botswana

In international and national forums, as well as in their daily relationships with their neighbors, the San maintain that they are the "first peoples" of the Kalahari, and this statement has been supported by a wide array of evidence (Henn et al. 2011). By the end of the first millennium, numerous groups occupied the Kalahari alongside the San, many of them peoples who engaged in agriculture and pastoralism (Tlou and Campbell 1997; Wilmsen 1989). The interactions among the San and these other groups varied considerably, ranging from situations in which San freely exchanged goods and services with other peoples to

Figure 4.1. People cooking in !Xere. Photograph by Robert Hitchcock.

relationships of greater inequality in which San worked as herders, field hands, domestic servants, and specialized hunters, trackers, and wage laborers (Lee and Guenther 1993; Solway and Lee 1990).

For purposes of this chapter, we concentrate on the western and central Kalahari region, now known as the Ghanzi District, one of Botswana's ten administrative districts. The Ghanzi District is approximately 117,910 km² in size, representing 20.3 percent of total surface area of Botswana (581,730 km²). In the past, the district was part of what was known as the Western Crown Lands, a sizable area of the country that had been set aside for the British Crown when the Bechuanaland Protectorate was established in 1885 (Gulbrandsen 2012).

At least a dozen San-speaking groups live in the western and central Kalahari, along with Bakgalagadi, Herero, Batawana, Barolong, Nama, Wayeyi, Kalanga, and Afrikaans and English speakers (Guenther 1986; Sapingoli and Hitchcock 2014). San groups in the Ghanzi region include Naro, !Xoo, /Haba, G/ui, G//ana, Tsila, and Ts'aokhoe (Barnard 1976; Guenther 1986). The G/ui and G//ana are sometimes referred to as central Kalahari San (Tanaka 1980:14; Takada 2005:86–87). Not only do they share land and language, they also have similar systems of kinship, marriage, beliefs, and rituals (Tanaka and Sugawara 1999, 2010). In addition to the G/ui and G//ana and other San in the central Kalahari, approximately a third of the population is made up of Baboalongwe Bakgalagadi (Ikeya 1999; Osaki 2001; Sapignoli 2012, 2015; Sheller 1977). The interactions among the G/ui, G//ana, and Bakgalagadi in the central Kalahari have been generally symbiotic but sometimes competitive, depending in part on factors such as wealth and livestock and small-stock holdings (Roy Sesana; Keiwa Setlhobogwa, personal communications 2013, 2011, respectively).

Most of the San who lived on the Ghanzi Ridge were dispossessed of their land when the Ghanzi farms were established in the 1890s (Russell and Russell 1979; Wily 1979). Some of them opted to work for the white farmers as herders or domestic servants in exchange for a place to live and often little more than food, clothing, and tobacco (Russell 1976).

Approximately 44 percent of what is now the Ghanzi District is made up of a protected area, the Central Kalahari Game Reserve. Established in 1961 by the Bechuanaland Protectorate administration on the recommendation of a government civil servant, George Silberbauer, the CKGR is the largest protected area in Botswana and the second largest in Africa.

The CKGR, which is 52,730 km² in size, was one of the few African game reserves, if not the only one, to allow people to reside within its borders and engage in subsistence hunting and gathering, something that was specifically forbidden in nearly all other African parks and reserves (Dowie 2009; Hitchcock 2001:144). At the time of its establishment, the CKGR supported some three thousand to five thousand people who lived primarily by hunting and gathering, although a few people cultivated melons and other crops and kept small herds of domestic animals, including goats, dogs, and poultry (George Silberbauer; Alec Campbell, personal communications 2011).

In 1958 George Silberbauer was appointed the Bushman survey officer of the Bechuanaland Protectorate so that he could conduct surveys that would lead to the drafting of recommendations for dealing with San issues. From 1958 to 1966 Silberbauer carried out ethnographic studies in the western and central Kalahari regions. Much of his work focused on a population of G/ui who were living around !Xade in the western part of the central Kalahari. One of the most important results of Silberbauer's work was the creation of the CKGR in 1961. The ideas behind the creation of the reserve, according to Silberbauer (2012: 201–202), were (1) to secure and protect the lifeways of the San and other people who lived in the region and (2) to conserve the wildlife, vegetation, and habitats of the region. As both a government officer and an anthropologist, however, Silberbauer (2012) was fully aware that the boundaries were artificial and that people recognized land outside the reserve as theirs for their use.

In December 1966, the same year of Botswana's independence, the researcher Jirō Tanaka began working in the !Xade area. Tanaka spent thirty-four months working in the central Kalahari between December 1966 and December 1974. Tanaka (2014:xvi) has undertaken a total of twenty-eight visits to the Kalahari, his most recent in 2006. His work, like that of Silberbauer, was ecologically oriented and demonstrated the complexities that faced populations residing in the central Kalahari.

Place and Movements

The central Kalahari is a semiarid area that receives between 170 and 450 mm of rainfall a year, usually in the period between November and April (Botswana Department of Meteorological Services data; Tanaka 1980:19–21). Rainfall is highly variable both in space and time, and the central Kalahari goes for long periods without surface water. Much of the Kalahari is an undulating sandy plain covered with trees, shrubs, and grasses (Thomas and Shaw 2010). It also contains geomorphological features such as ridges of calcrete, dunes, and pans—low-lying playa-like areas that have clay bottoms in which rainfall accumulates. In some cases, the pans were used for specialized purposes, such as ambushing animals that came to them to drink and consume mineral-rich earth. The pans were also the focal points of human settlement systems, with territories sometimes arranged in flower petal–like fashion around them (Albertson 2000; Hitchcock and Bartram 1998).

In a sense, pans can be seen as "islands" or "oases" that were crucial to the subsistence and settlement systems of the societies that utilized them. Landscapes in the undulating plains of the Kalahari were heterogeneous, and people used the land differentially depending on a whole series of factors, including season, natural resource type and density, their group size and composition, their health and nutritional status, and kinds of technology available to them. In very dry periods the San and Bakgalagadi who lived in the reserve would vacate the area and move out to neighboring places where there were villages or farms with wells. This kind of expansion and contraction pattern was common, especially in periods of alternating drought and rainfall (Sheller 1977).

In the 1950s and 1960s the aggregation and dispersal patterns of the peoples of the central Kalahari were such that they came together in large groups in the wet season and dispersed into small, family-sized groups in the dry season. This kind of settlement and mobility pattern was the exact opposite of that seen among the Ju/'hoansi of the northwestern Kalahari, who aggregated around pans with permanent water in the dry season and dispersed into small groups in the wet season (Lee 1979, chapter 3, this volume; Yellen 1977). Until a borehole was drilled at !Xade in the central Kalahari in 1962, the area had no permanent water holes.

In the 1960s and early 1970s, G/ui and G//ana mobility was relatively high, with residential moves occurring as often as ten to fifteen times per year, as compared to the Ju/'hoansi, who generally moved only three to six times per year and covered areas between 300 and 600 km² (Lee 1979:334). The peoples of the central Kalahari tended to range over sizable territories that averaged between roughly 900 and 4,000 km² (Silberbauer 1981a:193; Tanaka 1980:81), far larger than those of the Ju/'hoansi. The population density in the central Kalahari was one person per 10 km², while the foraging range was some 250–350 km from a residential camp.

Among the G/ui and G//ana, resources in the territory (*gu, g!u*) were supposed to be shared among the members of the landholding group; in other words, they were held communally. The sharing of resource areas and goods associated with territories was organized along lines of kinship, historical association, and specific local resource availability. In order for a group to enter another group's territory, the traveling group had to seek permission from representatives of the occupying group, usually those individuals who had resided in the territory the longest or who had the most familiarity with and historical connections to the area. In general, the person who was the most knowledgeable about the history of the territories and their use was the *ayako*, or local headman or headwoman, along with his or her relatives (Sapignoli 2012).

Networks of people are associated with spaces, and the people in these networks are linked to land and each other in a variety of ways. In the western and central Kalahari, people's territories were defined by (1) ascription (i.e., where they were born), (2) acquisition and achievement (e.g., links created through marriage and exchange and arrangements made between individuals and groups), and (3) inheritance (i.e., from one's parents or grandparents or from larger descent groups). What is important to note is that people have social ties that are crucial to their attachments to territory, which they attempt to maintain from one generation to the next. These ties are not just to the land and its resources and places of importance; they also include other people who may reside in different places. Visits to relatives and friends who lived long distances away from the central Kalahari were not uncommon. One of the advantages of these visits was that people were able to share information about the state of the natural and social environment in their own areas.

Groups made significant investments in order to create ties between themselves. They established trade relationships and exchange relationships through gift giving, by arranging marriages between people from distant places, and by engaging in ceremonies that included people from distant areas. Peoples of the western and central Kalahari made reciprocal, long-distance exchanges of ostrich eggshell beads and other goods, known among the G/ui, G//ana, and Naro as *//ai* (Barnard 1992:141–142; Sapignoli and Hitchcock 2014:56–58) and among the Ju/'hoansi as *hxaro* (Wiessner 2002). The exchange systems reduced risk for San populations whose mobility options were more limited in the latter part of the twentieth and early twenty-first centuries than they were in the 1950s and 1960s.

The G/ui and G//ana, like the Ju/'hoansi and other San, had relatively large social networks. We estimate that the total area involved in the gift-giving, ceremonial, and social alliance network for people in the central Kalahari was 170,000 km² in size. Individuals could call on their alliances with other people if they were in need, and they attempted to ensure that their social ties extended not only across space but across generations. In other words, the social maintenance of connections in space and time was seen as crucial to the well-being of local communities and individuals. These exchange relationships were not limited solely to San; they included Bakgalagadi and other groups in the western, eastern, northern, and southern Kalahari with whom the San exchanged goods and services (Ikeya 1999; Solway and Lee 1990).

In the 1980s, ecologists working in the central Kalahari suggested that people who were no longer living "traditional lives" and who were keeping domestic livestock and using modern technology should be removed from the area (see, for example, Owens and Owens 1981:28–31). Government officials took a similar position, saying that they were concerned about what they felt were precarious living conditions there (Spinage 1991). In 1985 the government of Botswana called for a commission of inquiry into the status of the CKGR. Although the Central Kalahari Game Reserve Commission suggested that people be allowed to stay in at least part of the reserve, the government decided in 1986 that the people of the central Kalahari should be relocated to places outside of the reserve where they could be provided with development assistance.

Over the next decade (from 1988 to 1997) the Botswana government attempted to convince the people of the central Kalahari to leave the reserve and when they did not do so, exerted pressures of various kinds, including cutting off food supplies and failing to fix the main borehole at !Xade when it broke down (Hitchcock 2002). The frequency of arrests of people in the central Kalahari for allegedly violating hunting laws increased, as did the number of legal cases brought against local people in the Ghanzi Magistrate's Court.

Resettlement

From May to June 1997, the government of Botswana moved 1,739 people out of the CKGR and into two nearby settlements on the periphery, one in eastern Ghanzi District (New Xade, K'goesakeni) and the other in northeastern Kweneng District (Kaudwane). Some 575 people in communities in the eastern part of the reserve refused to move out (Ikeya 2001:188). Many of the people who lived in !Xade in the western part of the reserve moved voluntarily (Kiema 2010: 48–49), but without being completely aware of what this movement implied.

In January 2002 the Botswana government informed the remaining residents of the CKGR that they were shutting down the wells, stopping all food deliveries, and relocating the balance of the population to resettlement sites outside of the reserve. In February 2002 the government began moving people and their possessions out of the central Kalahari. Trucks were brought into the reserve, and people were loaded onto them along with their possessions, including housing materials and livestock. By the middle of the first decade of the twenty-first century, some twenty-five hundred people lived in three resettlement sites outside of the reserve: New Xade (Ghanzi District), Kaudwane (Kweneng District), and Xere (Central District).

In the settlements (but not inside the boundaries of the CKGR) rations were distributed to individuals who had an identity card signifying their right to receive them. People who did not have a ration card were ineligible to receive rations. The fact that few jobs were available in the settlements and a limited number of people were receiving state support meant that a number of people were going hungry.

It is not surprising, therefore, that numerous people expressed the desire to return to the central Kalahari. The compensation program had failed to restore the livelihoods of people affected by the resettlement (Hitchcock et al. 2011), and in a large number of cases people were worse off after the relocation than they were before. A common complaint about the resettlement sites related to the high levels of conflict, violence, disease, and stress there. The presence of game scouts and police in all three settlements was also seen as problematic, as people could forage, and especially hunt, only at great risk. Hunting and gathering was a much more problematic means of earning a living in the settlements and essentially served as a buffering strategy.

Subsistence Strategies

In the past, subsistence strategies of the G/ui, G//ana, and other San of the western and central Kalahari were diversified and included a significant degree of dependence on wild plants (up to 80 percent of the diet), some hunting, and small-scale income-generating activities such as craft production. G/ui and G//ana exploited a large number of plants, over eighty different species (Silberbauer 1981a:79–94; Tanaka 1980:55–65). Particularly important were esculent plants, ones that contain moisture, such as the melons *Cucumis hookeri* and *Citrullus lanatus* (Ikeya 1996:86–88). People not only collected wild plants for food, moisture, medicine, and tool manufacture, but they also gathered wild plants for sale.

   In the late twentieth and early twenty-first centuries, the people of the western and central Kalahari engaged in a number of different kinds of hunting. While the Botswana government and some wildlife researchers (e.g., Owens and Owens 1981, 1984; Spinage 1991) maintained that people commonly hunted with guns, the evidence, at least in the CKGR, suggests otherwise. The types of hunting currently observed in the western and central Kalahari include (1) individuals hunting on foot with bows and poisoned arrows, spears, or clubs; (2) individuals running down animals on foot; (3) individuals and groups mounted on horses or donkeys and hunting with spears (see Osaki 1984); (4) individuals hunting with the aid of dogs (Ikeya 1994); (5) individuals hunting by ambush using traditional weapons; and (6) individuals snaring animals using traps made of sisal or fibers from branches of *Boscia albitrunca*. We have no evidence of residents of the reserve hunting with guns inside the CKGR, although people from the reserve encountered parties of hunters from villages such as Rakops in Central District and said that the outsiders were using rifles and vehicles for hunting. Residents of the reserve were concerned about the hunting done with guns since the use of guns led to animals staying farther away from people and the loud sounds of the guns attracted game scouts and police.

In order of frequency, the hunting techniques observed by Silberbauer (1981a: 206, 1981b) in the 1950s and 1960s were as follows: shooting with bow and poisoned arrow, snaring, catching (springhares) by hook, running down, spearing, clubbing, and meat robbing. The late twentieth- and early twenty-first-century hunting strategies were somewhat different, with more emphasis on night hunting, hunting with dogs, and using snares. Cooperative hunting was less common, in part because groups of people with horses and donkeys could be detected more easily by game scouts either on the ground or in the air.

In the early 1980s the area over which hunters ranged in search of game expanded to 5,000 km², and the number of group expedition hunts in which people attempted to obtain several large animals at a time increased significantly (Osaki 1984:53–56; table 4.1). Long-distance hunting was also facilitated by the use of donkeys to transport meat back to residential locations. These kinds of mounted hunting techniques are not allowed any longer under Botswana wildlife laws (Republic of Botswana 1992, 2014), although some people do engage in them surreptitiously.

Hunting has been a highly contentious issue in the CKGR (Hitchcock 2002; Owens and Owens 1981, 1984; Spinage 1991). In 1979 Botswana became the first country in Africa to allow people identified as being dependent on wild resources for survival to hunt for subsistence (Hitchcock and Masilo 1995). The legislation provided special game licenses (SGLs) to people who qualified for them based on a set of criteria that included whether or not wild animal meat was an important part of their diets. These SGLs let people hunt a selected set and number of different animal species, ranging from kudu (*Tragelaphus strepsiceros*) to steenbok (*Raphicerus campestris*).

However, a sizable number of people who were arrested for hunting in and around the CKGR had citizen hunting licenses or SGLs in their possession. Reports described how people who were detained for alleged hunting violations were mistreated and were sometimes tortured severely (see, for example, Workman 2009:76–82). Some of the people who were arrested were held in prison for extended periods without access to legal counsel. Although some wildlife officers and police were investigated, no formal charges were brought against them.

Over 120 people have been arrested since 2004 for hunting illegally, many of

Table 4.I. Wildlife obtained by a sample of subsistence hunters in the central Kalahari, 1958–1966.

Type of Animal	Scientific Name	Number Obtained	Meat Yield (kg)
African bullfrog	*Pyxicephalus adspersus*	67	0.1
Caracal	*Caracal caracal*	9	2.0
Duiker	*Cephalophus monticola*	65	6.0
Eland	*Taurotragus oryx*	4	267.0
Fox (bat eared)	*Otocyon megalotis*	18	2.0
Gemsbok	*Oryx gazella*	20	77.0
Genet	*Genetta genetta*	7	1.5
Giraffe	*Giraffa camelopardalis*	1	400.0
Hartebeest	*Alcelaphus caama*	11	45.0
Invertebrates	multiple species	many	277.0
Jackal (black backed)	*Canis mesomelas*	15	2.0
Kudu	*Tragelaphus strepsiceros*	3	111.0
Monitor lizard	*Varanus niloticus*	10	5.0[a]
Ostrich	*Struthio camelus*	2	63.0–145.0
Porcupine	*Hystrix africa-australis*	2	4.5
Springbok	*Antidorcas marsupialis*	30	13.0
Springhare	*Pedetes capensis*	222	0.7
Steenbok	*Raphicerus campestris*	68	7.0
Tortoise	*Geochelone pardalis*	67	0.1
Warthog	*Phacochoerus aethiopicus*	1	28.0
Wildcat	*Felis silvestris lybica*	7	3.0
Wildebeest	*Connochaetes taurinus*	12	86.0

Source: Campbell 1964, 1968, personal communication 2011; Silberbauer 1981a:209, table 4.
[a]Average yield.

whom were found outside of the CKGR in areas that are classified as Wildlife Management Areas and over which their communities have some degree of control (Republic of Botswana 1986). Dealing with the government in relation to the hunting arrests is a time-consuming and expensive process. Funds for lawyers are hard to come by, and some people have literally gone broke attempting to cover their legal fees. The lack of clarity on the subsistence hunting issue leaves San and other people vulnerable to arrest for following what they feel is the law.

Obtaining data on hunting in and around the central Kalahari was extremely difficult as people were reluctant to talk openly about their hunting activities, and we could not, in most cases, examine faunal remains in camps as people buried the bones for fear of being arrested for hunting violations. The presence

Table 4.2. Wild animals obtained by subsistence hunters in the central Kalahari, 2010–2012.

Type of Animal	Scientific Name	Number Allowed on Special Game License	Number Obtained
Caracal	*Caracal caracal*	10	4
Duiker	*Cephalophus monticola*	30	5
Gemsbok	*Oryx gazella*	4	2
Genet	*Genetta genetta*	50	3
Jackal	*Canis mesomelas*	50	2
Kudu	*Tragelaphus strepsiceros*	1	1
Monitor lizard	*Varanus niloticus*	10	4
Ostrich	*Struthio camelus*	2	1
Springbok	*Antidorcas marsupialis*	4	1
Steenbok	*Raphicerus campestris*	30	7
Tortoise	*Geochelone pardalis*	Unlimited	16
Warthog	*Phacochoerus aethiopicus*	3	1
Wildcat	*Felis silvestris lybica*	50	4
Wildebeest	*Connochaetes taurinus*	4	1

of game scouts, periodic visits by the Special Support Group of the Botswana police, and threats of Botswana Defense Force intervention ensured that people were very careful in their hunting activities. Some people admitted that they hunted small animals, often at night, in the vicinity of camps in the reserve, but they did not admit to long-distance expedition hunting. We did encounter a few hunting parties, which enabled us to ask what kinds of animals were being hunted and to obtain rough estimates of hunting returns for a portion of the central Kalahari population (table 4.2), though not for those in the resettlement sites, who were likely taking part in hunting parties in and around the reserve in addition to hunting smaller prey in the vicinity of the settlements.

Several things should be noted about the information presented in table 4.2. First, all of the animals hunted were considered legal under the National Parks and Wildlife Act of 1992 (Republic of Botswana 1992). Second, many of the animals obtained were smaller species and were nocturnal (for example, the wildcats). Third, only four of the antelopes killed (two gemsbok and two wildebeest) were obtained through hunting from horseback; the others were killed with poisoned arrows. Fourth, at least two animals were killed from hunting blinds at night. Dogs helped chase down some of the prey (including two of the warthogs), and other animals were obtained by women who were out on gathering trips (the monitor lizards and the tortoises). Meat from these animals was shared among kin and sometimes friends, but San people note that sharing networks are smaller today than they were in the past.

In 2011 approximately three thousand people resided in the three resettlement sites outside of the reserve: 1,269 in New Xade, 1,084 in Kaudwane, and 343 in Xere. Some of the people in the resettlement sites said that they were experiencing severe stress and that both adults and children had high levels of nutritional, health, and psychological problems. These problems were, in part, a result of the wrenching way in which the relocation was carried out in 1997 and 2002. In some cases, people who had resided together, often for generations, in communities inside the CKGR ended up in different settlements. Government officials at the gates were preventing the movement of food, livestock, water, and other goods into the reserve and arresting people who took food to relatives inside or outside of the reserve. The relationships between people inside of the reserve and outside in the resettlement sites were very important and continued to be so even as the government tried to prevent food deliveries inside the reserve.

Some of the people who returned to the central Kalahari after a lengthy legal case against the government that lasted two and a half years (2004–2006) did so in part because they wanted to engage in full-time hunting and gathering; they did not like life in the settlements, they wanted to avoid government control, and they wanted to be in places with which they were familiar and where their ancestors were buried (see also Lee, chapter 3, this volume). When they returned to their former territories, however, they found that the local habitats had changed, in part because of a reduction in fires in the region between the late 1990s and 2007. One of the ways that people responded to these changes was to expand their use of fire, something that was risky since the government of Botswana has a policy of preventing fires and arresting people who set them. Fire (*/e:* in G/ui and G//ana) is used for a number of purposes by San in the western and central Kalahari Desert, and people gave a number of justifications for setting fires. One of the most common was that burning served to modify the vegetation and helped to facilitate expansion in the numbers and types of wild animals in the region. Fire was seen as way to manage the environment in ways that were beneficial to both people and the habitats.

We were told that people purposely and spatially varied their fire setting so that they contributed to the development of a heterogeneous landscape. The timing of fires was variable: foragers tended to burn areas in the winter, while pastoralists set fires in the early part of the rainy season (roughly November to April) to encourage a flush of fresh green growth. Fire was sometimes used to smoke the meat of animals that had been killed, but the effectiveness of the smoking was said to vary by season, rainfall, and temperature. Although the reasons for setting fires were diverse, one point was raised by many of the people who were interviewed: fires were set not just to maximize hunting and gathering returns but also to produce goods for purposes of sharing (see also Bliege Bird et al., chapter 9; Codding et al., chapter 8, this volume). Hunting, gathering, setting fires, crop production, raising livestock, and trading were all seen as strategies for tying people together; in other words, they were parts of intricate social exchange systems.

Agriculture, Livestock, Mining, and Tourism: A Future for Foraging?

In the past, people moved in and out of the reserve depending on availability of resources, which were tied in part to cycles of rainfall. People also sometimes left the reserve to seek medical assistance, as occurred in 1950–1951 during a smallpox epidemic, or to obtain food and water from the Ghanzi farms (Alec Campbell, personal communication 2011; Sheller 1977; George Silberbauer, personal communication 2011). People living in the reserve in the period after 2007 said that they had to leave because few healers were available, some of them reportedly having died from tuberculosis or AIDS. People who were ill would go to the clinics in New Xade, Kaudwane, and Xere, but they often complained that the nurses and other health personnel were gone and that no medicines were available (Hitchcock et al. 2011; Sapignoli 2015).

In western and central Botswana farmers tended to be small-scale subsistence-oriented producers who engaged in low-input agriculture. Most of the food that was grown was used for domestic consumption. If people who raised crops were fortunate enough to generate a surplus, they either gave it away or sold it to generate some cash income. The central Kalahari farmers we studied faced a number of constraints that were both environmental (e.g., variability in rainfall, poor soil quality, competition from wild animals, pests, disease) and economic (e.g., lack of sufficient household capital to purchase seeds, agricultural implements, and fertilizers). Lack of labor was also a constraint. In the latter part of the first decade of the twenty-first century, approximately

30 percent of the households in the central Kalahari were raising crops in small rain-fed gardens. Based on our estimates of the returns from agricultural production, people in the central Kalahari derived approximately 5 percent of their subsistence from this source.

Livestock and small stock (sheep and goats) were kept by about a third (34 percent) of the households we documented in four of the five central Kalahari communities occupied in 2011 and 2012. Nearly half (45 percent) had donkeys, which they used primarily for transport; carrying water, melons, and other goods; and pulling plows and wagons. Goats were an important source of milk and meat and were sometimes given as bride price or sold to raise cash for household needs (goats were going for BWP$300.00 [USD$33.00] in the central Kalahari in 2012). No cattle lived in the reserve, although some people did own cattle and kept them in the resettlement sites or at cattle posts or villages outside of the reserve. We estimate that roughly 10–15 percent of the subsistence and income of people inside the reserve in 2011 and 2012 was based on livestock, depending on household livestock numbers and types. At least 30 percent of the households got no food or income from livestock whatsoever and said that they did not receive transfers of domestic animal meat or milk.

A particular problem for people in the central Kalahari and the resettlement sites was unemployment. Fewer than 10 percent of the people in the western and central Kalahari had jobs in the formal sector of the economy. Those people who did have jobs usually worked for the government, for example, as paid headmen or headwomen (*dikgosi*; $n = 3$), tribal police ($n = 2$), employees of the Remote Area Development Program (RADP; $n = 4$), teachers ($n = 2$), social workers in the district council offices ($n = 1$), or members of NGOs ($n = 3$). A total of seventeen people had jobs with the government in 2011. Salaries for different jobs varied. Table 4.3 presents data on the sources of employment and income for people in the western and central Kalahari in 2011 and shows that the three most important sources of income were farm and cattle-post work (22 percent), government employment (19 percent), and mining (17 percent).

A very important source of income was craft production, which was mainly done by women (16 percent). Women made ostrich eggshell beads and other jewelry, while men carved wooden toys, made bow and arrow sets, and, until it became too risky, manufactured skin clothing and blankets. Incomes were supplemented with food and cash from social safety net programs (Seleka et al. 2007). Pensions for the elderly were BWP$220 (USD$24.20) per month, but some people who had retired from jobs in the private sector got higher

Table 4.3. Employment and cash income for people in the western and central Kalahari, 2011.

	Employees				
	Full Time	Part Time	Total	Income (BWP)	Percentage
Crafts	56	0	56	260,000	16
Destitute payments (cash)	46	0	46	33,672	2
Devil's-claw collection	7	0	7	12,000	1
Farmworkers	21	4	25	360,000	22
Government employees	11	6	17	318,450	19
Government pensions	22	0	22	153,000	9
Mining	26	4	30	288,000	17
Miscellaneous jobs	3	7	10	97, 000	6
Safari hunting	8	1	9	92,000	6
Tourism	3	3	6	32,600	2
TOTAL	203	25	228	1,646,722	100

Note: A comparable table is presented by Wiessner (2003:154, table 4) on the Nyae Nyae region of Namibia, where the Ju/'hoansi reside. In the calculations shown here for the destitute payments, only the amounts paid in cash were included. Most of the funds for devil's-claw collection went to middlemen rather than the collectors.

pensions. Those people who got destitute rations also received cash payments of BWP$61.00 (USD$6.71) per month. The rations themselves were the equivalent of BWP$181.90 (USD$20.01) per month. In addition, people defined as destitute had school, health care, water, and electricity charges waived (Republic of Botswana 2002; Seleka et al. 2007). Those people who received cash for work in the labor-intensive public works projects were paid BWP$10.00 per day (USD$1.10), while supervisors were paid BWP$16.00 per day (USD$1.76).

Besides government and NGO jobs, some San in the central Kalahari and the resettlement sites worked in the tourism industry. Some of the tourism-related jobs were at safari camps, where people provided services such as cleaning. Others were in the safari-hunting industry, in which San acted as guides for safari company clients. A total of ten people, all men, worked for the safari companies, which tended to pay much better than the mobile safari operators or the tourist camps that mostly offered only low-end service jobs to San, who worked as janitors, maids, and camp cleaners. Fifteen people had jobs in the tourism and safari-hunting industries; their combined wages were BWP$124,600, 11 percent of the total income earned in the region in 2011–2012.

Mineral-prospecting companies from various countries working in the western, central, and northern Kalahari in the second decade of the twenty-first century hired temporary laborers (Sapignoli and Hitchcock 2014). These companies were constructing new prospecting tracks in the region, which has led to an increase in the number of outsiders operating there. One of the side effects of the presence of workers from outside of the area, according to local people, was an increase in resource depletion, toxic wastes on the landscape, interpersonal conflicts, sexually transmitted diseases, and HIV/AIDS. During this time one diamond mine, at Gope (Ghagoo), in the southeastern part of the reserve, was operating, and a copper-silver mine in the northwestern corner of the central Kalahari was being planned.

A question raised by people in and around the central Kalahari was how the presence of mining in the area might affect the willingness of tourists to come seeking "pristine habitats." The Botswana government was planning to lease out additional areas in the reserve for tourism purposes, but people from the central Kalahari were concerned that the government had made no announcements about whether they would be able to obtain community use rights to their areas inside the reserve. They were hoping that detailed mapping and documentation of their use of community areas, like that done in the late 1990s and early 2000s (see Albertson 2000) and initiated again in 2010 in the central Kalahari, would help convince the government to allow them to have rights over portions of the CKGR. One of the difficulties they faced, however, was that the government, under a set of policies on land and tourism announced in 2012, was aiming not only to stop hunting but also to do away with existing communal and commercial leasehold rights in the country and to issue new licenses to private companies that "had sufficient resources to develop them" (Sapignoli and Hitchcock 2013). What this meant, in effect, was that San communities, which by and large had relatively few funds, would be left out in the cold.

Transformations

The reestablishment of foraging and diversified livelihood strategies in the central Kalahari would not have been possible had the San and Bakgalagadi not gone to court to obtain them. Three court cases were filed by residents and former residents of the CKGR (Sapignoli 2012, 2015). The San and Bakgalagadi sought to obtain de jure (legal) rights to land and resources that had been promised to them "in perpetuity" with the establishment of the CKGR in 1961. They

Table 4.4. Population data for communities in the Central Kalahari
Game Reserve and resettlement sites outside of the reserve,
Botswana, 1988–2014.

Name of Community	1988–1989	1991	1996	1999	2002	2014
Bape	110	41	—	0	0	0
Gope	100	43	110	10	11	24
Gugamma	—	—	26	0	11	0
Kaudwane[a]	—	—	—	—	—	1,084
Kikao	104	98	30	25	13	25
Matswere	—	—	18	0	0	0
Menoatshe	50	—	—	0	0	0
Metseamonong	90	71	130	130	17	120
Molapo	202	61	113	130	14	130
Mothomelo	145	149	272	150	10	150
New Xade[a]	—	—	—	—	—	1,269
Serube	68	—	—	0	0	0
!Xade	791	528	701	0	0	0
Xaxa	—	30	0	0	0	0
Xere[a]	—	—	—	—	—	343
TOTALS	1,660	1,021	1,400	445	76	3,145

Note: The drop between 1996 and 2002 was due to the government's decision to
relocate people from the CKGR.
[a]Stands for the resettlement sites in Kweneng, Ghanzi, and Central Districts.

also sought the right to drill for their own water, to enter the reserve without restriction, and to keep small livestock in the reserve. What they aimed for, they told us, was to have the freedom to pursue the kinds of livelihood strategies that they chose for themselves.

Within two months of the high court decision in December 2006, people from the settlements began going back into the reserve, and by 2014 five hundred people were residing in five communities in the central Kalahari (table 4.4). People returned to their ancestral areas, and they established a mixed economy in which hunting and gathering generated 60–70 percent of the subsistence and income of local households, with the balance obtained through small-scale agriculture, herding, craft sales, pensions, and wage labor. One of the advantages of being in the central Kalahari was that there was less competition from other people; resource densities were also greater than in the resettlement sites and western Botswana.

The situations of the G/ui and G//ana in the twenty-first century are quite different than they were in the 1950s and 1960s. Whereas the central Kalahari San were previously mobile, they are now largely sedentary, ranging out from the settlements to hunt, gather, and obtain resources for consumption and occasionally for sale. This kind of tethered organizational strategy is like that seen among Inuit (Wenzel, chapter 2, this volume) and other northern and midlatitude hunter-gatherers who have been characterized by Binford (1980) as "collectors," as opposed to the "foragers" of the tropics and subtropics. However, some of the expedition hunts and gathering trips are of much longer duration than they used to be, with foraging trip distances averaging as much as 120–250 km.

It is interesting to compare the situation that exists today in the central Kalahari with that of Nyae Nyae in Namibia, another place in southern Africa where San moved into a government-sponsored settlement in the 1960s and 1970s before opting to go back to their ancestral areas in the 1980s and 1990s (see Biesele and Hitchcock 2013; Lee, chapter 3, this volume). Table 4.5 shows a number of similarities and differences between the central Kalahari and Nyae Nyae. One of the differences between the two areas has to do with land tenure: the former is a protected area (a game reserve), whereas the latter is located in communal land in Namibia. A second difference is that the communities in the central Kalahari have not yet been given permission by the Botswana government to form community trusts, locally based institutions that have the right to manage wildlife and benefit from tourism. In Namibia, on the other hand, conservancies are locally planned and managed multipurpose areas on communal land in which users have pooled their resources for wildlife conservation and utilization and tourism. The conservancy members are granted wildlife resource rights under an amendment to Namibia's Nature Conservation Amendment Act of 1996. Conservancy formation in Namibia requires a formal legal constitution, a representative conservancy committee elected by the members, a land use and management plan, and formally defined boundaries. The Nyae Nyae Conservancy (NNC) was the first communal conservancy established in Namibia in February 1998 (Lee, chapter 3, this volume). The central Kalahari communities today depend to a greater degree on hunting and gathering and receive less state and NGO assistance than do the thirty-six communities in Nyae Nyae. Other important differences between the two areas include the fact that safari hunting is allowed in Nyae Nyae, cattle are kept by people in

Table 4.5. A comparison of resource rights and natural resource management in the Central Kalahari Game Reserve (Botswana) and the Nyae Nyae region (Namibia).

Central Kalahari Game Reserve (CKGR) Botswana	Nyae Nyae Conservancy (NNC) Namibia
55,347 km², 5 communities, 700 people	8,992 km², 36 villages, 2,400 people
CKGR Residents Council (12 people)	Nyae Nyae Conservancy (1,180 members)
G/ui, G//ana, Tsila, G//olo, Kua, San, Baboalongwe Bakgalagadi	Ju/'hoansi San
Established July 1961	Established February 1998
Resource management done on the basis of communities according to traditional territories (/gu)	Resource management by NNC and local *n!ore kxaosi* (Ju/'hoan territorial overseers)
Right to return and to hunt won in 2006 Botswana High Court case	Subsistence hunting allowed: quota from government for "own use" and for safari hunting
No modern weapons allowed; traditional weapons used	Traditional weapons used, including bows and arrows with poison, spears
No snares or steel traps allowed	Traditional snares allowed
Use of dogs for hunting not allowed	Use of dogs for hunting not allowed
No mounted hunting (horses, donkeys) allowed	No mounted hunting (horses, donkeys) allowed
Ambush hunting not allowed	Ambush hunting allowed
No hunting of any kind allowed as of January 1, 2014	Limits on types and numbers of animals to be hunted
No quota allocated by the Department of Wildlife and National Parks	No quota for subsistence hunting, only for safari hunting, set by the Ministry of Environment and Tourism (MET)
No safari hunting allowed	Some safari hunting with a concession holder allowed
Problem animals (predators) controlled by the Department of Wildlife and National Parks outside of the CKGR	Shooting of predators by local people not allowed; problem animals controlled by MET
Collection of wild plants for domestic purposes allowed; no commercial exploitation of plants allowed	Collection of wild plants allowed, some of it for commercial purposes (e.g., devil's-claw, *Harpagophytum procumbens*)
Tourism controlled by the Department of Wildlife and National Parks and by private companies (e.g., Wilderness Safaris, Kwando Safaris); no direct community involvement in tourism at present	Tourism encouraged, in conjunction with communities and the NNC committee; benefits distributed to NNC members

Note: Data obtained from the NNC management committee, the Nyae Nyae Development Foundation of Namibia, the First People of the Kalahari, Tsamkxao ≠Oma, Leon Tsamkxao, Lara Diez, Richard Lee, Megan Biesele, Kazunobu Ikeya, Jumanda Gakelebone, Roy Sesana, and fieldwork in both areas.

Nyae Nyae, and the Ju/'hoansi in Nyae Nyae have greater control over their land and resources than do the people in the central Kalahari.

Discussion and Conclusions

The question of why foraging in the central Kalahari has seen a resurgence in the twenty-first century can be answered in several ways. First, the initial central Kalahari–related case to go to court made subsistence hunting legal, although admittedly, severe pressures are being brought to bear on people to curtail their hunting activities. Second, hunting and gathering is being carried out in what in many ways is a transitional landscape, one modified environmentally and socially. The establishment of tourism camps, roads, settlements, and a diamond mine have altered the physical and economic environments. Third, the social costs of abandoning foraging are viewed by many residents of the reserve as too great to make alternative livelihood pursuits worth the risk.

Many residents of the reserve see the expansion of foraging as a way to reclaim their identity and way of life. They also view it as resistance to the state. We should note that in many ways hunting and gathering in the reserve never stopped; what is different now are the numbers of people pursuing foraging as a significant part of their livelihoods. Unlike the situation of the Hadza in Tanzania (see Blurton Jones, chapter 5, this volume), the various efforts of the state to encourage people to become settled agriculturalists were partially successful, at least in terms of the size of the populations in the resettlement sites outside of the reserve. But people in both the resettlement sites and in the central Kalahari have expressed the desire to return to the bush and to take up foraging again. There is a far-reaching, rights-oriented dimension to this process of reclamation. The global discourse on indigenous rights and the discussions at the national and local levels on the San's access to territory and resources have helped to give foraging new meaning.

Another reason that foraging has expanded is that people in the central Kalahari itself have fewer alternatives than in the past; people are not getting food from the government unless they leave the reserve, and they have very few employment opportunities inside the central Kalahari, particularly since the tourism companies operating there refuse to hire people from the CKGR communities. Craft production is an important source of income for some, and this production involves the use of hunted and gathered products. Furthermore, transformations in the livestock industry and changes in access to livestock markets have reduced the numbers of jobs available to people living on the farms and cattle posts in western Botswana.

In both the western and central Kalahari people hunt and gather not just for economic gains but also for the many social benefits that come with this kind of subsistence. A number of G/ui and G//ana pointed out that foraging helped to sustain their social networks, binding people together in the face of challenging conditions. Maintaining knowledge of how to forage and live in transitional landscapes is seen as crucial, and people expended enormous energy to keep this knowledge alive. They viewed returning to the reserve and expanding foraging as strategies that could not only restore links to the land but also links to other people and to ways of life that many G/ui and G//ana prefer to pursue over the long term.

Acknowledgments

Support of some of the research upon which this paper is based was provided by the Department of Law and Anthropology in the Max Planck Institute for Social Anthropology, First Peoples Worldwide, the International Work Group for Indigenous Affairs, and Loci Environmental. We thank the government of Botswana for permission to carry out this work. We also thank Brian Codding and Karen Kramer for their excellent editorial work and for their kind invitation to take part in the School of Advanced Research seminar in May 2013. Sarah Soliz did a masterful job of copyediting our manuscript, which we appreciate greatly. We wish to express our deep appreciation to the people of the central and western Kalahari for their support, advice, and information, without which this discussion would not have been possible.

CHAPTER FIVE

Why Do So Few Hadza Farm?

NICHOLAS BLURTON JONES

Introduction

In this chapter I will discuss reasons for the Hadza rejection of farming during the last century. To set the scene I first describe some of the local variation in the circumstances of Hadza daily lives. We will see that even where the environment allowed successful farming, Hadza continued to live almost exclusively by hunting and gathering.

In 2002 Frank Marlowe wrote a paper for Sue Kent's (2002) *Ethnicity, Hunter-Gatherers, and the Other* called "Why the Hadza Are Still Hunter-Gatherers" in which he addressed many of the issues raised by "the Kalahari debate." He scoured the literature, which included reports of some twenty independent visitors since Baumann in 1892. I had done the same, also intending to determine whether the Hadza had always been hunter-gatherers. We were both impressed with how little had changed, despite clear evidence of continual Hadza contact with neighbors and six or more externally imposed attempts to make Hadza settle and farm. Camps in which we observed behavior and measured foraging success seemed very similar to those visited by Obst (1912) in 1911 and Woodburn (1968a, 1968b) in 1959–1961. The material culture showed little difference from Reche's (1914) and Woodburn's (1970) descriptions. Marlowe (2002) and Woodburn (1988) pointed out that Hadza foraging had persisted into the twentieth century partly because most of their land was too dry for farming and too heavily infested with tsetse flies for herding. In most of their range, then, hunting and gathering has been the best economic option for the Hadza. But in some locations farming was possible, and Hadza have rejected many opportunities to settle and farm. I will consider two situations: how an individual Hadza might decide to become "the first farmer" and how Hadza in general have responded

Figure 5.1. Hadza women collecting berries. Photograph by J. F. O'Connell.

to externally promoted settlement schemes. My main emphasis is on the conflict between farming and the Hadza sharing ethic.

An anecdote illustrates the plight of the solitary "first farmer." In 1965 a Hadza man, the late Mzee Danieli Tawashi, asked Rev. Bob Ward, a Lutheran missionary who had become interested in the Hadza, to help him and his family settle and farm. Ward (1999:210) describes the challenges faced by the first forager to farm: "A good harvest was forthcoming the first year. The only complaint I heard from Danieli was that tribal members came in from all directions and they were taking the harvest he had laid up for the dry season. It's impossible for one Tindiga [Hadza] to deny another in need if he makes a request for help." Thus, Danieli's early efforts appeared doomed. My conversations with Hadza in various parts of the Eyasi Basin suggest the same fate would await any lone effort at farming. "They will come" was a common response to my questions about sharing resources. But why cannot one Hadza refuse another? It is not enough just to label and describe the ethic. As a behavioral ecologist, my goal is to describe how circumstances promote one form of behavior or another, and different theories about sharing may predict different responses to the solitary farmer situation (Danieli's problem) or the external efforts to settle the Hadza (figure 5.1).

Ethnographic Background

I summarize the background under a number of headings. Readers should note that my remarks are restricted to the period up until the year 2000, the "anthropological present" in this chapter. I have not visited the Hadza since then. Subsequent to 2000, many more things have happened in the Eyasi Basin, several of them involving efforts to make the circumstances more as Hadza would like them to be. From what I hear, there have been some successes and some failures. Frank Marlowe has visited the Hadza almost every year since 2000, and we must hope that he and his students will someday have the opportunity to bring us up to date on events in Hadzaland.[1]

GEOGRAPHICAL BACKGROUND

The approximately one thousand eastern Hadza live within a roughly 80 km by 35 km rectangle southeast of Lake Eyasi in northern Tanzania. The lake is at an altitude of 1020 m in the bottom of a branch of the East African Rift valley. I refer to the lake and the immediately surrounding area where the Hadza live as the Eyasi Basin or as Hadzaland. Rainfall is low, about 500 mm per year, and vegetation is varied; most can be labeled as wooded savanna. The Eyasi Basin is enclosed by the steep slopes leading up to highlands, mountains and plateaus that rise to altitudes of 1800–3200 m, where rainfall is between 700 and 1,200 mm per year. Vegetation in the highlands includes areas of montane forest. Iraqw farmers and Maasai herders have lived in the highlands for hundreds of years. To the southwest the mountains and the rift wall are less pronounced and rainfall increases, allowing Isanzu, Iramba, and Sukuma farmers to thrive. The Eyasi Basin, at the bottom of the rift valley, where the land sank some 1000 m about a million years ago, includes its own small mountain ranges and plains. West of Lake Eyasi live another approximately 250 Hadza, who during my study period lived a rather confined life adjacent to high-priced shooting safari areas. I only visited them once, and therefore this chapter applies only to the eastern Hadza.

The eastern Hadza speak of their country as divided into three, sometimes four, "regions" (not to be confused with Tanzanian administrative regions). Hadza refer to Mangola, Siponga, and Tliika as regions and the people who live in them as belonging, respectively, to those regions. Sometimes Hadza refer to Han!abe, situated between Tliika and Mangola, as a fourth region. I also mention Munguli, at the southwestern end of eastern Hadza country, which was once a Hadza settlement and which now refers to an Isanzu village plus some other nearby villages where some Hadza lived during my study.

HISTORICAL BACKGROUND

When Obst (1912) stayed with Hadza and traveled about the Eyasi Basin in 1911, they apparently had the area to themselves. Neighboring Iraqw (Cushitic speakers) to the east, Maasai (Nilotic speakers) to the north, and the Isanzu, Iramba, and Sukuma to the south and southwest (all Bantu speakers) lived in areas surrounding but not overlapping the areas in which Hadza lived. Obst does report Hadza interactions with Isanzu and Isanzu living near Yaeda. He does not discuss Datoga, but it seems likely that some were living in the Eyasi Basin at that time, having been displaced from the nearby Ngorongoro crater by Maasai around 1840 (Bagshawe 1925; Borgerhoff-Mulder et al. 1989). The Hadza language, although it includes click consonants similar to those of Khoisan, is regarded as an isolate (Sands 1998), which attests to the extraordinary feat of cultural survival accomplished by the Hadza. Genetic studies suggest a separate Hadza identity through several tens of thousands of years and very little intermarriage with recent neighbors (Tishkoff et al. 2007; Tishkoff et al. 2009). Today's neighbors arrived between four thousand years ago (Cushitic speakers), two thousand years ago (Bantu speakers), and more recently (Nilotic speakers). Archaeologists find iron first appearing in the Eyasi Basin at 200 CE (Mabulla 2007).

During my study (1985–2000), Datoga lived in many parts of the Eyasi Basin, tending to prefer flatlands whereas Hadza prefer hills. By the end of my study other neighbors had encroached significantly. Most of the higher parts of the Siponga region had been cultivated by Iraqw and deserted by Hadza. A large number of non-Hadza immigrants were farming by irrigation in the Mangola region, using springs fed from the forested slopes of Oldeani Mountain (3,214 m). Two large non-Hadza villages, Qang'dend and Barazani, had grown up next to the irrigated fields. At the southwest end of eastern Hadza country in the early 1990s, many Hadza deserted Munguli and moved deeper into eastern Hadza country. Occasional non-Hadza pioneer farmers moved into other parts of Siponga and Tliika, cleared land, tried to farm, and usually failed, leaving only bare ground behind them. Around 1995 tourists began to visit the Hadza, mostly at bush camps in Mangola region. One or two tourist companies took a limited number of visitors to Hadza camps in Tliika. Tourism may have been the most influential change in Hadza life during the twentieth century.

LATE TWENTIETH-CENTURY CONDITIONS IN HADZA LAND

At the end of the twentieth century Hadza life had been little altered other than by the occasional tourist visits. Unlike the Aché, they had experienced no clear disjunction, such as settlement in a permanent village (Hill and Hurtado 1996). But between 1965 and 1991 six externally funded and guided attempts were made to encourage Hadza to settle and become farmers. All failed. Hadza came to the settlements for free food, tilled some fields, and then left when the free food ran out or when sickness increased and children died or when too many non-Hadza moved in. None of these settlements included the entire Hadza population. During each settlement attempt, only a few families stayed more than a year or two. Schooling was offered at two of these settlements (Yaeda and Munguli) in the 1960s, and in the early 1990s some children were taken away to boarding school at Endamagha. Few children stayed long; they simply walked home through the bush.

No lasting, major economic change, such as welfare payments or regular government food, has been introduced among the eastern Hadza—unlike in the Kalahari (Hitchcock and Sapignoli, chapter 4; Lee, chapter 3, this volume). Rural health clinics are available at Yaeda, Endamagha, and Munguli, often more than 15 km away from where Hadza live, but between 1985 and 2000 the availability of medicines at the clinics was unpredictable and Hadza used the clinics infrequently. In 1999, 41 percent of interviewed women had been to a clinic at some time in their lives (very few more often than once) and 9 percent to the district hospital. Other health-promoting facilities, such as piped water and electricity, are not available. Hadza are mobile foragers who travel exclusively by foot (they had two bicycles briefly). They hunt with bows and arrows of traditional design (Reche 1914) and of their own construction but use no guns. All Hadza make use of wild foods. Modern communications are not accessible; from time to time, a few Hadza have obtained a radio, but batteries are difficult to get, and the radios do not last long in the dust and rain.

Hadza in all locations speak Hadzane to each other. Most men also know Swahili well and sometimes a third language of one of the larger neighboring Isanzu or Iraqw populations. While Hadza have their own name for each of the neighboring populations, they commonly refer to any non-Hadza as "Swahili." I follow their usage here, which is a reference to the national language, not to the coastal peoples more properly known as Swahili.

The 2,500 km² area in which eastern Hadza live is fairly easily identified. As of 2000, their area had contracted only about 400 km² compared to the earliest accounts. Despite poor agricultural conditions in most of Hadza country, it has been invaded by a large number of farmers and has an increasing population of herders. Some of the agriculture in northern Tanzania is based on irrigation, which has a long history in the area (Sutton 1990; Westerberg et al. 2010), and Sutton (1986) found rock irrigation channels at Endamagha at the north end of Hadza country that date from 1500 to 1700 CE. The northeastern shores of Lake Eyasi and a row of springs at Qang'dend are fed from Oldeani Mountain and the Ngorongoro Crater rim (so long as the forests endure). Between the 1970s and today, irrigation farming in this area has grown extensively.

The number of non-Hadza living in and around Hadza country has increased even faster than the national population's 3.0 percent per annum and much faster than the Hadza's own 1.5 percent per annum (Tanzania Population and Housing Census 1978).[2] Given this population pressure, it is not surprising that neighboring farmers were prepared to move into the "unclaimed" parts of the Eyasi Basin. But nonirrigation farming depends on rainfall, which in the Eyasi Basin averages only 500 mm per year. Rainfall in East Africa varies dramatically (Spinage 2012), and the level was substantially lower in the first half of the twentieth century than from 1961 onward.

As farmers spread into the bush, the Hadza gained trading partners and a few brief employment opportunities (such as guarding fields) but lost natural resources. So far, the impact on the plant resources has not been great. Of more immediate concern to Hadza, however, are effects on game animals. Datoga modify water holes in ways that make them more difficult for wild animals to access, and the clearing of fields and building of "Swahili" houses deprive wildlife of food. Poachers move in, hunting with guns, snares, and vehicles.

Hadza readily sit together and talk angrily about these factors impacting their daily lives, but they are powerless to intercede. However, their objections do not prevent them individually from striking the best short-term bargain they can with immigrant farmers. Too often we neglect the difference between generosity in food sharing and cooperation in communal matters. In what follows I discuss the idea that a failure to make this distinction may impair settlement efforts. The letters that groups of Hadza several times dictated to me and instructed me to deliver to relevant local authorities fell on deaf ears. Among officials, aid workers, and others in the highlands, ignorance about the Eyasi Basin is profound. For example, European aid workers in Mbulu (the district capital) saw a letter from Hadza in Tliika as a threat to the onion productivity of Mangola (50–60 km away). Eventually, plant foods will diminish as goats clear the vegetation, herders burn it, regeneration ceases, and more non-Hadza with donkeys come to collect baobab pods. The probable future is not as Hadza would like to see it.

DIFFERENCES BETWEEN HADZA REGIONS

Researchers often prefer to look at the least disturbed portion of their study populations, although they can miss some valuable "natural experiments" by doing so. Hadza observed by Hawkes, O'Connell, and myself from 1985 to 1989 in Tliika, and by Marlowe and his students subsequently in Tliika and Siponga, were living in the most remote parts of Hadzaland and had the least contact with domesticates. Farm food comprised a very small part of the diet, 5 percent in 1985–1986 (Hawkes and O'Connell, personal communication 1991). Marlowe (2010:36) reports that of the food weighed as it arrived in the fourteen camps in which he stayed (up to 2005), only 5.7 percent was of agricultural origin, and all was obtained by trade. Contacts with people of other tribes were quite limited. Hadza we observed day to day interacted with anthropologists, the environment, and each other, but rarely with outsiders.

My demographic surveys covered the entire eastern Hadza population, exposing me to a wider array of local circumstances, summarized in table 5.1. The table also compares Tliika in the 1980s with Tliika in the 1990s and adds Munguli and its nearby villages. Mangola and Munguli stand out as different from Tliika, Siponga, and each other. Munguli was the longest enduring settlement, and several Hadza families farmed there for years. Bleek's (1930) notebooks hint that Hadza in that general area "had gardens" in the 1930s and that some were married to Isanzu. Kaare and Woodburn (1999:200) write, "Precise numbers [of Hadza] are difficult to determine owing to the flexible ethnicity of peripheral persons," which applies well to the southern extreme of Hadza country but not elsewhere.

Siponga, where Woodburn did much of his fieldwork in 1959–1961, had lost all of its higher areas to Iraqw farmers by 1985. A few Hadza families lived on the mountain slopes and sometimes worked for these farmers, guarding their fields and eating maize and impalas. I briefly visited one such group of families in their rock shelters in February 1989. They used the rock shelters like houses—as somewhere to sleep, hide their things, and have a fire. Farmers have since moved down the Udahaya River, felling its gallery forest. But two hundred or so Hadza still live relatively unimpaired lives in the lower parts of Siponga.

Table 5.1 shows the striking differences between Mangola and Tliika. Mangola is the most heavily occupied by non-Hadza, who outnumber Hadza sixteen

Table 5.1 Circumstances of Hadza life during the period 1985–2000 (mean census counts are on average 65 percent of the mean number of Hadza known to be alive at the time).

Circumstance	Tliika, 1982–1989	Tliika, 1990–2000	Siponga	Mangola	Munguli	Total Eastern Hadza population
Alcohol use	None	Rare	Rare	Abundant since 1995	Regulated?	Increasing?
Batteries available	No	No	Yes, at Yaeda	Yes, in 2 dukas	?	Not for long
"Become a Hadza"	0	0 (1 Iraqw wife)	1	1 plus 2 men nearly	0	2 men
Births, 1985–2000, with non-Hadza father (%)	?	?	?	?	43	16 (no change)
Communications	Word of mouth	Word of mouth	Word of mouth	Private e-mail (1997), cell phones (2000)	Word of mouth	Almost exclusively word of mouth
Cultivation	None	None	1989–1991	3 brief episodes	1965–2000	Some
Digging stick use	Every woman	Every woman	Every woman	Every woman	?	Every woman
Emigration from core area	?	?	?	?	3 men, 11 women	16 men, 18 women
Epeme dances held	Yes	Yes	Yes	Yes	?	Ubiquitous?
Epeme feasts held for men	Yes	Yes	Yes	?	?	"Normal"
Farm foods available (%)	5	5	?	More	?	9 (1995)
Firearms (non-Hadza) available	0	0	Maybe 1	0	1 old rifle	2
Flashlights available	2–3	2–3	2–3	More?	?	Few
Go to the Swahilis	?	?	?	2 families	?	?
Health services available	Very seldom used, 8–15 hour walk	Very seldom used, 8–15 hour walk	Yaeda	Available, 0.5–5 hour walk	Available, 0.5 hour walk	Used ever in lifetime by 41% of women

HIV	No evidence	No evidence	Not reported	1991 non-Hadza, 2010 Hadza	?	?
Homicide	0	1	1	?	0	33/100,000 persons/year
Housing	Grass houses	Same	1–3 larger houses	1–3 larger houses	Some larger	Mostly traditional, rock shelters used in some localities
Immigration to core area	?	?	?	?	22 men, 27 women	12 men, 15 women
Immunizations	Some old smallpox scars	Few polio and measles in 1992	?	Available, rate unknown	Available, rate unknown	Few
Manufactured clothing and footwear use	Mostly	Mostly	Mostly	Mostly	Mostly	Widespread, motor tire sandals
Married women with non-Hadza husbands (%)	0	2	7	6	24	6
Mean census count	206	191	173	174	84	622
Meet a Datoga	1/month	More	Daily	Frequently	? seldom	?
Radio receiver available	1–2	1–2	1–2	1	?	Few
See a Swahili	0	0	Weekly	Daily	Daily	
STDs	Handful of cases	Handful of cases	Some	Probably more	?	4% primary sterility
Tourists	No	Few	Few	Many since 1995	No	See text
Traditional clothing use	Some	Little	Little	None	None	Rare
Water supply	Many small, natural sources	Many small, natural sources	Small, natural, Datoga wells in sand rivers	Springs, sand rivers, tank in Ngorongoro Conservation Area	Well, for a while	

thousand to two hundred. Nonetheless, Hadza live in their separate camps and subsist predominantly on bush foods. From 1995 to 1996 Marlowe visited camps in different regions, including camps in Mangola that were located near "Swahili" villages. At that time only 6.6 percent of the calories brought into camp came from domesticates, obtained through trade, indicating a surprising degree of economic separation between Hadza and non-Hadza even in Mangola, where Hadza are so outnumbered by non-Hadza immigrants.

Starting in 1995, tourists began to visit Mangola-area bush camps almost daily. After a tourist visit, adult camp members, who were paid in cash by tour leaders, headed immediately to the nearest "hoteli" in search of alcohol. There they would stay until drunk and all the money gone. Alcohol brings violence and promiscuity and can rapidly multiply homicide rates. Foreign tourists thus seem likely to accomplish what no others before them have: the extinction of Hadza culture. Two other surprises accompanied the arrival of tourism in the Mangola area. A group of teenage boys made themselves headdresses of baboon skins, which they wore to impress the tourists, and women began to make beads from discarded plastic containers, melting the plastic on a long wire held over the fire. We do not know who came up with the idea but doubt that it would have flourished without tourists to buy the beads and villagers to discard their broken plastic buckets.

The cut-price tourists who rent drivers and aging Land Rovers see an obviously contrived and limited display on their bone-shaking day trip to Mangola from Karatu. Their cash will reach the alcohol suppliers within minutes. They will leave drunkenness and debauchery in their wake. Tourists with more time and money may join select groups that go far into the bush and camp. Here tourists will see Hadza camps very similar to those in which we worked in the 1980s and do much less harm with their cash. Until very recently, alcohol was too far away and cash was saved up for a two- to three-day walk to a traveling rural market, where it could be exchanged for a knife, axe, cold chisel (for making arrowheads), or aluminum cooking pot. But alcohol now reaches the "remote" areas where we worked in the 1980s. Awful tragedies lay ahead for some of the children whom I observed back then.

Although tourists have destructive effects on the Hadza, they have given the Hadza (and, less needy, the Datoga) a commercial value to their Swahili neighbors, people in the towns, and even the government. Although Hadza are officially citizens, and equally entitled to vote, without tourism and researchers the Hadza would have no influence and no voice.

Attempts to have Hadza paid in a currency other than cash have failed. Hadza often complained that cash was controlled by non-Hadza, yet no Hadza was able to take on the role of handling the transactions with tour companies and the distribution of cash. Arrangements for Hadza to make their case at local meetings have also failed. Hadza agreed to speak, prepared, and then failed to show up or just sat in silence. It is as if the dangers of taking the lead, of speaking for the whole group, are too much for them. These phenomena are somehow related to the fear of individuals setting themselves above others, just as Lee (1979) has described among the Zhun/twa. Woodburn (1979) described a variety of rare un-Hadza-like episodes of "bullying" linked to dealings with the "outside." These imply that the Hadza fear of individuals setting themselves above others is realistic.

SETTLEMENT SCHEMES AND HADZA MOBILITY

Around the time of Danieli's unsuccessful experience in 1965, a series of heavy-handed efforts to bring Hadza "in from the bush" began. The aim was to persuade them to settle and farm. The intention was to provide schools and health services and to bring Hadza into the national mainstream. These were not the first such attempts, nor the last (McDowell 1981). But despite the investment of considerable resources, all these efforts have failed. The majority of Hadza left settlement communities and resumed their mobile foraging lives. However, each settlement attempt had two longer-term consequences. First, a few Hadza families remained in settlement communities or close by. Second, a number of non-Hadza families moved in, farmed successfully enough, and became the majority of voters and users of the newly provided facilities. As a consequence, the Hadza lost more territory.

The sedentism of life in the settlements contrasts with the mobility of Hadza life in the bush. There, Hadza move camp frequently, every two to five weeks. Camp size averages about thirty people, and the composition of camps changes continually. During any camp move, some members may go to different destinations. Between camp moves, members may leave. Others may arrive and join the camp. A sociometric study showed that while Hadza name more people who live closer to them as those they would like to camp with, they also identify some people in camps scattered throughout Hadza country (Apicella et al. 2012). My censuses showed that on average, an individual was 17 km from where I last saw them a year or two years previously; however, the distribution has a long tail, and some are 100 km away. Movement between Hadza regions is slower but significant. Forty-one percent of later sightings were in a different region from the one in which an individual was seen in 1985. Woodburn (1968b) comments that one well-known older woman, who tended not to move very frequently, nonetheless camped with sixty-seven different people over three years of observation. I tried to replicate his finding by sampling all women in all regions born before 1975 and seen during my censuses between 1985 and 2000. Although individual scores varied, the central tendency was very close to Woodburn's. Women seen in four or more censuses were recorded with a median of 65 different adults (mean 68.9, range 10–144, n = 171 women). (Women seen five or more times had a median of 69 and a mean of 71.9; those seen three times, 65 and 66.5, respectively.) These figures suggest no meaningful change since Woodburn's 1960s observations and help show the great rate at which Hadza switch camp mates. Mobility rules.

This pattern of flexibility in camp composition means that eastern Hadza are continually exposed to choices about who to live with. Given that there are advantages to living with some people, and perhaps disadvantages to living with others, and everyone is free to live where they like, Hadza are clearly embedded in an extensive and continuous "biological market" for camp mates. They may continually try to be in camp with those of value to them and try to avoid those with whom they are in dispute or who are of less value to them (Barclay 2013; Noë and Hammerstein 1994; Noë et al. 2001).

In contrast to the mobile bush life, in a settlement or village an individual has much less choice of immediate neighbors. He or she can try to ignore some and curry favor with others, but the situation is very different from that of high residential mobility. It may be easier and more rewarding to keep track of individuals and debts in a settlement rather than a mobile setting. A bush-living Hadza hunter waiting for another individual to reciprocate may have to wait hundreds of days to find out whether he will in fact be reciprocated, based on our observed frequency and unpredictability of catches. His computations will be further complicated by the high likelihood that those to whom he "gave" meat will be living somewhere else when they make their next catch. Reciprocal exchange of small items in a village, or other settlement, may be more feasible. We should expect different kinds of goods to be subject to different ecological-economic processes and patterns of sharing.

To account for the Hadza reluctance to farm, we should contemplate the pre-adaptations to farming that some have proposed. Anthropologists distinguish between hunter-gatherers who are egalitarian, mobile, and share food widely from those who store food, have stable residences for at least part of the year, and tend to be less egalitarian and in some cases are quite stratified. Testart (1982) drew attention to ecological differences, contrasting the dispersed and unpredictable foods of the mobile egalitarian foragers with the synchronized, seasonal "gluts" (such as acorn harvests and salmon runs) that are associated with storage societies. He found that storage was neither confined to nor universal in extremely cold climates. Testart suggested that storage societies were pre-adapted to farming, which is impossible without storage and tends to require residence near crops, just as the storage foragers lived close to rivers or migration routes. This distinction fits closely with the "tolerated theft" model (Blurton Jones 1987). Foods that arrive unpredictably, in large packages and at different times, may not be worth defending from others who have no other food source. Each will contest and consume "according to their needs." When everyone experiences food arriving all at once in large amounts, in a kind of synchronized glut, no one gains from contesting his or her neighbor's stash. Storage and the social recognition of ownership might follow easily.

Woodburn (1982, 1988) similarly categorized foragers into "immediate return societies" and "delayed return societies." The core of his dichotomy was "ownership" and the construction and ownership of "facilities" such as fish weirs.[3] Woodburn's labels also suggest a difference in attitude to the future that may attract some consideration. I will neglect it as an outcome of ecological conditions that we seek to understand, although Tucker (2006) has shown "discounting the future" to be an important feature of Mikea farming and foraging decisions. Like Testart, Woodburn suggested that the less egalitarian delayed return societies were pre-adapted to farming, and these works suggest we look for obstacles to farming in the nature of resources and the system of sharing.

Why Not Settle and Farm?

The Hadza entered the late twentieth century as hunter-gatherers who rejected agriculture partly because rainfall is too low in most of the Eyasi Basin for farming and also because the bush had too many tsetse flies for herding. However, these environmental constraints are probably only part of the reason Hadza have not become farmers.

LACK OF OPPORTUNITY OR RESISTANCE?

Hadza have been in the Eyasi Basin for a very long time, and some locations have always had suitable soil, water, and climate for farming. In those locations recent migrants from neighboring tribes successfully grow onions, tomatoes, sweet potatoes, millet, and maize. For at least one hundred years, trade contact with neighboring farmers was probably sufficient for Hadza to acquire adequate seeds and knowledge to farm themselves. But as far as we know Hadza only ever farmed in the extreme south where rainfall is a little higher (Kaduna 1982) and where they mixed with Isanzu farmers. Hadza did not make use of these opportunities en masse.

In recent decades, Hadza have been subjected to six settlement attempts. At each settlement, Hadza received seed, hoes, and free food until at least the time of their first harvest. Most of the settlements required Hadza to give up foraging in an environment that supported them well for farming in an environment in which farming was only marginally successful. We may wonder what would have happened if the choice was between continued Hadza foraging in their present environment and farming in a more agriculturally productive location. The Mikocheni settlement was in a productive location, yet it, too, failed to endure.

While immigrant farming and tourism were developing around Mangola village, Hadza still had camps in Mangola where people tried to live a traditional life. They hunted and gathered in the depleted region and made very little use of agricultural foods. We must conclude that even if the opportunity is now lost, for some decades they actively resisted farming.

Hadza often say they do not know how to farm, but enough of them have had experience during the settlement attempts to question this claim. They have had opportunities at least as good as those taken by the farmers who migrated from surrounding regions. Several families did successfully become farmers, at the cost of being referred to by Hadza as "lost among the Swahilis." Most did not.

THE RICHNESS OF THE BUSH AND THE POVERTY OF FARMING

The Hadza habitat is rich in wild resources (Vincent's [1985] tuber transects are some of the strongest evidence). In "The Global Process and Local Ecology" (1996), my colleagues and I suggested that the balance of costs and benefits is different when the bush provides a rich living than when it provides a more frugal one. We argued that the Hadza have a richer environment than the !Kung, mainly because the Hadza environment has many small water sources and therefore shorter distances between water, camp, and food. Because dry season water sources for the !Kung are few and far from their staple foods, !Kung often add gardening to their subsistence strategy. The !Kung and the Hadza also have different relationships with herders. The !Kung live alongside, work for, and marry Herero and have accumulated some livestock. Such relationships could make it easier for !Kung to supervise their gardens. Hadza do not have a close social or economic relationship to Datoga. I know of only two Hadza women who ever married Datoga men. Disagreement over Datoga modification of water holes is severe, and Datoga have sometimes tried to capture Hadza children to tend their herds. We may wonder why the relationships are so different between these two forager-herder pairs. Some of the possible answers may lie in the more militaristic history and traditions of the Datoga.

WOMEN'S EXPERIENCE WITH FARMERS:
WHO CONTROLS THE RESOURCES?

Although Hadza women sometimes marry Swahili farmers, and some move outside Hadzaland with them, more than half come back and bring most of their children to be raised as Hadza. These women complain about the relative servitude of life as a farmer's wife. They are outraged at beatings and perhaps annoyed by the difficulty of acquiring simple domestic resources like firewood. Among neighboring farmers, men have much more control over the acquisition and distribution of resources than do Hadza men.[4] Hadza women have free access to plant foods, water, firewood, and meat killed by any man wherever they go in Hadzaland. This autonomy may be threatened by life as a farmer's wife,[5] and this difference in resource control may be the reason why Hiernaux and Hartono (1980) found that Hadza women were better nourished relative to men than women elsewhere in Africa. Draper (1975) discusses the autonomy of !Kung women in the bush and the evident reduction of autonomy among !Kung women who have adopted a village life. The threat to women's autonomy could be one reason why Hadza resist settled life.

AVOIDING "SWAHILIS"

An older woman arrived from Munguli and was living in Tliika with her many younger kin and with her co-wife of their late husband. Quite a large number of Hadza had deserted Munguli at that time, and I asked her why she had left the comforts of that place. Her answer was simple: "To be with my people." It is not unusual to hear Hadza explain that they left a settlement because there were "too many Swahilis," which was particularly true of the major settlements of the 1960s: Yaeda, Endamagha, and Munguli. In each of these communities a school and clinic were built. Many non-Hadza quite quickly arrived, settled, and made a sufficient living as farmers to enable them to stay permanently. Recently, however, the farming population of Yaeda has declined as less water flows from the nearby highlands.

The Hadza comment about "too many Swahilis" is extremely "politically incorrect" in Tanzania, where the predominant task of the government has been to weld over two hundred language groups into a nation. But neighbors do, almost universally, look down on Hadza as "primitive and lazy" and unwilling to "develop." The interactions are not necessarily unpleasant, but the attitudes are clear, and most Hadza just avoid them. On a visit to Mbulu (the district capital) with Gudo Mahiya, we were asked, pleasantly, by a woman we had both met and had had friendly interactions with before why Hadza insisted on living in the bush and not taking up the comforts of village life. The discussion was quite lengthy and good natured. Gudo's answers that the bush is clean, safe and, peaceful and they like to eat meat seemed sound reasons, but they were clearly beyond our friend's comprehension. Other Hadza and other authors (e.g., Woodburn 1988, 1997) have reported much less enjoyable, even openly insulting, interactions.

AVOIDING EXTERNAL CONTROL AND THE DANGER POSED BY WELL-CONNECTED INDIVIDUALS

Woodburn (1979, 1988) described several instances in which a Hadza with close connections to the outside world tried to control other Hadza, sometimes in extreme and bizarre ways. The memory of these instances may have been refreshed at the time of the 1989 settlement attempt when a group of young men were sent about to persuade Hadza to join the settlement. Informants described extreme and objectionable methods, and I witnessed one such recruiting visit to a bush camp. Young men, some of whom I knew quite well, disported themselves in an un-Hadza-like and personally uncharacteristic rough and authoritarian manner. Eventually, they left empty handed, having seen that all my papers were in order and having decided that my research was important for the history of their people and thus the camp members could stay where they were.

Woodburn ascribed the source of these unusual incidents to connection with the outside world, and memory of these events may add to the reluctance of most Hadza to act in leadership roles (as described in connection with tourism). But resistance to an individual setting himself above others probably predates these settlement attempts. It has been described in other foragers, notably the !Kung (Lee 1979, chapter 3, this volume) and may be one source of the "leadership problem" of egalitarian foragers that is mentioned by several authors in this volume.

!Kung and Hadza often settle disputes—about who got how much or whether a debt was returned—by moving away. Moving away is relatively difficult for the !Kung during the dry season because water is scarce and camps far apart, but it is easier for !Kung in the wet season and easy all year round for the Hadza. It is much more difficult for a farmer who has cleared his fields, built his house, and stored his harvest in the darkness of the rafters. At the settlements, Hadza who come into conflict can adopt their traditional solution and leave the settlement. If they are to stay they must do without this primary means for resolving conflicts. Decreased mobility also deprives an audience of its traditional sanction of a budding despot, which is to desert him. As Betzig (2004) remarked so clearly, despots arise when people cannot get away from them. If Hadza cannot, or are not willing to, leave the settlement, despots can arise. But Hadza do leave, perhaps sometimes for this very reason.

AID WORKERS MAY HAVE MISUNDERSTOOD SHARING AS COOPERATION

After Tanzania's independence in 1961, all land was publicly held. Recently, however, economic advisers have pressed the Tanzanian government to consider individual land ownership because of the common belief that private owners will take better care of their land. Meanwhile, Hadza supporters have argued in favor of legal status for communally held land. Given this background and the widespread notion of foragers as sharing, communally minded people, I suspect that all of the settlement attempts (funded externally by various aid organizations) tried to promote communal labor and communally owned fields and stores (a communal storeroom was built at Mono and at Munguli). Whether or not this was the case, sharing among the Hadza is not the same as cooperating. I mentioned that Hadza will sit together and grumble about immigrant farmers, but individually they will welcome these farmers into personal economic agreements.

Contrasts with Datoga illustrate the difference between sharing and cooperating. Datoga communally maintain their water holes for their livestock, organize teams of young men to pass up buckets of water from the deeper wells, and organize groups of young men to carry sick patients to the hospital two days' walk away. Hadza almost never cooperate in such labor (though I heard of one instance of a man, badly injured by a buffalo, being tracked down and carried home by a group of friends). Draper (personal communication 1988) described the contrast between !Kung and Herero reactions when a water bucket fell to the bottom of a well. While !Kung appeared unable to respond, Herero immediately organized a team to retrieve it and repair the rope. The !Kung and Hadza ability to share food widely and apparently ungrudgingly does not mean they have a penchant for all forms of cooperation. By assuming that food sharing implies a mechanism for labor cooperation, unity of response, or disinterested leadership, settlement organizers may have doomed their efforts from the outset. However, Hadza farming persisted at Munguli, where each family appeared to have its own small garden plot.

THE SHARING ETHIC

Details of Hadza sharing, particularly large-animal meat sharing, are still debated (Wood and Marlowe 2013). From the wide range of processes by which sharing could evolve (Noë and Hammerstein 1994; Stevens and Gilby 2004), only two have absorbed the attention of human behavioral ecologists: variance-reducing reciprocal altruism and costly signaling. But in writing about the "show-off" hypothesis and the "hierarchy of virtue," respectively, Hawkes (1990) and Bliege Bird and colleagues (2012b) have developed the idea of "competitive altruism" (Roberts 1998) as an important feature of hunter-gatherer societies.

Reciprocal altruism refers to a situation in which, for example, giving is advantageous because it sufficiently increases the probability that the recipient will return the favor in kind, or in another currency, in the future. An extensive literature has shown the limited circumstances in which this phenomenon can arise and persist, and few examples have survived rigorous tests. Costly signaling is a process in which a costly act can be favored by natural selection if it is a reliable signal of some quality of the signaler that is important to the audience. Its costliness makes it expensive to fake and thus reliable to the audience. Show-off refers to the view that some hunting is economically suboptimal for the hunter but selected because it serves as a reliable and highly salient signal that conveys information about the hunter's value as a mate or competitor. Competitive altruism suggests that when individuals can choose their social partners, they compete for the most altruistic partners and nonaltruists may become ostracized. Altruism can then arise outside the narrow requirements for reciprocal altruism. Competitive altruism implies that individuals are in a "market" for social partners. In a market, value and scarcity are important, and Noë and colleagues (2001) have shown how this idea can be used to account for otherwise surprising aspects of behavior. Competitive altruism takes us close to Bird's hierarchy of virtue in which individuals strive to achieve and maintain a reputation as good altruists. This framework brings us quite close to the idea of an ethic and much closer to sociological formulations of giving, such as Titmuss 1973, and classical anthropological descriptions of giving and sharing, such as Sahlins's (1974) over-cautiously labeled "generalized reciprocity" and "demand sharing."

Hadza display a prosharing ethic. They say, "We are Hadza. We share because our hearts are good." Whatever one's theory of food sharing, it is hard to deny that Hadza have this powerful belief. If someone asks, you must give. A good person gives. A bad person is someone who does not share properly. Hadza agree that everyone should share, even though sometimes they will try not to. Sometimes, when a man came home apparently empty handed, he would later summon us surreptitiously to weigh the bird or baobab pod full of honey that he had hidden in his house. Woodburn (1998:56) and Marlowe (2010) have described similar events. When I asked women whether they could keep a bird for their children, most said they should share something the size of a guinea fowl but not the size of a dove. I asked whether they could say the guinea fowl was just for their children. That would be very bad, I was told. Any "ethic" is littered with "exceptions" or "special cases," and again we must require adequate theories of sharing to account for detailed variation. We should aim to explain why, for example, some things are shared, some "owned," some loaned, and some apparently redistributed in games of chance.

Classically, an ethic is most noticeable when broken. Among the Hadza, this transgression can lead to a surprising response: an aggressive tirade against a familiar visitor who gave too much. I have been the recipient four times. The most memorable was when, after several years, I saw a young woman whom I had often followed around when she was a busily foraging child. I very discretely gave her a larger present than the others. A prolonged grumble followed: "We used to think that Nicholas was a good person. Now we know he is not." On another occasion, after a young man had been particularly helpful on a drive through an un-navigable mountainous area, he asked me to bring something for his mother, using her name to persuade me it was not just for his next flirtation. I made sure it was a generous present, and a year or two later I gave it to her discretely packaged. She looked at it scornfully, replying at a volume only older Hadza women can attain, "How can you give me this paltry thing when I'm standing here in front of you in these rags and tatters?" While reminiscent of Lee's account in "Eating Christmas in the Kalahari" (1969), in the Hadza context it was not so much that I might think I had done too well, but that others might think the recipient received an unfairly large gift. Perhaps the other side of the coin is that no one begrudged our practice of giving children who refused to be measured a cup of maize meal "just for trying."

Woodburn has described and discussed Hadza sharing, especially sharing meat from large animals, in some detail:

> It has often been suggested that meat-sharing is simply a labor-saving form of storage. The hunter surrenders his rights to much of his kill in order to secure rights over parts of the kills of other hunters in future. There are problems with this formulation: as I have already mentioned, hunting success is unequal. Donors often remain on balance donors and may not receive anything like an equivalent return. Entitlement does not depend in any way on donation. Some men who are regular recipients never themselves contribute. Instead of seeing the arrangement as being in the interest of the donor, I think we should be clear that it is imposed on the donor by the community. [Woodburn 1982:441]

> To treat such sharing as any form of exchange or reciprocity is inappropriate when donation is obligatory and is disconnected from the right

to receive. To describe such sharing as exchange or reciprocity does not accord with local ideology or local practice among the Hadza. [Woodburn 1998: 50]

The situation described by Woodburn, in which it is impossible to refuse shares, is similar to "tolerated theft" (Blurton Jones 1984, 1987), and both are susceptible to a serious freeloader problem: why not be the one who sits home and still continues to get chunks of meat on demand? Why continue to go out and hunt dangerous buffalo or scavenge from lions when you have little influence over where the proceeds go? Recognizing this problem, Hawkes (1990) proposed a series of potential advantages to the hunter of large animals.[6] The very large amount of meat available when a hunter kills a buffalo, zebra, or eland attracts much attention. People come to the kill site from neighboring camps as well as the hunter's camp, and most carry away several kilos of meat. People know who shot the animal. They have consistent opinions about who often hunts successfully, and the opinions correlate positively with observed rates of hunting success (Blurton Jones et al. 1997; Marlowe 2010). Hawkes (1990) originally suggested that the audience may self-interestedly treat the hunter, or his wife or his children, better in order to keep him in camp and the meat bonanzas flowing. They may prefer him as a neighbor over other individuals. By hunting large, even dangerous, prey, the hunter may also be signaling his vigor, intelligence, and energy or more subtle qualities that make him a more formidable adversary and a potential mate whose children might inherit some of his vigor. Hawkes's (1990) suggestion became known as "show off," despite our having seen exactly the displays of humility by successful hunters that Woodburn (1998:59) described.

As E. A. Smith (1993, 2004) pointed out, some of the benefits proposed for the successful hunter suffer a "secondary" freeloader problem. Why be the one to make the costly concessions when everyone apparently benefits equally? The show-off process was then narrowed down to costly signaling (Bliege Bird et al. 2001; Hawkes and Bliege Bird 2002). Costly signaling, as it was proposed, suffers no freeloader problem since it is to the advantage of each member of the audience to take account of the indications of a hunter's quality as an adversary or a mate.

Some of the "concessions" to the hunter proposed in early versions of Hawkes's "show off" (treating his wife or children better, trying to keep him as an ally and desirable neighbor) may have anticipated the newer series of ideas referred to as "biological markets" (Noë and Hammerstein 1994). A key aspect of these models is that when individuals can choose their partners (camp mates), aspects of sharing (and other more subtle relationships) evolve more easily. The good hunter may be more inclined to stay in camp with someone who makes concessions than with someone who does not. Because good hunters are scarce, and others numerous, these others are in competition to get a good hunter as a camp mate. Anyone who does not give a good hunter special treatment may quickly be replaced by someone who does. Whether these market forces would solve the "secondary" freeloader problem associated with the concessions made to keep the hunter as a neighbor has not been rigorously tested. Intuitively, I would suggest that given the ease with which either the Hadza hunter or audience can move or change camp, the "secondary" freeloader problem may have been overestimated.

The market for camp mates (and spouses) requires only that some be better than others and all be mobile or otherwise selectable. Among other ground-foraging primates, it may be significant that living alone is quite dangerous, as it probably was for most of our bipedal ancestors. But occasionally Hadza do live alone. Woodburn mentions examples, and during my study period one youth was well known for living in the bush on his own and an older man and his wife were famous for disappearing into the bush for extended periods. While people had their concerns about the youth, they had only admiration for the old man, a second husband to a woman who headed a very large family of siblings, daughters, and granddaughters but who, at that time, often did not live with them.

Most Hadza settlement attempts involved a large number of people living in one place. The size and constancy of group membership enforced by the settlements may have been part of what led to their downfall. That is, the audience could no longer vote with their feet. Without the option to move camps and find more desirable neighbors, biological market forces are weakened. Payoffs for the successful, active hunter diverge less from payoffs to the inactive or unsuccessful hunter than they would in a mobile population. Those who were succeeding in the hierarchy of virtue stood to lose in the settlement. In fact, proportionally more of the good hunters (scored from women's responses to the question, "Can you tell me the names of some expert hunters, people who often hit large animals?") stayed away from the Mono settlement in 1990. In the settlement they would have had a reduced opportunity to hunt but also have lost the opportunity to select their audience. Good hunters could also have more formidably resisted the "posse" that herded people into the settlement.

The sixteen good hunters who initially went to the settlement mostly had connections or history in the Siponga region, where the settlement was sited; only five remained there in 1991 and three in 1992.

Different theories of sharing may predict different responses to the loss of mobility. If reciprocal exchange was a large component of Hadza sharing, it could continue under the conditions of the settlement. Reciprocity apparently persists successfully in village settings;[7] however, the frequency of exchanges might be lower as the variance and asynchrony in food availability are much reduced. This factor would also reduce the frequency of transfers due to tolerated theft or harassment (Stevens and Stephens 2002). Reduction in the frequency of such exchanges does not necessarily motivate resistance to or departure from the settlement. But derangement of the traditional process of partner choice, which on the one hand restrains would-be despots and on the other enables the biological market that maintains sharing, is a compelling reason for the repeated failure of settlements. Those who are not successful as competitive altruists may be more inclined to settle. Among the unsuccessful hunters, some had, of their own accord, gone "outside" seeking employment among "the Swahilis," at least for a few months or years.

Discussion and Conclusions

I have reviewed several possible reasons why in most of their range Hadza have rejected opportunities to settle and farm. But farming by Hadza in the extreme south of their range in and around Munguli has not been explained, beyond the mention of slightly higher rainfall levels, separate household gardens, and a possibly longer history. To some extent farming was achieved by intermarriage with Isanzu and the retention of both Hadza self-identification (when convenient) and continued farming by adult children. Something similar may have happened to foragers all over Africa during the Bantu expansion.

However, several issues remain unaddressed. Hadza relationships to Datoga may have made the addition of small livestock to their resources impossible. But why does this relationship differ from the relationship of !Kung to Herero (Lee, chapter 3, this volume)? Also, two newly developing features could be expected to reduce Hadza mobility: camping where tourists can find them and an increasing population living at increased density. I have seen the effects of neither in my data. Recent visitors may be able to document further consequences.

For the majority of eastern Hadza, resistance to farming is most likely related to their sharing ethic and to their "competitive altruism," which depends upon mobility and flexibility in camp membership. I propose that the incompatibility of the Hadza sharing ethic and settled life is the main reason Hadza have repeatedly rejected settlement. Other chapters in this volume show how the sharing ethic supports the persistence of hunting and gathering in much more modernized circumstances than those of the Hadza. Several of them include mobility enhanced by motor vehicles (cars, boats), obviously useful for hunting, but perhaps reducing residential mobility (Codding et al., chapter 8; Coxworth, chapter 7; Wenzel, chapter 2, this volume). Insofar as their circumstances include lower residential mobility, these cases may contradict my argument. Among Hadza, the cost of failure to participate in the sharing ethic appears to be gradual, un-acclaimed, de facto ostracism. Like the one enduring Hadza family of sweet potato farmers in Mangola region, the outcome is gradually becoming referred to by Hadza as "lost among the Swahilis."

Notes

1. The results of a series of eight censuses of the Hadza that I conducted between 1985 and 2000 are reported in Burton Jones 2016. Numbers and statements in this chapter that have no cited sources all come from this book.

2. Mangola ward had 6,846 people in 1978 and 16,568 in 2002; Mwangeza ward, which is the area around Munguli, went from 2,445 to 12,414.

3. Woodburn (1988) categorized Aboriginal Australian societies as "delayed return societies" because men claimed "ownership" of women and the ability to transfer ownership. Researchers on Australia represented in this volume would probably dispute his decision.

4. Hawkes and colleagues (2001a) and Woodburn (1998) concluded that Hadza men have very little control over the meat of the large animals they kill.

5. Much as Leacock (1982b) argues that a change in relations between the sexes accompanied the rise of fur trade among the Montagnais-Naskapi.

6. Woodburn (1998:60) appears to reject the idea that Hadza hunters gain social benefits, claiming that the hunter receives no benefit except the intrinsic pleasure of success at a difficult task. Woodburn thus ignores the behavioral ecologist's question: how did natural selection make this rewarding?

7. Among the Aché, see Allen-Arave et al. 2008; Gurven et al. 2002. Among the Lamalera, see Nolin 2010, 2012.

CHAPTER SIX

In Pursuit of the Individual
Recent Economic Opportunities and the Persistence of Traditional Forager-Farmer Relationships in the Southwestern Central African Republic

KAREN D. LUPO

Introduction

Throughout forested portions of central Africa, foragers (historically called pygmies) are characterized as forest specialists who have long-standing and well-established interethnic relationships with settled farming populations. The interrelationships between these populations are quite complex and have important political, social, and religious dimensions (Hewlett 1990). The most highly visible aspect of these interactions is the economic exchange of forager-procured forest products (especially meat) for village products (usually manioc [*Manihot utilissima*]). For decades the link between forager and farmer was so complete in anthropological thought that questions about why foragers foraged were narrowly focused on the idea that the economic exchange of domesticated crops for meat from wild animals was a functional response to rain-forest resource insufficiency, especially the availability of wild starches (Bailey et al. 1989; Bailey and Headland 1991). This view cast forest forager and farmer interrelationships around the world as functionally mutualistic. Forest foragers hunted prey and procured meat to trade for starches produced by settled farmers, who were unable to obtain sufficient meat on their own. This view implied that full-time independent foragers could not have existed in the forest before the advent of domesticated crops and always existed as part of a dyad with Bantu-speaking farmers.

Although this view had popular appeal, archaeological, biomolecular, and historical linguistic studies (which I will summarize) show that foragers occupied forested regions before the advent of domesticated foods (Lupo et al. 2014;

Mercader 2002). Ethnobotanical surveys conducted in forested portions of west-central and central Africa identified high densities of wild edible starches in the form of yams (*Dioscorea* spp.) that were utilized by foragers (Bahuchet et al. 1991; Caudell 2011; Dounais 2001; Hladik et al. 1984; Hladik and Dounais 1993; Sato 2001). Ethnographic studies showed that some forest foragers survived for long periods of time without access to domesticated starches (Ichikawa 2012; Kitanishi 1995; Yasouka 2006a, 2006b, 2009a, 2009b). Furthermore, from the early to middle part of the twentieth century, forest foragers throughout western and central Africa increasingly turned to growing their own crops in response to governmental mandates and policies, local economic changes, and habitat constriction (Bahuchet 1985; Ichikawa 1991; Kitanishi 2003, 2006). Even though some foragers can produce sufficient crops to meet their own demands, many continue to forage for wild resources and maintain traditional ties with farmers. Studies suggest that while forager-farmer dyads may serve mutual needs, the emergence, nature, or persistence of these interactions cannot be explained by an appeal to functional nutritional requirements (e.g., Bahuchet et al. 1991; Hladik and Dounais 1993).

In this chapter I argue that the resiliency of forager-farmer dyads is linked to the social benefits derived from these relationships. Forest foragers continue to forage because of a shared identity deeply rooted in the forest, an established place in an ancient system that involves multidimensional relationships with neighboring farmers and has economic and social value (also see Blurton Jones, chapter 5, this volume). However, the persistence of forager-farmer dyads throughout forested regions of western and central Africa cannot be viewed as a homogenous response to ecological or socioeconomic conditions. These relationships differ in scale, scope, and intensity because the costs and benefits of sustaining these relationships vary as a function of different historical processes and ecological and socioeconomic contexts.

I present data showing that despite the relatively recent emergence of forager-farmer dyads in prehistory, these relationships have been maintained over time, albeit in modified forms. Data spanning the historical period, through 2003 CE, show that the nature of these relationships is dynamic and responsive to change yet sustained by both populations through large-scale sociopolitical, economic, and ecological shifts. I also present quantitative data showing the dynamic nature of forager-farmer relationships in the village of Grima in the southwestern Central African Republic from 1999 to 2003. In the study discussed here,

Figure 6.1. A Bofi man making a net. Photograph by Karen Lupo.

reductions in the availability of key prey (e.g., blue duikers [*Cephalophus monticola*]), increased market opportunities, and random demographic changes had the cumulative effect of changing how forest meat was procured. Specifically, the frequency of cooperative net-hunts decreased (figure 6.1), and the use of individual hunting strategies (especially the use of snares) increased among foragers. The development of a road allowed for greater and more regularized access of commercial koko (*Gnetum africanum*) vendors to the village and increased the sales of koko by foragers to vendors. If forager-farmer relationships were solely based on economic or nutritional need, then an emphasis on individualized production in concert with increased access to commercial markets should decrease the interrelationship, as foragers could directly purchase comestible and utilitarian items. However, data presented here (and elsewhere) suggest that although prey depression and changes in hunting technology reduced the amount of meat available for exchange, these processes did not have an appreciable impact on forager-farmer exchanges. In this village, relationships were maintained with plant foods replacing meat as the basis of exchange.

Forest Foragers in the Congo Basin

Groups of forest foragers currently occupy regions spanning thirteen different countries in central and western Africa with a total population estimated
to be between three hundred thousand and six hundred thousand individuals
(figure 6.2). These groups are ethnolinguistically diverse but share a distinctive
cultural identity, a long-standing connection to the forest (Bahuchet 1993), and
a common, albeit complicated, genetic heritage (Batini et al. 2007; Batini et al.
2011a; Batini et al. 2011b; Patin et al. 2009; Verdu et al. 2009). Many are closely
associated with settlements inhabited by ethnically distinct farming populations who speak Bantu, Obanguian, or Central Sudanic languages. The forest
foragers who neighbor these villages speak the same languages as the farmer
populations and retain limited vocabulary from their indigenous languages,

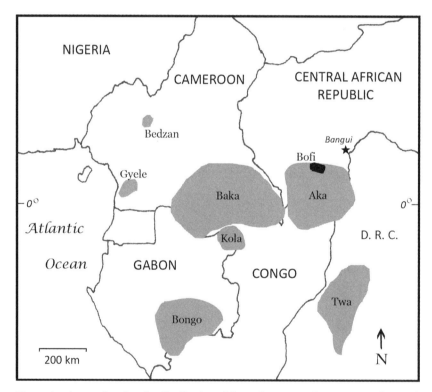

Figure 6.2. A map showing the distribution of forest foragers in the western and central
Central African Forest.

suggesting a long span of interactions between these populations (Bahuchet 1993), perhaps reaching back some two thousand to four thousand years.

Ethnographically, interrelationships of foragers and farmers were often described as patron-client-type arrangements with forager clients providing forest resources (meat and honey) and labor to their farmer patrons in exchange for village products such as domesticated foods, cloth, salt, and oil (Bahuchet 1985). Nevertheless, foragers retain their ethnic distinctiveness in material culture, social and political organization, ritual beliefs, and economic organization.

Forest forager lifeways continue to undergo rapid transformation in response to government policies mandating settling and farming, habitat restriction and destruction, industrialization, and especially the commoditization of forest products (i.e., the bushmeat trade). The impacts of and foragers' responses to these processes are, however, highly diverse and vary according to local historical, ecological, and sociopolitical circumstances. For instance some groups, such as the Babongo in Gabon, are integrated with their farmer neighbors through high rates of intermarriage (also see Knight 2003; Verdu et al. 2009). Other groups, such as the Baka in Cameroon (Kitanishi 2003; Köhler 2005; Yasouka 2006a, 2006b), Mbendjele Yaka in northern Congo (Lewis 2005), and Bakoya in Gabon (Soengas 2009), have undergone significant economic transformation and practice a mixed economy by growing their own domesticated crops and hunting part time yet still maintain barter-based relations with settled farmers.

BEFORE AND AFTER FARMING:
A LONGITUDINAL CONTEXT FOR FOREST SPECIALISTS

Archaeological, linguistic, and biomolecular data suggest that forest foragers occupied the forest for long stretches of time punctuated by periods of isolation, population migration, and contact among groups. Dispersed and small populations of indigenous foragers likely occupied at least some portions of the Congo Basin as early as eight hundred thousand to nine hundred thousand years ago (Gotilogue 2000; Mercader 2002), with the earliest specialized technological adaptations to the rain forest in evidence some three hundred thousand years ago (Barham 2001; Taylor 2011). Biomolecular studies of contemporary forest peoples show that foragers shared a common ancestor with Bantu farming populations seventy-one thousand to ninety thousand years ago (Batini et al. 2007; Batini et al. 2011a; Batini et al. 2011b; Patin et al. 2009) and that the groups diverged approximately thirty thousand to seventy thousand years ago, when daughter populations become isolated from one another by adapting to separate ecological habitats (e.g., rain forest versus grasslands) and via sociocultural barriers. Forager populations subsequently separated further, possibly in response to a climate-driven reduction in rain-forest habitat (Bahuchet 1993), giving rise to two subpopulations that occupied the eastern and western parts of the Congo Basin after forty thousand years ago (Batini et al. 2011a; Batini et al. 2011b).

Biomolecular studies identify major demographic changes and establish temporal intervals for the origins of contemporary forest populations but reveal very little about the nature of forager lifeways prior to the advent of farming (Lupo et al. 2014). Bahuchet's (1993) historical linguistic analysis, in contrast, identified the common vocabulary of the protolanguage (Baakaa) of forest foragers that predates the Bantu expansion by as much as forty thousand years and shows that their ancestors were always forest specialists. A shared vocabulary includes terms related to communal spear hunts, the use of bows and poisoned arrows, honey acquisition, and the hunting of elephants (*Loxodonta africana*). The number of common terms relating to the composition of elephant groups and the widespread and highly regarded position of elephant hunter (*tuma*) indicate that elephant hunting was an important prehistoric activity (Bahuchet 1993:42). Thus, we have evidence of rain-forest occupation over several millennia by mobile forest specialists who also pursued big game and, in some areas, had long-standing contact with outlying forager populations well before the arrival of farming populations.

The emergence and nature of the relationship between forest foragers and agricultural populations are purportedly linked to the migration of Bantu-speaking peoples (the putative earliest farmers) and date to the last two thousand to five thousand years (Berniell-Lee et al. 2009; Eggert 2002; Holden 2002). Traditional archaeological reconstructions link Bantu migrations to the spread of ceramics, domesticated products, and sometimes metal objects, all of which are widely viewed as desirable trade items that solidified the economic interrelationships among forest populations (but see Lupo 2011–2012; Lupo et al. 2014). Nevertheless, we have little direct archaeological evidence of prehistoric exchange between Bantu immigrants and indigenous foragers (but see Barham and Mitchell 2008; Mercader et al. 2000a; Mercader et al. 2000b). Much stronger evidence of early interactions between Bantu immigrants and indigenous foragers comes from biomolecular studies that imply that Bantu populations with high levels of population growth pushed foragers into undesirable habitats, thus reducing gene flow and effective population size (Destro-Besol

et al. 2004). Among western forager groups evidence of genetic drift resulting from population contraction and isolation occurs approximately 2,625 and
2,900 years ago (Verdu et al. 2009). Several other biomolecular studies also
reveal evidence of hypergyny—the mating pattern well known in ethnography
whereby forager women marry or mate with farmer men—emerging within the
last two thousand to five thousand years (Anagnostou et al. 2013; Destro-Bisol
et al. 2004; Quintana-Murci et al. 2008).

The earliest written accounts of forest populations in central Africa date to
the historical period (1610 to 1885 CE), which was punctuated by catastrophic
demographic, economic, social, and political upheaval (Bahuchet 1985; table
6.1). Although historical sources are limited, most depict forest foragers as
nomadic big-game hunters occupying independent camps in remote regions of
the forest or living near villages associated with farmers, but engaged in external
trade for goods (e.g., iron, millet, oil, and salt; see Quatrefages 1895).

The colonial period in the Central African Republic (CAR) began in 1885,
when the Europeans arrived and established concessions to exploit ivory, rubber, copper, and other products (Bahuchet 1985). Bahuchet (1985; table 6.2)
views the events associated with and stemming from the colonial period as the
most pivotal for forager-farmer interactions and as creating the ethnographic
pattern. Among these events, it was the establishment of rubber plantations
around 1910 that most significantly altered the interrelationships of foragers
and farmers. Farmers were forced to labor on the rubber plantations under
brutal and harsh conditions, which limited their ability to obtain food, and they
become reliant on the exchange of forest products, especially meat, with foragers. Between 1924 and 1945 many Bantu farmers moved to remote areas of the
forest to escape colonial labor and taxation and came to live in close proximity
to foragers (Guille-Escuret 1998). Some groups of Aka foragers in the Lobaye
region of the southwestern CAR began growing their own crops in the 1930s, but
many eventually abandoned their fields, and others failed to produce sufficient
food to meet their needs (Guille-Escuret 1998). From 1918 through the 1950s,
the exportation of duiker skins to Europe, where they were used to manufacture clothing and carriage rugs, increased the hunting of these animals (Christy
1924). To capitalize on this market, Bantu farmers gave hunting nets to foragers
and compelled them to procure duikers for the farmers (Bahuchet 1985). During the postcolonial period (post-1960s–1970s), many farmers established coffee plantations, and because labor was in short supply, they employed foragers
as laborers, who for the first time earned wages and were able to purchase goods

Table 6.1. Selected historic (1610–1885) descriptions of forest foragers.

Date	Group/Area	Description of Foragers	Source
1610	Mbaka	Used poisoned arrows and bows, darts; hunted elephants and gorillas; paid tribute to Mani Kesock in ivory and elephant tails; women carried bows and arrows and hunted with men	Battell 1967[1625]
1686	Bakké-Bakkés	Elephant hunters in the interior of central Africa	Dapper 1686[a]
1854	Sierra Leone	Hunted elephants and generously traded big-game meat for grain; also hunted monkeys, baboons, wild hogs, and deer	Koelle 1854
1863	Babongo/Gabon	Established relationships with Ashango but lived in separate villages (round huts); hunters used traps to capture monkeys and other small game; traded meat for cloth, cooking utensils, and iron; tolerated as skilled hunters but no intermarriage with farmers	Du Chaillu 1899
1871	Akka	Informant mentions nine tribes each with a chief or king, all hunters; men possessed a spear and bow and arrow	Schweinfurth 1874
1886		Lived in bands composed of families; houses made from reeds; lived in temporary camps in forest but usually within reach of villages; hunted elephants and buffalo and used meat, animal hides, and feathers to barter for grain, oil, native beer, and other necessities	Pasha 1888
1885	Batwa/Lulua River	First mention of dependent and independent foragers; some Batwa lived close to Bakuba villages; each village had a sub-chief and a Batwa village assigned to them, whose inhabitants supplied him with palm wine and meat; independent Batwa lived in the forest and bartered dried meat for manioc or maize at periodic markets on neutral ground	Wolf in Sun 1889[b]
1886	Batwa/Sankura	Nomadic, lived in groups of up to eight or more families; hunted with dogs and used pit traps with stakes to hut big game; also used spears, bows and arrows	Wissman in Sun 1889[b]
1885–1886		Traded meat for weapons, brass rings, beads, grain, and vegetables; purchased wives; ambushed large prey with spears; some intermarriage with Bakuba	Von Francois in Sun 1889
1889	Batwa	Two nomadic groups of Batwa, Batwa Bankonko and Batwa Basingi; described as good warriors but did not grow crops	Bateman 1889
1902		Trapped small animals; collected honey and insects; hunted monkeys and birds with snares; used arrows; traded for iron with neighbors; lived in forest but did not practice agriculture or intermarry with Bantu	Johnston 1902

[a] As reported by Bahuchet and Guillaume (1979:21).
[b] As reported by Werner (1890).

Table 6.2. Major colonial and postcolonial impacts on Bofi and Aka lifeways in the southwestern Central African Republic.

Time Range	Description	Source
	CHANGES IN ECONOMICS	
1910–1940s	Establishment of rubber plantations and forced labor resulted in farmers becoming more reliant on foragers for forest products	Bahuchet 1985
1918–1950s	Demand for duiker skins in Europe increased value of duikers; foragers intensified hunting efforts for those species	Bahuchet 1985
Post-1960	Establishment of coffee plantations; foragers hired as labor and worked for cash wages	Bahuchet and Guilluame 1982
	Commercial demand for meat increased: by mid- to late 1970s 50% of all meat acquired in Lobaye being sold; by 2000 43% of the biomass taken sold to markets. Some foragers (Aka) in some areas begin to grow their own crops	Bahuchet 1985; Dethier and Ghiurghi 2000
	CHANGES IN HUNTING TECHNOLOGY	
Colonial period	Crossbow replaced traditional bow and arrow	Bahuchet 1985
1918	Increased use of cooperative hunting nets by foragers	
1950s	Guns and snares came into common use among farmers but were less commonly used by foragers	
1970–1980s	Elephants and other large game drastically declined due to uncontrolled hunting; reduced importance of the tuma, or great hunter, a traditional position of prestige	Maisels et al. 2013; Milner-Guiland and Beddington 1993
	CHANGES IN MOBILITY	
Post-1960s	Foragers became semisedentary and moved closer to villages	Bahuchet 1985

(Bahuchet and Guillaume 1982). This moment marked an important turning point in forager-farmer relationships because foragers moved to farming villages, became more sedentary, and began to view their own labor as generating money. Foragers also gained more autonomy and purchasing power then they had previously experienced.

More recently, habitat depletion from logging operations, industrialized and artisanal mining, and the commoditization of forest products continue to constrain the availability of resources. High levels of political upheaval and poverty and low infrastructural development have greatly increased the demands for forest resources such as bushmeat, koko, and dried caterpillars in villages and larger cities. Rural foragers and sometimes farmers collect these resources, which are sold to middlemen and then transported to the cities.

ECOLOGICAL CONTEXT: NGOTTO FOREST

Data reported here were collected between 1999 and 2003 from Bofi foragers and farmers occupying the study village of Grima as part of an ethnoarchaeological study of hunting and food sharing. The village is located on the northern border of the Ngotto Forest, a 3,250 km² triangular area in the Lobaye Prefecture that lies between the Lobaye and Mbaéré Rivers and is situated on the extreme northern edge of the Congo Basin. This part of the central African forest is classified as a dry Guinea-Congolian rain forest (F. White 1983) and is comprised of a complex, heterogeneous mosaic of tropical microenvironments (Bahuchet and Guillame 1982). High average annual temperatures (around 77°F), humidity (70–90 percent), and precipitation (in excess of 1,600 mm) characterize this area.

From 1998 until 2010, the Ngotto Forest was co-managed by ECOFAC (Ecosystèmes Forestiers d'Afrique Central) and logging companies with the goal of balancing preservation and sustainable harvests (Runge 2009). Although the ECOFAC project is finished, two large-scale logging companies continue to operate and harvest high-value timber such as *Entandrophragma cylindricum* and *E. utile* (Ngasse 2003; Runge 2009). The village of Grima, discussed here, is located in a managed zone where traditional hunting and agriculture activities are permitted (see Bahuchet 1985).

THE STUDY VILLAGE OF GRIMA

At the time of this study, Grima was occupied by approximately 100–150 foragers and 200 farmers. The village had been in existence for at least the last sixty years according to village inhabitants and vintage topographic maps from the 1950s. According to oral tradition, Grima was settled by farmer families who migrated into the area approximately two hundred years ago. This tradition also relates that the ancient farmers brought the foragers with them as their slaves. During the study, the foragers occupied dome-shaped branch-and-leaf structures clustered into small subvillages that surrounded, but were on the outskirts of, Grima proper. Grima consisted of approximately fifty permanent rectangular mud-brick or mud, wood, and leaf structures that were occupied by farmer families. The village was bisected by a dirt road (which will be discussed further), and a few families occasionally offered a limited selection of durable goods (oil, salt, matches) for sale. Itinerant salesmen walked through the village at least once a week selling a variety of small transportable items (mostly clothing). Two large-sized towns, Bambio and Ngotto, were located 20 and 24 km, respectively, from Grima and could be reached via the road on foot or by bicycle.

Services such as medical care and educational opportunities were locally available. A small medical clinic operated in Grima and was manned by a trained nurse. Most of the services were offered free of charge or for a very nominal fee. Farmer families readily made use of the clinic, but most foragers did not go to the clinic or purchase medicines and relied instead on traditional medicines provided by local practitioners (*ngangas*). A small school was in operation from 1999 to 2002 in Grima, but the chance to attend was only offered to local farmer children. The school closed in 2002 because farmer families neglected to pay the school fees and salary of the teacher.

ETHNOGRAPHIC CONTEXT: BOFI FOREST FORAGERS

Although the Bofi are an ethnolinguistically distinct group, they claim a close ancestry with Aka foragers who occupy the southern portion of the forest. The two groups share a large number of cultural beliefs and material traits (Hewlett 1990). At the time of this study, approximately half of the Bofi diet was composed of wild forest plants, insects, and meat from forest animals. The economic unit of production is the family with men, women, and children often foraging

Figure 6.3. Bofi children on their way to exchange koko. Photograph by Karen Lupo.

and hunting together, especially on cooperative net-hunts. Married couples frequently cooperate in the acquisition of collected resources, especially koko and insects.

Important edible wild plant resources include koko, wild yams, several varieties of mushrooms (Pleurotaceae), various fruits, and nuts, especially *Trecula africana*, *Irvingia robur*, and *Irvingia gabonensis* (figure 6.3). Insects including termites, caterpillars and butterfly pupa, and land snails, along with honey from several species of stinging and stingless bees, are important collected resources. The most common prey species are small game (<10 kg live weight; see Lupo and Schmitt 2004, 2005). Bofi hunters often commented on the rarity of larger game in the vicinity, and several reported that more large game was available only a generation ago. Although we have no quantitative data demonstrating a decline of big game in this area, one very gross measure of prey reductions can be extrapolated from the hunting descriptions of Aka foragers in the Lobaye forest as reported by Bahuchet (1985) in the mid-1970s. He detailed the exploitation of large-game (>25 kg) species such as elephant, chimpanzee (*Pan troglodytes*), bongo (*Tragelaphus eurycerus*), red buffalo (*Syncerus caffer nanus*), gorilla (*Gorilla gorilla*), sitatunga (*Tragelaphus spekii*), and aardvark (*Oryctero-pus afer*), which are now very rarely encountered in this area and are no longer exploited by foragers in this part of the forest.

Unlike the Aka, very few Bofi foragers grow crops. Only a handful of foragers have fields, and no one produces enough food to be self-supporting. However, the lack of productivity of forager fields is clearly not explicable by a lack of knowledge or experience because most work as farm laborers for villagers. Low productivity of fields is largely due to a lack of time and labor investment. Of the fields we visited, most were very small (fewer than five manioc plants) and poorly tended and produced minimal amounts of food. Domesticated foods, especially manioc, are largely obtained via barter with local farmers and comprise at least half of the diet. None of the foragers keep domesticated animals, except dogs. On a handful of occasions we witnessed Bofi foragers attempting to keep chickens obtained via barter. These are always short-lived enterprises. The chickens are either very quickly sold or bartered or become victims of forest predators. The Bofi foragers do not eat chickens or their eggs.

Hunting Technologies. The Bofi use a range of hunting technologies including handmade fiber hunting nets, metal-tipped spears, metal-tipped poisoned arrows, unpoisoned wooden darts, crossbows, several types of traps, and wire snares as well as capturing prey by hand (Lupo and Schmitt 2005). While a few farmers own guns and often hire foragers to hunt for them, only one forager owned two guns but both were in disrepair. Some hunting equipment, such as nets, wire snares, guns, and crossbows, is relatively new and was introduced within the last one hundred years (see table 6.2). The only traditional equipment (i.e., precolonial) still in use includes spears, poisoned arrows and darts, and fiber traps.

The most widely used cooperative hunting technique today is the net-hunt. Net-hunts are well described in the literature (Harako 1976; Noss 1998; Putnam 1948; Schebesta 1936; Tanno 1976; Turnbull 1965) and consist of groups of up to thirty-five people, including men, women, and children, using nets placed end to end to encircle and capture prey (see Lupo and Schmitt 2002, 2005). This technique generally targets small duikers, especially blue duikers. A more diverse range of cooperative hunting activities was used in the recent past. Describing hunts by the Aka in the Lobaye region in 1976–1977, Bahuchet (1985) describes cooperative spear hunts targeting chimpanzees, six different types of net-hunts, and the use of constructed wooden palisades to capture large fossorial insectivores (e.g., giant pangolins and aardvarks). None of these techniques are used or even known by foragers in the area today.

Individual hunting can involve one to three people and includes the use of spears, traps, snares, crossbows, and hand capture. Foragers use snares made from metal cable despite its high cost, and these kinds of hunting activities target a wider range of prey than the nets (see Lupo and Schmitt 2005). Individualized hunts may take place as isolated bouts on specific days, but hunters on net-hunts sometimes abandon their nets and switch strategies to pursue certain kinds of prey using individualized strategies (Lupo et al. 2013).

Different carcass acquisition strategies are associated with different meat-sharing rules. Animals captured in nets during a communal hunt are subject to very specific cultural sharing rules. People receive specific shares based on their relationship to the hunter or tool owner and their role in acquiring, butchering, or transporting the animal. These sharing rules are extensive and can account for between 20 percent and 40 percent of the meat associated with a carcass (e.g., Bahuchet 1985, 1990; Ichikawa 2005; Kitanishi 1998; Lupo and Schmitt 2002, 2005). There are, however, no obligatory sharing rules associated with prey acquired by individuals. Carcasses acquired by individualized techniques are usually consumed by the hunter's family or sold to vendors or exchanged with farmers. Consequently, hunters using nets distribute meat more widely than hunters using individual techniques (also see Hewlett 1991; Lupo and Schmitt 2004).

Money and Barter Exchange. Bofi foragers have few opportunities to earn cash outside of selling forest products such as meat, koko, and, occasionally, honey. During our study interval, only two men earned wages as trackers for a primatologist, and this work was temporary. Women occasionally earn small amounts of cash by making and selling corn whiskey (*embacko*). The bushmeat trade in Grima is limited, and only a few farmers act as middlemen, selling meat procured by foragers. A handful of commercial meat vendors seasonally travel to Grima to purchase meat from farmers and the foragers. As will be discussed further, koko is a product in high demand, and commercial vendors from the surrounding area visit the town and purchase harvested leaves directly from the foragers.

Money earned from selling forest products is generally used for special purchases, such as tobacco and especially imported alcohol, and is rarely used for utilitarian items such as tools and food (also see Kitanishi 2006; Köhler 2005). Nonlocal and commercial products such as clothing, soap, beads, cooking pots, cable for snares, and metal tools are available for purchase at local kiosks and from itinerant salesmen. Occasionally, foragers purchased utilitarian items with cash or by barter. However, most foragers obtain these items secondhand through exchange with or as gifts from farmers. Foragers rarely use money to purchase food. Barter is the traditional and main economic interaction with local neighboring farmers and the primary means for obtaining domesticated foods and utilitarian items.

Population Mobility. Bofi foragers are nomadic for at least six months of the year, when they use a series of temporary camps for procuring forest products. Temporary forest camps can be used throughout the year but are most often visited during the dry season, when hunters are more actively engaged in capturing prey. Permanent residential camps next to the farmers' village are maintained nearly year round by some individuals, although the population in these camps is highly variable and fluid. Residential groups usually consist of clusters of one to twelve families who are members of or affiliated with the same clan.

Traditional and Nontraditional Positions in Bofi Society. Bofi foragers have few recognized positions of social prestige. Although some men are reputedly good hunters, little prestige and no power are ascribed to these individuals. Bofi foragers do, however, recognize ngangas, people with great healing abilities (Hewlett 1991) who often possess other supernatural powers (e.g., the ability to see the future, identify sorcerers, or craft hunting charms). In the recent past, forest foragers recognized the position of tuma, elephant hunter or great hunter, but this position is no longer active due to reductions in large prey species. The Bofi foragers recently elected a chief who serves as a representative at village functions, but this position was only created at the behest of local and regional administrators and carries no real power or prestige.

ETHNOGRAPHIC CONTEXT: BOFI FARMING POPULATIONS

Most farmers make a subsistence living by growing crops. Some men earn wages working for local lumber companies or as ecoguards. Others supplement their income by producing specialized products for local sale, such as bricks or baskets, or by illegal activities such as hunting and diamond mining. Women may add to the household income by producing and selling corn whiskey and selling prepared food, excess crops, or firewood. Both men and women occasionally work their neighbors' fields for wages.

Almost every farmer family maintains one or more fields of manioc that are usually identified as belonging to the women in the household. Many families also grow other crops for sale (i.e., cash crops), such as coffee (*Coffea* spp.), peanuts (*Arachis hypogaea*), maize (*Zea mays*), and tobacco (*Nicotiana* spp.). Manioc cultivation and processing dominate the daily activities of the farmers, particularly women, who work six days a week to produce a constant supply of manioc for their families and surpluses to exchange with foragers. Livestock is limited and consists of chickens and goats, which are rarely consumed, and dogs used for hunting (see Lupo 2011).

Even though farmers obtain forest produce via trade with foragers, many procure resources from the forest directly, especially meat through illegal hunting activities that involve metal cable snares. In fact, most farmers have one or more snare lines in close proximity to their fields. Hunting permits are available, but very few men are willing to pay the cost of the license. Because guns are difficult to obtain and the cartridges are very expensive, very few village men regularly hunt with guns. Those that do are considered specialists and hunt at night using a flashlight to dazzle animals. Only one man in Grima was a professional hunter who used guns and snares to regularly and illegally procure prey.

Traditional Positions of Prestige. Unlike foragers, farmers recognize important differences in social status based on kinship and the acquisition of material items (see Schmitt and Lupo 2008). The village chief is a traditional post of leadership and in the past was hereditary. Today chiefs are elected by popular vote, but elections in smaller villages are highly informal affairs and certain families often monopolize the position for long periods of time. A chief's tenure may last for a set period of time or until the incumbent dies. In the recent past the position of chief carried a great deal of power and prestige, but today the position is minimized. However, chiefs still act as local liaisons who dispense justice, grant land concessions, and settle disputes.

Interethnic Relationships. Bofi foragers maintain complex, multidimensional relationships with neighboring Bofi farmers. The populations are ethnically distinct, and despite the close nature of these relationships, social distances are maintained and reinforced by differences in material wealth, access to education, societal beliefs, and residential segregation. Most farmers, for example, have the economic resources to purchase better-made clothing and material possessions and to send their children to school (see Schmitt and Lupo 2008). Farmers view foragers as uncultured primitives yet admire their sharing ethic, hunting skills, and magical abilities. Foragers defer to farmers in public settings but view them as aggressive and loud and often mock them in private. Farmer men may have liaisons with forager women, but intermarriage is uncommon. Forager woman who marry farmers are usually second wives, and the unions frequently end in divorce. Liaisons between farmer women and forager men are a social taboo and purportedly never happen.

Forest foragers have two types of interrelationships with settled farmers: dependent and so-called independent relationships. Dependent relationships are viewed as the common and purportedly traditional pattern among foragers and farmers. Independent relationships are often portrayed as uncommon and are believed to be a more recent phenomenon. However, dependent and independent forest foragers were reported as early as 1885 by Wolf (cited in Sun 1889; see table 6.1; see also Guille-Escuret 1998), and although the historical records are unclear on this point, it is entirely plausible that both kinds of arrangements have always existed. In the 1970s, Bahuchet (1985) reported that there were few independent foragers but that the numbers appeared to be increasing in the Ngotto Forest. Grima, for example, had an equal number of independent and dependent foragers.

In so-called dependent relationships, agriculturalists and foragers maintain a relationship that is passed from one generation to the next and share a fictive kinship by adopting the same clan name (Bahuchet 1985). Farmers hold recognized land-use rights that extend to the exploitation of specific forest tracts, while forager clans have recognized boundaries in the form of trails that crisscross the forest. For farmers, use rights include permission to clear and cultivate land and extract resources (e.g., meat, plants, honey), and these rights extend to foragers who share the same clan name as the farmer. In addition to land-use rights, farmers have important social obligations to foragers and often provide assistance in obtaining the bride price or gifts for forager marriages (Bahuchet 1985; but see Lewis 2005:62). Farmers attend forager weddings and funerals and play important roles in rituals such as circumcision (Hewlett 1990). The interrelationship also offers political advantages to foragers who are represented in village disputes by their farmer partners. Foragers who have traditional interrelationships are obligated to exchange their products with and supply field labor to their village "patrons." Even so, foragers have considerable autonomy in habitation location, degree of mobility, and in the timing and duration of labor (Bahuchet 1985:550).

Independent foragers do not have hereditary relationships with patrons, are not obligated to sell to or exchange with any particular villager, and do not have clan affiliations. Nevertheless, they still exchange with local villagers and maintain social interactions through gift giving, visiting, and shared social events. Although independent foragers are under no obligation to work for specific farmers, they often maintain long-standing interactions with one or two people and are sometimes bound to a particular family by debts.

Results

From the brief historical overview presented here, it is clear that forager-farmer interactions have been sustained throughout turbulent historical and more recent events and have been dynamic and responsive to a variety of different demographic, ecological, and social challenges (also see Kleinman 1999). Importantly, these interactions continue to be malleable and sensitive to local circumstances.

CHANGING FOREST ENVIRONMENTS AND DYNAMIC INTERACTIONS

From 1999 to 2000, Grima was only accessible by a very poorly maintained jeep trail that often became impassible after the rains. Drivers rarely used the trail because it was a notorious sand trap, and from 1999 to 2000 we rarely observed more than one vehicle per week on the road. But in 2001 a local lumber company decided to improve the trail with a grader that plowed the substrate once a week. The number of vehicles that used the graded road greatly increased (to more than five per day) and even included public taxis that came through once a week. By 2003, road access allowed increased amounts of outside goods to reach the village, and several small shops opened. The road also facilitated access of commercial marketers, especially koko vendors, and permitted them to visit Grima with greater regularity and more readily transport forest goods to outside markets.

Road development in remote forested regions is widely recognized as a factor impacting territorial and migratory animal populations and can influence recruitment patterns, leading to decreasing abundances of selected species

(Laurance et al. 2006). Roads also facilitate increased access to remote areas by commercial and local hunters, resulting in increased hunting pressure or overexploitation (Wilkie et al. 2000; Wilkie et al. 1992; Wilkie et al. 2005). In addition to road development, random demographic changes in the forager population of Grima had the cascading effect of changing the productivity of different kinds of cooperative ventures and led to an increase in individualized hunting efforts and overall changes in how carcasses were acquired.[1]

CHANGES IN TARGET PREY:

NETS VERSUS INDIVIDUALIZED TECHNIQUES

Data discussed here were collected over 119 days: 41 days during the dry season of 1999–2000, 25 days in the dry season of 2001–2002, and 53 days in the wet to early dry season in 2003. During these intervals we collected observational data on fifty-eight focal follows, conducted 137 interviews and forty-six tool-kit household inventories, and collected some thirty-eight hundred animal bones from individual and family meals. Although all of the foragers included in this study considered themselves to be independent, most, but not all, maintained economic and social interactions with neighboring farmers.

These data show that from 1999 to 2003, hunting patterns changed in part in response to declining availability of certain kinds of species. In 1999–2000, more animals of all kinds were taken in comparison to 2001–2002 and 2003 (mean = 5.88, s = 4.38, n = 26 hunts; t = 2.9947, p = 0.0048 and t = 2.68, p = 0.0098, respectively). On average, fewer animals of any kind were taken between 2001 and 2002 (mean = 2.58, s = 1.37, n = 17 days) and in 2003 compared to 1999–2000 (mean = 3.1, s = 3.24, n = 30; table 6.3). Average encounter rates with blue duikers, a common prey species, as measured by the number of animals captured or seen per hour differed between 1999–2000 and post-2000 intervals (1999–2000 mean = 0.361, s = 0.544; 2001–2003 mean = 0.253, s = 0.405), but not significantly.

The declining availability of key prey especially changed the productivity and frequency of net hunting. Net hunting was among the least productive hunting technologies as measured by post-encounter return rates (table 6.3). However, the decreased use of nets after 2000 was partly a response to the declining efficacy of the technique as measured by the number of prey killed in nets (table 6.4). For example, in 1999–2000 there is no statistically significant difference between the number of prey killed in nets and those killed by individual

Table 6.3. The average post-encounter return rates for prey.

Technology	Target Prey[a]	N[b]	Post-encounter Return Rate[c]	Rules of Sharing[d]
Hand	Giant pouched rat	30	561	No
Hand[e]	Various	15	352–5,543	No
Nets	Small duikers	42	106	Yes
Snares	Various	18	4,909	No
Spears	Medium duikers	15	6,769	No
	Small duikers	13	3,044	No
	Brush-tailed porcupine	8	2,152	No
Traps	Brush-tailed porcupine	10	1,037	No

Source: Lupo and Schmitt 2005.
[a]The animal most often caught with this technology.
[b]Number of observations.
[c]Mean post-encounter return rate as measured by kcal per hour.
[d]Communal net-hunts are the only hunts with strict rules about who receives specific shares based on their relationship to the hunter and participation in hunt. Other hunting techniques mentioned here are considered individual. People may nevertheless share carcasses according to their own wishes.
[e]Includes small birds, tortoises, bats, civets, and pangolins.

hunting techniques, such as hand and spear capture, during net-hunts ($t = 1.135$, df = 46, $p = 0.2621$). But after 2001, significantly more animals were taken by individual techniques than nets during net-hunts ($t = 2.729$, df = 45, $p = 0.0089$). Part of this decline is linked to hunt frequencies. Fewer net-hunts were conducted in the dry season of 2001–2002 than 1999–2000 ($n = 14$ and $n = 24$, respectively). The 2003 interval had even fewer net-hunts ($n = 7$), but this period spanned the late wet season, when rains often prevented net hunting. However, the differences in prey taken by different kinds of techniques on net-hunts (outlined previously) suggest that the declines were not entirely due to hunt frequencies.

CHANGING HUNTING TECHNOLOGIES: FROM NETS TO SNARES

As net hunting declined, Bofi foragers increased their use of cable snares. This change in technology is reflected by tool-kit inventories collected from forty-six foragers (men and women) in 1999, with follow-up inventories collected in 2003 (table 6.5). Tool kits include the range of tools that individual foragers reported owning, and we collected the inventories by interview, with hunts followed by visual validations to ensure accuracy.

Table 6.4. The number of prey taken from 1999 to 2003.

Prey	1999–2000	2001–2002	2003
Bats	0	0	2
Birds	0	0	2
Blue duiker	76	12	26[a]
Civet	2	0	0
Giant pouched rats	35	24	42
Medium duiker (bay or Peters's)	6	2	4
Monkey (unspecified)	1	1	8[a]
Murid mice	11	0	0
Porcupine	15	2	15
Snake	0	0	1
Tortoise	2	1	1
Tree pangolin	5	1	0
Yellow-backed duiker	1	0	0
TOTAL[b]	154	43	101

[a]Four of the duikers and seven of the monkeys were killed with a gun by a forager hired by a farmer. The gun belonged to the farmer.
[b]These counts do not include prey killed by farmers during our study intervals. The following animals were shot or snared by farmers: two duikers, one monkey, seven medium-sized duikers, one hornbilled bird, three porcupines, one mongoose, ten giant pouched rats, and two snakes.

Table 6.5. A comparison of hunting inventories of Bofi foragers in Grima.

Item	1999	2003
Crossbow	2	1
Knife	21	15
Net	23	11
Other	1[a]	6[b]
Snare	7	247
Spear	17	24
Trap	59	72
TOTAL	130	376

[a]Axe.
[b]Two guns in disrepair, one fish trap, one fishhook, two slingshots.

Fewer foragers owned nets in 2003 than in 1999, but some of the decrease in net ownership was due to local demographic circumstances. For instance, of the people who owned nets in 1999, four had died and two moved away by 2001. By 2003, two additional people had sold their nets and several others had given their nets away to relatives in other villages. Furthermore, the average size (as measured by length) of nets significantly decreased between 1999 and 2003. In 1999 the average net length was 43.48 m ($s = 11.17$, $n = 14$), and although some people had or were making nets in 2003, the average length was significantly smaller at 14.00 m ($s = 12.67$, $n = 8$, $t = 5.8005$, df $= 20$, $p < 0.0001$). The decline in the use and size of nets was offset by a rise in the use of individualized hunting technologies, especially the dramatic increase in the use of metal cable snares. In 1999 only one forager man possessed a few rusty cables that he found abandoned in the forest. Most forager men did not use snares because the cost of purchasing the metal cable was prohibitive.[2] By 2003, fourteen hunters were using cable snares, and many of them were men who had previously used nets. Many of these men possessed large numbers of individual cable snares (mean $= 15$). In general, tools classified as individualized technologies, such as spears, traps, and snares, increased in frequency from 1999 to 2003. The number of individualized hunting technologies represented in tool inventories in 2003 was significantly higher than the number recorded in 1999 ($X^2 = 58.11$, $p < 0.0001$), largely due to the rise in the number of snares.

Changes in the use of different hunting technologies in Grima from 1999 to 2003 are linked, in part, to the longitudinal effects of prey depression, road construction, and the influx of marketing opportunities. But random changes in demography, like the loss of hunting partners (through death or migration in 2001), also played a role in the ability of Bofi hunters to carry out cooperative hunts. By extension, these losses likely influenced the decision of other foragers who subsequently sold or gave away their nets. Ethnographic studies throughout the Congo Basin consistently report that net-hunts require at least ten nets and twenty participants to be successful (Terashima 1983) and that larger hunting groups are more successful than smaller ones (Harako 1976; Ichikawa 1983; Noss 1995; Tanno 1976). Furthermore, successful net-hunts are usually conducted by groups of related individuals, especially men, and changes in the number of male kin resources (Hewlett 1991) can have particularly disruptive effects on cooperative groups (Turnbull 1965). Male kin and other close relatives are preferred partners in group hunts because thick vegetation prevents visual contact among hunters, and familiarity with the techniques of neighboring hunters allows for quick, coordinated, and effective responses to prey (Turnbull 1965). Thus, changes in the frequency of different kinds of hunts can also be related to changes in demography.

In 2001–2002 and 2003, Bofi foragers often complained about their inability to execute net-hunts because of the lack of nets in the village, and on several occasions Grima men went to neighboring villages to recruit additional hunters. This practice was unpopular because the recruited individuals were often unrelated to the Grima foragers, and on at least one occasion a fight broke out among the hunt participants over the disposition of the catch.

The increase in individualized hunting is not surprising given the reduction in cooperative net-hunting partners. Despite the high cost of the cable, snares offer several advantages over nets. Snares do not require the cooperation of close kin or a large labor force and only need to be checked once every two to three days after the snare is set. This kind of technology allows individuals to pursue other opportunities, such as harvesting koko to sell to itinerant vendors.

The overall productivity of cooperative net-hunts, as measured by post-encounter return rates (kcal/h), is significantly lower in comparison to most hunts executed with individualized technologies, especially snares (see table 6.3). Therefore, one might expect the use of snares to increase individual foraging efficiency. However, at least in 2003, Bofi foragers were phenomenally unsuccessful at snare hunting largely because they failed to check their snares at regular intervals and lost meat largely to putrification and scavenging carnivores (also see Noss 1995). Less commonly, some animals managed to escape from the snares. But snares can be productive when properly deployed. For instance, in 2003 we recorded only one animal taken by a forager snare, yet over the same time period farmers took twenty-four animals with the same technology. Given the short time span in which the Bofi have been using this technology, improvements in technological deployment may take several years to manifest.

RESOURCE DISTRIBUTION AND FORAGER-FARMER FOOD EXCHANGE

A shift from cooperative to individualized hunting can potentially have far-reaching consequences for forager-farmer exchange relationships. Hewlett (1991), for instance, found that Aka men who regularly participated in cooperative net-hunts maintained more traditional dependent relationships with farmers than men who pursed individualistic activities. Recall that individualistic hunters are not bound by obligatory sharing rules and have flexibility in how meat is distributed. This flexibility may translate into greater opportunities to sell meat and use the cash to purchase items, in contrast to men who pursue cooperative ventures and are obligated to share meat. Given cultural sharing norms, we might expect that an increase in the use of individualistic technologies would lead to one or more of the following consequences: higher levels of meat consumption by individual families, lower frequencies of forager-farmer exchange, or higher frequencies of meat sales to commercialized vendors.

We monitored hunted and collected foods from the point of acquisition through distribution and tracked the distribution of 298 carcasses and all of the plants, insects, and nuts obtained by the foragers in our sample. After food is acquired it is immediately transported to a forest camp or the village, where it can be distributed in a variety of different ways. For example, carcasses or portions thereof can be consumed and shared, exchanged for food (usually manioc), given as gifts, used to pay debts, or sold for money.

Food consumption (excluding manioc) by foragers varied in response to the availability of prey (table 6.6). Overall, less meat was consumed by foragers after 2000 because fewer carcasses were taken by hunters. But we found no differences in the mean amount of meat consumed between 1999–2000 and 2001–2002 ($t = 0.7140$, $p = 0.4764$). Significantly, however, more meat was consumed in 1999–2000 compared to 2003 ($t = 2.203$, $p = 0.0285$). More plant foods were consumed in 2003, when meat was less available. Despite fluctuations in the availability of meat, exchanges with farmers were sustained. The mean amount of meat exchanged for manioc did not significantly vary during our study intervals (1999–2000 and 2001–2002, $t = 0.4023$, $p = 0.6879$; 2001–2002 and 2003, $t = 1.0172$, $p = 0.3108$; 1999–2000 and 2003, $t = 0.3782$, $p = 0.7056$). This trend is further reflected in the amount of vegetables and insects that were exchanged for manioc. The exception is 2001–2002, when few vegetable products were exchanged. The presence of vendors increased the amount of koko collected and sold, especially in 2003, but there was no difference in the amount of plants and insects exchanged for manioc in comparison to 1999–2000 ($t = 1.4513$, $p = 0.1475$).

Other kinds of food distributions (table 6.6) shed additional light on forager-farmer interactions. For instance, farmers often extend credit to foragers against future resource acquisition, resulting in debts. Although the total amount of food of any kind used to repay debts did not differ among the study intervals, a significantly higher number of forager-to-farmer debts were repaid with meat in

Table 6.6. Distributions of forest food proportions by Bofi foragers.

Year/Resources	Sold	Exchanged (Manioc)	Exchanged (Other Products)	Consumed	Gifted	Debt	Other	Total (Rounded to Nearest Whole Number)
1999–2000								
Meat	94,050.0	44,385.2	6,735.6	279,114.6	0	5,910.0	23,163.0	453,358
Plant/insect	8,265.0	4,369.5	361.0	6,071.5	0	1,000.0	461.0	20,528
Total	102,315.0	48,754.7	7,096.6	285,186.1	0	6,910.0	23,624.0	473,886
2001–2002								
Meat	11,776.1	10,302.3	0.0	61,882.0	1,195	0.0	7,917.1	94,677
Plant/insect	0.0	22,153.0	594.0	22,363.0	170	0.0	1,400.0	46,680
Total	11,776.1	32,455.3	594.0	84,245.0	1,365	0.0	9,317.1	141,357
2003								
Meat	29,165.0	33,952.7	2,909.5	119,315.2	0	1,195.2	45,629.9	232,168
Plant/insect	118,035.0	65,820.0	5,740.0	146,103.0	3,426	26,765.0	0.0	365,889
TOTAL	147,200.0	99,772.7	8,649.5	265,418.2	3,426	27,960.2	45,629.9	598,056

Note: The values show the weight (g) of different foods acquired by the Bofi.

2001–2003 in comparison to 1999–2000. Meat is a more highly valued resource than plant products, and increases in debt payments of meat when prey was less available could reflect greater economic interactions between foragers and farmers. Table 6.6 also shows that foragers gave more food gifts (mostly plants) to farmers in 2001–2003.

Thus, exchanges between foragers and farmers were sustained even with an increase in the use of individualized hunting technologies and access to commercial vendors. This sustained interaction between foragers and farmers is even more apparent when one considers the underlying economics of the exchanges and value of different products. Over the last four decades, as shown in table 6.7, the cash value of meat has greatly increased, but the exchange value of meat in manioc has decreased. The increased cash value for meat reflects the reality of a competitive market for limited resources. Decreases in the manioc exchange values of meat could indicate that the surplus production of manioc by farmers has a lower threshold today than it did in the 1970s. But these values could also reflect the underlying reality that farmers today have the ability to obtain meat by hunting or purchasing it from neighbors. Illegally obtained meat was available in Grima throughout the year, and sometimes when foragers were not successful they actually purchased meat from farmers (also see Kitanishi 2006). In fact, foragers could actually purchase larger amounts of manioc with cash earned from selling different products, such as koko, than they could obtain through the exchange of meat with farmers (table 6.7). This means that the barter between foragers and farmers, while materialistic in nature, was not necessarily driven by traditional economic rationales.

FROM COOPERATIVE VENTURES TO INDIVIDUAL PURSUITS

Changes in the hunting technologies and modes of production explored in this chapter did not appreciable influence forager-farmer exchanges, although the overall reduction in the availability of prey resulting from long-term over-exploitation and recent road construction has impacted the kinds of forest products available for exchange, access to commercial vendors, and access to cash. The regular influx of vendors and sale of koko gave foragers sufficient amounts of cash to be able to purchase domesticated foods grown by farmers. Yet cash was rarely used in this fashion, and exchanges with farmers continued even though foragers could have purchased larger amounts of food with cash

Table 6.7. Exchange values of different food commodities.

Item	1999–2003		1976–1978	
	CFA Francs	Manioc (kg)	CFA Francs[a]	Manioc (kg)[a]
Blue duiker (½)	750–1000	1.700–2.000	50–300	6.0
CFA (100)	—	0.500–1.000	—	—
CFA (200)	—	1.200	—	—
Day's work (½)	2–500	1.200–1.500	—	—
Giant pouched rat	3–500	0.600–0.850	—	—
Koko (200–250 g)	25	0.450–0.500	—	—
Medium duiker (¼)	1–1,500	3.000–3.400	50–600	10.0
Mushrooms (650 g)	100–150	0.750–1.000	—	—
Porcupine	1–1500	1.200–1.500	20–300	2.0–3.0

Note: The exchange values for manioc are approximate. Even though we measured amounts using a set of spring scales, village economic exchanges are often informal approximations.
[a]Data from Bahuchet 1985.

than they actually received through exchanges. The data presented here invite a reexamination of the question posed by this volume: why do foragers forage? In this case, commoditization of forest products and access to cash allow foragers to function as independent and autonomous entities.

Previous studies point to the ability of forest foragers to grow their own crops as an important factor in whether or not foragers continue to forage (Guille-Escuret 1998; Kitanishi 2003). It might be argued that the Bofi foragers discussed here grow insufficient quantities of foods and continue to forage to obtain domesticated foods from farmers. However, a number of forest-foraging groups in other portions of western and central Africa—such as the Baka, Bakoya, Aka, and Babongo (see Hewlett 1991; Kitanishi 2003; Knight 2003; Köhler 2005; Soengas 2009; Yasouka 2006a, 2006b)—grow sufficient quantities of domesticated plants and yet still collect forest products. In many of these cases, foragers sell forest products but also continue to maintain exchange relationships with farmers. The ability to produce sufficient quantities of crops does not explain why foragers continue to forage or why they maintain ties to farmers.

In past publications, I have argued that the use of hunting nets by foragers acted as a kind of costly signal of affiliation with farmer clans (Lupo and Schmitt 2002). If this inference is correct, the demise of net hunting undermined the value of that signal but not the value of the affiliation. As I have discussed here, farmers fill many valuable sociopolitical and ritual roles in forager society, including acting as liaisons in village disputes. In the context described here and throughout the Congo Basin, foragers have no political leaders and a restricted ability to be economically and socially mobile, and they are viewed as an under-class. In contrast, farmer populations have a long history of hereditary leaders, status differences within their population, and control over desirable resources, which disenfranchises foragers in relation to specific items and in complex social interactions (see Lupo et al. 2014). One way foragers can accommodate this circumstance is to form ongoing partnerships with farmers. Foragers' bar-tering with farmers is one way they show and maintain affiliation even when the exchanges themselves are disadvantageous to the foragers. As I have shown, these exchanges do not maximize the amount of manioc that can be obtained for meat, and researchers in different parts of the Congo Basin have also noted the disparity in the amount of manioc (and other products) obtained by for-agers via barter in comparison to the amount that can be directly purchased (e.g., Bahuchet and Guillame 1982; Ichikawa 1991; Köhler 2005).

I argue that these systems are maintained because of the additional social currency gained by both parties, beyond the caloric and nutritional value of the food items involved. For farmers, widespread poverty and unemployment limit their ability to leave the villages. Farmers who leave villages and attempt to earn a living in the city often fall back to the countryside, especially in times of strife. In short, this society does not provide much opportunity for upward mobility, and traditional deference from foragers in economic and social inter-actions may provide farmers with incentives to maintain relationships, even on a minimal level (Schmitt and Lupo 2008). For foragers, having a local liaison or trading partner within the dominant and more controlling social group has obvious advantages as well.

Importantly, the nature and scope of forager-farmer relationships clearly vary throughout forested areas in central and western Africa, suggesting that the value relative to the costs of these relationships is not uniform and changes as a function of historical processes and ecological and sociopolitical contexts. Kitanishi (2003), for example, reports that the Baka in southwestern Cameroon do not have close economic relationships with farmers. The Baka in this area work for farmers for wages and material items but always expect payment. In southwestern Cameroon governmental policies forced Baka foragers to become sedentary agriculturalists as early as the 1950s. Most grow a sufficient quantity of crops (in this case plantains) to meet their own needs and do not need to exchange forest products with farmers. Nevertheless, these foragers continue to collect wild foods that they consume or sell. It is not clear if or how this change in economic focus influences other social aspects of forager-farmer interactions. In fact, most ethnographic studies on forest foragers' transition to agriculture have focused almost exclusively on economic transactions with farmers and provide very little information on how economic changes impact the social, political, and ritual dimensions of forager-farmer dyads (Guille-Escuret 1998; Kitanishi 2003).

Conclusions

Recent changes in forager hunting technologies in response to prey depletion can influence core social relationships among and between populations. Some of these changes have resulted in the demise of traditional features of forager society in this portion of the forest, such as cooperative hunting and meat-sharing patterns. Despite the changes, however, forager and farmer dyads that first emerged some two thousand years ago continue to persist. As described here (and elsewhere), these relationships have been maintained, albeit in modified forms, through economic, social, and political upheavals during the historical, colonial, and postcolonial periods. The fact that these interrelationships continue to survive throughout the Congo Basin suggests a resiliency in this bond that transcends nutritional need and specific historical events.

Notes

1. By 2007, with the opening of the Quatiéme parallel road, the road's route had been changed to completely avoid Grima. This cutoff was developed by a logging concession to avoid sand traps and was located approximately 5 km from Grima. By 2010, the entire village had been abandoned, and most of the inhabitants had moved to a new location, "New Grima," located along the new road. In 2010 we were able interview many of the former residents who cited sorcery as the main reason for abandoning the old village.

2. Metal cable cost about XAF$300 per yard. One yard of metal cable yields four or more two-strand snares or ten single strand snares that can last for up to two years (Noss 1995).

CHAPTER SEVEN

What Now?

Big Game Hunting, Economic Change, and the Social Strategies of Bardi Men

JAMES E. COXWORTH

Introduction

Of the varied behaviors that men use to attain social standing, big game hunting has received special attention (Alvard and Gillespie 2004; Bliege Bird et al. 2001; Kaplan and Hill 1985; E. Smith 2004; Smith et al. 2003), including among hunter-gatherers (Hawkes 1993; Hawkes et al. 2001b; Wiessner 1996, 2002). The links between hunting and reproductive success (RS) are of particular interest to evolutionary anthropologists due to their fitness implications (Gurven and Von Rueden 2006; E. Smith 2004). Yet hunting is not the only way that men pursue status (Barkow 1975, 1989; Ellis 1993a, 1993b; Henrich and Gil-White 2001; Hill 1984). Nor is big game hunting the only status-linked behavior that correlates positively with RS (see reviews in Hopcroft 2006; Perusse 1993). In this chapter, I investigate the links between male RS, hunting, and a pair of other status-linked behaviors, making money and negotiating with bureaucrats, among the Bardi—a group of part-time foragers in northwestern Australia.

Bardi country encompasses the northern tip of the Dampier Peninsula and includes coastal waters and close-lying islands. Most Bardi live in one of three major communities: Djarindjin, Lombadina, or One Arm Point. Residence is flexible, and people frequently move between these communities, family-owned outstations, and the local population centers of Broome and Derby. This chapter will focus on Djarindjin and its associated outstations, where I collected interview and census data in 2010 and 2011.

The array of opportunities for men to pursue status in Djarindjin has been heavily influenced by the region's colonial past. The hunting of marine turtles and dugongs appears to have a long history in Bardi country (Rouja 1998) and constitutes a substantial portion of the contemporary economy (Buchanan et al. 2009). The increasing availability of inexpensive store-bought food, however, has diminished the importance of hunting large marine game for subsistence, despite the introduction of efficiency-boosting technology. Alongside changes to long-standing practices such as hunting, increased interaction with the Western world has opened new pathways to social status. The monetary economy presents one such path. Today, Bardi men gain status by earning money in the private and public sectors, which then flows to other group members through demand sharing (Peterson 1993). In addition, the bureaucracy that resulted from the 1972 policy shift to self-determination, though cumbersome for some Djarindjin residents, provides a venue for men to exert their influence, direct the flow of outside resources, and build their reputations. Like individual incomes, these resources flow to a range of community members, although in comparison to wages, individual men may have even less control over these returns since outside organizations ultimately dictate resource allocation.

These changes make Djarindjin an ideal setting in which to investigate the links between RS and big game hunting. Previous research has been conducted in places where subsistence depended on the acquisition of big game (e.g., Alvard and Gillespie 2004; Hawkes et al. 2001b; Kaplan and Hill 1985; Smith et al. 2003). Though the Bardi were entirely dependent on wild foods until the late 1800s, diets in Djarindjin now incorporate a large proportion (60–90 percent) of store-bought food. As a result, contemporary subsistence depends more on access to money than on acquisition of wild foods. A substantial body of literature (e.g., Cronk 1991; Hopcroft 2006; Irons 1979; Mace 1996; Turke and Betzig 1985) indicates that, like hunting success, access to material wealth correlates positively with men's RS. Substantial wealth differences are not apparent in Djarindjin, but both negotiating with bureaucrats and wage labor are effective means of accessing resources (though in neither case does increased access necessarily mean increased control). Men in Djarindjin may therefore have a trio of pathways to higher RS. Given previous findings, I have developed a set of initial hypotheses:

H1. Male RS will correlate positively with hunting.

H2. Male RS will correlate positively with wage labor.

H3. Male RS will correlate positively with the ability to negotiate with local bureaucracy.

Figure 7.1. Trevor Sampi, a senior Bardi man and well-regarded hunter, looks on as young Torrey James points to a bull dugong (*Dugong dugon*) from a neighboring dinghy. The hunters pursued this animal but lost it in deeper water just out of frame. Photograph by James Coxworth.

Before investigating these hypotheses, I begin with an ethnographic overview of life in Djarindjin, paying close attention to contemporary foraging practices and factors influencing family size. I then provide detailed descriptions of the competitive venues under consideration, including local governance, wage labor, and big game hunting. After relating these behaviors to previous investigations of male status and RS, I report the data and methods used as well as the analytical results. The discussion that follows takes a detailed look at the implications of the main findings for understanding why men who live in Djarindjin continue to hunt big game.

Ethnographic Background

Bardi country encompasses the land, intertidal regions, and outlying islands of the northern tip of the Dampier Peninsula—a broad triangle pointing north of

Broome, Western Australia (WA). Local ecology is complex and encompasses both marine and terrestrial environments. The northern peninsula averages 770.5 cm of rain annually, with the majority (569.2 cm or 74 percent) falling between January and March (Australian Bureau of Meteorology 2013). Inland areas are primarily made up of dry monsoonal woodlands dominated by acacia and eucalypt species. Coastal ecosystems are more diverse in both plant and animal resources. They include a number of ecological communities such as monsoonal vine thickets, tidal mud flats, mangrove swamps, and rocky shorelines (see Smith and Kalotas 1985 for review). The marine environment surrounding Bardi country is equally rich. Sandy beaches, sea grass beds, coral reefs, and an extensive system of islands surround the northern peninsula, making up a complex array of aquatic habitats—a complexity compounded by the largest tidal swings in the southern hemisphere (Rouja 1998).

Like their neighbors, Bardi historically spoke a Nyulnyulan language that is mutually intelligible with surrounding languages (Dixon 2002). Most residents of Djarindjin now speak a Bardi-English creole, while a small minority speaks Bardi fluently. This linguistic transformation is just one example of the substantial postcontact changes that have affected the Bardi and other Aboriginal peoples throughout the West Kimberley region.

The rich marine environment first led to intensive contact between Bardi and non-Aboriginal people starting in the late 1880s (Glaskin 2002). Europeans arrived in search of *Pinctada maxima*, the world's largest pearl oyster, which is native to the waters surrounding Bardi country. The arrival of pearling crews began the process of colonization and led to the establishment of two missions— one at Lombadina on the western coast and another based on Sunday Island or Iwanyi, the largest island in a small archipelago east of One Arm Point. These early contacts brought researchers to Bardi country. Their work spans a range of topics including linguistics (Aklif 1999; Bowern 2008, 2012), land tenure (Glaskin 2007; Robinson 1973) and native title (Glaskin 2002), ritual life (Campbell and Bird 1915; Elkin 1933, 1935; Worms 1950, 1952; Worms and Nevermann 1986), social organization (Elkin 1932; Robinson 1979), ethnoarchaeology (Akerman 1975a, 1975b, 1976; M. Smith 1983, 1984, 1987), ethnobotany (Smith and Kalotas 1985), and contemporary foraging practices (Buchanan 2013; Buchanan et al. 2009; Rouja 1998). Glaskin (2002), Robinson (1973), and Rouja (1998) provide useful ethnographic overviews.

Home to approximately 250 residents, Djarindjin sits on the western edge of the peninsula and is separated from the ocean by an extensive dune system.

It abuts the community of Lombadina, from which it split in the 1980s. Roads are dirt, services are basic, and the government owns all of the homes, which are occupied by extended families and are generally overcrowded. Residence is highly flexible, often out of necessity as local housing is chronically scarce. Individuals and families often move between the Bardi communities, family outstations, Broome, Derby, and Australian capital cities. Children attend the Djarindjin-Lombadina Catholic School from kindergarten through grade ten; some pursue more advanced schooling in Broome or Perth. A small office and a grocery store in the center of the community function as communal gathering places. Doctors and dentists regularly visit the medical clinic, which is sited on the border of Lombadina and Djarindjin and staffed by a pair of registered nurses.

CONTEMPORARY FORAGING

Until the early 1880s, all Bardi lived as full-time foragers focused on coastal ecosystems, as did their NyulNyul and Jawi neighbors to the south and the east (Elkin 1932). Hunting was an important part of subsistence, and it still makes a substantial contribution to the local economy (Buchanan et al. 2009), but contemporary foraging involves a range of strategies in addition to hunting (Rouja 1998). Men, women, and children all commonly participate in line fishing and the collection of shellfish and mollusks. Spearfishing, either with Western spear guns or more traditional hand spears, is another common, typically male, pursuit. A number of foraging practices, such as fish poisoning (Rouja 1998) and the use of stone weirs (M. Smith 1983), have become rare today. Foraged foods make up 10–40 percent of diets in Djarindjin, and this percentage shows substantial intra- and inter-individual variation.

Residents of Djarindjin have ready access to inexpensive, calorie-rich foods that challenge even the most profitable wild resources for a place in the diet. During a visit in June 2013, I found that meat ranged from $11.89 per kilogram of mutton to $6.90 per kilogram of chicken (all prices in Australian dollars). Root vegetables were priced from a low of $2.40 per kilogram of onions to a high of $3.80 per kilogram of potatoes. Rice, a carbohydrate staple in many Djarindjin households, cost $4.50 per kilogram. Relative to the otherwise high costs of living in this remote Aboriginal community, these food prices are quite affordable. Though I did not collect household income data, I did ask fifty-one Bardi men in the course of structured interviews how much money they made.

Respondents' weekly incomes averaged $377.53 (standard error of the mean or sem = $62.01, maximum = $2,500), with a substantial minority of men (20/51 or 39 percent) relying solely on social welfare payments.

These statistics likely underestimate the importance of subsidies, however, since women receive more money from such programs—mostly due to their role as the primary caretakers of dependent children (Commonwealth of Australia 2012)—which they then share with family members. In some cases, women's incomes underwrite men's hunting by paying for fuel and equipment (also see Wenzel, chapter 2, this volume). Even families with two working adults whose earned income makes up the majority of the budget partake of public assistance by, for example, living in government-built housing (the primary kind of housing in Djarindjin) or collecting payments for residing in a remote area (called the Remote Area Allowance; see Department of Human Services 2012). These forms of governmental assistance make store-bought foods less expensive in real terms and therefore more attractive.

FACTORS INFLUENCING FAMILY SIZE

Contemporary Aboriginal Australia is characterized by high fertility (Johnstone and Evans 2012). In 2012 Aboriginal women (defined as females fifteen and older) in WA had a total fertility rate (TFR) of 3.10, the highest rate in the commonwealth (Australian Bureau of Statistics 2013). Female fertility is slightly lower in Djarindjin than the rest of Aboriginal WA, with women reporting an average of 2.85 children ($n = 67$, sem = 0.29, maximum = 8). Birth control is readily available at the local clinic, and its use is encouraged by clinic staff, which may explain Djarindjin women's lower average number of offspring when compared to the rest of Aboriginal WA. Yet female fertility in Djarindjin is still substantially higher than WA's overall TFR of 1.91 (Australian Bureau of Statistics 2013). It is also slightly higher than the TFR of the men in this sample ($n = 51$, mean = 2.24, sem = 0.35, maximum = 11).

A number of factors may influence male fertility in Djarindjin. Age at first birth varies substantially among the Bardi men for whom I could reliably estimate this statistic ($n = 24$, mean = 21.83, sem = 0.95, minimum = 15, maximum = 36), with older men tending to have later ages at first birth. Dividing this sample of fathers at the median age of 33.5 reveals that the older half has an average age at first birth of 24.60 (95 percent confidence interval or CI = 21.41, 27.25), whereas the younger half averages 19.33 (CI = 18.03, 20.64)—

a statistically significant difference (p < 0.01, two-sample t-test). Community members have suggested that this trend is due to the gradual relaxation of traditional rules of marriage. Though the rules may have changed in recent years, marriage still constitutes an important determinant of male fertility. The majority (39/51 or 76.5 percent) of men reported having been married at least once in their lifetimes. In an age-controlled generalized linear model or GLM, ever-married men had 1.88 (CI = 0.77, 3.35; p < 0.01) more children than their never-married counterparts.

Status, Authority, and the Relationships between Bardi Men

The authority of adult men in some Aboriginal Australian groups, rooted in ritual life but branching deeply into the secular world, appears to distinguish them somewhat from hunter-gatherers elsewhere (Bird and Bliege Bird 2010; Hawkes 2000; Keen 2006). Rules of proper conduct (Meggitt 1965), marriage and social organization (Hart et al. 1988), food distribution (Rouja 1998), and land and resource use (Myers 1982) were traditionally, and in some cases continue to be (see Bliege Bird et al., chapter 9, this volume), grounded in ritual concerns and dictated by elders (for a discussion of variation in Aboriginal men's authority, see Hiatt 1996). Unlike immediate-return foragers (Woodburn 1982) on other continents, among whom an egalitarian ethic pervades social life (Boehm 1999; Fried 1967; Sahlins 1959; Woodburn 1982), Bardi men assert their authority and contest that of their peers. Men in contemporary Djarindjin, while continuing to rely on traditional behaviors (e.g., big game hunting) to gain status, also use relatively novel behaviors such as negotiating with bureaucrats and making money.

HUNTING

Evidence from Australia's northern coast suggests that Aboriginal hunters have pursued dugongs and marine turtles since well before contact with Europeans (Haddon 1890; McNiven and Feldman 2003; Thomson 1934). This kind of hunting appears to have an equally long history among the Bardi (Rouja 1998). The most common method of hunting—chasing turtles or dugongs with an aluminum dinghy and outboard motor—owes much of its current form to the advent of Western technologies (table 7.1). These technological changes may have increased the efficiency of big game hunting by increasing encounter rates

Table 7.I. Key technological shifts in the twentieth century and their effects on big game hunting.

Traditional Tool	Contemporary Tool	Effects on Big Game Hunting
Mangrove raft	Aluminum dinghy	Increased encounter rate, reduced handling costs
Paddle	Outboard motor	Increased encounter rate
Wooden spear	Slip-tip harpoon	Reduced handling costs

with turtles and dugongs while, in the language of optimal foraging theory (Pyke et al. 1977), reducing post-encounter handling costs (i.e., making successful captures more likely). For example, hunters used to employ wooden spears when hunting turtles (Rouja 1998), which meant they had to aim only at the soft parts between shell and carapace. Harpoons, however, easily penetrate shells and have therefore increased the effective target size for turtle hunters.

Men usually hunt turtles by patrolling likely spots with the boat motor at a fast idle. On dugong hunts, men head for a likely spot and then shut off the motor. They scan the surrounding water for dugongs and, if they find some, use a transom-mounted paddle to scull quietly over and investigate. As with turtles, hunters chase dugongs with the motor at full throttle after deciding to pursue them. These high-speed chases can last upward of twenty minutes. Men chase turtles whenever the weather and tides allow, while dugong hunts are constrained to the cooler months of May, June, and July (Rouja 1998).

Chasing these animals is not the only way to acquire them; men also harvest mating turtles or *oondoord* between October and early December (Smith et al. 2003). Taking mating turtles seems to have a long history in northern Australia (Haddon 1890:350; Thomson 1934:246) and can be done mostly from shore, with hunters and their families watching expectantly from headlands and dunes. Once a mating pair is spotted, the men take a dinghy out to investigate. If the female looks worthwhile, one of the hunters will either try to harpoon her or swim over and wrestle her from under the male. Men also walk the beaches looking for nesting turtles, which they then grab either on the beach or in the shallows. These hunts occur during a brief nesting season that overlaps with the end of oondoord season and only during bright phases of the moon, since turtles usually haul out onto the beach at night and moonlight is the only way to spot them at a distance.

Residents of Djarindjin often complain that meat distribution after successful hunts is haphazard when compared to the "old ways." My observations support these complaints, as the distribution of meat varies dramatically between and within families. In his 1998 thesis, Rouja describes strict rules of distribution for both types of animal, with named portions going to specific recipients (often according to ritual ties) and distributions directed by senior men. Some follow these practices today; traditional distributions of meat seem more likely if the hunter is older and involved in ritual life and if the animal is a dugong. In contrast, some animals—especially turtles—are distributed almost exclusively within the nuclear family. Most meat distributions fall between these extremes. It is unclear whether these deviations from sharing norms are new or if individuals manipulated food transfers in the past. Convenient methods of meat storage and transport, owing to chest freezers and four-wheel-drive trucks, may foster a greater degree of individual control over hunting returns (Rouja 1998).

BUREAUCRACY

An elected council governs Djarindjin locally and selects and advises a community CEO. In turn, the CEO oversees daily operations and executes the council's strategic vision. Most councilors are middle-aged or older community members who are both well regarded and members of large families. This profile also holds true for the Prescribed Body Corporate, a council set up after the establishment of native title that oversees land issues throughout Bardi country. The politics of governance are often a topic of conversation among community members. Theirs is not just idle talk, however, as senior men can have substantial impacts both on the composition of governing bodies and the decisions they make (Coxworth 2013).

One of the more important duties of these local governance bodies is to negotiate with outside organizations. The number of nongovernmental organizations, private corporations, and governmental agencies hoping to operate in Djarindjin has expanded greatly since 1972, when the Whitlam government adopted a policy of Aboriginal self-determination. These groups, which together constitute the so-called indigenous sector (Rowse 2002), influence "all facets of existence in remote communities" (Sullivan 2010:1) such as Djarindjin through a dense bureaucracy. The obligations imposed by these organizations constitute a very real draw on people's time and limit the number of hours available for other pursuits.

For Bardi men, however, the bureaucracy offers an opportunity. Despite the red tape, organizations in the indigenous sector do provide real benefits and these benefits flow differentially between Bardi communities and families within these communities. To an extent, local politics influences these flows, which provides a chance for men to manipulate the bureaucracy in ways that suit their needs. The most direct consequence of gaining influence in this sector is the ability to affect service delivery. Apart from influencing the flow of resources, dealing well with bureaucrats carries a number of indirect benefits such as opportunities to meet with policy makers, paid consulting positions or employment as a cultural adviser, and access to vital information (e.g., the emergence of new welfare eligibility requirements).

MAKING MONEY

The contemporary work environment in Djarindjin, which was also heavily influenced by the policy shift to self-determination (Altman and Sanders 2006[1991]), differs substantially from that of the past. Unlike the mission days when missionaries provided rations for labor, Bardi people now work for pay. The old missionary policy of "no work, no food" has little place in the current network of social welfare, job training, and special employment programs that structure the monetary economy. Involvement with this economy is shaped primarily by governmental programs and policies aimed at increasing Aboriginal employment (Altman et al. 2004; Biddle et al. 2008; Taylor 2006, 2008).

One such program, Community Development Employment Projects or CDEP, is the single largest employer of Aboriginal people in the region today (Taylor 2006). Not only does CDEP keep a large fraction of the community gainfully employed, it ensures the continuing performance of essential services in Djarindjin. CDEP also supports some of the most highly sought-after jobs in Bardi country, including the Bardi-Jawi rangers (Buchanan et al. 2009). However, most CDEP-based employment in Bardi country, as elsewhere in Australia, entails part-time, unskilled work for low pay (Taylor 2006) and only rarely leads to more profitable or rewarding positions.

In addition to work funded through CDEP, Bardi men and women take advantage of local private sector jobs such as those offered at the Djarindjin airstrip and helipad, Lombadina Catholic School, and area pearl farms (Rouja 1998). Residents of Djarindjin also find jobs in two sectors that led a recent economic boom in the Kimberley area (Taylor 2006): tourism and resource extraction. Jobs in the latter industry are the most lucrative available, and the men and women who have them are widely known as big earners—and big spenders. However, having to be away from the community so frequently and for such extended periods makes work in the mining industry unattractive, despite the large paychecks (see also Codding et al., chapter 8, this volume; Taylor 2008).

For some, tourism offers a promising alternative. One avenue of employment in the tourism sector runs through Kooljaman, the community-owned resort at Cape Leveque. Apart from Kooljaman, a number of families have entered the tourist sector by setting up their own tourism operations. These are typically cooperative affairs with a rotating roster of "employees" (usually family members) led by a matriarch or patriarch who handles the finances and takes primary responsibility for advertising, scheduling, and leading the tours.

Status and Reproductive Success

A number of studies show that good hunters accrue substantial social rewards for their successes (Alvard and Gillespie 2004; Hawkes et al. 2001b; Kaplan and Hill 1985; Smith et al. 2003; Von Rueden et al. 2008; Wiessner 2002). Of particular interest to evolutionary anthropologists are the reproductive benefits of being a good hunter (Gurven and Von Rueden 2006; E. Smith 2004). Though the mechanisms underlying the correlation between hunting and reproductive success remain controversial (Gurven and Hill 2009; Hawkes et al. 2010), evidence points to the importance of status and reputation (Gurven and Von Rueden 2006; Hawkes and Bliege Bird 2002; E. Smith 2004; Von Rueden et al. 2008, 2011; Wiessner 1996).

Hunting is one behavior that Bardi men employ to gain status, but is not the only option. Diverse theoretical perspectives suggest that individuals gain social standing through behaviors that benefit other members of their group, even when these behaviors entail substantial costs for the focal individual (Barclay 2013; Bliege Bird and Smith 2005; Hawkes 1993; Hawkes and Bliege Bird 2002; Noë and Hammerstein 1994; Roberts 1998; Smith and Bliege Bird 2000, 2005; Zahavi 1977). A number of such opportunities have emerged in the last fifty years and may affect Bardi men's involvement in big game hunting. I focus on two: making money and engaging with bureaucracy.

In the case of making money, other community members benefit through the practice of demand sharing (Peterson 1993). By making repeated claims on a man's income, which he is rarely able to deny, an array of community members benefit from his hard work. In Djarindjin, therefore, a reputation for making money is less about controlling resources and more about having direct access to them. This sets money in Djarindjin somewhat apart from other status- and fitness-linked types of wealth such as land among agropastoralists (e.g., Borgerhoff Mulder 1987; Voland 1990) and income in postindustrial societies (Hopcroft 2006). Like income from wage labor, the returns from bureaucratic engagement (e.g., funding, job training, employment opportunities) are widely dispersed through the community. These resources are allocated by outside agencies to the entire community or classes of individuals within it (e.g., children who use the day-care center), which makes control by individual Bardi men difficult, if not impossible.

DATA

I employ three types of data in the following analyses. The first is census data, which I use to estimate men's number of living offspring. The second type is nominations. These data come from eighty-nine interviews with fifty-one men and thirty-eight women (average ages = 32.86 and 40.87, respectively). During these interviews, I asked participants to name as many good hunters, men who make good money, and men who deal well with bureaucrats as they could think of without, in the case of male interviewees, naming themselves. This technique, known as free listing (Bernard 2011), allowed participants to be as inclusive or exclusive as they liked. In contrast to pile sorts, free listing does not require participants to rank anyone. As a means of verification, I used self-reported indexes of success in hunting (number of turtles and dugongs harvested in the past year), wage labor (weekly income), and bureaucracy (number of committees currently served upon) collected among the fifty-one male interviewees. Of these fifty-one men, four engaged all three behaviors, twenty pursued two, twenty-six did one, and one man did none of them.

ANALYSES AND RESULTS

I conducted all analyses in R 3.0.1 (R Core Team 2013). To investigate the ties between nominations and reproductive success, I first controlled for age effects by regressing both nominations and surviving offspring on age using GLMs. Since both surviving offspring and nominations are overdispersed counts, I assumed a negative binomial error distribution for each model (Bolker 2008).

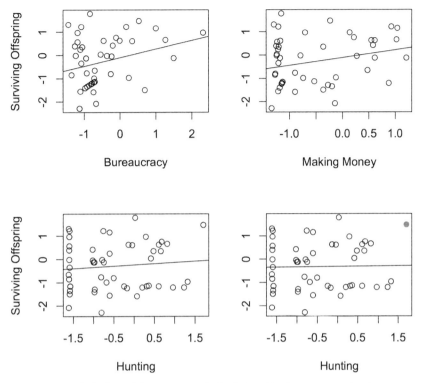

Figure 7.2 Residual plots of the age-controlled relationships between nominations in three status-linked activities and surviving offspring. Solid lines indicate linear regressions. The correlation coefficient for bureaucracy nominations is 0.14 (95 percent CI: 0.03, 0.25; p = 0.01). Making money is 0.10 (CI: 0.02, 0.18; p = 0.02). The correlation between hunting and surviving offspring is 0.05 (CI: −0.04, 0.15; p = 0.26) when including all individuals. After removal of an outlier (filled gray circle in the upper-right corner of the plot), the correlation drops to 0.01 (CI: −0.1, 0.11; p = 0.92).

After fitting these models, I compared their residuals using linear regressions with normally distributed error (figure 7.2).

Hunting nominations correlate positively with surviving offspring. Surprisingly, however, this correlation is quite weak, as demonstrated by the large p value and a 95 percent CI spanning both positive and negative numbers. The observed relationship between hunting nominations and surviving offspring becomes even weaker after removing an influential outlier, identified via hat

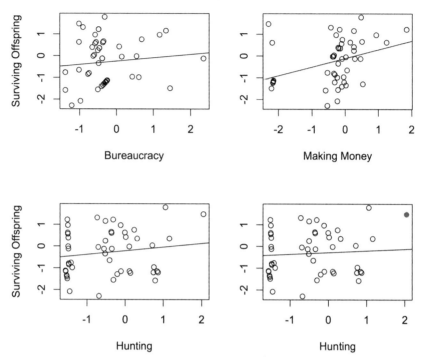

Figure 7.3. Residual plots of age-controlled relationships between self-reported success in three status-linked activities and surviving offspring. Solid lines indicate linear regressions. Correlation coefficients are as follows: Current Committees = 0.16 (95 percent CI: −0.26, 0.57; p = 0.45), Hunting Returns = 0.17 (CI: −0.14, 0.48; p = 0.28), Weekly Income = 0.40 (CI: 0.13, 0.67; p = 0.001). After removal of an influential outlier, the coefficient for hunting returns becomes 0.08 (CI: −0.25, 0.41; p = 0.63).

values (Venables and Ripley 2002), from the data set (see the lower right panel of figure 7.3). This result differs from findings reported elsewhere, which have shown a strong relationship between hunting success and offspring (Alvard and Gillespie 2004; Hawkes et al. 2001b; Hill and Hurtado 1996; Kaplan and Hill 1985; Marlowe 1999; Smith et al. 2003; Von Rueden et al. 2008; Wiessner 2002).

If RS is tied to status, as many have suggested (Gurven and Von Rueden 2006; Hawkes and Bliege Bird 2002; Henrich and Gil-White 2001; Hill 1984; Irons 1979; E. Smith 2004; Von Rueden et al. 2008, 2011; Wiessner 1996), then status-linked behaviors aside from big game hunting should have positive reproductive outcomes. As shown in figure 7.3, reputations as a wage earner and a man who deals well with bureaucracy are positively linked to surviving offspring (though nominations for making money are only marginally significant). This result echoes the findings of other studies showing that status-linked behaviors other than big game hunting lead to more surviving offspring (e.g., Betzig 1992, 1995; Borgerhoff Mulder 1987; Casimir and Rao 1995; Chagnon 1979; Cronk 1991; Flinn 1986; Hewlett 1988; Hopcroft 2006; Irons 1979; Low 1990; Mace 1996; Perusse 1993; Turke and Betzig 1985).

I also analyzed the ties between surviving offspring and self-reported measures of success (e.g., weekly income, annual big game harvest) to verify the links between nominations and reproductive success. The statistical procedure for these analyses was identical to that for nominations (i.e., regressing dependent and independent variables on age using GLMs, then analyzing the residuals using linear models). I found two meaningful differences between the results of these analyses and those using nominations. First, regarding bureaucracy, the correlation between surviving offspring and self-reported success is much weaker than surviving offspring's correlation with nominations. Second, weekly income is a better predictor of surviving offspring than nominations for making money. The previous year's hunting returns (measured as total turtles and dugongs taken) are just as unreliable a predictor of surviving offspring as are hunting nominations.

These analyses suggest a degree of mismatch between nominations and self-reports. In relation to bureaucracy, the difference likely reflects a deficiency in the self-reported measure (i.e., committees currently served upon). Skill in negotiating with bureaucrats involves more than this index captures, in which case nominations are a more reliable guide. In the case of making money, it seems that nominators may have incomplete information about men's incomes or are not basing their nominations on income alone. On the first count, money is easier to hide than other resources, which makes it difficult (though far from impossible) to infer individual incomes. In addition to income, nominations for making money could be partly based on perceived generosity, since sharing is a major aspect of social life here as elsewhere in Aboriginal Australia (e.g., Bird and Bliege Bird 2010; Peterson 1993; Schwab 1995).

Discussion

Unlike findings from ethnographic situations in which hunting underpins subsistence (Alvard and Gillespie 2004; Hawkes et al. 2001b; Hill and Hurtado 1996; Kaplan and Hill 1985; Marlowe 1999; Smith et al. 2003; Von Rueden et al.

2008; Wiessner 2002), reputations for big game hunting are not associated with reproductive success among men in Djarindjin (H1 unsupported). However, both negotiating with bureaucrats and making money correlate positively with surviving offspring, providing support for H2 and H3. In conjunction, these findings suggest that since hunting success seemingly does not improve Bardi men's fitness, men should allocate resources away from hunting and toward those behaviors that correlate with more offspring. Yet few men pursue wage labor or engagement with the bureaucracy to the exclusion of hunting (Coxworth 2013). This observation turns Bardi men's pursuit of big game into a riddle: why hunt if it does not lead to more surviving offspring? There are three distinct possibilities.

The first is purely economic; perhaps it costs less to acquire meat via hunting rather than buying it at the store. The abundance of inexpensive store-bought food, including meat, undermines such an argument, as does the high cost of fuel—something that chasing turtles and dugongs requires lots of. Between June 2010 and June 2011, when I gathered interview data, unleaded petroleum, which hunters use in their outboard motors, averaged 155.8 Australian cents per liter in the regional hubs of Broome and Derby (Western Australian Department of Commerce 2013). Diesel, the most common fuel for off-road vehicles used to tow boats to the beach, averaged 152.2 cents (Western Australian Department of Commerce 2013; prices are generally 10–40 cents higher in Djarindjin). When I returned in June 2013, fuel costs had risen to 172.2 cents per liter of petroleum and 170.8 cents per liter of diesel (Western Australian Department of Commerce 2013). The costs of hunting can generate conflict within families, especially when unemployed men use too much money hunting (also see Wenzel, chapter 2, this volume). In addition to fuel costs, hunting exposes expensive equipment (i.e., outboard motors and aluminum dinghies) to wear and tear and entails inherent risks of injury, including drowning (Rouja 1998; Smith and Bliege Bird 2000). Spending hours at sea also carries opportunity costs. Despite these considerations, economic explanations remain plausible in the absence of reliable quantitative estimates of dugong and turtle hunting's relative costs.

Men also might continue to hunt because once a venue of competition is widely pursued, as big game hunting has been in Djarindjin, individuals find it detrimental to withdraw. Commenting on the success of some Tsimane men in multiple competitive domains, Von Reuden and collaborators (2011:2230) suggest that abandoning a venue might allow others to "gain ascendancy" and thereby undermine one's social standing. From this perspective, status-seeking behavior entails a runaway process in which once a competitive domain is established, men must devote resources to it even if their efforts yield suboptimal returns. This explanation seems most likely where returns from a given behavior vary between individuals, so that some men gain a lot when others gain less. In such a scenario, those who profit most drive participation, while men who profit less must continue to invest in order to avoid falling too far behind their competitors. It is not clear, however, whether any men gain much—at least in terms of surviving offspring—from big game hunting.

This interpretation suggests the possibility that surviving offspring are an inappropriate currency with which to measure the fitness-linked benefits of big game hunting. In a range of ethnographic settings, hunting success advances men's social standing (Gurven and Von Rueden 2006; E. Smith 2004; Wiessner 1996), and the influence that accompanies increased social standing affects a range of fitness-linked outcomes. A substantial body of research (e.g., Apostolou 2008; Borgerhoff Mulder 1998; Harris et al. 1998; Hawkes et al. 2001b; Shenk and Scelza 2012) suggests that status may shape men's fitness in ways that are not captured by counting numbers of surviving offspring. In the most relevant such study of male influence and reproduction, which took place among the Martu (distant southern neighbors of the Bardi; see Bliege Bird et al., chapter 9; and Codding et al., chapter 8, this volume), a father's presence led to a lower age at initiation for his sons, perhaps due to the influence fathers exerted in the ritual domain. This reduction correlated with earlier ages at first birth and increased age-specific fertility (Scelza 2010).

This and other studies point to the varied ways in which status and influence affect male fitness. Any one of the pathways illuminated by previous work may help explain the persistence of big game hunting in Djarindjin. An important lesson from previous research is that the outcomes of social standing are context specific. Like many of the ethnographic situations described in this volume, substantial economic shifts make the Bardi setting a compelling one in which to investigate the social benefits of hunting. The findings I have presented and the contrasts I have drawn with previous work underline the importance of identifying alternate mechanisms by which hunters might benefit from their successes in contemporary Djarindjin.

Summary and Conclusions

The hunting of large game persists as part of Djarindjin's mixed economy, despite the availability of inexpensive store-bought foods. The consequences of big game hunting for male status and reproductive success may help explain hunting's persistence. Yet in contrast to other ethnographic settings, men with reputations as good hunters do not have more surviving offspring. Reputations earned through relatively novel opportunities for status, such as wage labor and engagement with bureaucracy, correlate positively with surviving offspring. These findings leave three alternative explanations for Bardi men's continued pursuit of large game. One is that hunting may persist due to its economic benefits (i.e., hunted meat is less expensive than store-bought meat). Another possibility is that the individual costs of withdrawing from such a widely practiced competitive activity may encourage men's continued pursuit of big game. The third possibility is that fitness-linked benefits aside from surviving offspring may underwrite men's allocation of time, energy, and resources to hunting.

Acknowledgments

I would like to express my gratitude to the organizers of this seminar (and editors of this volume) as well as my fellow participants; this chapter and my knowledge of contemporary foragers benefitted greatly from their insightful comments. Thanks also to the residents and traditional owners of Djarindjin, who have welcomed me into their community and made my research there possible. This work was supported by a Leakey Foundation general grant.

CHAPTER EIGHT

Alternative Aboriginal Economies
Martu Livelihoods in the Twenty-First Century

BRIAN F. CODDING, REBECCA BLIEGE BIRD,

DOUGLAS W. BIRD, AND DAVID W. ZEANAH

Introduction

In the western deserts of Australia, hunting and gathering endures as an important social and economic activity. That foraging persists within the boundaries of developed industrialized nation-states may come as a surprise to those who evaluate foraging as less profitable than agricultural or market alternatives (or to those who see it as a somehow inferior economic mode; e.g., Morgan 1877). However, the tendency to dismiss foraging as a less viable mode of production may be an error given the evidence that foraging can sometimes be the best option within certain constraints (e.g., Kramer and Greaves, chapter 1, this volume; Tucker et al. 2010). If this is the case in Australia, then the maintenance of foraging into the twenty-first century may be as much an economic decision as one aimed at maintaining social relations, identity, and connections to traditional lands and practices.

Determining whether foraging is indeed a viable economic alternative to those embedded within state and market economies requires comparable data across each mode of production. To date, these data have been lacking because quantitative ethnographic research into Aboriginal economies has tended to focus either on the internal dynamics of foraging practices (e.g., Altman 1987; Bliege Bird and Bird 2008; Gould 1980; O'Connell and Hawkes 1984) or the external impacts of market economies and government schemes (Altman and Gray 2010; Fijn et al. 2012; Martin 2001). Recently, an approach that seeks to understand the interactions between traditional and external factors came out of the Centre for Aboriginal Economic Policy Research at Australian National University, where Altman (2001, 2003, 2007, 2010) proposes a hybrid economy

Figure 8.1. A Martu grandson and grandfather warming by a morning fire at an extended foraging camp outside of Parnngurr community, 2010. Photograph by Brian Codding.

model. In this model, traditional, state, and market options are viewed as complementary. Traditional practices feed markets (e.g., art, tourism), and the state supports these activities through subsidies (e.g., welfare, pensions, state-run jobs) and market expenditures (e.g., taxes), with some traditional practices (e.g., land management) feeding back to support the state.

Within this three-mode economic framework, individuals face trade-offs between engaging in one economic arena versus another. To evaluate these trade-offs, we examine the relative benefits of alternative economic pursuits in remote Western Desert Aboriginal communities today. Specifically, we evaluate the relative costs and benefits of foraging, working for a wage, and producing paintings for sale. First, we establish estimates of relative efficiency for each task. Then, we examine how individuals allocate their time to each of these activities. Finally, we evaluate how time allocation for these activities varies as a function of the decisions of co-residing spouses and the number of co-residing dependents. These final analyses allow us to determine if individuals coordinate tasks within the household as an economic unit and evaluate which activities people focus on in order to provision dependents. If foraging provides a complementary income to other activities, then the contemporary division of labor between men and women may be a function of coordinated work choice. Further, if foraging activities are more compatible with child care than the alternatives, this compatibility may provide an additional explanation for the retention of foraging. These results provide insights into how individuals negotiate between these alternative economies to fulfill subsistence needs while meeting social obligations to others in the community. Our findings outline how individual decisions aggregate to create the contemporary shape and structure of Aboriginal economies observed in remote communities today.

Ethnographic Background

Martu (also *Mardu* or *Mardujarra*) is the term most frequently used to refer to a group of Aboriginal Australians belonging to one of five dialect groups: Manyjilyjarra, Kartujarra, Warnman, Putijarra, and Kiyajarra. Collectively, the dialects are known as Martu Wankga or "Martu Speak." While individuals maintain their identities as belonging to one or some combination of these and other dialects, there is a still larger Martu identity, which seems to have emerged as members of these five dialect groups came into increasing contact with each other after the European incursion into the deserts. During this process, the hybrid economy also developed through the interactions of Martu with outsiders and their alternative economies.

INVASION, ABANDONMENT, AND RETURN: THE EMERGENCE OF A MARTU IDENTITY AND A HYBRID ECONOMY

Contact with European Australians occurred in multiple events with different groups from the early decades of the twentieth century through the 1960s (Davenport et al. 2005). Reporting on the Aboriginal economy during the contact period, Tonkinson (1993) suggests that individuals spent about half the day foraging, which left ample time for other activities. Women's labor provided the majority of daily foods and sometimes focused on tree and grass seeds and other times on small vertebrates like sand monitor lizards; men focused on less reliable resources including hill kangaroos, which frequently resulted in failed hunts (Tonkinson 1993). Contact-era bands were centered on women's cooperative groups, often sororal co-wives (Scelza and Bliege Bird 2008). Reliable access to plants, especially seeds, required the use of fire to increase habitat heterogeneity and plant diversity (Bliege Bird et al., chapter 9, this volume; Walsh 1990). These broad patterns appear to have been common in the Western Desert: Gould (1967, 1969a, 1969b) reports similar finds among Ngatatjarra foragers to the south of Martu country.

At the time of contact, Aboriginal economies were based solely on foraging. But this traditional economy and way of life shifted as people began to leave the desert and were taken to surrounding mission settlements. Some Martu and their relatives went north to the Catholic La Grange Mission (Bidyadanga community), whereas others went into Papunya, but the majority of those (and their descendants) now in Martu communities left their homes in the desert and went to the station at Jigalong. Jigalong was originally established as a depot to supply crews constructing the Rabbit Proof Fence. Later, it also became the site of an epistolic mission (Tonkinson 1974, 1990). The mission's purpose was to convert the Aboriginal population then exiting the desert, and it attempted to do so by schooling the youth, encouraging a disciplined life among adults, and providing rations to all. Using a "capture by flour" strategy, missionaries and government operators introduced market goods as a means of making individuals abandon foraging economies and become reliant on these purchased goods. This practice ushered in the first elements of a hybrid economy, which coincided with a growing recognition that individuals from each dialect group shared a common Martu identity (Tonkinson 1974). This period ended with the mission's withdrawal in 1969. In many ways, missionary efforts were a failure as they converted only one individual over the twenty-five years of operation (Tonkinson 1974, 2007).[1] The unintended consequences of the mission period included the realization by Martu that they had a collective interest in opposing outsiders and the economic alternatives forced upon them. It was in this context that Martu began their return to the desert.

The period of "self-determination" or "autonomy" began with the return of Martu to the desert, where they established three communities within their ancestral lands: Punmu, Kunawaritji (Well 33 along the Canning Stock Route), and Parnngurr. This work focuses on Parnngurr community, which was established gradually as residents of Jigalong began camping near Parnngurr Rockhole to protest a mining operation that was testing for uranium in the area. While the initial occupation was not permanent, it sent a serious message to government and mining officials and resulted in the eventual establishment of

Parnngurr community in the mid- to late 1980s. Parnngurr School (Parnngurr Martukurnu Kuul) was founded soon after in 1988 (Davenport et al. 2005; Tonkinson 1993; Walsh 1987, 2008). With government support, the hybrid economy further expanded. Although individuals relied heavily on foraging (Walsh 2008), government funds also supported community infrastructure.

The government supported this "outstation movement" by providing subsidies and infrastructure including a community store, a government office, and generators. While this support facilitated community development, Martu did not yet have title over the land. Traditionally, individuals gain and maintain rights to tracts of land known as estates (Stanner 1965). Through birth, initiation, marriage, and other means, men and women gather a collection of estates through their lives (Tonkinson 1993). The combined Martu estates center on the Karlamilyi River and extend to the Percival Lakes and Lake Disappointment. With growing commercial (particularly mining) interests in the area, Martu have sought to articulate their traditional system of land tenure with the Australian legal system. Through persistent efforts lasting into the twenty-first century, Martu were awarded native title over most of their traditional estates in 2002–2003. Although the Australian government now recognizes basic Aboriginal land rights, problems related to self-governance, political autonomy, and economic independence are far from over.

Martu are still struggling with land issues on at least two fronts. First, they continue to have conflicts with mining companies that seek to extract resources (including, once again, uranium) within the native title determination area. Current disagreements between mining companies and various members of the communities will likely continue as the potential benefits and costs of mining are debated. The second issue of sovereignty concerns the governance of Karlamilyi National Park, which is situated within the center of the Martu native title area. The Karlamilyi River is one of the most important areas to Martu, and especially to Warnman-speaking people, but the Australian government did not return these lands to Martu as part of their native title. Currently, government land managers are interested in incorporating Martu into future management schemes, and a few Martu are participating in a nongovernmental organization (NGO)–sponsored ranger program that pays individuals to monitor parts of the region frequented by tourists as a kind of "caring for Country" initiative (Morrison 2007). However, most Martu simply assert their sovereignty over the park by traveling in and out of its borders without notice—burning, hunting, and camping along the way.

Despite these issues surrounding formal sovereignty and autonomy, individuals maintain their traditional rights to Country by maintaining their traditional foraging economies. Today, however, these practices cannot be continued without subsidies from the state. While state funds continue to support the community, many government officials still lack insight into what is actually happening on the ground in these remote communities. Frequently this lack of understanding leads to misinterpretations of a community's needs, wants, and values (Folds 2001; Tonkinson and Tonkinson 2010). Perhaps as a result of these misunderstandings, policies can sometimes tend to be paternalistic and even outright hostile toward Aboriginal ways of life (see Altman and Hinkson 2007; Maddison 2008). Some suggest that events such as "the intervention" may mark the beginning of the end of the self-determination era, though this fact is far from evident in the remote communities of Western Australia. Here, ill-planned and mishandled government schemes more generally result in wasted funds and humorous stories of cross-cultural misunderstanding. Some relief from these repeated failures may come out of the recent rise of locally managed NGOs, though these are still quite new and only time will tell what their impacts truly are. As it now stands, basic government support of the community is integral to the maintenance of traditional foraging economies, a hallmark of the hybrid economy in remote communities today.

COMMUNITY LIFE IN PARNNGURR TODAY

On any given day, Parnngurr community has between two and two hundred plus residents. Populations shift between communities, towns, and ephemeral camps in the desert, and many of their movements are based on the same factors that would have pushed and pulled populations throughout the desert for thousands of years: food, water, family, and social and ritual obligations. Now with motor vehicles, individuals can travel large distances over short periods of time; for example, individuals may reside in one of the communities but still maintain daily access to their traditional hunting grounds over an hour's drive away. Food may dictate some movements at larger scales as well: many young families with bilocal ties between the desert and coast may temporarily relocate from one to the other based on which resources are "on." People are also likely to make such moves in order to maintain social ties between dispersed family and friends and to fulfill ritual obligations associated with initiations and funerals.

When in Parnngurr, *hearth-groups* consisting of collections of individuals generally live in *camps*, which are centered at house structures (mostly pre-fabricated) supplied by the government or donated by one of the local mining companies. Each generally has a kitchen, two to four bedrooms, a bathroom, and possibly a main living-type room. Anyone can rent a camp from the community, though the majority of camps are maintained by senior community members. Camps generally have a core set of residences, though many people shift between multiple camps as they come and go from the community. People usually sleep outside in the warm months, inside in the cold months. When outside, people cluster under bough sheds, sharing a single open space. When inside, rooms are shared based on kin and age classification (e.g., single men, co-habiting spouses perhaps with children, older co-wives or sisters, single parents with children, grandparents with grandchildren). Rarely is anyone left with a room to themselves, both out of tradition and personal preference. However, those who share space do not necessarily extend that relationship into the daily economic or social sphere. Rather, it signifies merely that they co-reside.

Alternative Economies: Foraging, Painting, and Wage Labor

Martu living in the remote community of Parnngurr have several work alternatives that vary in the benefits they provide. Here we discuss three main alternatives: foraging, painting, and wage labor.

FORAGING

Foraging is a major occupation of remote community residents today. Someone goes out foraging from the community nearly every day, and women and men spend about 13.3 percent and 17.4 percent, respectively, of all days foraging (Codding 2012). It remains as important for food as it is for maintaining social relations, individual identities, and ties to traditional life. While many aspects of foraging have changed over the last forty years, most of these changes are predictable from a simple cost/benefit perspective. Seeds have dropped from the diet, replaced by processed flour (O'Connell and Hawkes 1984). Metal tools have mostly replaced those made of wood and stone. Rifles have largely replaced spear-throwers. Perhaps most important, vehicles have become central to aspects of travel, transport, and, for some resources, search.

While Martu will still sometimes walk out from the community to forage for nearby resources, vehicles allow them to maintain a relatively centralized residential base in the community while also accessing traditional foraging locations (or hunt regions) distributed up to about an hour away. Perhaps as an unintended consequence of the adoption of vehicles, hunting tracks have become central corridors of movement through the desert. The main tracks head out of the community in four named cardinal directions and branch out from there in what initially seems like an innumerable combination of connections and loops. A detailed knowledge of these four-wheel-drive hunting tracks is not only a skill required for navigation, but also a source of pride for those who raise and lower a hand, tick a finger, and point with their lips to indicate prior knowledge of every bump, twist, turn, and landmark along the way. Equally important is the creation of new, straight tracks into long unvisited foraging locales and the correction of old, unnecessarily curving roads. Depending on the foraging activity and the season, Martu may travel out from the community and begin searching for resources immediately (e.g., bustards, camels), subsequently returning to the community to process and cook their catches. But for most resources, Martu head out of the community and establish a temporary *dinnertime camp* (Bird et al. 2009; Bird et al. 2013; Bliege Bird and Bird 2008; Bliege Bird et al. 2009; Codding 2012; Codding et al. 2010).

Dinnertime camps are the economic and social locus of foraging. Foragers decide on the hunt region that they are going to travel to and choose the location of the dinnertime camp on arrival. Generally, this choice is made through unassuming consent, though arguments over the ideal locale do sometimes occur. The average dinnertime camp composition includes 2.3 ± 1.1 men, 3.6 ± 0.8 women, and 2.1 ± 1.4 children (Bliege Bird et al. 2012b). Upon arrival, some may immediately depart from the vehicle to start foraging, others may collect firewood (*waru*), and some may wait around for a bit before departing. Depending on the activity, foragers may work together or separately and may be accompanied by children or may leave their dependents behind at the temporary dinnertime camp. The duration of their foraging venture is here referred to as a *foraging bout*. A foraging bout includes the time a forager is in the process of searching for food, pursuing it, and traveling back to the dinnertime camp.

When people return from hunting and collecting wild resources, they typically sit around the fire processing their harvest over discussions of the bout and perhaps a cup of tea. With smaller resources like sand monitor lizards, foragers typically process their own catch and sometimes the catches of others. For larger resources like kangaroos, the hunters will deposit their prey at the edge of camp and take a seat with the others; a senior individual will typically take over processing from there (Bird and Bliege Bird 2010; Bird et al. 2009; Bliege Bird and Bird 2008; also Gould 1967). Hunters cook animal resources following the Law passed down by the Dreaming ancestors (the Jukurrpa): they first singe the animal's hair or skin in the hot flames of a burning fire; then allow a portion of the fire to burn down to coals, heating the sand in the process; and then dig a hole to accommodate the animal, which they then carefully place and cover with hot sand and coals. Sometimes a senior woman may bring a bowl, flour, and baking powder in order to make an unleavened bread called a damper (similar to traditional seed dampers), which is also cooked in the fire either in a depression in the sand (following the method used to cook game) or in a cast-iron pan. After processing and cooking are completed, resources are generally shared between all present. Sharing around a hearth takes on a ritual appearance as individuals pass lizards, cuts of meat, fruit, torn-off bits of damper, and store-bought items like crackers or a can of baked beans. Based on the high probability that they will fail to capture risky prey items (Bird et al. 2009; Bliege Bird and Bird 2008; Bliege Bird et al. 2009; Codding et al. 2011), some individuals will typically rely on the foraging income of others (Bird and Bliege Bird 2010; Bliege Bird et al. 2012b). However, Martu gladly share with those who do not contribute. After everyone is satiated (or earlier if late in the day), the foragers load up in the vehicle and begin the return trip to the community. Departure from dinnertime camp is sometimes discussed but is frequently abrupt, based on some comment or a consensus of full stomachs. Occasionally, if the foraging is very productive and the obligations elsewhere limited, a dinnertime camp may extend into an overnight camp, though more frequently, overnight or multiday camps are planned in advance. While these longer duration camps extend the size and scope of dinnertime camps, they typically maintain the same basic characteristics.

PAINTING

While Martu art originated long ago in a noncommercial context, it has transitioned over the years from traditional mediums, including the body, cave walls, and sand, to acrylic on canvas aimed at a national and international art market. While this process began gradually, the production of art-for-sale expanded rapidly with the formation of the Martu arts cooperative (Martumili) in 2006. Since then, painting and, to a lesser extent, basketmaking and carving have become a major economic and social force in the community.[2] Martu art is uniquely situated within the desert art tradition, and particular individuals are becoming artists celebrated by a growing community of critics, scholars, and buyers.

Martu see painting as a way of maintaining and sharing traditional knowledge while simultaneously producing a product for market. Paintings are most frequently expressions of particular Dreaming tracts (or "song lines") of estates (or Country) over which individuals have traditional rights, though to the artist, the paintings are more than mere representations. According to Myers (2002), desert art is not so much a story that can be decoded or a representation of some discrete event or place; rather (to those initiated), it *is* what it represents. Carty has made a similar case, arguing that Martu artistic expression is more than representation (Davenport et al. 2010). When discussing a collaborative painting of four important water sources from *Kunawarritji to Wajaparni*, Martu artist Jeffery James remarked, "This is our family tree—this painting" (Davenport et al. 2010; field notes). Here, place is family is Jukurrpa; the social landscape, the physical landscape, and the metaphysical landscape are one and the same, as are their representations in paint. Lest these be judged excessively artful interpretations, we would point out that this alternative ontology has a strong foundation. In remarks on Aboriginal philosophy, Elkin (1969) notes that Jukurrpa and things in the world do not have a direct cause-and-effect relationship because the two exist simultaneously as the same. This idea may be extended to painting—acrylic on canvas is not any less the Jukurrpa than Country is the Jukurrpa. This is at the core of why artistic production and sharing are so important. The Law passed down from the Dreaming ancestors requires the maintenance of these traditional practices and encourages them to be shared widely. Akin to performative representations in traditional dance and song in which knowledge of Country is shared with others, paintings are distributed widely across the world to serve a similar function, though in a different medium, to a different audience (one that may never be able to visit or learn more of that Country), and at a much larger scale (Carty 2012; Myers 2002). From a source of income to an extension of the Dreaming, desert Aboriginal art holds multiple meanings, each of which has implications for the future of remote communities and Aboriginal identity (Carty 2012; Dussart 2006; Myers 2002).

Though it is difficult to overemphasize the social and ritual importance of painting, economics is also central to individual decisions to paint or produce baskets. The time required to produce a painting depends greatly on the size of the canvas. Likewise, the price depends both on the size of the painting and the renown of the artist. Celebrated artists may routinely fetch about $10,000 for a medium-sized painting, and extraordinary collaborative paintings sell for upward of $100,000 (all prices in Australian dollars). But these exceptional works are rare. Based on our observations, conversations with artists, and interviews with members of the art community, we would say that the average painting takes two to four weeks to produce (the artist painting nearly every day) and can be sold for $1,000 to $5,000. Smaller paintings may take only a week to produce and sell for about $250 to $1,000. Paintings sold through the cooperative return about 70 percent of the profit to artists, which suggests that talented artists may be able to bring in about $500 per week if they opt to engage in painting full time. While likely accurate, these figures should only be considered rough estimates.

Baskets, like painting, are a new medium for Martu. They are generally produced from grasses that are collected, bundled, wound, and woven together with colorful yarn. A basket generally requires less time to produce than a painting (though individuals do spend a good deal of time searching for and collecting appropriate grasses) and generally sells for less than a painting. Baskets take about one week to produce and can be sold for about $500 on average. One traditional medium, wood, is also used to carve secular objects that sell also for about $500 (e.g., nulla-nullas, boomerangs), though very few people are currently doing this kind of work in Parnngurr.

While people could paint or make baskets nearly every day (as long as the materials are available), people generally paint incrementally. They sometimes spend many consecutive days sitting in front of their camp, in the art shed, or at the arts cooperative office in town, but other times individuals start a painting, work on it for half the day, then go out hunting in subsequent days, leaving the painting partially finished for weeks. Such a staccato rhythm may have to do with other social obligations, but it may also have to do with how individuals weigh alternative economic pursuits. Indeed, the economics of painting and how it ties in with alternative livelihoods is an open topic that demands further exploration.

WAGE LABOR

Opportunities to engage in wage labor are limited in remote Aboriginal communities. The most common form of employment comes from the state through the Community Development and Education Program (CDEP). While every unemployed member of the community receives either a welfare stipend through Centrelink or a "pension" if they are of retirement age, those who choose to work for CDEP can double their welfare payments from about $500 to $1,000 per fortnight. CDEP jobs are generally off-and-on based on the presence or absence of someone to organize them. Tasks include cleaning the community, dumping rubbish bins from individual camps at the tip (dump), assisting in the operation of the government office, and cooking meals at the center for the elderly.

Martu may also receive wages from nonprofit organizations, partially funded by the government through grants. Tasks include cultural awareness training for miners, monitoring of endangered species, and ranger work along the heavily toured Canning Stock Route. These pay well, about $100 per day, but opportunities are inconsistent. Thus, working for a nonprofit probably provides about the same weekly rate as topping off unemployment benefits with CDEP wages, providing about $1,000 per fortnight. One exception is a ranger program that was started by the nonprofit organization Kanyrninpa Jukurrpa in 2009. If funding continues, it may provide a few people with regular work directed at preserving natural and cultural resources in the Martu native title and Karlamilyi National Park. But as with most government-sponsored employment schemes, funding can be lost, programs cut, and wages disappear. In reality, the irregularity of employment is not necessarily a bad thing as Martu place a greater value on so many other aspects of life than earning regular wages. When employment comes into conflict with social, ritual, and family obligations, wage work rarely takes precedent.

While the data we will examine cover only wage labor in the community, wage opportunities can also be found outside of the community, and these can draw people away for extended periods of time. Options include work in cattle stations (particularly to the north near Bidyadanga), but more frequently people take up work in one of the regional mining operations. Martu who work in the mines earn about $3,000 per fortnight, with one or two weeks off in between shifts. Such rigid schedules frequently conflict with important obligations, including initiations and funerals. Moreover, time away from family is a serious added cost. Frequently, individuals will take a job for a brief rotation in order to acquire enough funds for a particular item or event. Often though, the early departure is not planned but emerges out of conflicts between job requirements and familial obligations or longing for home. As Burbank (2006) has written about Aboriginal communities in southern Arnhem Land, paid work is sometimes avoided *because* of the obligation to be on a schedule.

Methods

Understanding why foraging may continue within remote Aboriginal communities requires comparable data across each work alternative. To this end, we collected data on community demographics, caloric returns associated with different activities, time allocation, and evaluations of those choices based on other co-varying factors (spouses' work decisions and the number of co-residing dependents).

We collected weekly census data between the third week of April and the first week of June in 2010 to capture a bit of the variability in the distributions of populations. Since individuals move within and between communities, we thought this census period would provide a measure of mobility and the shifting residence patterns that determine community populations. We collected these data on the same day of the week and always in the morning. Accuracy was checked by multiple independent counts and through conversations with community members. While accurate over the observation period, these figures do not necessarily capture all of demographic variability we would expect even over a typical year as the community population may swell for particular events (e.g., funerals, initiations) and drop when such events draw people elsewhere.

To understand how people spend their time in the community, we recorded the activities of fifty individuals per day for two months across April, May, and June of 2010. For each observation period, the sample includes individuals occupying at least four spatially discrete camps of varying demographic compositions in order to limit geographic covariance. Camps were selected to provide a broad sample of individuals from each age and sex category. Each day, we recorded whether individuals allocated time to foraging, wage labor, or painting. While coarse grained, this per-day scale should also be accurate as each activity either requires more than half of a day or an individual tends to allocate more than half of their day to one of these activities. As such, each activity is essentially mutually exclusive per day. The sampling procedure was designed to capture patterning in community life: if individuals left the community, they were recorded as absent and ignored for the rest of the sample week or until they returned (unless they took up residence at a different camp that was outside the sample when they returned). If all the members of a camp left in the course of a week, each individual was recorded as absent until the next week, when another camp was selected for observation.

Fine-grained data on individual foraging decisions and returns are discussed in greater detail elsewhere (Bird et al. 2005; Bird et al. 2009; Bird et al. 2013; Bliege Bird and Bird 2008; Bliege Bird et al. 2008; Bliege Bird et al. 2009; Bliege Bird et al. 2012a; Bliege Bird et al. 2012b; Bliege Bird et al. 2013; Codding 2012; Codding et al. 2010; Codding et al. 2011; Codding et al. 2014; Scelza et al. 2014). Our data collection included focal individual follows with hunters and continuous camp scans of all individuals leaving and returning to the dinnertime camp (Altmann 1974). We measured or estimated from counts the weights of acquired foods and converted these to kilocalories following standard nutritional data calculations (e.g., Brand Miller et al. 1993).

To make foraging, wage labor, and painting comparable, we translated the costs and benefits of each activity into two variables: time and calories. Whereas these variables are direct measures of foraging effort and productivity, we converted the money acquired from the production and sale of art and from wage labor into calories based on cost per calories at the community shop. Individuals generally make routine, even daily, visits to the community shop; the alternative would be to make a trip to the town of Newman to purchase food at a major grocery store (Woolworths). However, individuals are frequently limited by access to a vehicle capable of making the long trip and the funds to purchase the large amount of fuel required. Thus, the community shop is the most reliable place at which to purchase food. While fresh fruits, vegetables, cheese, and eggs are typically available shortly after the arrival of the resupply truck, they run out of stock quite quickly and so were excluded from this inventory. To convert cash into calories, we divided the total nutritional value of each shop item by its unit cost, thereby calculating kilocalories per dollar. We used shopping patterns from Scelza (2012) to calculate a weighted mean and median to represent the amount of energy (kcals) individuals acquired with each dollar spent.

Because these are count data assumed to take a Poisson distribution, statistical inference was made through the use of generalized linear models with a Poisson error structure. We ran these models in R (R Core Team 2013). Model results include the likelihood r-square value (R_L^2) and the alpha or *p* value (for more information, see Crawley 2007; Faraway 2006; Grafen and Hails 2002; and Menard 2002).

Results

Here we present the results of our study outlining community demographics, benefits of work, time allocation, and determinants of work choice.

COMMUNITY DEMOGRAPHICS

Over the seven-week census period, we recorded data on 138 different individuals, though the community never contained that many people all at one time. At any given time, the number of people in the community ranged from forty-one to eighty-five (figure 8.2a, table 8.1). The increase over the observation window is not linear as such fluctuations are truly typical and caused by multiple factors. While community population can easily spike into the hundreds — usually during "footy" (Australian rules football) competitions, initiations, or funerals — no such events occurred during this window of time.

A total of twenty camps were occupied off and on during the census period. Only four camps were occupied during all seven weeks, and the majority of camps were occupied only two of the seven weeks. Some individuals never settled at any camps; instead, they floated between camps or resided in common areas.

On average, camps included between four and five individuals, though camps with two people were recorded most frequently (figure 8.2b). Married individuals had their spouses present about 40 percent of the time. The average camp had between one and two dependents ranging from zero to five at any given time (figure 8.2c). Across all camps, each nondependent adult had an average of 0.5 dependents.

BENEFITS OF WORK

Martu typically return from foraging well fed. While foraging returns vary substantially depending on the resource and season, returns averaged 2,506.3 kcals per foraging bout across 1,876 bouts, including all foraging activities recorded from 2000 to 2010. If only successful hunts are included, this number increases to 3,632.5 kcals per bout averaged over 1,224 successful bouts. With the average foraging bout lasting 2.41 hours, the mean overall return rate (including both successful and failed bouts) is 1,200.31 kcals per hour. Hypothetically, if foragers

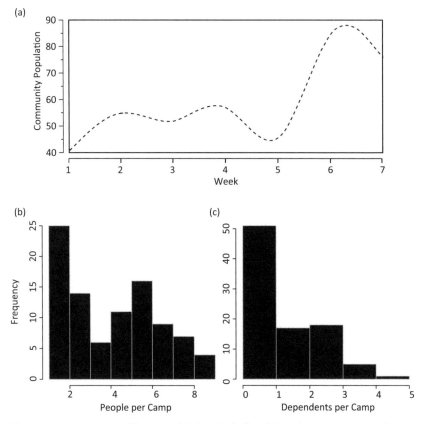

Figure 8.2. A summary of demographic data including (a) total community population across the census period by observation date with between observation values interpolated with a smoothing spline ($\lambda = 1$; see data in table 9.1), (b) distribution of the number of people in each camp, and (c) the number of dependents per camp per week.

were to extend a bout to an eight-hour period, they could expect returns upward of 9,600 kcals per day.

To make foraging, painting, and wage labor comparable, we converted dollars into calories based on the prices of items in the community store and their caloric values. Store items range from a low of about 50 kcals per dollar for frozen chicken breasts or canned vegetables to a high of about 1,456 kcals per dollar for flour (table 8.2). That flour has the highest return rate per dollar is particularly interesting given that it has largely replaced wild seeds as the primary grain source, a common trend in Aboriginal societies (O'Connell and Hawkes

Table 8.I. A summary of census data by age class and gender.

Week	Young	Adult	Senior	Women	Men	Total Individuals
1	15	19	7	16	25	41
2	18	27	10	22	33	55
3	16	24	12	24	28	52
4	14	25	18	24	33	57
5	13	27	6	22	24	46
6	30	38	17	39	46	85
7	22	34	20	33	43	76

Table 8.2. The cost (Australian dollars) and energetic value (kcal) of items at the community shop.

Item	Kcals	Unit Cost ($)	Kcal/$
Diet cola*	5	2	3
Tomato sauce	102	5	20
Sports drink	200	5	40
Chicken breasts	1,100	23	48
Cola	100	2	50
Canned vegetables*	210	4	52
Instant noodles	296	5	59
Beans in tomato sauce	328	4	82
Meat pies	684	8	86
Spaghetti noodles	631	6.5	97
Chickpeas	604	5	121
Stew chops	2,150	17	126
Kangaroo tail	1,670	10	167
Hamburger	2,444	12	204
Pearl barley	1,239	5	248
Rice	1,755	5	351
Honey	1,254	3	418
Sausages	4,050	9	450
Dry red lentils*	3,377	5	675
Canola oil	6,089	5	1,218
Flour	7,280	5	1,456
Mean			284
Median			121
Weighted mean			224
Weighted median			199

*Expired item at time of recording.

1981). Most Martu camps have a bucket of flour around, and people frequently make flour damper (a bread made with only water, flour, and baking powder) in place of what would have traditionally been seed damper (collected and ground wild seeds and water). While bleached flour is surely less nutritious than wild seeds, it is still healthier than many of the other high-calorie items like oil and sausages. Frequently purchased items, like meat pies, actually have a relatively low return per dollar, most likely because they are processed meals ready to eat after being warmed (frequently in their tins, on the fire).

To calculate the amount of energy an individual can expect to acquire for each dollar spent at the shop, we calculated a weighted mean and median based on spending patterns. Scelza (2012) reports that shop expenditures are distributed nonrandomly across food categories. On average, 47 percent of dollars spent go to general grocery items (flour, canned food, dried goods, snacks), 19 percent to cool drinks (cola, sports drinks), 13 percent to meat, 13 percent to tobacco, 4 percent to fruit and vegetables, and 4 percent to water. Using these values to weight mean and median values of energy per dollar spent, we found that a dollar spent at the shop returns an average of 224 kcals and a median of 199 kcals. Given the skewed distribution of shop items, the weighted median value was used to estimate central tendency.

The base income received from welfare comes to about $36 per day (table 8.3). Based on the weighted median value of shop items, a community member receiving welfare could acquire 7,107 kcals per day if they spent 100 percent of their income. More realistically, those on welfare could bring in about 1,777 kcals per day by spending 25 percent of their income, with other funds going to rent, vehicle maintenance, fuel, and additional living expenses. Assuming that the average person requires about 2,000 kcals per day and given the average 0.5 dependents per nondependent adult across the community for the census period, the average person would need to bring in about 3,000 kcals per day to cover themselves and their dependents (unless they purchased high-return items such as flour and sausages exclusively). As the estimates show, this number of kilocalories would be difficult to acquire on a welfare stipend alone. By taking advantage of alternative options, individuals could increase their income by choosing to work for the community, producing paintings for sale, or foraging to supplement their cash income with bush foods.

Those who choose to work for the community can double their welfare income, bringing in about 3,553 kcals per day (table 8.3). But as foraging results in an average of 2,892 kcals per day, individuals would be better off using their

Table 8.3. Estimated wages earned (Australian dollars) and estimated energetic returns (kcal) per day for subsistence-related activities.

	Australian Dollars			Kilocalories		
	Month	Week	Day	100%	50%	25%
Foraging[a]	—	—	—	9,602.5	4,801.2	2,400.6
Foraging and welfare	—	—	—	16,709.6	8,354.8	4,177.4
Painting[b]	2,000.00	500.00	71.40	14,214.3	7,107.1	3,553.6
Painting and welfare	3,000.00	750.00	107.10	21,321.4	10,660.7	5,330.4
Wage labor[c]	1,000.00	250.00	35.70	7,107.1	3,553.6	1,776.8
Wage Labor and welfare	2,000.00	500.00	71.40	14,214.3	7,107.1	3,553.6
Welfare/pension	1,000.00	250.00	35.70	7,107.1	3,553.6	1,776.8
Mining	4,500.00	1,125.00	150.00	29,850.0	14,925.0	7,462.5

[a]*Foraging* assumes average returns per hour with "100%" indicating an eight-hour foraging bout.
[b]*Painting* assumes an artist working exclusively on painting can produce a small painting in one week.
[c]*Wage labor* assumes an individual working eight hours per day for CDEP over five work days; amount per day is divided by seven days.

welfare or pension money to purchase items (such as flour) at the shop and supplementing these items with foraging, thus bringing in a total of about 4,177 kcals per day—more than enough to cover self and 0.5 dependents. Two other alternatives include basketmaking and painting. While basketmaking (and perhaps carving) provides an average return at the same level as community wage labor, painting exclusively would bring in returns in excess of 5,000 kcals per day (table 8.3). This estimate for painting is rather high, however, and would only come from securing stable sources of supplies and buyers. While we have included mining in table 8.3 for reference, it is not considered a substitutable alternative as it requires people to be away from the community for extended periods of time.

Overall, these results suggest that individuals do need to supplement their welfare incomes and that they would be best off doing so through the production and sale of art. However, while anyone *can* paint, not everyone has the requisite skills to consistently produce high-quality paintings that will sell. Thus, we expect that some skilled individuals will specialize in painting. The majority of those for whom painting is not a realistic alternative should, we predict, opt to forage rather than work wage labor jobs in order to supplement their incomes.

We will test these predictions by examining how individuals allocate their time between these different activities and how their choices vary as a function of the variability in camp and community demographics. Specifically, we examine how individuals alter their work decisions in coordination with a co-residing spouse or as a function of the number of co-residing dependents.

TIME ALLOCATION

We observed between seventeen and thirty-seven persons in one of our focal activities per day, resulting in 899 person-days for which an activity was recorded and 357 person-days in which individuals were scored as absent, totaling 1,256 person-days overall. Individuals were divided into three age classes: pre-initiate (young), adult, and senior adult.

Adults spent about 39.0 percent of all days either foraging, painting, or engaged in wage labor, whereas senior adults spent 57.8 percent of their days working in one of these activities (Codding 2012). All other days were spent in pursuit of some other activity, including ritual, vehicle repair, or rest.

Of the days allocated to one of our focal productive activities, adult and senior individuals together divided their time unevenly, with approximately 52 percent of days dedicated to foraging, 39 percent to wage labor, and 9 percent to painting or producing other traditional goods for sale. These results show that adult and senior individuals spend disproportionately more of their time foraging, as we predicted based on the benefits of the alternatives. However, we also found a good degree of variability. One woman and several men only spent time in wage labor, another group of individuals only in foraging, and one woman was only observed painting. To understand what might drive this variability, we next examine how the presence or absence of a co-residing spouse and the number of co-residing dependents predict time allocation across these different activities.

DETERMINANTS OF WORK CHOICE

To determine what explains variability in work-choice decisions, we examined individual time allocation relative to household demographics. First, if foraging provides better outcomes compared to other activities, then coordinated work choice by men and women could help explain the maintenance of foraging as well as variability across individuals. Second, if foraging individuals choose to allocate more time to foraging when they reside with more dependents, then foraging may be a more compatible option than other work alternatives and may support the retention of foraging practices.

If spouses specialized in complementary activities, then we would expect the activities of co-residing spouses to negatively covary (Gurven and Hill 2009). However, an examination of paired spousal data suggests that individuals do not coordinate their labor at all, either negatively or positively.[3] The time allocated to different work alternatives does not positively or negatively covary between co-residing spouses, suggesting that husbands and wives do not coordinate as economic units. Complementarity across work alternatives does not seem to predict variability in time allocated to work and does not help explain the retention of foraging.

If individuals care for and provision co-residing dependents (regardless of relatedness), then they should increase their work effort as a function of the number of co-residing dependents. Although we should not necessarily predict a linear increase given the possibility of shared child care (Kramer 2011), work choice should still be partially directed by the needs of dependents. The results show that neither the number of individuals working for a wage ($R_L^2 = 0.02$, $p = 0.189$) nor the number of people painting ($R_L^2 < 0.01$, $p = 0.434$) changes as a function of the number of co-residing dependents. However, people do increase the number of days they spend foraging with up to three co-residing dependents ($R_L^2 = 0.07$, $p = 0.0033$; figure 8.3), suggesting that individuals provision dependents through foraging rather than wage labor or painting.

Discussion

While foraging is often dismissed as a nonviable economic alternative, our results show that foraging appears to be one of the best economic alternatives available in remote desert Aboriginal communities today. But because foraging now requires travel in four-wheel-drive vehicles and because these vehicles require monetary inputs for fuel and maintenance, foraging is only viable in combination with wage-producing tasks or reliance on the state, as is the case among the Inuit (Wenzel, chapter 2, this volume). Considering these factors, we think Altman's (2001, 2003, 2007, 2010) "hybrid economy" may aptly describe conditions in remote communities today. Rather than suggesting that Aboriginal populations should work to articulate their traditional economies with the

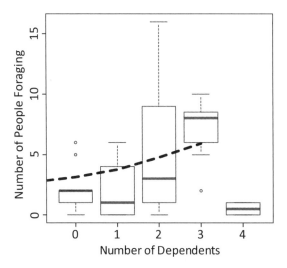

Figure 8.3. The number of foraging individuals per camp per week as a function of the number of co-residing dependents. The dashed line shows predicted trend from a Poisson generalized linear model. Box plots show the distribution of counts.

market (through painting) or the state (through co-management of natural resources), these results suggest that individuals should be left to engage with their traditional economies in ways that best suit their needs.

Given the benefits of foraging, we should not be surprised that individuals in Parnngurr allocate more time to foraging than to any other economic pursuit. Variability across individuals seems to be partially determined by household demographics. Though spouses do not seem to coordinate their work efforts, individuals do choose to forage more to care for more dependents, which is likely the result of immediate returns gained from foraging and the fact that foraging provides a social environment more compatible with caring for children than the alternatives, especially when extended family members, particularly grandmothers, may be available to share in the costs of child care (Scelza 2009). Furthermore, the approximately two children per dinnertime camp would receive not only basic care but also food and education on traditional practices from foraging adults. While not all foraging activities are equal in their propensity to reliably provide food or in their compatibility with child care, many of the foraging activities undertaken most by Martu do indeed meet these requirements. Women's sand monitor hunting, which also provides long-term environmental benefits (see following; Bliege Bird et al., chapter 9, this volume), may be particularly important.

ON THE FORAGING MODE OF PRODUCTION

In his classic treatise, Sahlins (1972) proposed that hunter-gatherers were the *original affluent society*. This proposal was based on, among other things, the observation that Aboriginal foragers in Arnhem Land (see McCarthy and Mac-Arthur 1960) worked only a few hours to provide for their *limited wants and limited needs*. We raise this point not to prolong the stereotype but to illustrate an alternative interpretation of this observation in light of the data we have presented. Foraging as an economic alternative may be driven not by limited wants, but by the benefits it affords individuals, by a basic economic evaluation of the costs and benefits of foraging relative to the alternatives. Even in the twenty-first century, foragers may be able to work fewer hours for parallel rewards. Thus, we should not be surprised to see so many individuals foraging so frequently in remote communities today.

These trends make particular sense when viewed through the lens of human behavioral ecology (Smith 2013; Winterhalder and Smith 1981, 1992, 2000), which typically assumes that individual decisions are made to optimize outcomes within constraints. By quantifying the trade-offs associated with different activities, we are able to gain better insight into the costs and benefits individuals experience. In the context of twenty-first-century hunting and gathering, as in any economic context, it is not hard to see why working less for equal rewards may be a better strategy. Add a social context within which accumulation is not rewarded but punished (Bird and Bliege Bird 2010; Myers 1986, 1989), and the continued importance of a foraging mode of production is understandable. Indeed, the social costs imposed on those who opt out of a traditional economy—in which individuals gain wealth by sharing widely—may be equally important in explaining why individuals continue to forage (Bliege Bird et al., chapter 9; Blurton Jones, chapter 5; Coxworth, chapter 7; Wenzel, chapter 2, this volume).

While foraging may be able to satiate limited wants and limited needs, some from "mainstream" Australian society do not understand remote community life and consider foraging to somehow be "backward." Some individuals use this interpretation as support for cultural assimilation (see McGregor 1999; Myers 1988), and their ideas continue to linger in the background of contemporary debates about "development" that center on economic integration (Altman 2010).

ON DEVELOPMENT AND CONSERVATION

Our findings suggest some specific reasons to continue government support for remote communities and the traditional activities that occur in and around them. As others have noted, various indicators of health, wealth, and well-being all show that those living in remote communities may be better off than their urban counterparts (Burgess et al. 2005; Garnett et al. 2009; Tonkinson and Tonkinson 2010). However, many of the efforts to "help" Martu in remote communities may actually impede the behaviors that are causing these benefits.

Contemporary government policies frequently encourage remote community residents to engage in the market economy, which detracts from traditional strategies for making a living and caring for children. As we have shown, Martu may be much better off foraging than engaging in government employment schemes—choosing to forage is a rational economic decision. Instead of trying to stop people from hunting and gathering wild resources, government policies may do better to support traditional practices. Rather than providing job training, in-town education, and "opportunities" to work, the government should, both for people and the environment, encourage and support life in these remote communities. Support of foraging may be particularly important as foraging from a central community incurs greater monetary costs (see also Wenzel, chapter 2, this volume), most likely due to a (relatively) large population that is likely to deplete resources around the community, leading to higher travel and transport costs to and from productive foraging locations (e.g., Codding et al. 2014). Funding the diesel for vehicles that allow individuals to travel to more remote locales may be crucial to an increase in food sovereignty in these remote communities. Unfortunately, the government and even private organizations have begun to downplay and even disallow expenditures for the purchase of vehicles, vehicle maintenance, or diesel. The opposite should in fact be a priority if people want to ensure Martu livelihoods in these communities, and doing so may also provide added benefits to individual health and the environment.

Because foraged foods are typically healthier than low-quality store items (particularly those that are affordable) and because foraging itself generally leads to greater levels of exercise than would be found in most jobs, individuals serve to gain on multiple fronts by maintaining a foraging lifestyle. The maintenance of this lifestyle may further lead to reductions in the overall health-care costs that are currently dominated by treatment rather than preventative measures. In addition, the support rather than stigmatization of this traditional mode of economic production may lead to mental health benefits. Because foraging is equally valued for social as well as economic reasons, stigmas on foraging can be particularly harmful—and breaking down these stigmas could be particularly beneficial.

Not only does foraging serve to benefit individual health, it also promotes the health and biodiversity of the desert environment. As discussed elsewhere (Bliege Bird et al., chapter 9, this volume; Bliege Bird et al. 2008; Bliege Bird et al. 2012a; Bliege Bird et al. 2013; Codding 2012; Codding et al. 2014), desert ecologies coevolved with Martu hunting, collecting, and burning practices, and so biodiversity tends to increase with Martu foraging. The restructuring of vegetation resulting from Martu burning practices may be particularly beneficial to many now threatened small mammal populations. This issue is something that government agencies express interest in addressing, whether or not they actually do so. Attempts to incorporate Aboriginal insights and participation into government-sponsored environmental management schemes typically involve turning individuals into Western-style land managers—a trend sometimes referred to as the "caring for country" movement. However, at least in the Martu case, it is what Martu just *do* that promotes biodiversity. Formal programs designed to make people "care" may simply get in the way of the real environmental benefits that result from Martu hunting, gathering, and burning in an ecology that evolved with humans performing those very activities (Bliege Bird et al., chapter 9, this volume; Codding 2012; Walsh 2008). In essence, agencies do not need to pay people not to hunt so that they can work to "manage" the land. Instead, agencies should encourage hunting—biodiversity will follow (Bird 2009).

Policies that create disincentives to forage will likely have negative consequences—less food sovereignty; declines in physical, mental, and social health; and reductions in biodiversity—the opposite of what such policies intend to accomplish. Policies that support foraging, on the other hand, will likely have positive effects on community health, social cohesion, and the desert environment.

Summary and Conclusions

Models of twenty-first-century foraging economies tend to either ignore external dynamics, instead focusing on foraging activities alone, or examine state and market alternatives without treating foraging as a viable alternative. By examining the trade-offs between foraging, painting, and wage labor within a remote desert Aboriginal community, we show, contrary to many common assumptions, that foraging is one of the most productive economic alternatives within the community. While co-residing spouses do not seem to coordinate labor across activities, individuals do forage significantly more frequently as a function of the number of co-residing dependents. This finding suggests that while households are not economic units per se, individuals do adjust their work levels based on the need to provision dependents through foraging because of its immediate returns and the compatibility between child care and foraging within a dinnertime camp structure. These results suggest an answer to the question posed in the title of this book. People continue to forage because it is a viable economic alternative. Development efforts may be best directed at facilitating traditional foraging practices, which will in turn supply profound social and environmental benefits.

Acknowledgments

Thanks to our Martu friends for all of their support and collaboration. This work has benefited tremendously from the support of Bob and Myrna Tonkinson, Peter Veth, John Carty, and Brooke Scelza. Thanks to all of the participants of the SAR seminar on twenty-first-century hunting and gathering and especially Karen Kramer and George Wenzel for comments on an earlier version of this chapter. This chapter was improved by comments from two anonymous reviewers — we thank them for their careful reading of this work.

Notes

1. Ironically, after the missionary's departure Tonkinson (2007:513) came to see himself as a "secular missionary" who began "shamelessly preaching to the initiated men against gambling and alcohol, and passionately urging them to maintain the integrity of their unique culture" for the love of what he came to know as Martu society. This period of time saw several such individuals, many of whom may have aided or at least encouraged the self-determination movements.

2. Many individuals, like Martumili Arts director Gabriel Sullivan, helped to inspire and foster the current art movement in Martu communities. It was also certainly influenced by earlier movements in the desert (Myers 2002) and by

visiting artists like Galiano Fardin, who was one of the artists, if not the first, to bring canvases, paint, and encouragement out to Parnngurr.

3. Models examining all combinations of work choice between co-residing spouses result in z values ranging from -0.003 to 0.003 and p values from 0.9967 to 1.0000.

CHAPTER NINE

Economic, Social, and Ecological Contexts of Hunting, Sharing, and Fire in the Western Desert of Australia

REBECCA BLIEGE BIRD, BRIAN F. CODDING, AND DOUGLAS W. BIRD

Introduction

In the remote desert regions of Australia, Aboriginal foragers continue to practice some of their traditional lifeways and livelihoods. Their practices include economic pursuits focused on hunting and gathering wild resources, activities that are intertwined with the maintenance of social relations and ritual obligations. Among Martu, Aboriginal inhabitants of the Great and Little Sandy Deserts and traditional owners of one of the largest native title regions in Australia, one of the most important foraging activities is also one that carries important social and environmental benefits: women's sand monitor lizard (*Varanus gouldii*) hunting. Sand monitor hunting not only provides a reliable source of food, it brings people closer together in tight cooperative and sharing networks.

Women light fires while hunting sand monitors in the wintertime, and these have cascading trophic consequences in this fire-adapted landscape. Anthropogenic burning creates small-scale fire mosaics (patches of ground burned at different times) that buffer against lightning-caused wildfires and support a wide range of species. In this chapter, we expand on other economic explanations of why Martu continue to forage well into the twenty-first century (Codding et al., chapter 8, this volume) by showing how women's burning practices are central to the continued productivity of hunting and gathering. Martu modify their environment with fire in order to create the network of economic, ecological, and social interactions that supports their foraging way of life.

Figure 9.1. Martu women hunting for sand monitor lizards with fire near Parnngurr community. Photograph by Rebecca Bliege Bird.

ETHNOHISTORICAL BACKGROUND

In the arid center of Australia, human hunting and human fire may have been part of the landscape for the last thirty-six thousand years or more (M. A. Smith 2013; Smith et al. 2008). At contact, small to medium-sized mammals, lizards, and snakes, along with seed grasses, acacia beans, geophytes, and bush fruits, underwrote daily subsistence, with larger prey (hill kangaroo, *Macropus robustus*; plains kangaroo, *M. rufus*; and emu, *Dromiceius novae-hollandiae*) providing an occasional feast (Cane 1987; Gould 1969, 1991; Kayberry 1939; Meggitt 1965; O'Connell et al. 1983). Throughout the desert, people used broadcast fires (fires intended to expose at least 1 ha of ground) in the cool dry season to clear areas of mature spinifex (*Triodia* spp.) in sand-plain and dune country and facilitate their search for burrowed prey, especially sand monitors and other lizards and snakes, but also small mammals such as bilby (*Macrotis lagotis*), mulgara (*Dasycercus cristicauda*), burrowing bettong (*Bettongia lesueur*), and rufous hare-wallaby (*Lgorchestes hirsutus*; Gould 1971; Jones 1969; Kimber 1983;

Latz and Green 1995). Smaller spot fires were used for flushing prey during hunts for larger monitors (*V. giganteus* and *V. panoptes*), brushtail possums (*Trichosurus vulpecula*), and feral cats (*Felis catus*).

Until about the mid-1960s, Martu moved across an extensive landscape, concentrating their hunting and burning around sources of water and moving on along established tracks to new camps when hunting returns declined. According to the reports of early explorers, precontact landscape-level fire mosaics were localized around heavily used campsites near springs, wells, and rockholes; such a pattern was so evident that European explorers linked the appearance of fire mosaics to the proximity of water (Gammage 2011).

In 1906, after Alfred Canning established the stock route linking Wiluna in the south with Halls Creek in the north and with the subsequent construction of the No. 1 Rabbit Proof Fence, Aboriginal depopulation of the western and central desert began, proceeding along with the spread of pastoralism around the desert's margin from the south and east to the north and west. The Aboriginal exodus in the mid-twentieth century was driven both by the pull of resources available at settlements and by the push of an increasingly arid climate, made more difficult to endure by population loss. Several years of low and erratic rainfall had caused water sources to dry up, and without a large population present to maintain them, they gradually were disappearing under vegetation or filling with silt. Fire mosaics were breaking down, as fewer bands moved across the landscape burning and hunting. Invasive species were spreading into the arid interior: cats specializing in mice and small mammals, rabbits around clay pans and salt lakes, foxes in the southern regions, and, most recently, feral dromedaries. Atomic testing in the south left many poisoned and ill, contributing to increased social isolation. By 1960, fewer than two hundred mobile foragers were probably left in the northern half of the western desert, some of whom were first contacted during government patrols during the establishment of the Blue Streak missile testing range (Davenport et al. 2005; Peterson and Long 1986; Scelza and Bliege Bird 2008). By the mid-1970s, nearly all desert nomads had moved to centralized settlements such as Jigalong (Davenport et al. 2005), and although they continued forays into the desert margins, great expanses of the interior were entirely abandoned (see Codding et al., chapter 8, this volume, for additional ethnographic details).

In the mid-1980s, Martu returned to their homelands after a twenty-year exile in the missions and settlements on the desert fringe and took up permanent residence at the site of a uranium lease at Parnngurr Rockhole that was owned by an Australian subsidiary of the international mining company Rio Tinto. This group of about sixty people included several families from the Kartujarra, Manyjiljarra, and Warnman linguistic groups, who felt their claim to the area was quite strong. Unlike other parts of Australia, the Great and Little Sandy Deserts had been spared ecological degradation resulting from pastoralism, agriculture, and development; in their absence, the desert had been silent, the only visitors mining exploration teams intent on gold and uranium. Even so, Martu returned to an ecosystem far different from the one they had left, one in which most of their important subsistence resources, both plant and animal, had vanished. Paradoxically, the Martu hiatus from their homeland coincided with the local extinction of twenty-one species of native marsupial and the decline of forty-three more (Burbidge et al. 1988; Burrows et al. 2006; Finlayson 1961). Gone were several small marsupials that had been common prey—the rufous hare-wallaby (*mala*), brushtail possum (*wayuta*), burrowing bettong (*jamparn*), and golden bandicoot (*minkajurru, Isodon auratus*)—and in their place were feral housecats, camels, donkeys, and foxes. These new landscapes were dominated by extensive lightning fires that burned ten to one hundred times larger than the fires the Martu were used to (Burrows et al. 2006).

Martu coped with the extensive scale of these new landscapes by using vehicles to reduce the cost of travel, adapting to the new realities of settlement life by increasing their mobility across vast distances. As Martu continued to hunt and burn around camps, they reestablished fire mosaics (albeit in more restricted areas near vehicle tracks) and complaints about resource scarcity diminished.

To explain why Martu continue to forage today, we first need to understand their relationship with fire. The productivity of hunting and gathering is dependent upon Martu being able to use fire across the landscape in ways consistent with those of their long history. Unlike nearly all hunter-gatherer populations in other regions of the world, Martu in remote desert communities face no conflicts of interest with neighbors about burning; the region contains no pastoralism, no agriculture, no non-Aboriginal settlements, no developed infrastructure aside from their own communities, and very few tourists. Martu employ fire not to construct landscapes but as a hunting tool used in particular ecological contexts for particular kinds of animal prey.

FORAGING AND FIRE

Contemporary foraging among Martu is an important component of a hybrid economy (Altman 2010) that includes some wage labor, arts and crafts production, and social security payments. On any given day, 23 percent of community members are out foraging (Scelza et al. 2014). Contemporary foraging practices are shaped primarily by the search for five staple animal prey: hill kangaroos (*kirti-kirti*, 24.7 percent of total production by whole weight), bustards (*kipara, Ardeotis australis*, 24.1 percent), sand monitors (*parnajarlpa*, 19.1 percent), large varanids (*maruntu* and *yalapara*, 2.7 percent), and feral house cats (1.5 percent; see Bird et al. 2009; Bliege Bird and Bird 2008; Bliege Bird et al. 2008; Codding et al. 2011; Veth and Walsh 1988).

Including all foraged foods, the average Martu forager acquires 2,506 kcal per foraging day. By far, the majority of daily calories come from sand-plain hunting, which targets mainly sand monitors. This primarily female activity provides an average of 73.2 percent of the daily foraging income, with a standard deviation across 368 camp days of 35 percent. Mean per capita harvest sizes per hunting day average 1,298 ± 1,251 kcal per person. Sand monitor is a staple resource primarily because harvests are reliable: out of 368 camp days, sand monitors were hunted on 166. There were only eight days when no hunter acquired any sand monitor, an additional twenty-one days when per capita returns were lower than 400 kcal per person per day, and thirty-two days when returns were greater than 2,000 kcal per person per day. But although sand monitor hunting is consistent, the chance of a very large harvest is low: daily returns exceeded 4,000 kcal per person only on two hunting days.

Contrasting with sand monitor hunting is kangaroo hunting, which is primarily a male activity. Men hunted kangaroos on seventy-two camp days, providing 2,127 ± 6,622 kcal per person per hunting day. On fifty-eight of those days, no one acquired any kangaroos, and on ten days the per capita return was greater than 4,000 kcal per person per day.

Sand monitor hunting is economically important both because it is reliable on a daily basis and because harvest sizes are predictable: the longer a forager hunts, the larger the harvest, which means harvests can be adjusted to need on a daily basis (Bliege Bird and Bird 2008; Codding et al. 2010). Variance discounting models show that sand monitor return rates have a higher utility than kangaroo returns for a forager who values meat primarily for its consumption benefits (as opposed to the benefits of sharing, storing, or sociopolitical gain;

Jones et al. 2013). Within the context of a hybrid economy, which includes reliance on purchased goods, sand monitor hunting responds to economic scarcity: more women hunt more often when money is short (Scelza et al. 2014). Hunting monitor lizards is also an important way for women, especially postmenopausal women, to invest in their grandchildren and other dependents (Bliege Bird and Bird 2008; Scelza 2009; Scelza and Bliege Bird 2008).

In order to achieve such high and consistent returns, foragers need to locate suitable hunting habitat. Burrowing prey are primarily found in long unburned spinifex grasslands on sand plains, dunes, and pockets of sand in upland areas. Foraging efficiency in the hunt for burrowing prey is constrained by den visibility, so foragers either target spinifex in the early stages of recovery following fire (early successional habitat) or set a broadcast fire in long unburned patches. Sand monitors enter a period of near dormancy during the cool dry season (May to September), remaining mostly underground and living off stored fat; most hunting fires are set at that time. Summer-season hunts when varanids are mobile target early successional habitats with good track visibility, to avoid the need to dig the animals out. Hunters (more often women) work alone or in small cooperative groups, probing areas around burrows with long, narrow digging sticks to search for the resting chambers, which lie 10–20 cm below the ground.

Hunters set broadcast fires primarily in the winter season because they significantly increase sand monitor foraging returns. In the winter, when pursuits involve mainly den spotting, foragers gain 348 kcal per hour of search and pursuit within late-successional patches of regrowth and 1,613 kcal per hour if they burn those patches (table 9.1). In the summer, when foragers pursue lizards by tracking, access to ground burned earlier in the season is critical: returns drop with more plant cover as tracks become more difficult to see. Although foragers do some burning when lizards are active, summer burns tend to be more difficult to control at the beginning of the season, when fuels are dry; more difficult to spread at the end of the season, when fuels are wet; and costlier to hunt in, as new fires drive lizards into their deep summer dens, which require extensive digging at high energetic cost. However, summer burns can be a fallback strategy if foragers are unable to find decent patches of early successional vegetation to hunt in. They can also return to a summer burn a few days later, when lizards have emerged from their dens to hunt again on the surface. The number of fires lit in regions where people are hunting cannot be predicted simply from where people travel on the landscape, nor by whether or not they are foraging in

Table 9.I. Least-squares mean and return rates by habitat type and season.

Type of Pursuit	Successional Stage	LS kcal/h	Mean SE	N	Lower 95% CI	Upper 95% CI
Tracking in summer	Early	1,950	412	14	1,084	2,816
	Mid	369	491	9	−636	1,374
	Late	96	602	5	−1,111	1,304
Den spotting in winter	Early	343	513	8	−694	1,381
	Mid	725	367	41	−101	1,552
	Late	348	380	32	−488	1,185
	Burn late	1,613	332	61	829	2,398

Note: LS means derived from LS regression mixed model (forager random effect): $n = 170$ patches, model $r^2 = 0.325$, Pursuit Type (successional stage) effect test, F-ratio = 7.31, $p < 0.0001$. Return rates calculated as kcal/h in search and pursuit within each patch type.

a location, but only by the amount of time they devote to sand monitor hunting (Bliege Bird et al. 2008).

FIRE AND THE LANDSCAPE

These consistent and high returns from sand monitor hunting are dependent not just on the immediate use of fire, but on the history of fire and how it— along with other Martu subsistence activities—has shaped the structure of environmental variation.

The main fuel burned in desert sand-plain fires is highly flammable hummock grasses (mainly *Triodia schinzii* and *T. basedowii*) that dominate the sand-plain and sand-dune regions of the arid interior of Australia, covering 86 percent of the total land area. Spinifex hummock grass coexists with a dispersed overstory of shrubs and trees, mainly acacias (*A. pachycarpa*, *A. ligulata*, and *Cassia* spp.), with mulga (*A. aneura*) woodlands on lateritic uplands and clay-dominated soils (2.4 percent) and *Eucalyptus* (mainly *E. victrix* and *E. microtheca*) in watercourse margins and floodplains (3.2 percent). Spinifex is slow growing but an excellent competitor, and it slowly crowds out most other species by about seven to ten years after a fire, depending upon rainfall (Burrows and Christensen 1990).

As burned ground recovers from fires, different plants and animals recolonize and grow at different rates. Martu classify these colonization and growth phases into five successional stages defined by their utility to humans and other animals. *Nyurnma* is a freshly burned area. *Waru-waru* is an early successional stage characterized by the presence of *yukuri*, or green shoots of new and diverse growth, which provides high-quality food for browsing and grazing animals. *Nyukura* is a mid-successional stage reached at approximately one to three years following rain, characterized by high densities of edible seed grasses, flowering shrubs, acacia seedlings, fruit, and other edible plants that are high-quality foods for gramnivores and frugivores. Nyukura gradually fades into the late successional stage of *manguu*, or mature spinifex, as the slowly growing spinifex begins to crowd out edible plants, about five to seven years following the first rain. Manguu is important for animals that depend on woody shrubs and trees for nectar and seeds as well as shelter from predators. As the spinifex ages to *kunarka*, it begins to die in the center. Generally, only manguu and kunarka contain enough fuel to feed a broadcast fire.

Patches in different stages of regeneration following fire are associated with different community compositions (Latz and Green 1995; Pianka and Goodyear 2012). Plants like *Solanum diversiflorum* and other bush tomatoes, along with seed grasses like woolybutt (*Eragrostis eriopoda*) are most abundant in early and early to mid-successional stages (one to four years after fire), whereas late successional (ten or more years) shrubs and trees and spinifex grass increase in density over time (Parker et al. n.d.).

Animals, too, show differential fire responses: some animals move away after a fire, whereas others move in. Bustards come to freshly burned ground to feed and also enjoy the *Solanum* fruits so abundant in mid-successional patches. Termite specialists such as *Ctenophorus nuchalis*, the netted dragon, a 50–100 g slow-moving lizard, are more prevalent in recent burns, while *Ctenophorus isolepis*, which requires mature spinifex for refuge and thermoregulation, is more abundant in long unburned areas (Letnic et al. 2004; Masters 1996; Pianka and Goodyear 2012). Large insects may also show differential fire responses: scorpions may be larger and more abundant in mid-successional patches (Smith and Morton 1990), and large beetles may be disadvantaged by fire (Blanche et al. 2001). Thus, many different patches at different postfire stages (a fire mosaic) together make up a good indicator of both animal and plant species diversity at the landscape scale.

Sand monitor hunting is dependent upon an anthropogenic fire mosaic, which is created primarily through several years' worth of hunting fires. Hunters use spot fires to pursue feral cats, bustards, and large monitors, but broadcast

Table 9.2. Fire size and nearest neighbor distances in lightning fire–dominated and Martu fire–dominated landscapes.

	Median Size (ha)	Mean Size (ha)	Distance between Fires (m)	Number of Fires
WET SEASON				
Lightning	46.9	1,910 ± 325	5,400 ± 3,594	647
Martu	4.1	326 ± 83	1,248 ± 874	1,342
DRY SEASON				
Lightning	16.9	6,255 ± 3,099	12,832 ± 15,589	163
Martu	3.3	109 ± 41	661 ± 335	2,514

fires set for hunting sand monitors have huge ecological effects across the landscape. In two Martu communities, Parnngurr and Punmu, anywhere from 60 to 240 individuals hunt. Hunters set a broadcast fire once every three to four days on average, producing about 360 hunting fires per year of about 100 ha in size across an area of nearly 500,000 ha (Bliege Bird et al. 2012a).

The hunting fires that people light are very different from lightning fires, which dominate this seasonally dry and climatically variable landscape. A comparison of landscapes marked by Martu hunting fires and those marked by lightning fires reveals that hunting fires are smaller and closer together: Martu hunting fires average 969 ± 723 m apart, whereas nearest neighbor distances in the lightning regime average 8.93 ± 11.41 km (Bliege Bird et al. 2012a). Seasonally, both mean and median hunting fire sizes are significantly smaller than lightning fires (table 9.2).

Hunting fires are smaller for a number of reasons. First, Martu light fires mostly under conditions when fire size can be more easily controlled—where downwind firebreaks are nearby, when winds are more consistent throughout the day, and when temperatures are lower. Under conditions unfavorable to the control of fire, hunting fires tend to be larger. Lightning fires are large because they tend to start mainly when temperatures are high and winds are unpredictable. The size of lightning fires is limited mainly by the amount and contiguity of fuels, as measured by antecedent cumulative rainfall, which does not predict the size of Martu hunting fires (Bliege Bird et al. 2012a). When the grass is thick, Martu simply light a larger number of smaller fires because thick grass reduces lizard-hunting search efficiency. Because burned vegetation requires several years to regrow thickly enough to fuel a fire again, the small, patchy fires set throughout the landscape by Martu hunters have the incidental effect of creating firebreaks that prevent the spread of large lightning fires during seasons when they threaten.

Martu fires are also smaller because people light fires within social contexts as well as ecological and climatic ones. While the incentive to burn is supplied by the immediate boost to foraging returns, many of the disincentives to burn are socially imposed. Despite the fact that among Martu burning is an important signal of ownership and a demonstration of one's rights to manage Country, burning without foraging is considered wasteful and costly: it destroys resources others might want to collect and exposes animal dens to predators such as dingoes, who also take advantage of fire clearings to hunt. Being able to control a fire is important because the rights to burn Country for hunting are held collectively, but individual hunters are responsible for fires that burn areas to which they do not hold such rights. A hunter whose fire shifts with the wind and threatens a sacred site in an area where his or her burning rights are deemed less than legitimate is subject to severe punitive procedures governed by the collective body of owners, which today involve ritualized physical punishment and monetary compensation.

A Martu fire regime produces a landscape significantly different from one that is burned primarily by lightning ignitions. In 1953, when several Martu bands still lived nomadically in the region, aerial photography taken near Kurta Kurta Soak revealed a tight vegetation mosaic created from 135 small fires that had burned that year or the year prior in an area of 119,236 ha. In this region, an area of sand dunes to the south of Karlamilyi River and to the west of Kurta Kurta Soak, fire size averaged 52.7 ± 118 (33–73, 95 percent CI) ha, with a median size of 15.9 ha. Only 14 percent of all fires were above 100 ha in size, and only 1 percent were above 1,000 ha. Today, the Kurta Kurta region is dominated by lightning fires and is not under a Martu fire regime. Between 2000 and 2009 the region had only 137 fires in total, averaging 798 ± 3,568 (604–992, 95 percent CI) ha, with a median size of 11 ha. Twenty-four percent of all fires were above 100 ha in size, and 9 percent were above 1,000 ha. The coefficient of variation in fire size doubled from 225 to 446.

The fire regime has shifted from one of small, consistent fires to one of quite variable fire size, with a mean skewed by extremely large fires (>3000 ha in size) that occur every few years. Similar patterns have been observed in other regions of the desert following Aboriginal population loss (Burrows et al. 2006). However, other regions visible in the 1953 aerial photography show no significant differences in mean fire size or number of fires per year compared to the present day. The Yulpul region (figure 9.2) has been intensively hunted ever since Martu returned to Parnngurr in 1984, and mean fire size in that region today is not significantly different. Between 1952 and 1953, there were 227 fires averaging 40.1 ± 218 (12–69, 95 percent CI) ha, with a median of 6.3 ha; 7.5 percent of all fires were above 100 ha (in a region covering 138,493 ha). Between 2000 and 2009, Yulpul saw 1,279 fires averaging 88 ± 706 (25–151, 95 percent CI) ha, with a median of 3.2 ha and 6.7 percent of all fires above 100 ha. While the coefficient of variation in mean fire size has increased, from 543 to 798, it has not increased to the same extent seen in the Kurta Kurta region.

Anthropogenic fires not only restructure the distribution of successional mosaics and attendant vegetation, but also the distribution of animals. Transect surveys show that sand monitor density is increased in regions with greater environmental heterogeneity. The higher the density of habitat edges—contrasts between new burns, regrowing vegetation, and old growth—the higher the density of sand monitors (Bliege Bird et al. 2013). Because Martu hunting fires increase the density of such contrasts, the mean percentage of plots with lizards present in unburned hummock grassland increases with human use. That is, lizards are more abundant in landscapes where they are more intensively hunted. This increase in abundance, in turn, increases Martu hunting returns. Mean returns of sand monitors are 1.6 times higher in more heavily hunted regions than they are in regions that are rarely visited by Martu hunters, and success rates are six times higher. An increase in patch diversity from one to two successional stages encountered per hour more than doubles foraging returns, from 541 ± 827 to 1,256 ± 675 kcal per hour (Bliege Bird et al. 2013).

The increase in lizard density with human use of landscapes is likely a function both of improvements to habitat through burning, which reduce the movement costs of foraging and predation and increase the availability of high-ranked prey, and of the effects of human predation on species that eat lizards. Monitor lizards in smaller-scale fire mosaics may be able to switch more easily to preying upon alternative high-ranked species in neighboring patches, thus increasing their overall return rates within the habitat. Increases in sand monitor density under higher human hunting pressure may be caused by interference-related competition (or direct predation) between humans and other predators of sand monitors, particularly the larger monitor lizards, which are actively hunted by

5km   1954: 19±46 ha   1973: 6255 ha   2000: 15±36 ha

Figure 9.2. Recent fires (white) in a subset of the Yulpul region: in 1954, when Martu were nomadic foragers; in 1973, when all Martu had left the region seven years previously; and in 2000, when Martu had been hunting and burning since their return in 1985. Remote sensing analysis performed by Rebecca Bliege Bird.

Martu. *V. giganteus*, the perentie, is the largest varanid in Australia and reaches 2 m in length and 17 kg or more in weight (Pianka 1995).

Martu hunting fires also shape population distributions of other desert species that benefit from access to a more diverse set of successional stages at smaller spatial scales. Hill kangaroos (*Macropus robustus*) are more likely to be found in early successional patches characterized by newly emerging green shoots and in mid-successional patches, where they are able to target fruiting and herbaceous browse (Codding et al. 2014). Hill kangaroo scat density is linked significantly to successional-stage heterogeneity: scat counts increase both with remotely sensed measures of successional richness and with on-the-ground observations of successional edge density.

Characteristics of many of the animal species that disappeared or are in decline suggest that they, too, may have been advantaged by Martu fire mosaics. Hare-wallabies are browsers that rely on plants in many different successional stages and require mature spinifex hummocks for nesting and predator protection. Prior to the 1960s, they were abundant and widespread throughout the spinifex sand plains and were hunted frequently. The continued persistence of the population has been argued to be dependent on continued patch mosaic burning for access to early successional habitat adjacent to mature spinifex (Lundie-Jenkins 1993; Lundie-Jenkins et al. 1993a; Lundie-Jenkins et al. 1993b). The brushtail possum, which formerly was one of the most abundant small mammal prey for human hunters, seems to have been able to persist in more marginal desert regions only where its habitat, riparian eucalyptus woodlands, has been protected from extensive fire through Aboriginal patch mosaic burning (Kerle et al. 1992). In addition, access to a variety of successional stages appears to be important for possums, as they seem to prefer the same high-ranked early successional *Solanum* fruits that people do (Pickett et al. 2005).

THE SOCIAL CONTEXT SUSTAINING HUNTING

The landscape-level effects of fire sustain Martu social interactions via food sharing. Fire shapes a more productive anthropogenic landscape, but embedded in this productivity is a tradeoff: the more one acquires, the more one must give away. A sand monitor hunting bout is followed by sharing with other non-cooperating individuals 77 percent of the time (69/90 acquisitions; see Bliege Bird et al. 2012b for details of the sharing database). Hunters share whenever harvest size is over about 500 g; the average size of an unshared harvest is

401 ± 186 g, and a shared one averages 1,309 ± 764 g. Sharing proceeds with each hunter distributing her harvest (after having divided it with her cooperation partner, if any) to all those sitting around the same hearth at the *ngurra* (camp or hearth), not just those who were unsuccessful, but those who were successful as well (Bliege Bird et al. 2012b). Women exchange lizards with other hunters, as if reluctant to consume their own, not in the form of immediate dyadic exchanges, in which two individuals pass each other lizards simultaneously, but in the form of sequential one-way distributions from each hunter to each member of the ngurra. Women must place their trust in the other members of the ngurra, that if they give up their own lizards, others will do so as well (a trust that is usually, but not always, rewarded, especially for better hunters, as we will describe). This form of reciprocity is not dyadic: a woman may receive from someone she did not even give to, and the goal is not to repay the hunter for her gift, but to ensure a roughly even distribution of meat among all consumers.

Shares of meat are distributed in ways that defuse the "power of the gift" (Mauss 1954). This power is muted in several ways typical of "immediate return economies" (Woodburn 1982) that disassociate the hunter with ownership of the food he or she has acquired, create egalitarian distributions of economic goods, promote tolerance of free riding, encourage cooperation, and discourage contingency in the sharing of food. First, any prey regardless of species that is larger than about 1–2 kg (including feral cats, perenties, and other small animals that can reach this size) is routinely given to another individual to cook and distribute. Second, with the temptation to benefit one's self removed by lack of control over distribution, hunters receive no more than anyone else in the distribution of prey they have acquired (Bird and Bliege Bird 2010; Bliege Bird et al. 2012b). Those who acquire more than everyone else do not predictably benefit from their overproduction; in fact, better hunters share a larger proportion of their harvest and do so routinely (Bliege Bird et al. 2012b). Even for prey smaller than 1 kg, which is usually distributed by the hunter, the amount shared is a strongly linear function of the amount acquired: 89 percent of the variability in amount shared is predicted by amount acquired ($p < 0.0001$, $n = 153$ individuals). The proportion of a harvest given away increases with harvest size as well (figure 9.3). The successful small-game hunter does eat more but not at the expense of everyone else; a very successful hunter increases not only her own consumption portions, but those of everyone else at the ngurra equally (Bird and Bliege Bird 2010). Third, the power of the gift is also muted by sharing the opportunity to give. We have previously shown that better hunters

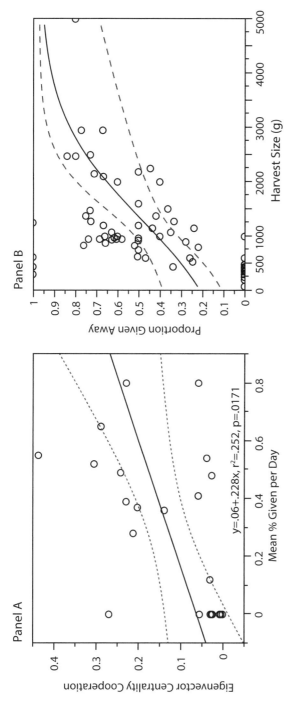

Figure 9.3. Panel A: The proportion of a sand monitor hunter's harvest (whole weight) given to other dinner-camp members (with whom one did not cooperate). The best-fit line is estimated by a generalized linear model with a binomial logit link function, $\beta = 0.001$, $\chi^2 = 9.61$, $p = 0.0019$. The cluster of points at 0 and 1 represent harvests in which nothing was shared (most 500 g or less) and all was shared, respectively. While few harvests in this sample ($n = 153$ individuals in sand monitor hunting camps) were larger than 3 kg, proportions shared likely reach an asymptote at around 80–90 percent above about 4–5 kg. Kangaroo harvests, which are routinely above 20 kg, average 90 percent shared. Panel B: Sharing following cooperative sand monitor hunts ($n = 168$ cooperative, 226 solitary hunts) reveals that those who share more generously, that is, have a higher mean proportion of their acquisition given away to others, are also those who have higher centrality in the cooperative hunting network—they are more cooperative and cooperate more with other cooperative people.

cooperate more than expected (Bliege Bird et al. 2012b). They cooperate and split the resulting harvest evenly among group members, even though disparities in hunter ability or effort mean that better hunters tend to end up subsidizing the poorer ones, who contribute less to the common pot. But the better hunter has given the poorer hunter the opportunity to give, in effect sharing social capital and defusing the tensions that arise from being the "tall poppy."

The costs sustained by the better hunters who eat little, share most, and cooperate extensively with poor hunters are compensated by the social benefits they receive. Martu say that the benefit of producing is the happiness created through sharing and kinship ties with people who are not necessarily closely related (*pukurrpa*). Although we cannot measure pukurrpa, we can measure the social networks of interaction—relationships of trust and cooperation that build family ties—that are created through sharing. Those who are more generous on average have higher centrality scores in the cooperative hunting network, meaning they cooperate more with more others who are also cooperative (see figure 9.2; see also Bliege Bird and Power 2015). More generous sharers are thus able to create a social network of strong ties between connected individuals. One may thus pay a cost to cooperate with a poor hunter, but one cooperates with a poor hunter who is also a more generous hunter, willing to share her poor harvest evenly with her partner. The benefit better hunters gain from looking after others in this way is a position on the hierarchy of virtue, rather than material accumulation (Bliege Bird et al. 2012b). Better hunters, *mirtilya*, signal their disinterest in pecuniary gain in order to convince others that they really do have the best interests of everyone at heart.

For Martu, the goal of mirtilya is generosity, and the benefits of generosity (pukurrpa) come indirectly from being at the center of a wide, cohesive social network. In sharing widely and generously, one supports an extensive family from which one might draw a variety of indirect benefits, including help in child rearing, protection from intergroup aggression, and improved health and well-being. Trust is also crucial in garnering support for meting out ritualized punishments, retaliating against sorcery, defending rights to land, and gaining access to higher levels of ritual knowledge. Where "generosity is the main measure of a man's goodness" (Hiatt 1982:14), building and maintaining a reputation for virtue generates trust in many different dimensions of social life. Foragers share a greater percentage of their harvest the larger it is, feeding and holding those who cannot or will not forage for themselves. This is how Martu gain a measure of social prestige and become respected as those strong in the

Law: by disengaging with property (Tonkinson 1988) and fostering egalitarian material relationships in the "holding" of Country and family—by living the Dreaming (Bird and Bliege Bird 2010).

Conclusions: Why Martu Still Hunt and Gather

As Codding and colleagues (chapter 8, this volume) describe, the social, ecological, and metaphysical landscapes exist simultaneously for Martu, inextricably intertwined in a complex web of interaction. Sand monitor hunting is integral to the maintenance of Martu social networks and ultimately sustains both kinship and cooperation and structures gender relations. Martu today rely on hunting and gathering because it is economically efficient (Codding et al., chapter 8, this volume) and because hunting supplies both social and ritual benefits through sharing and the holding of Country and family. However, hunting and gathering is possible only within an environment where small animals flourish, which requires the intervention of human fire. Fire makes women's hunting highly productive, increasing both predictability and return rates in the hunting of small animals, which gives women some measure of economic autonomy and enhances their importance in the subsistence economy. The foraging benefits supplied by fire-maintained habitats are invested into social relationships via food sharing. Fire sustains the generosity of the mirtilya, supports the kinship that emerges from generosity, and fosters stronger social ties between individuals, generating trust and facilitating cooperation. Anthropogenic fire links the realms of the economic, the social, the ritual, and the ecological.

The act of setting a broadcast fire not only binds family together, it also resonates with ecological implications. Martu serve as trophic regulators, both in their hunting of smaller predators, which prevents overexploitation of many prey species, and in their fire-mediated disturbance of plant communities. Their fires have widespread effects on the ecosystem, creating small-scale habitats that prevent the spread of very large fires and buffer small ground-dwelling mammals from both the effects of climate-driven fire and the heavy predation that ensues when animals are exposed in burnt areas. Martu burning creates more and smaller patches of unburned habitat that reduce the distance small animals must travel between food and shelter. In areas where traditional owners have returned to their homelands and actively hunt, burn, and share food, there is evidence of increased availability and diversity of habitat niches that favor endemic species, a reduction in climate-related variability in fire size and predation risk, and an increase in density of critical plant and animal species that support both people and many other animals. Productive foraging and the egalitarian social relationships that underpin a foraging economy require that Martu continue to hunt and gather, burn and share, as they have for generations. That Martu are able to continue to maintain at least a part-time foraging economy today is due to some extent to their ability to burn: fire makes hunting and gathering sustainable in the western Australian desert.

Cross-Cultural Demographic and Social Variables for Contemporary Foraging Populations

KAREN L. KRAMER, NICHOLAS BLURTON JONES, REBECCA BLIEGE BIRD,

BRIAN F. CODDING, JAMES E. COXWORTH, RUSSELL D. GREAVES,

ROBERT K. HITCHCOCK, KAREN D. LUPO, AND GEORGE W. WENZEL

Introduction

This appendix provides information on demographic and social variables for the foraging groups discussed in this book. Each variable was selected to provide a quantified perspective of the key themes and topics discussed in the preceding chapters. These codings are provisional and are not intended to capture the complexity of some of the social and cultural variables, but to give readers a sense of relative context.

Variable Descriptions

Group: preferred autodenomination
Country: modern nation-state of residence
GDP: gross domestic product per capita, a measure of national economic status
  (figures come from https://www.cia.gov/library/publications/resources/
  the-world-factbook/rankorder/2004rank.html, accessed October 2013)
Period: years or decades to which codes refer

EDUCATION

Traditional skills: are children trained in traditional skills?
  Y = yes
  N = no

Schools: do children have access to education?

    0 = no access to education

    1 = access to lower school

    2 = access to lower–middle school

    3 = access to lower–upper school

    4 = access to lower higher education

Literacy: are children (younger than twenty) literate?

    0 = no literacy

    1 = minority (under 50 percent) of children literate

    2 = majority (over 50 percent) of children literate

First language: what is a child's (younger than twenty) first language?

    T = traditional/native language

    N = regional/national language

National language fluency: do children (younger than twenty) speak the language of the nation-state in which they live?

    0 = do not speak national/regional language

    1 = minority (under 50 percent) of children are fluent

    2 = majority (over 50 percent) of children are fluent

LIFE HISTORY

e_0: life expectancy at birth, combines males and females, population value if available; otherwise

    H = over seventy

    M = fifty to seventy

    L = under fifty

Infant mortality: infant deaths (from birth to age one) per one thousand live births if available; otherwise

    H = over 10 percent of live births

    M = 5–10 percent of live births

    L = under 5 percent of live births

Child mortality: child deaths (ages one to five) per one thousand births if available; otherwise

    H = over 10 percent of live births

    M = 5–10 percent of live births

    L = under 5 percent live births

Preference for child's sex:

    T = traditional

IM = increase in male bias

IF = increase in female bias

Polygynous marriage

    0 = not present

    C = common (over 20 percent of marriages)

    UC = uncommon (under 20 percent of marriages)

Female age at marriage: age at first marriage, average age in parentheses if known; otherwise

    1 = under twelve years (or before puberty)

    2 = twelve to fifteen years (i.e., at puberty)

    3 = sixteen to nineteen years (after puberty)

    4 = over eighteen (i.e., as adults)

Male age at marriage: age at first marriage, average age in parentheses if known; otherwise

    1 = under twelve years (or before puberty)

    2 = twelve to fifteen years (i.e., at puberty)

    3 = sixteen to nineteen years (after puberty)

    4 = over eighteen (i.e., as adults)

Male/female contribution to subsistence base:

    T = traditional (unchanged)

    IM = increase in male participation

    IF = increase in female participation

HEALTH CARE

Contraception: is modern contraception available?

    0 = no contraception available

    1 = contraception available

Bottle feeding: are baby bottles used to feed children?

    Y = yes

    N = no

Access to health services: are health-care facilities available?

    0 = no health services available

    1 = available but seldom or never used (e.g., for emergencies or every couple years)

    2 = available and occasionally used (about once a year)

    3 = available and regularly used (>once a year)

Distance to health services:

    n/a = no health services available

    1 = 0–10 km

    2 = <100 km

    3 = >100 km

Babies born:

    0 = at home

    1 = in clinic/hospital

EFFECTS OF EXTERNAL FORCES

Use of surnames:

    Y = yes

    N = no

Increase in monogamy:

    Y = yes

    N = no

Regional status: what is the status of the foragers within the regional hierarchy?

    H = high

    M = medium

    L = low

Female autonomy: what is female status, relative to males, within the foraging group?

    E = equality

    NE = nonequality

Change in female autonomy: has there been a change in female status in recent years?

    0 = stayed the same

    I = increased

    D = decreased

Legal system: has there been a change in the local forager legal system or means by which individuals may be sanctioned?

    T = traditional

    NT = nontraditional/imposed

NGO presence: do foragers have access to NGO programs and funds?

    0 = no presence

    1 = presence

Aid: is outside aid available?

    0 = none

    1 = receive monetary aid

    2 = receive monetary and/or other aid

STRATIFICATION AND LEADERSHIP

Intrapopulation variability in somatic wealth: within the forager population, are there individual differences in wealth?

    H = high

    M = medium

    L = low

Change in variation: has there been a recent change in wealth?

    0 = stayed the same

    D = decreased

    I = increased

Variation in wealth:

    T = traditional

    NT = emerging class differences

Leadership: what is the local form of leadership?

    T = traditional

    NT = nontraditional

Headman: what is the local form of headman?

    T = traditional

    NT = paid spokesperson from outside

Table A.I. Cross-cultural demographic and social variables for contemporary foraging populations.

Group	Country	GDP (dollars)[a]	Period	Traditional Skills	Education			
					Schools	Literacy	First Language	National Language Fluency
Bardi	Australia	43,300	2008–2013	Y	4	2	T	2
Martu	Australia	67,463	2000–2010	Y	1	1	T	2
Inuit	Canada	51,964	1971–2014	Y	4 (mandatory)	2	T	2
Bofi	CAR	333	1999–2005	Y	0	0	T	1
G/ui G//ana	Botswana	73,150	1999–2013	Y	1	1	T	1
Ju/'hoansi	Namibia	5,693	1990–2013	Y	1	1	T	1
Hadza	Tanzania	912	1985–2000	Y	3 (sporadic)	0	T	2
Pumé	Venzuela	13,200	1990–2007	Y	0	0	T	0

Life History

Group	e₀ at Birth	Infant Mortality	Child Mortality	Preference for Child's Sex	Polygynous Marriage	Female Age at Marriage	Male Age at Marriage	Adult Contribution to Subsistence Base
Bardi	67.7[b]	7.49[c]	L[d]	T	0	4	4	T
Martu	60.0–75.0	8–15	~5.0	T	UC	3 (15–20)	3 (15–20)	T
Inuit	mid-60s	~40	—	T	0	3	3	T
Bofi	L	H	H	T	UC	2	2	T
G/ui G//ana	32.0	300	H (38% don't survive to age 15)	T	UC	2	3	T
Ju/'hoansi	51.0	200	H (45 % don't survive to age 15)	T	UC	3	4	T
Hadza	32.7	218.3	138.4	T	UC	3 (18.5)	4 (25)	T
Pumé	30.0	346	H (45% don't survive to age 15)	T	UC	2 (14.5)	2	T

Health Care

Group	Contraception	Bottle Feeding	Access to Health Services	Distance to Health Services	Babies Born
Bardi	1	Y	3	1	1
Martu	1	N	3	1 for clinic and 2 for hospital	1
Inuit	0	Y	3	3	1
Bofi	0	N	1	1	0
G/ui G//ana	1	N	2	3	0
Ju/'hoansi	1	N	2	2	0
Hadza	0	N	1	1	0
Pumé	0	N	0	n/a	0

Effects of External Forces

Group	Use of Surnames	Increase in Monogamy	Regional Status	Female Autonomy	Change in Female Autonomy	Legal System	NGO Presence	Aid
Bardi	Y	Y	—	NE	0	NT	1	2
Martu	Y	Y	L	E	0	T + NT	1	2
Inuit	Y	Y	H	NE	1	NT	0	0
Bofi	N	Y	L	E	0	T	1	0
G/ui G//ana	N	N	L	E	0	T	1	0
Ju/'hoansi	Y	N	L	E	D	NT	1	1
Hadza	N (just beginning)	N	L	E	0	T + NT	1 (sporadic)	0
Pumé	N	N	L	E	0	T	0	0

Stratification and Leadership

Group	Intrapopulation Variability in Somatic Wealth	Change in Variation	Variation in Wealth	Leadership	Headman
Bardi	M	I	NT	NT	T
Martu	M	D	T + NT	T + NT	T + NT
Inuit	H	I	NT	T + NT	T
Bofi	L	0	T	T	T
G/ui G//ana	M	I	NT	T	T
Ju/'hoansi	M	I	NT	T	T
Hadza	L	0	T	T	T
Pumé	L	0	T	T	T

[a] GDP taken from World Bank website: http://data.worldbank.org/indicator/NY.GDP.PCAP.CD, accessed May 23, 2015.

[b] Reported by Australian Bureau of Statistics for indigenous residents of Western Australia.

[c] Rate reported by Australian Bureau of Statistics for all indigenous children ages 0–1.

[d] Rate reported by Australian Bureau of Statistics for all indigenous children ages 1–4.

Economic Activities of Twenty-First-Century Foraging Populations

RUSSELL D. GREAVES, KAREN L. KRAMER, DOUGLAS W. BIRD,
REBECCA BLIEGE BIRD, NICHOLAS BLURTON JONES, ADAM H. BOYETTE,
BRIAN F. CODDING, JAMES E. COXWORTH, KIRK ENDICOTT,
MAXIMILIEN GUEZE, THOMAS N. HEADLAND, BARRY S. HEWLETT, KIM HILL,
ROBERT K. HITCHCOCK, THOMAS S. KRAFT, RICHARD B. LEE,
KAREN D. LUPO, LUCENTEZZA NAPITUPULU, MARIA SAPIGNOLI,
DAVE N. SCHMITT, IVAN TACEY, BRAM TUCKER, VIVEK VENKATARAMAN,
GEORGE W. WENZEL, POLLY WIESSNER, AND BRIAN M. WOOD

Introduction

Table B.1 is designed to provide recent data on a number of hunter-gatherer populations in the twenty-first century. The data were collected by researchers from 2000 onward and serve two primary purposes. First, they provide updated information on the subsistence and technological behaviors of many groups who still are frequently characterized as using practices from the mid-twentieth century, some of which are thought to be remnants of older practices. The second, and perhaps most important, goal of this table is to identify how populations that still engage in hunting and gathering have adopted new practices and technologies that keep foraging a viable economic activity in the modern world.

During the SAR seminar, we discussed the ways that many groups strategically have adopted and employed a range of modern opportunities that derive from interactions with outsiders and the global market as it reaches these locations, demonstrating both the dynamic, innovative flexibility of hunting and gathering and the viability of older practices. Some practices (e.g., the adoption of specific cultivated plants, novel hunting methods, the collection of resources with market value, new technologies) actually extend the ability of hunter-gatherers to continue relying on significant amounts of wild resources. Other behaviors (e.g., changing residential and foraging mobility, wage work, trade and exchange opportunities) have substituted for past foraging activities but may be successfully (or not) combined with continued hunting and gathering.

The table provides a range of quantitative and qualitative data that present a fresh outlook on the changing dynamics of hunting and gathering. This important perspective contrasts with older views that hunter-gatherers represent remnant economic practices from the human evolutionary past. All past foragers periodically adopted new practices, technologies, and interactions with and from other populations. The pace of those changes has certainly accelerated in the twentieth and twenty-first centuries. However, they also provide unique opportunities for us to examine how and why hunter-gatherers can or cannot adjust a range of social, subsistence, and labor behaviors to the economics of foraging, food production, work activities, or exchange and which wild resources may remain productive sources of their livelihoods.

Variable Descriptions

Group: preferred autodenomination
Ecology:
    Coastal (Tropical, High Latitude)
    Desert
    Forest
    Savanna
    Woodland

Land Tenure:
    Unprotected (UP) = Indigenous lands are not protected, and no recent efforts have been or are being made toward resolving this problem. The group may or may not recognize the issue of land protection.
    Secure (S) = Efforts have successfully resulted in protection of at least some portion of indigenous lands. Legal status is stable, although there may still be some internal or external conflicts regarding land tenure issues.
    Contested (C) = Some recent attempts have been made to establish a level of protection of indigenous lands. The process remains either unresolved or stalled, or no current efforts are being made. At least some members of the group recognize that efforts have been or could be directed toward resolving the issue.

Residence:

> Traditional = The settlement pattern is relatively similar to that either of periods before significant influence by outsiders or of relatively longstanding past with some structured interactions with outsiders (nomadic, semi-nomadic, seasonal shifts). Some architectural forms might have changed, but the overall pattern of architecture is similar or serves a similar purpose (e.g., temporary shades using metal laminate rather than leaves).

> Mixed = Some aspects of the residence pattern have changed in the relatively recent past, most likely due to effects of interaction with outsiders, settlement, or attraction of market items. However, noticeably "traditional" aspects of residence are still practiced (some seasonal mobility, analogous household membership, or pattern of household formation and fissioning is still practiced to some extent or by approximately half the community population). Architecture may or may not be significantly altered from past house forms.

> Settled = An altered residential pattern is based on the forced or negotiated settlement of populations and involves a significant if not total reduction in most mobility. Architecture may be significantly altered from past forms, and household organization may be different from that of the past.

Mobility:

> Foraging (Y/N) = Foraging activities still involve comparable daily, seasonal, or annual movements that are similar to past or "traditional" patterns. Alternatively, foraging mobility is no longer practiced (which implies a significant shift in an economy in which only very minimal hunting, fishing, or collecting of plant foods or of raw materials ever occurs anymore).

> Residential (Y/N) = Residential movements are/are not still similar to past or "traditional" patterns. The number of residential moves per year is included if known.

> # = The number of residential moves per year.

Traditional Foraging: This column identifies which aspects of behaviors that include foraging and subsistence technology still are practiced in a manner that can be considered similar to past foraging practices. These data represent a qualitative judgment about the overall pattern of how these behaviors compare with past behaviors and are not intended to track all changes (e.g., use of metal arrowpoints would still be considered "traditional" technology, as long as bows and arrows are still the dominant hunting implement). This evaluation identifies the ways that many recent foragers are changing or the ways they may retain or modify traditional practices. Two authors provided some relative percentages of these categories for this column.

Food (F) = Is a significant part of the diet still derived from foods that are hunted, fished, or gathered? This notation includes a qualitative assessment of whether the current combination of traditional and outside foods is somewhat or very analogous to circumstances before the availability of outside cultivated (i.e., rice, grain, farmed meat) or manufactured (flour from various grains, pasta, canned goods) foods.

Medicine (M) = Are some traditional medicines still used? Even with some access to or use of commercial medicines, the practice of some traditional medicine may signal how a society copes with irregular supply, high cost, or inaccessibility of Western medicine. It seems that all traditional societies are aware of Western medicine, its efficacy in treatment of various diseases or pain, and would want more access to it. This variable identifies whether (despite the awareness of commercial medicines) indigenous practices are still common enough to be observed during recent fieldwork.

Raw Material (RM) = Are traditional raw materials still collected in relative abundance? Even with some decrease in frequency due to access to and use of industrialized implements, this notation identifies whether groups are still making and using a significant amount of technology they construct from collected materials and whether wild (or cultivated or semicultivated) raw materials are still collected.

Technology (T) = Are traditional forms of technology still dominant? All groups now use new tools and technological systems, but many such tools (knives, machetes, other steel tools, clothing, flashlights, music devices) do not necessarily alter the overall technological system when they are present in a relatively low frequency or used in ways that do not alter dominant technological uses.

Foraged Foods Retained in Diet: This category is a rough evaluation of which foods that are obtained by hunting and gathering are still moderately common to very common dietary elements, independent of whether newer market foods are now a significant or infrequent contribution to the overall diet. New technologies (e.g., guns, vehicles [see column in table], flashlights, steel shovels, machetes, fishing line, commercial hooks) may have replaced some or many native technologies. However, the listed activities represent those that are still relatively similar to past subsistence activities (i.e., in their overall activity organization, frequency, return profile, and foraging role). Some foods may be accessed in traditional ways, but their exploitation is quite different because of other changes. If the role of the food is different in the overall diet or economy but the means of accessing it is analogous to past behavior, then it is considered as retained but identified as a novel foraging opportunity in the next column. If the activity represents behavior that is strikingly different from past gathering, fishing, or hunting, then it will not appear in this column.

Fish (F) = Fishing is still an important part of subsistence. If fishing has recently become more important (i.e., because of increased sedentism or loss of other foraging opportunities), it is coded as retained but may also be identified with a novel role in the following column. If fishing methods, technologies, frequencies, or catch sizes have dramatically altered (or become important in a group that did not fish much previously) in response to changes in the contributions of other foods in the diet or to market or trade opportunities, fishing is not coded as a retained behavior but noted in the novel foraging column. The approximate percentage contribution to the total diet is identified if known.

Honey (H) = Honey was or is an important dietary item, and people still commit time to pursuing this resource. As with other resources, if commercial or trade specialization on honey uses traditional methods but is much more frequent than under a more traditional foraging diet, it is identified as such in the following novel foraging activity column. The approximate percentage contribution to the total diet is identified if known.

Meat (M) = Most wild game meat is still coming from hunting rather than trade or purchase. If hunting is a relatively rare event, performed only by a much smaller number of individuals than in the past or is practiced in such an impoverished environment that it only provides a very infrequent contribution, then it is not identified as still coming from traditional foraging efforts. If hunting activities have significantly increased in response to an outside market or trade demand, it is coded as retained only if this commercialization involves an additional surplus of meat based on "traditional" technologies and hunting methods that still primarily bring in meat for community consumption. If the development of hunting schedules, parties, technologies, or techniques appear to be focused almost exclusively on trade and does not resemble subsistence hunting, then it is not coded as a traditional form of hunting but may be identified as a novel foraging opportunity in the next column. The approximate percentage contribution to the total diet is identified if known.

Plants (P) = Wild plant foods are still important in the diet. Even if fewer gathered plants are part of the diet, if most still come from collection they are identified as retained. If horticulture, agriculture, or trade has significantly supplanted the gathering of wild plant foods, then plants are not identified as retained in the diet through foraging. Some collected plants may now be collected in greater quantity because of changing subsistence economics or new trade or market opportunities. If such plants dominate current gathering behavior but are collected traditionally, and if their collection methods are still relatively similar to past activities, they are identified as retained. However, any novel context is noted in the next column. New plant targets and significantly novel collection technologies or activities that have developed are identified as a novel foraging opportunities in the next column. The approximate percentage contribution to the total diet is identified if known.

All = All of the above resources are still obtained primarily by relatively traditional foraging methods from subsistence-focused trips, and little additional detail is available.

Novel Foraging Activity: This category follows the coding parameters for the previous column (Foraged foods retained in diet) and identifies any novel contexts that involve exploitation of *wild* resources. N/A = no novel wild resource foraging activities.

Nonforaged Food Sources: These nonforaged foods are used in addition to whatever a mix of traditional or semitraditional foraging still produces. The percentage contribution to the total diet is identified if known.

Animals (A) = Some domesticated animals are raised, or fresh domesticated meat or animals for slaughter are purchased/acquired through trade. The adoption of a small number of chickens (or other small animals) is not included. For example, when only a small number of households have any chickens, coding animals as a source of nonforaged foods may misrepresent their importance and overall dietary contribution. If most households have even one chicken (or other small domesticate), then animals are coded as nonforaged foods. The organizational changes involved in having one or a very small number of cows, pigs, goats, or other larger animals will generally result in their presence being used to identify animals as a non-foraged food source. However, there will be cases in which such a situation only occurred infrequently or for a short period of time, without any long-term change in the adoption of domesticated animals as a food source. Such circumstances that seem to be situational but unsuccessful adoptions are not coded as representing the adoption of animals as nonforaged foods. Dogs are not included, unless they have become a novel food item. The approximate percentage contribution to the total diet is identified if known.

Crops (C) = Labor is invested in growing crops (at a horticultural or agri-cultural intensity level), or fresh agricultural foods are purchased/traded from others. The approximate percentage contribution to the total diet is identified if known.

Market (M) = This notation refers to any regular presence (beyond very infrequent contributions) of some purchased or exchanged market foods, meaning processed, nonfresh foods (i.e., flour, pasta, dried cere-als, canned goods, frozen foods, junk food, soda).

How Long? What is the relative estimated time period that the nonforaged foods in the previous column have been part of the diet of the group?

1 = 0–20 years ago

2 = 20–50 years ago

3 = >50 years ago

4 = prior to colonial contact

Source of Nonforaged Foods: Based on our evaluation of what nonforaged foods have become a part of the forager diet, these are the ways those resources have been incorporated into the economy.

Adoption (A) = The group of foragers has adopted the cultivation of crops or raising of domesticated animals, including cases in which the crop food or domesticated animals (except dogs) are long-term and potentially stable contributions as fallback or important foods that do not detract from the importance of overall foraging-based subsistence.

Labor (L) = Labor exchange, either for cash or direct payment in food goods, is the primary source for some nonforaged foods.

Trade/Exchange (T) = The source of a nonforaged food is primarily through the exchange of a commodity. This could be a traditionally collected food, handi-craft, wild raw material, or newer resource such as recently adopted crops or domesticated animals or their products traded for other food goods.

Aid (Aid) = The source of nonforaged foods is either commodities or cash that is used to purchase nonforaged foods provided by a government, NGO, religious, charity, or other outside source.

Commercial Foraging: This column complements information provided in the Foraged Foods Retained in Diet and Novel Foraging Activity categories.

Yes (Y) = Some foods, raw materials, medicines, or other natural products are extracted from the environment for commercial sale or exchange. This should include small-scale exchange (i.e., exchanges with one or two families of outsiders or with members of one's own ethnicity if not performed in a traditional/semitraditional fashion) if it is a frequent activity.

No (N) = There is no such opportunity or practice in the group.

Exchange Currency: This category identifies the form of any commodity that is exchanged by the forager group and may be used to obtain any nonforaged resources or outside goods that are the focus of trade or exchange relationships with outsiders. This variable does not simply identify established ("traditional") means of exchange, but ways that modern hunter-gatherers are accumulating the needed currency for newer exchange opportunities. As noted, some of these also are traditional ways of obtaining goods from others within or outside the foraging group. These currencies may also be part of economic changes and begin to dominate exchange relationships within a foraging group itself in ways distinct from past practices. Some of these activities (especially minor surplus, labor, or craft currencies) can be part of generalized or delayed reciprocities in hunter-gatherer groups. This variable focuses on commodity exchange and seeks to identify trade or exchange activities that result in a tangible, immediate, or clearly brokered "purchases" of some good or service.

Minor Surplus (MS) = This category identifies an excess that can be collected with minor additional effort during normal subsistence activities that support the forager community and distinguishes relatively minimal overproduction from the next category of systematic foraging for an exchange or market system.

Targeted surplus (TS) = Intentional overproduction structures acquisition activities so that the majority of returns are intended for exchange. Examples include bushmeat, particular plants as food or medicine, and large amounts of raw materials obtained with the primary goal of trading, selling, or exchanging them for other goods.

Cash (C) = Foragers use cash, obtained through any source, as the currency they employ to obtain nonforaged foods, tools, medicine, clothing, or any other goods or services. "Cash" relates primarily to exchanges outside the community; however, it may also signal changes in exchanges between members of a community or foraging ethnicity for resources that formerly were part of internal trade or sharing systems. Some goods function very much like cash in forager economies, but this category only codes for the use of money.

Labor (L) = Labor is the primary means of obtaining goods for many groups. Time or a particular quantity of realized labor may be the unit determining the exchange value. Labor can be a common component of traditional hunter-gatherer exchange networks that may be part of delayed reciprocal relationship, or other forms of contributed effort toward a common pool of obligations and interdependence. However, this variable identifies labor that is commonly directed toward obtaining a planned exchange good and does not resemble traditional or low frequency work for outsiders.

Craft (CR) = Several modern foraging populations have been encouraged to enter the craft market as a source of cash or for trade. Craft specialization is not uncommonly a part of traditional forager work as an activity for older (or sometimes younger) individuals with lower subsistence productivity, who use craft production as a contribution toward subsistence success. This activity can be periodic (e.g., making a number of arrows to give once or twice a year to potential exchange partners) or a dedicated practice of impaired or low-productivity individuals. This column identifies when craft production is directly tied to exchange in novel ways as a form of obtaining goods distinct from the common traditional ways outlined briefly. It may be that craft production is usually entirely devoted toward obtaining cash. If that is the case, then "Craft" and "Cash" are both used.

All (A) = All of the above forms of exchange commodity are used by foragers trading for another good.

Cash Source: This column identifies how hunter-gatherers obtain any cash that may be used by them for any purpose and refers only to activities that can result in obtaining money. Although this category may pertain primarily to interactions with outsiders, in some cases it may apply to interactions within a particular foraging society. However, no distinction is made between internal or external source as long as foragers obtain money directly in relation to the activity specified.

Aid (A) = This explicitly refers to outside sources of cash from governments, NGOs, or religious, charitable, or other kinds of organizations.

Crafts (C) = This category refers to the production of any traditional craft or modified traditional craft item (e.g., Aboriginal Australian bark art; "tourist" bows and arrows that are smaller, have fewer components to reduce cost and investment in production, or that are made of materials and in ways that make them nonfunctional) that can be sold.

Labor (L) = This is the category normally identified as wage labor. As noted, it can refer to work for outsiders or work within a foraging society if that is a source of wages. Wages must be direct (cash), not for reimbursement in goods, to use this variable.

Sale of Products (S) = This category includes any foraged animal or plant foods, medicine, raw materials, or other products that are sold following their capture or collection that may resemble or be embedded in normal foraging or represent a specialized activity to obtain materials for sale.

Tourism (T) = Because some hunter-gatherers have been encouraged to participate in the tourism market or lend their presence to "ecotourism" or other kinds of "adventure" travel, we are interested in finding out what kinds of societies or environments are engaging in this practice. In general, tourism can involve posing as traditional foragers (Labor), working for tourism organizers (Labor), selling provisions to tourism organizations (Sale of Products), being recipients of "help" activities for tourists to feel involved in "assisting" traditional populations (Aid), or creating crafts for direct or indirect tourism consumption (Crafts).

Other (O) = Any cash source not identified by the above categories is Other.

Type of Labor: This variable identifies several ways that employment is available to foraging populations and may include individuals who have left the community to take a government position or employment elsewhere. If those individuals are drawn from the population that is currently foraging, then they are considered to have taken opportunities that are available as an alternative to hunting and gathering and as a measure of whether and how the global market has developed a presence among a group of foragers. Wage labor away from the community is a very common form of employment opportunity. Some participants in such a system may never return to their community after they engage in such labor. This variable identifies jobs that reduce hunting and gathering opportunities by those performing these roles. Government jobs, business employment, or other kinds of wage labor that only draw on nonforaging portions of the population (from "acculturated" communities or fully agricultural or pastoral segments of a population that does still contain foragers in other communities) are not included in this sample.

Entrepreneurial Jobs (E) = These include jobs such as those in a storefront, involving transportation of goods from a community to market, or in which the participant has a capital stake in the venture (even if that comes from an aid, government, NGO, or other source), some managerial role, and must make business decisions about what the business does, costs, credit, etc. This is distinguished from the many forms of wage labor in which the worker has no stake or responsibility in the business and is usually only exchanging physical labor for a wage based on time or productivity.

Government Job (G) = This is any national or local government job, full or part time. It may involve work away from the individual's community or activities with a home population or group of communities. Such a job may also be part of novel organizational changes creating very localized government agencies, no matter how informal, within indigenous communities. It can be opportunistic, such as census work, help with aid distribution, work in a national park, or work as a cultural informant.

Tourism (T) = Many of these may be strictly wage labor positions but can represent somewhat novel opportunities involving the creation of tourism employment opportunities for hunter-gatherers.

Wage Labor (W) = As noted, this includes many kinds of work that primarily involve physical labor for established remuneration based on time worked or productivity and excludes those wage labor jobs that pay individuals from a government funding source (those are coded as Government Job). Any form of employment that does not fit into the other three categories is coded as Wage Labor.

None (N) = No form of nontraditional labor is practiced.

Number of Wage Labor Jobs: If known, this provides either a relatively precise or approximate ratio representing the number of persons who have a wage job of any kind in relation to the population estimate (the pool in which those jobs represent a portion of some functional, bounded unit). This provides a relative measure of the availability of employment for some segment of the population.

Foraging Technology: This column has a minimal set of options that characterizes technology as being "traditional," using guns, or including the use of a vehicle. Significant debate and discussion of many examples determined that whether foragers include the use of their traditional foraging technologies, whether guns are present, and whether vehicles are used in foraging activities contained important information about forager flexibility in using modern technologies.

Traditional (T) = This identifies whether some traditional technologies are still employed in subsistence foraging. This is primarily a presence/absence variable, but extremely low-frequency retention of such technology among a minor segment of the population (e.g., a few old men) might mean that traditional technology is not identified as still being used in foraging. The categories identify not only hunting technologies (bow and arrows, blowguns, and spears), but they also pertain to women's foraging technologies. Minor changes in technology that include some foreign manufactured elements (steel tips on digging sticks, steel arrowpoints, nylon string, plastic buckets, etc.) may still support an overall technology that is structured and used in ways analogous to past times, when such items or components were unavailable. This category evaluates whether foragers still use traditional tools or forms of subsistence that would contrast with examples where guns (or other projectiles) or vehicles are used to gather, hunt, or fish.

Gun (G) = Because guns have become ubiquitous tools in many part of the world and are available to many hunter-gatherers, their presence offers some insight into the reach of the global market. The opportunity to code traditional technologies and guns in this column (and date of adoption of novel activities in other columns) provides a sense of whether they may be a replacement or complementary technology. Guns change some aspects of hunting, the need for a supply of ammunition, and may have broader implications, such as for other economic behaviors undertaken to maintain gun use.

Vehicle (V) = One very interesting finding of the SAR seminar was that vehicles do not always signal a shift away from traditional foraging. Several groups that were discussed are employing a range of motorized craft (see the next column) to continue to target traditional food resources or to reinstate the viability of hunting, gathering, and fishing through travel that overcomes localized resource depletion. This was one of the most exciting comparative examples of ways that hunter-gatherers either modify past social or labor organizational means of funding technology, mobility decisions, or transportation, or how they create new mobility strategies to continue taking wild resources.

Other (O) = Most foraging and other technologies are nontraditional and
consist primarily of items obtained through market or other exchange
sources. This can include retention of some traditional technologies.

Vehicle Types: This category includes what types of vehicles are employed in
subsistence activities. It is not intended to identify vehicles that are not used in
support of gathering, hunting, fishing, or other traditional subsistence and raw
material collection activities. This can include the use of vehicles to transport
goods to markets or trade locations. Vehicles that are only used for travel to
other communities, towns, or to commercial markets for purchases (not sale
of foraged items) are not included (even if vehicles may be present in the community but are not used in any subsistence-related activity). Travel to other
communities or transport of individuals may support foraging if they involve
moving gathering, hunting, or fishing labor to a point of access for those activities in ways that cannot be done without them.

Bicycle (BC) = This is any form of bicycle used in foraging mobility.

Boat (B) = This specifically identifies motorized watercraft used for fishing
or travel to foraging locations.

Motorcycle (M) = A motorcycle is any motorized two-wheel vehicle used for
subsistence mobility.

Snowmobile (SM) = This includes snow machines and any other motorized
vehicle that travels over snow.

Truck (T) = Any four-wheeled vehicle that is used in terrestrial forging quali-
fies for this category, including cars. Trucks may be used primarily to go
to foraging locations away from any community settlement, to transport
labor groups to places that stage parts of forging trips, to move foragers
from multiple communities in novel ways, or move goods to markets.

N/A = Either no vehicles are present or they are not used in support of any
foraging activities.

Vehicle Use: This column codes whether vehicles are used for mobility within a
relatively traditional form of subsistence activity or if they are used for a novel
opportunity. Some vehicle uses change mobility and make an activity distinctly
different enough to consider the vehicle support novel. For example, vehicle
travel may result in different numbers of people involved and in changing the
ways that resource are targeted or exploited. Transportation in vehicles may
result in both men and women traveling together and foraging or engaging in

other labor in ways that alter not only the extraction activity but other aspects of food availability, processing, consumption, or sharing. Conversely, some of the changes resulting from vehicle use may be relatively minor and the vehicle-supported activity considered an extension, with some modification, of traditional foraging.

Support Traditional Activity (TA) = Although some changes may occur because of the use of a vehicle, the general activity is considered similar enough to a traditional activity to consider the vehicle as an aid to continuing (or reinstigating) a traditional foraging activity or target pursuit.

Novel Activity (NA) = The vehicle use involves a new kind of food target, raw material acquisition activity, or labor movement, or vehicle use has changed a significant number of behaviors related to exploiting traditional target and represents a novel reorganization of these activities.

None (NO) = No vehicles are used.

(Tables begin on page 256)

Table B.I. Economic activities of twenty-first-century foraging populations.

Group	Ecology	Land Tenure	Residence
AFRICA			
Aka (Bagandou)	Forest	UP	Mixed
Aka (Ndele)	Forest	UP	Mixed
Bofi (Grima)	Forest	UP	Mixed
G/ui and G//ana	Savanna	Game reserve	Traditional
Nyae Nyae Ju/'hoansi	Savanna	S	Settled
Hadza Mang'ola 2000	Savanna	C	Traditional
Hadza Siponga and Tliika 2000	Savanna/woodland	C	Traditional
Hadza (Kipamba)	Savanna/woodland	C	Mixed
Hadza (Mang'ola)	Savanna/woodland	UP	Mixed
Hadza (Siponga)	Savanna/woodland	UP	Mixed
Hadza (Tli'ika and Han!abe)	Savanna/woodland	C	Traditional
Hadza (Yaeda)	Savanna/woodland	S/C	Mixed
Mikea	Forest	C	Mixed
ASIA			
Batek (exterior/border Taman Negara)	Forest	C	Mixed/settled
Batek (interior Taman Negara)	Forest	C	Traditional
Casiguran Agta (Dumagat)	Forest	C	Mixed
Punan Tubu	Forest	UP	Settled
AUSTRALIA			
Bardi	Woodland/tropical coastal	S	Settled
Martu	Desert	S	Mixed
NORTH AMERICA			
Inuit (Baffin Island)	High latitude coastal	S	Settled
SOUTH AMERICA			
Aché	Forest	S	Settled
Hiwi	Savanna	S	Mixed
Pumé (savanna)	Savanna	UP	Traditional
Hoti	Forest	UP	Mixed/settled
Nukak	Forest	UP	Traditional/settled

	Mobility	
Residential	Foraging	Traditional Foraging
Y	Y	F, M, RM, T
Y	Y	F, M, RM, T
Y	Y	F, M, RM, T
Y, 2	Y	F, M, RM, T
N	N	F, RM
Y	Y	F, M, RM, T
Y	Y	F, M, RM, T
N	Y	F (20%), M (100%), RM (100%), T (100%)
N	Y	F (20%), M, RM, T
N	N	F (50%), M, RM, T
Y	Y	F (90%), M, RM, T
N	Y	F (50%), M, RM, T
Y	Y	F, M, RM, T
N	Y	F, M, RM, T
Y	Y	F, M, RM, T
N	Y	F, M, RM,
N	N	F, RM
N	Y	F, M, RM
Y	Y	F, M, RM
Y	Y	F
N	Y	F, M, RM, T
N	Y	F, M, RM, T
Y, 6	Y	F, M, RM, T
Y	Y	F, M, RM, T (80% for all)
Y, 70	Y	F, M, RM, T

Group	Foraged Foods Retained in Diet	Novel Foraging Activity
AFRICA		
Aka (Bagandou)	F (2%), H (15%), M (25%), P (36%)	N/A
Aka (Ndele)	All	N/A
Bofi (Grima)	All	N/A
G/ui and G//ana	M (10%), P (50%)	N/A
Nyae Nyae Ju/'hoansi	H (<5%), M, P	Collecting of devil's-claw
Hadza Mang'ola 2000	H, M, P	N/A
Hadza Siponga and Tliika 2000	H, M, P	N/A
Hadza (Kipamba)	H, M	Trading meat and honey to non-Hadza
Hadza (Mang'ola)	H, M	Tourist hunting and gathering; helping fishermen for fish
Hadza (Siponga)	H, M	Hunting while guarding fields for agriculturalists; trading honey
Hadza (Tli'ika and Han!abe)	H, M, P	N/A
Hadza (Yaeda)	H, M	Hunting while guarding fields for agriculturalists; trading honey
Mikea	F, M, P	Collection of wild silk
ASIA		
Batek (exterior/border Taman Negara)	F, H, P	Collecting various nontimber forest products
Batek (interior Taman Negara)	All	Collecting various nontimber forest products
Casiguran Agta (Dumagat)	F, H, P	Rope-snare hunting of deer and pigs
Punan Tubu	F, M	N/A
AUSTRALIA		
Bardi	F (19%), H (1%), M (10%)	Collecting *Trochus* shells for sale
Martu	H, M, P	H, M
NORTH AMERICA		
Inuit (Baffin Island)	F (15%), M (35%)	N/A
SOUTH AMERICA		
Aché	F (100%), H (100%), M (50%), P (5%)	N/A
Hiwi	F (100%), H (100%), M (90%), P (90%)	N/A
Pumé (savanna)	F (15%), M (10%), P (60%)	N/A
Hoti	F (9%), M (27%), P (16%)	N/A
Nukak	F (10%), H (5%), M (10%), P (60%)	N/A

Nonforaged Food Sources	How Long?	Source of Nonforaged Foods
C (22%<N>55%), M (<1%)	Crops = 4, L, T Market = 2	
C	4	A, T
C	4	T
C (15%), M (<1%)	4	L, T, Aid
C (<10%), A (25%), M (40%)	2	A, L, Aid
C	4	L, T
C (<1%)	4	T
C (70%)	2	A, L, T, Aid (10%)
M (50%)	2	L, T, Aid (30%)
C (50%)	2	A, L, T, Aid
C	2	T, Aid (10%)
C (25%)	2	A, L, T, Aid (25%)
A, C, M	4	A
C, M	4	A, L, T, Aid
C, M	4	A, T
C, M	2	A, L, T
A (<5%), C (90%), M (<5%)	3	A, Aid
M (70%)	3	L, Aid
M	2	L, Aid
M (50%)	3	L, T, Aid
A (50%), C (90%), M (50%)	2	A, L
C (5%), M (5%)	2	A, L
C (10%), M (<1%)	4	A, L, T
C (20%)	3	A, L, T, Aid
C (15%), M (<1%)	3 or 4	A, T

Group	Commercial Foraging	Exchange Currency	Cash Source	Type of Labor	Number of Wage Jobs	Foraging Technology	Vehicles Types	Vehicle Use
AFRICA								
Aka (Bagandou)	Y	TS, L	L, S	WL	<1%–10%	T, G	N/A	NO
Aka (Ndele)	Y	LS, L	S	N	0	T	N/A	NO
Bofi (Grima)	Y	LS, L	S	N, WL	2	T	N/A	NO
G/ui and G//ana	Y	MS	A, C, L, T,	E, T, WL	32	T	T	TA
Nyae Nyae Ju/'hoansi	Y	C, CR, L	A, C, L, T	G, T, WL	40–<150/3,000	O	T	NA
Hadza Mangola 2000	N	MS	T	G, WL	1	T	BC (1)	NO
Hadza Siponga and Tliika 2000	N	MS	T (rare)	Y (rare)	1–2 (Siponga)	T	BC (1)	NO
Hadza (Kipamba)	Y	All	L, S	W	Unknown	T	N/A	NO
Hadza (Mang'ola)	Y	All	All	G, E, T, W	Unknown	O	N/A	NO
Hadza (Siponga)	Y	MS, L	C, L, S	W	Unknown	T	N/A	NO
Hadza (Tli'ika and Hanlabe)	N	MS	A, C, S, T	E, T	Unknown	T	N/A	NO
Hadza (Yaeda)	Y	All	A, C, L, S, T	E, G, T, W	Unknown	T	N/A	NO
Mikea	Y	All	C, L, S	WL	Unknown	T	N/A	NO
ASIA								
Batek (exterior/border Taman Negara)	Y	All	All	G, T, WL	<5%	T, V	B, M	TA
Batek (interior Taman Negara)	Y	MS, TS, C	A, S	N	0	T, V	B	TA
Casiguran Agta (Dumagat)	Y	All	C, L, S,	W	~30	T, G,	N/A	NO
Punan Tubu	Y	C	A, C, S	E, G	0	T, G, V	B	TA, NA

AUSTRALIA								
Bardi	Y	TS, C, CR	A, C, L, S, T	E, G, T, WL	30 men and 51 women	T, G, V	B, T	TA, NA
Martu	Y	C, CR, L	A, C, L	G, WL	5	T, G, V	T	TA, NA
NORTH AMERICA								
Inuit (Baffin Island)	N	TS, CR, L	A, C, L, T	G, T, WL	75/1,050	T, G, V	B, SM	TA
SOUTH AMERICA								
Aché	N	C, L	L, O, T	WL	30/600	T (75%), G (25%)	B (5%)	NO
Hiwi	N	C, L	L	WL	3/130	T	N/A	NO
Pumé (savanna)	N	L, MS	L	WL	0/800	T	N/A	NO
Hoti	N	L	A, L	WL	11/900	T	N/A	NO
Nukak	N	CR	A?, L?	WL?	unknown	T	N/A	NO

Group	Source[a]
AFRICA	
Aka (Bagandou)	Boyette and Hewlett
Aka (Ndele)	Lupo and Schmitt
Bofi (Grima)	Lupo and Schmitt
G/ui and G//ana	Hitchcock, Lee, and Sapignoli
Nyae Nyae Ju/'hoansi	Wiessner
Hadza Mangola 2000	Blurton Jones
Hadza Siponga and Tliika 2000	Blurton Jones
Hadza (Kipamba)	Wood
Hadza (Mang'ola)	Wood
Hadza (Siponga)	Wood
Hadza (Tli'ika and Han!abe)	Wood
Hadza (Yaeda)	Wood
Mikea	Tucker
ASIA	
Batek (exterior/border Taman Negara)	Kraft, Venkataraman, Tacey, and Endicott
Batek (interior Taman Negara)	Kraft, Venkataraman, Tacey, and Endicott
Casiguran Agta (Dumagat)	Headland
Punan Tubu	Gueze and Napitupulu
AUSTRALIA	
Bardi	Coxworth
Martu	Codding, Bliege Bird, and Bird
NORTH AMERICA	
Inuit (Baffin Island)	Wenzel
SOUTH AMERICA	
Aché	Hill
Hiwi	Hill
Pumé (savanna)	Greaves and Kramer
Hoti	Zent and Zent 2007, 2008
Nukak	Politis 2007

[a]The data come from unpublished syntheses of information collated by the authors specifically for this table (some may be previously published but most are not), except for information from Zent and Zent 2007, 2008 and Politis 2007.

ADAMS, D. C., AND C. D. ANTHONY

1996   Using Randomization Techniques to Analyse Behavioural Data. Animal
        Behaviour 51:733–738.

ADAMS, R. L.

2004   An Ethnoarchaeological Study of Feasting in Sulawesi, Indonesia. Journal of
        Anthropological Archaeology 23:56–78.

AGI (ARCHIVO GENERAL DE INDIAS)

1776   Caracas 252, letter from Fr. Thomas Bernardo de Castro, December 16.
        Seville, Spain.

1786   Caracas 135, letter from Fernando Miyares y Gonzáles, September 24. Seville,
        Spain.

1787   Caracas 135, letter from Fernando Miyares y Gonzáles, July 12. Seville, Spain.

1788   Caracas 135, letter from Fernando Miyares y Gonzáles, May 10. Seville, Spain.

AKERMAN, K.

1975a   Baler Shell Implements from North West Australia. Mankind 10:16–19.

1975b   The Double Raft or Kalwa of the West Kimberley. Mankind 10:20–23.

1976   Fishing with Stone Traps on the Dampierland Peninsula. Mankind 10(3):182.

AKLIF, G.

1999   Ardiyooloon Bardi Ngaanka: One Arm Point Bardi Dictionary. Halls Creek,
        WA: Kimberley Language Resource Centre.

ALBERTSON, A.

2000   Traditional Land-Use Systems of Selected Traditional Territories in the Cen-
        tral Kalahari Game Reserve. Report to First People of the Kalahari, Ghanzi.

ALLEN-ARAVE, W., M. GURVEN, AND K. HILL

2008   Reciprocal Altruism, Rather than Kin Selection, Maintains Nepotistic
        Food Transfers on an Ache Reservation. Evolution and Human Behavior
        29:305–318.

ALTMAN, J. C.

1987   Hunter-Gatherers Today: An Aboriginal Economy in North Australia. Can-
        berra: Australian Institute of Aboriginal Studies.

2001   Sustainable Development Options on Aboriginal Land: The Hybrid Econ-
        omy in the Twenty-First Century. Discussion Paper, 2001. Canberra: Centre
        for Aboriginal Economic Policy Research.

2003   People on Country, Healthy Landscapes and Sustainable Indigenous

Economic Futures: The Arnhem Land Case. Drawing Board: An Australian Review of Public Affairs 4:65–82.

2007   Alleviating Poverty in Remote Indigenous Australia: The Role of the Hybrid Economy. Topical Issue, 10. Canberra: Centre for Aboriginal Economic Policy Research.

2010   What Future for Remote Indigenous Australia? Economic Hybridity and the Neoliberal Turn. *In* Culture Crisis: Anthropology and Politics in Aboriginal Australia. Jon Altman and Melinda Hinkson, eds. Pp. 259–280. Sydney: UNSW Press. http://caepr.anu.edu.au/sites/default/files/Altman/Chapters/2010_CultureCrisis_Altman.pdf, accessed August 23, 2013.

ALTMAN, J. C., N. BIDDLE, AND B. HUNTER
2004   Indigenous Socioeconomic Change, 1971–2001: A Historical Perspective. CAEPR Discussion Paper, 266. Canberra: Centre for Aboriginal Economic Policy Research, Australian National University.

ALTMAN, J. C., AND M. C. GRAY
2010   The Effects of the CDEP Scheme on the Economic Status of Indigenous Australians: Some Analyses Using the 1996 Census. Discussion Paper, 195. Canberra: Centre for Aboriginal Economic Policy Research.

ALTMAN, J. C., AND M. HINKSON, EDS.
2007   Coercive Reconciliation: Stabilise, Normalise, Exit Aboriginal Australia. North Carlton: Arena.

ALTMAN, J. C., AND W. SANDERS
2006 [1991]   From Exclusion to Dependence: Aborigines and the Welfare State in Australia. CAEPR Discussion Paper, 1. Canberra: Centre for Aboriginal Economic Policy Research, Australian National University.

ALTMANN, J.
1974   Observational Study of Behavior: Sampling Methods. Behaviour 49:227–267.

ALVARD, M. S., AND A. GILLESPIE
2004   Good Lamalera Whale Hunters Accrue Reproductive Benefits. Research in Economic Anthropology 23:225–247.

ALVARD, M. S., AND D. A. NOLIN
2002   Rousseau's Whale Hunt: Coordination among Big-Game Hunters. Current Anthropology 43:533–559.

ALVAREZ, H. P.
2004   Residence Groups among Hunter Gatherers: A View of the Claims and Evidence for Patrilocal Bands. *In* Kinship and Behavior in Primates. B. Chapais and C. M. Berman, eds. Pp. 420–442. Oxford: Oxford University Press.

ANAGNOSTOU, P., C. BATTAGGIA, M. CAPOCASA, I. BOSCHI, F. BRISIGHELLI,
C. BATINI, G. SPEDINI, AND G. DESTROL-BISOL

2013   Reevaluating a Model of Gender-Biased Gene Flow among Sub-Saharan
        Hunter-Gatherers and Farmers. Human Biology 85(4)597–606.

ANDERSON, M. K.

2005   Tending the Wild: Native American Knowledge and the Management of
        California's Natural Resources. Berkeley: University of California Press.

APICELLA, C. L., F. W. MARLOWE, J. H. FOWLER, AND N. A. CHRISTAKIS

2012   Social Networks and Cooperation in Hunter-Gatherers. Nature 481:497–501.

APOSTOLOU, M.

2008   Bridewealth and Brideservice as Instruments of Parental Choice. Journal of
        Social, Evolutionary, and Cultural Psychology 2(3):89–102.

AUSTRALIAN BUREAU OF METEOROLOGY

2013   Monthly Rainfall: Cape Leveque. Canberra: Commonwealth of Australia.

AUSTRALIAN BUREAU OF STATISTICS, ED.

2013   Births, Australia, 2012. Canberra: Commonwealth of Australia.

BAGSHAWE, F. J.

1925   The Peoples of the Happy Valley (East Africa): The Aboriginal Races of Kon-
        doa Irangi; Part II: The Kangeju. Journal of the African Society 24:117–130.

BAHUCHET, S.

1985   Les Pygmées aka et la forêt centrafricaine. Paris: CNRS and SELAF.

1990   Food Sharing among the Pygmies of Central Africa. African Study Mono-
        graphs 11:27–53.

1993   History of the Inhabitants of the Central African Rainforest: Perspectives
        from Comparative Linguistics. *In* Tropical Forests, People and Food: Biocul-
        tural Interactions and Applications to Development. C. M. Hladik, A. Hla-
        dik, O. F. Linares, H. Pagezy, A. Semple, and M. Hadley, eds. Pp. 37–54. Man
        and the Biosphere, 13. Paris: UNESCO and Parthenon.

BAHUCHET, S., AND H. GUILLAUME

1979   Relations entre chasseurs-cueilleurs Pygmées at agriculteurs de la forêt de
        nord-ouest de Bassin Congolais. *In* Pygmées d'Afrique centrale. S. Bahuchet,
        ed. Pp. 103–109. Paris: SELAF.

1982   Aka-Farmer Relations in the Northwest Congo Basin. *In* Politics and History
        in Band Societies. E. Leacock and R. Lee, eds. Pp. 189–212. Cambridge: Cam-
        bridge University Press.

BAHUCHET, S., D. MCKEY, AND I. DE GARINE

1991   Wild Yams Revisited: Is Independence from Agriculture Possible for Rain
        Forest Hunter-Gatherers? Human Ecology 19:213–243.

BAILEY, R. C., AND R. AUNGER JR.

1989   Net Hunters vs. Archers: Variation in Women's Subsistence Strategies in the Ituri Forest. Human Ecology 17:273–297.

BAILEY, R. C., G. HEAD, M. JENIKE, B. OWEN, R. REICHMAN, AND E. ZECHENTER

1989   Hunting and Gathering in Tropical Forests: Is It Possible? American Anthropologist 91:59–82.

BAILEY, R. C., AND T. N. HEADLAND

1991   The Tropical Rain Forest: Is It a Productive Environment for Human Foragers? Human Ecology 19:261–285.

BALIKCI, A.

1989   Ethnography and Theory in the Canadian Arctic. Études/Inuit/Studies 13(2):103–111.

BARCLAY, P.

2013   Strategies for Cooperation in Biological Markets, Especially for Humans. Evolution and Human Behavior 34(3):164–175.

BARHAM, L. S.

2001   Central Africa and the Emergence of Regional Identity in the Middle Pleistocene. *In* Human Roots: Africa and Asia in the Middle Pleistocene. L. Barham and K. Robson-Brown, eds. Pp. 65–80. Bristol: Western Academic and Specialist Press.

BARHAM, L. S., AND P. MITCHELL

2008   The First Africans: African Archaeology from the Earliest Toolmakers to the Most Recent Foragers. Cambridge: Cambridge University Press.

BARKOW, J. H.

1975   Prestige and Culture: A Biosocial Interpretation. Current Anthropology 16(4):553–572.

1989   Darwin, Sex and Status: Biological Approaches to Mind and Culture. Toronto: University of Toronto Press.

BARNARD, A.

1976   Nharo Bushman Kinship and the Transformation of Khoi Kin Categories. PhD dissertation, University of London.

1992   Hunters and Herders of South Africa: A Comparative Ethnography of the Khoisan Peoples. Cambridge: Cambridge University Press.

BARREIRO, J. A., O. BRITO, P. HEVIA, C. PÉREZ, AND M. OROZCO

1984   Utilización de la semilla del chigo (*Campsiandra comosa*, Benth) el la alimentación humana. II. Proceso de fabricación artesenl de chiga. Archivos Latinoamericanos de Nutrición 34:531–542.

BARTON, H., T. DENHAM, K. NEUMANN, AND M. ARROYO-KALIN

2012   Long-Term Perspectives on Human Occupation of Tropical Rainforests. Quaternary International 249:1–3.

BATEMAN, C. S. L.

1889   The First Ascent of the Kasäi: Being Some Records of Service under the Lone Star. London: George Philip & Son.

BATINI, C., V. COIA, C. BATTAGGIA, J. ROCHA, M. M. PILKINGTON, G. SPEDINI,
D. COMAS, G. DESTRO-BISOL, AND F. CALAFELL

2007   Phylogeography of the Human Mitochondrial L1c Haplogroup: Genetic Signatures of the Prehistory of Central Africa. Molecular Phylogenetics and Evolution 43:635–644.

BATINI, C., G. FERRI, G. DESTRO-BISOL, F. BRISIGHELLI, D. LUISELLI, P. SÁNCHEZ-DIZ,
J. ROCHA, T. SIMONSON, A. BREHM, V. MONTANO, N. E. ELWALI, G. SPEDINI,
M. E. D'AMATO, N. MYERS, P. EBBERSEN, D. COMAS, AND C. CAPELLI

2011b   Signatures of the Preagricultural Peopling Process in Sub-Saharan Africa as Revealed by the Phylogeography of Early Y Chromosome Lineages. Molecular Biology and Evolution 28(8):2603–2613.

BATINI, C., J. LOPES, D. M. BEHAR, F. CALAFELL, L. B. JORDE, L. VAN DER VEEN,
L. QUINTANA-MURCI, G. SPENDINI, G. DESTRO-BISOL, AND D. COMAS

2011a   Insights into the Demographic History of African Pygmies from Complete Mitochrondrial Genomes. Molecular Biology and Evolution 28(2):1099–1110.

BATTELL, A.

1967 [1625]   The Strange Adverntures of Andrew Battell of Leigh in Angola and the Adjoining Regions. *Reprinted from* Purchas His Pilgrims. E. G. Ravenstein, ed. Wiesbaden: Lessing-Druckerei.

BELLWOOD, P.

2005   First Farmers: The Origin of Agricultural Societies. Malden, MA: Blackwell.

BERNARD, H. R.

2011   Research Methods in Anthropology: Qualitative and Quantitative Approaches. Lanham, MD: AltaMira Press.

BERNIELL-LEE, G., F. CALAFELL, E. BOSCH, E. HEYER, L. SICA, P. MOUGUIAMA-
DAOUDA, L. VAN DER VEEN, J. J. HOMBERT, L. QUINTANA-MURCI, AND D. COMAS

2009   Genetic and Demographic Implications of the Bantu Expansion: Insights from Human Paternal Lineages. Molecular Biology and Evolution 26(7):1581–1589.

BESNERAIS, H. L.

1948   Algunos aspectos del río Capanaparo y de sus indios Yaruros. Memoria de la Sociedad de Ciencias Naturales La Salle 8(21):9–20.

BETTINGER, R.

1991   Hunter-Gatherers: Archaeological and Evolutionary Theory. New York: Plenum Press.

BETZIG, L.

1992   Roman Polygyny. Ethology and Sociobiology 13(5–6):309–349.

1995   Medieval Monogamy. Journal of Family History 20:181–216.

2004   Where's the Beef? It's Less about Cooperation, More about Conflict. Behavioral and Brain Sciences 27(4):561–562.

BIDDLE, N., J. TAYLOR, AND M. YAP

2008   Indigenous Participation in Regional Labor Markets, 2001–06. CAEPR Discussion Paper, 288. Canberra: Centre for Aboriginal Economic Policy Research, Australian National University.

BIESELE, M., AND R. HITCHCOCK

2011   The Ju/'hoan San of Nyae Nyae and Namibian Independence. London: Berghahn Books.

2013   The Ju/'hoan San of Nyae Nyae and Namibian Independence: Development, Democracy, and Indigenous Voices in Southern Africa. Oxford: Berghahn Books.

BINFORD, L. R.

1977   Olorgesailie Deserves More than the Usual Book Review. Journal of Anthropological Research 33(4):493–502.

1980   Willow Smoke and Dogs' Tails: Hunter-Gatherer Settlement Systems and Archaeological Site Formation. Journal of Anthropological Archaeology 1(1):4–20.

1984   Bones of Contention: A Reply to Glynn Isaac. American Antiquity 49:164–167.

1985   Human Ancestors: Changing Views of Their Behavior. Journal of Anthropological Archaeology 4:292–327.

1988   The Hunting Hypothesis, Archaeological Methods and the Past. Yearbook of Physical Anthropology 30:1–9.

2001   Constructing Frames of Reference. Berkeley: University of California Press.

BINFORD, L. R., AND J. F. O'CONNELL

1984   An Alyawara Day: The Stone Quarry. Journal of Anthropological Research 40:406–432.

BIRD, D. W.

2009   The Inherent Value of Foraging: Why the Martu People Love Foraging and Manage Their Estate as Well. Arena 98:30–33.

BIRD, D. W., AND R. BLIEGE BIRD

2010   Competing to Be Leaderless: Food Sharing and Magnanimity among Martu Aborigines. *In* The Evolution of Leadership: Transitions in Decision Making from Small-Scale to Middle-Range Societies. K. J. Vaughn, J. W. Eerkens, and J. Kantner, eds. Pp. 21–49. Santa Fe, NM: SAR Press.

BIRD, D. W., R. BLIEGE BIRD, AND B. F. CODDING

2009   In Pursuit of Mobile Prey: Martu Hunting Strategies and Archaeofaunal Interpretation. American Antiquity 74(1):3–29.

BIRD, D. W., R. BLIEGE BIRD, AND C. H. PARKER

2005   Aboriginal Burning Regimes and Hunting Strategies in Australia's Western Desert. Human Ecology 33:443–464.

BIRD, D. W., B. F. CODDING, R. B. BIRD, D. W. ZEANAH, AND C. J. TAYLOR

2013   Megafauna in a Continent of Small Game: Archaeological Implications of Martu Camel Hunting in Australia's Western Desert. Quaternary International 297:155–166.

BIRKET-SMITH, K.

1929   The Caribou Eskimos: Material and Social Life and Their Cultural Position. Report of the Fifth Thule Expedition, 1921–24, vol. 3, no. 3. Copenhagen: Gyldendalske Boghandel.

BLANCHE, K. R., A. N. ANDERSEN, AND J. A. LUDWIG

2001   Rainfall-Contingent Detection of Fire Impacts: Responses of Beetles to Experimental Fire Regimes. Ecological Applications 11(1):86–96.

1930   Notebooks from Hadza Language Project Lake Eyasi, Tanzania. Cape Town: Cape Town University Library Archives.

BLIEGE BIRD, R., AND D. W. BIRD

2008   Why Women Hunt: Risk and Contemporary Foraging in a Western Desert Aboriginal Community. Current Anthropology 49(4):655–693.

BLIEGE BIRD, R., D. W. BIRD, B. F. CODDING, C. H. PARKER, AND J. H. JONES

2008   The "Fire Stick Farming" Hypothesis: Australian Aboriginal Foraging Strategies, Biodiversity, and Anthropogenic Fire Mosaics. Proceedings of the National Academy of Sciences 105(39):14796–14801.

BLIEGE BIRD, R., B. F. CODDING, AND D. W. BIRD

2009   What Explains Differences in Men's and Women's Production? Determinants of Gendered Foraging Inequalities among Martu. Human Nature 20:105–129.

BLIEGE BIRD, R., B. F. CODDING, P. KAUHANEN, AND D. W. BIRD

2012a   Aboriginal Hunting Buffers Climate-Driven Fire-Size Variability in Australia's Spinifex Grasslands. Proceedings of the National Academy of Sciences 109(26):10287–10292.

BLIEGE BIRD, R., AND E. POWER

2015   Prosocial Signaling and Cooperation among Martu Hunters. Evolution and Human Behavior 36:389–397.

BLIEGE BIRD, R., B. SCELZA, D. W. BIRD, AND E. A. SMITH

2012b   The Hierarchy of Virtue: Mutualism, Altruism and Signaling in Martu Women's Cooperative Hunting. Evolution and Human Behavior 33:64–78.

BLIEGE BIRD, R., AND E. A. SMITH

2005   Signaling Theory, Strategic Interaction, and Symbolic Capital. Current Anthropology 46(2):221–248.

BLIEGE BIRD, R., E. A. SMITH, AND D. W. BIRD

2001   The Hunting Handicap: Costly Signaling in Male Foraging Strategies. Behavioral Ecology and Sociobiology 50:9–19.

BLIEGE BIRD, R., N. TAYOR, B. F. CODDING, AND D. W. BIRD

2013   Niche Construction and Dreaming Logic: Aboriginal Patch Mosaic Burning and Varanid Lizards (*Varanus gouldii*) in Australia. Proceedings of the Royal Society B: Biological Sciences 280(1772).

BLURTON JONES, N. G.

1984   A Selfish Origin for Human Food Sharing: Tolerated Theft. Ethology and Sociobiology 5(1):1–3.

1987   Tolerated Theft, Suggestions about the Ecology and Evolution of Sharing, Hoarding and Scrounging. Social Science Information 26:31–54.

2016   Demography and Evolutionary Ecology of Hadza Hunter-Gatherers. Cambridge: Cambridge University Press.

BLURTON JONES, N. G., K. HAWKES, AND J. F. O'CONNELL

1996   The Global Process and Local Ecology: How Should We Explain Differences between the Hadza and the !Kung? *In* Cultural Diversity in Twentieth-Century Foragers. S. Kent, ed. Pp. 159–187. Cambridge: Cambridge University Press.

1997   Why Do Hadza Children Forage? *In* Genetic, Ethological and Evolutionary Perspectives on Human Development: Essays in Honor of Dr. Daniel G. Freedman. N. L. Segal, G. E. Weisfeld, and C. C. Weisfeld, eds. Pp. 279–313. Washington, DC: American Psychological Association.

2002   Antiquity of Postreproductive Life: Are There Modern Impacts on Hunter-Gatherer Postrerproductive Life Spans? American Journal of Human Biology 14:184–205.

BOAS, F.

1888a   The Central Eskimo. Bureau of American Ethnology Annual Report, 6. Washington, DC: Government Printing Office.

1888b   The Central Eskimo. Sixth Annual Report of the Bureau of American Eth-
         nology for the Years 1884–1885. Pp. 399–669. Washington, DC: Smithsonian
         Institution.

BODENHORN, B.
1990   "I'm not the great hunter; my wife is": Inupiat Anthropological Models of
         Gender. Études/Inuit/Studies 14(1–2):55–74.

BOEHM, C.
1999   Hierarchy in the Forest: The Evolution of Egalitarian Behavior. Cambridge,
         MA: Harvard University Press.

BOLKER, B. M.
2008   Ecological Models and Data in R. Princeton, NJ: Princeton University Press.

BOLLONGINO, R., O. NEHLICH, M. P. RICHARDS, J. ORSCHIEDT, M. G. THOMAS, C. SELL,
Z. FAJKOŠOVÁ, A. POWELL, AND J. BURGER
2013   2000 Years of Parallel Societies in Stone Age Central Europe. Science
         342:479–481.

BORGERHOFF MULDER, M.
1987   On Cultural and Reproductive Success: Kipsigis Evidence. American
         Anthropologist 89(3):617–634.

1998   Brothers and Sisters: How Sibling Interactions Affect Optimal Parental Allo-
         cations. Human Nature 9(2):119–161.

BORGERHOFF MULDER, M., D. SIEFF, AND M. MERUS
1989   Disturbed Ancestors: Datoga History in the Ngorongoro Crater. Swara
         2(2):32–35.

BOTSWANA DEPARTMENT OF METEOROLOGICAL SERVICES
N.d.   Botswana Climatic Data. Gaborone: Botswana Department of Meteorologi-
         cal Services, Ministry of Environment, Wildlife, and Tourism.

BOWERN, C.
2008   Bardi Arguments: Referentiality, Agreement, and Omission. *In* Discourse
         and Grammar in Australian Languages. I. Mushin and B. Baker, eds.
         Pp. 59–86. Studies in Language Companion Series. Amsterdam: John
         Benjamins.

2012   A Grammar of Bardi. Berlin: Walter de Gruyter.

BOWLES, S.
2011   Cultivation of Cereals by the First Farmers Was Not More Produc-
         tive than Foraging. Proceedings of the National Academy of Sciences
         108(12):4760–4765.

BRAND MILLER, J., K. W. JAMES, AND P. M. A. MAGGIORE
1993   Tables of Composition of Australian Aboriginal Foods. Canberra: Aboriginal
         Studies Press.

BRIA (BAFFIN REGIONAL INUIT ASSOCIATION)

1981   Summary of Harvests Reported by Hunters in the Baffin Region, Northwest
           Territories for 1980. Unpublished report by the Baffin Regional Inuit Asso-
           ciation, Iqaluit.

1982   Summary of Harvests Reported by Hunters in the Baffin Region, Northwest
           Territories for 1981. Unpublished report by the Baffin Regional Inuit Associa-
           tion, Iqaluit.

1983   Summary of Harvests Reported by Hunters in the Baffin Region, Northwest
           Territories for 1982. Unpublished report by the Baffin Regional Inuit Associa-
           tion, Iqaluit.

1984   Summary of Harvests Reported by Hunters in the Baffin Region, Northwest
           Territories for 1983. Unpublished report by the Baffin Regional Inuit Associa-
           tion, Iqaluit.

1985   Summary of Harvests Reported by Hunters in the Baffin Region, Northwest
           Territories for 1984. Unpublished report by the Baffin Regional Inuit Asso-
           ciation, Iqaluit.

BRIGGS, J.

1974   Eskimo Women: Makers of Men. *In* Many Sisters: Women in Cross-Cultural
           Perspective. C. Matthiasson, ed. Pp. 264–304. New York: Free Press.

BROSIUS. J. P.

1991   Foraging in Tropical Rain Forests: The Case of the Penan of Sarawak.
           Human Ecology 19:123–150.

BUCHANAN, G.

2013   Hybrid Economy Research in Remote Indigenous Australia: Seeing and Sup-
           porting the Customary in Community Food Economies. Local Environment
           19(1):10–32.

BUCHANAN, G., ET AL.

2009   "Always Part of Us": The Socioeconomics of Indigenous Customary Use and
           Management of Dugong and Marine Turtles; A View from Bardi and Jawi
           Sea Country, Western Australia. *In* NAILSMA Knowledge Series, Research
           Report. Darwin: North Australian Indigenous Land and Sea Management
           Alliance.

BURBANK, V.

2006   From Bedtime to On Time: Why Many Aboriginal People Don't Especially
           Like Participating in Western Institutions. Anthropological Forum 16:3–20.

BURBIDGE, A. A., K. A. JOHNSON, P. J. FULLER, AND R. I. SOUTHGATE

1988   Aboriginal Knowledge of the Mammals of the Central Deserts of Australia.
           Wildlife Research 15(1):9–39.

BURCH, E. S., JR.

1975   Eskimo Kinsmen: Changing Family Relationships in Northwest Alaska. American Ethnological Society Monograph, 59. St. Paul, MN: West Publishing.

1994   The Future of Hunter-Gatherer Research. *In* Key Issues in Hunter-Gatherer Research. E. S. Burch and L. J. Ellanna, eds. Pp. 441–455. Oxford: Berg.

BURGESS, C., F. JOHNSTON, D. M. J. S. BOWMAN, AND P. WHITEHEAD

2005   Healthy Country: Healthy People? Exploring the Health Benefits of Indigenous Natural Resource Management. Australian and New Zealand Journal of Public Health 29(2):117–122.

BURROWS, N. D., A. A. BURBIDGE, P. J. FULLER, AND G. BEHN

2006   Evidence of Altered Fire Regimes in the Western Desert Region of Australia. Conservation Science Western Australia 5:272–284.

BURROWS, N. D., AND P. CHRISTENSEN

1990   A Survey of Aboriginal Fire Patterns in the Western Desert of Australia. Fire and the Environment: Ecological and Cultural Perspectives, US Department of Agriculture Forest Service, General Technical Report, SE-69. Pp. 20–24. Asheville, NC: Southeastern Forest Experimental Station.

CAMPBELL, A. C.

1964   A Few Notes on the Gcwi Bushmen of the Central Kalahari Desert, Bechuanaland. Nada 9(1):39–47.

1968   Gcwi Bushmen: Some Notes on Hunting with Poisoned Arrows. Botswana Notes and Records 1:95–96.

CAMPBELL, W. D., AND W. H. BIRD

1915   An Account of the Aboriginals of Sunday Island, King Sound, Kimberley, Western Australia. Journal of the Royal Society of Western Australia 1:55–82.

CANE, S.

1987   Australian Aboriginal Subsistence in the Western Desert. Human Ecology 15:391–434.

CARNEIRO, R. L.

2000   The Evolution of the Tipití: A Study in the Process of Invention. *In* Cultural Evolution: Contemporary Viewpoints. G. M. Feinman and L. Manzanilla, eds. Pp. 61–93. New York: Kluwer Academic/Plenum.

CARTY, J.

2012   Creating Country: Abstraction, Economics and the Social Life of Style in Balgo Art. PhD dissertation, Department of Anthropology, Australian National University.

CASIMIR, M. J., AND A. RAO

1995   Prestige, Possessions, and Progeny: Cultural Goals and Reproductive Success among the Bakkarwal. Human Nature 6(3):241–272.

CAUDELL, M.

2011   Tuber Foraging and Forager/Farmer Interactions. MA thesis, Department of Anthropology, Washington State University.

CHAGNON, N. A.

1979   Is Reproductive Success Equal in Egalitarian Societies? *In* Evolutionary Biology and Human Social Behavior: An Anthropological Perspective. N. A. Chagnon and W. Irons, eds. Pp. 374–402. North Scituate, MA: Duxbury Press.

CHRISTY, C.

1924   Big Game and Pygmies: Experiences of a Naturalist in Central African Forests in Quest of the Okapi. London: Macmillan.

COCK, J. H.

1982   Cassava: A Basic Energy Source in the Tropics. Science, n.s., 218(4574):755–762.

CODDING, B. F.

2012   "Any Kangaroo?" On the Ecology, Ethnography and Archaeology of Foraging in Australia's Arid West. PhD dissertation, Department of Anthropology, Stanford University.

CODDING, B. F., D. W. BIRD, AND R. BLIEGE BIRD

2010   Interpreting Abundance Indices: Some Zooarchaeological Implications of Martu Foraging. Journal of Archaeological Science 37:3200–3210.

CODDING, B. F., R. BLIEGE BIRD, AND D. W. BIRD

2011   Provisioning Offspring and Others: Risk-Energy Trade-Offs and Gender Differences in Hunter-Gatherer Foraging Strategies. Proceedings of the Royal Society B: Biological Sciences 278(1717):2502–2509.

CODDING, B. F., R. BLIEGE BIRD, P. G. KAUHANEN, AND D. W. BIRD

2014   Conservation or Co-evolution? Intermediate Levels of Aboriginal Burning and Hunting Have Positive Effects on Kangaroo Populations in Western Australia. Human Ecology 42:659–669.

COMMONWEALTH OF AUSTRALIA

2012   Income Support Customers: A Statistical Overview 2011. Statistical Paper, 10. Canberra: Research Publications Unit.

CONKLIN-BRITTAIN, N. L., C. D. KNOTT, AND R. W. WRANGHAM

2006   Energy Intake by Wild Chimpanzees and Orangutans: Methodological Considerations and a Preliminary Comparison. *In* Feeding Ecology in Apes and Other Primates: Ecological, Physical and Behavioural Aspects. G. Hohmann,

M. M. Robbins, and C. Boesch, eds. Pp. 445–465. Cambridge: Cambridge University Press.

COOK, L.
2013   The Mushroom Hunters: On the Trail of an Underground America. New York: Ballantine Books.

COPPENS, W.
1983   Los Hoti. *In* Los aborígenes de Venezuela, vol. 2. R. Lizarralde and H. Seijas, eds. Pp. 243–301. Caracas: Fundación La Salle de Ciencias Naturales.

COXWORTH, J. E.
2013   First among Equals: Male-Male Competition among the Bardi of Northwestern Australia and Its Implications for Human Evolution. PhD dissertation, Department of Anthropology, University of Utah.

CRAWLEY, M.
2007   The R Book. Hoboken, NJ: John Wiley and Sons.

CRONK, L.
1991   Wealth, Status, and Reproductive Success among the Mukogodo of Kenya. American Anthropologist 93(2):345–360.

DALTON, G.
1961   Economic Theory and Primitive Society. American Anthropologist 63(1):1–25.

1962   Traditional Production in Primitive African Economies. Quarterly Journal of Economics 76:360–378.

DAMAS, D.
1963   Igluligmiut Kinship and Local Grouping: A Structural Approach. Bulletin 196. Ottawa: National Museum of Canada.

1972   Central Eskimo Systems of Food Sharing. Ethnology 11(3):220–240.

2002   Arctic Migrants/Arctic Villagers: The Transformation of Inuit Settlement in the Central Arctic. Montreal: McGill-Queen's Press.

DAPPER, O.
1686   Description de l'Afrique. Amsterdam: Wolfgang Waesberge, Boom & Van Someren.

DAVENPORT, C., M. L. FONTAINE, AND J. CARTY
2010   Yiwarra Kuju: The Canning Stock Route. Exhibit catalog. Canberra: National Museum Australia.

DAVENPORT, S., P. JOHNSON, YUWALI, WOOMERA ROCKET RANGE
2005   Cleared Out: First Contact in the Western Desert. Canberra: Aboriginal Studies Press.

DEPARTMENT OF HUMAN SERVICES

2012   Remote Area Allowance, vol. 2012. Canberra: Government of Australia.

DESTRO-BISOL, G., V. BOSCHI, I. VERGINELLI, F. CAGLIA, A. PASCALI, V. SPENDINI, AND
G. CALAFELL

2004   The Analysis of Variation of mtDNA Hypervariable Region 1 Suggests that
          Eastern and Western Pygmies Diverged before the Bantu Expansion. Ameri-
          can Naturalist 163(2):212–226.

DETHIER, M., AND A. GHIURGHI

2000   Étude de la chasse villageoise dans le secteur ouest (route Mambélé-Ndelé)
          de la zone d'intervention du projet. Yaounde: ECOFAC.

DIAMOND, J., AND P. BELLWOOD

2003   Farmers and Their Languages: The First Expansions. Science 300:597–603.

DIXON, R. M. W.

2002   Australian Languages: Their Nature and Development. Cambridge: Cam-
          bridge University Press.

DOUNAIS, E.

2001   The Management of Wild Yam Tubers by the Baka Pygmies in Southern
          Cameroon. African Study Monographs, suppl., 26:135–156.

DOWIE, M.

2009   Conservation Refugees: The Hundred Year Conflict between Global Conser-
          vation and Native Peoples. Cambridge, MA: MIT Press.

DRAPER, P.

1975   !Kung Women: Contrasts in Sexual Egalitarianism in Foraging and Seden-
          tary Contexts. In Toward an Anthropology of Women. R. R. Reiter, ed.
          Pp. 77–109. New York: Monthly Review Press.

DU CHAILLU, P.

1899   Adventures in the Great Forest of Equatorial Africa and the Country of the
          Dwarfs. New York: Harper and Brothers.

DUSSART, F.

2006   Canvassing Identities: Reflecting on the Acrylic Art Movement in an Aus-
          tralian Aboriginal Settlement. Aboriginal History 30:1–13.

EDER, J. F.

1978   The Caloric Returns to Food Collecting: Disruption and Change among the
          Batak of the Philippine Tropical Forest. Human Ecology 6:55–69.

1988   Batak Foraging Camps Today: A Window into the History of a Hunting-
          Gathering Economy. Human Ecology 16:35–55.

EDGINGTON, E. S., AND P. ONGHENA

2007   Randomization Tests. 4th edition. Boca Raton, FL: Chapman & Hall/CRC.

EGGERT, M. K. H.

2002   Southern Cameroun and the Settlement of the Equatorial Rainforest: Early Ceramics from Fieldwork in 1997 and 1998–99. *In* Tides of the Desert: Contributions to the Archaeology and Environmental History of Africa in Honor of Rudolph Kuper = Gezeiten der Wüste : Beiträge zu Archäologie und Umweltgeschichte Afrikas zu Ehren von Rudolph Kuper. Tilman Lenssen-Erz et al., eds. Pp. 507–522. Cologne: Heinrich-Barth-Institut.

ELIZALDE, G., J. VILORIA, AND A. ROSALES

2007   Geografía de suelos de Venezuela. *In* GeoVenezuela, vol. 2. Pp. 402–537. Caracas: Fundación Empresas Polar.

ELKIN, A. P.

1932   Social Organization in the Kimberley Division, North-Western Australia. Oceania 2(3):296–333.

1933   Totemism in North-Western Australia (the Kimberley Division), Part II. Oceania 3(4):435–481.

1935   Initiation in the Bardi Tribe, North-West Australia. Journal of the Proceedings of the Royal Society of New South Wales 69:190–208.

1969   Elements of Australian Aboriginal Philosophy. Oceania 40:85–98.

ELLIS, L.

1993a   Conceptually Defining Social Stratification in Human and Nonhuman Animals. *In* Social Stratification and Socioeconomic Inequality, vol. 1: A Comparative Biosocial Approach. L. Ellis, ed. Pp. 1–14. Westport, CT: Praeger.

1993b   Operationally Defining Social Stratification in Human and Nonhuman Animals. *In* Social Stratification and Socioeconomic Inequality, vol. 1: A Comparative Biosocial Approach. L. Ellis, ed. Pp. 15–35. Westport, CT: Preager.

EMBER, C. R.

1983   The Relative Decline in Women's Contribution to Agriculture with Intensification. American Anthropologist 85:285–304.

ENDICOTT, K.

1979   Batek Negrito Religion: The World View and Rituals of a Hunting and Gathering People of Peninsular Malaysia. Oxford: Clarendon Press.

ENDICOTT, K., AND P. BELLWOOD

1991   The Possibility of Independent Foraging in the Rain Forest of Peninsular Malaysia. Human Ecology 19:51–185.

FARAWAY, J.

2006   Extending the Linear Model with R: Generalized Linear, Mixed Effects and Nonparametric Regression Models. New York: Chapman and Hall.

FIJN, N., I. KEEN, C. LLOYD, M. PICKERING, EDS.

2012   Indigenous Participation in Australian Economies II: Historical Engagements and Current Enterprises. Canberra: ANU Press.

FINLAYSON, H. H.

1961   On Central Australian Mammals, part IV: The Distribution and Status of Central Australian Species. South Africa: Government Printer.

FLANNERY, K. V.

1969   Origins and Ecological Effects of Early Domestication in Iran and the Near East. *In* The Domestication and Exploitation of Plants and Animals. P. J. Ucko and G. Dimbleby, eds. Pp. 73–100. Chicago, IL: Aldine.

FLINN, M. V.

1986   Correlates of Reproductive Success in a Caribbean Village. Human Ecology 14(2):225–243.

FOLDS, R.

2001   Crossed Purposes: The Pintupi and Australia's Indigenous Policy. Sydney: University of New South Wales Press.

FRIED, M. H.

1967   The Evolution of Political Society: An Essay in Political Anthropology. New York: Random House.

GAMMAGE, B.

2011   The Biggest Estate on Earth: How Aborigines Made Australia. Crows Nest: Allen & Unwin.

GARNETT, S., B. SITHOLE, P. WHITEHEAD, C. BURGESS, F. JOHNSTON, AND T. LEA

2009   Healthy Country, Healthy People: Policy Implications of Links between Indigenous Human Health and Environmental Condition in Tropical Australia. Australian Journal of Public Administration 68:53–66.

GEMICI, K.

2008   Karl Polanyi and the Antinomies of Embeddedness. Socio-Economic Review 6(1):5–33.

GIFFEN, N.

1930   The Roles of Men and Women in Eskimo Culture. Chicago: University of Chicago Press.

GLASKIN, K.

2002   Claiming Country: A Case Study of Historical Legacy and Transition in the Native Title Context. PhD dissertation, Department of Archaeology and Anthropology, Australian National University.

2007   Claim, Culture and Effect: Property Relations and the Native Title Process. *In* The Social Effects of Native Title: Recognition, Translation, Coexistence. B. R. Smith and F. Morphy, eds. Pp. 59–77. CAEPR Research Monograph, 27.

Canberra: Centre for Aboriginal Economic Policy Research, Australian National University.

GOMBAY, N.

2010   Making a Living: Place, Food and Economy in an Inuit Community. Saska-
        toon: Purich.

GOMES, A. G.

1982   Ecological Adaptations and Population Change: Semang Foragers and Teme-
        huan Horticulturalists in West Malaysia. Research Report, 12. Honolulu, HI:
        East-West Environment and Policy Institute.

GOTILOGUE, S.

2000   État de recherches archeologiques en Republique Centrafricaine. Recent
        Research into the Stone Age of Northeastern Africa. Studies in African
        Archaeology, Poznan Archaeological Museum 7:239–257.

GOULD, R. A.

1967   Notes on Hunting, Butchering and Sharing of Game among the Ngatatjara
        and Their Neighbors in the West Australia Desert. Kroeber Anthropological
        Papers 36:41–66.

1968   Living Archaeology. Cambridge: Cambridge University Press.

1969a   Subsistence Behaviour among the Western Desert Aborigines of Australia.
        Oceania 4:253–274.

1969b   Yiwarra: Foragers of the Australian Desert. New York: Charles Scribner's
        Sons.

1971   Uses and Effects of Fire among the Western Desert Aborigines of Australia.
        Mankind 8(1):14–24.

1978   The Anthropology of Human Residues. American Anthropologist 80(4):
        815–835.

1980   Living Archaeology. New Studies in Archaeology. Cambridge: Cambridge
        University Press.

1981   Comparative Ecology of Food-Sharing in Australia and Northwest Califor-
        nia. *In* Omnivorous Primates: Gathering and Hunting in Human Evolution.
        R. S. O. Harding and G. Teleki, eds. Pp. 422–454. New York: Columbia Uni-
        versity Press.

1991   Arid-Land Foraging as Seen from Australia: Adaptive Models and Behav-
        ioral Realities. Oceania 62(1):12–33.

GOWDY, J., ED.

1998   Limited Wants, Unlimited Means: A Reader on Hunter-Gatherer Economics.
        Washington, DC: Island Press.

GRABURN, N.

1969   Eskimos without Igloos: Social and Economic Development in Sugluk. Bos-
        ton, MA: Little, Brown.

GRAEBER, D.

2014   Debt: The First Five Thousand Years. Brooklyn, NY: Melville House.

GRAFEN, A., AND R. HAILS

2002   Modern Statistics for Life Sciences. Oxford: Oxford University Press.

GRAGSON, T. L.

1989   Allocation of Time to Subsistence and Settlement in a Ciri Khonome Pumé
        Village of the Llanos of Apure, Venezuela. PhD dissertation, Pennsylvania
        State University.

GRAY, P. B., AND K. G. ANDERSON

2010   Fatherhood: Evolution and Human Paternal Behavior. Cambridge, MA: Har-
        vard University Press.

GREAVES, R. D.

1997a   Ethnoarchaeological Investigation of Subsistence Mobility, Resource Target-
        ing, and Technological Organization among Pumé Foragers of Venezuela.
        PhD dissertation, Department of Anthropology, University of New Mexico.

1997b   Hunting and Multifunctional Use of Bows and Arrows: Ethnoarchaeology of
        Technological Organization among Pumé Hunters of Venezuela. *In* Projec-
        tile Technology. H. Knecht, ed. Pp. 287–320. New York: Plenum.

2006   Forager Landscape Use and Residential Organization. *In* Archaeology and
        Ethnoarchaeology of Mobility. F. Sellet, R. D. Greaves, and P. L. Yu, eds.
        Pp. 127–152. Gainesville: University Press of Florida.

GREAVES, R. D., AND K. L. KRAMER

2014   Hunter-Gatherer Use of Wild Plants and Domesticates: Archaeological
        Implications for Mixed Economies before Agricultural Intensification. Jour-
        nal of Archaeological Science 41:263–271.

GREMILLION, K. J.

2004   Seed Processing and the Origins of Food Production in Eastern North
        America. American Antiquity 69:215–233.

GRIFFIN, P. B.

1984   Forager Resource and Land Use in the Humid Tropics: The Agta of North-
        eastern Luzon, the Philippines. *In* Past and Present in Hunter-Gatherer
        Studies. C. Schrire, ed. Pp. 95–121. New York: Academic Press.

GUENTHER, M. G.

1986   The Nharo Bushmen of Botswana: Tradition and Change. Hamburg: Helmut
        Buske Verlag.

GUILLE-ESCURET, G.

1998   La révolution agricole des Pygmées Aka: De la structure dans l'événement et réciproquement. L'Homme 147:105–126.

GULBRANDSEN, O.

2012   The State and the Social: State Formation in Botswana and Its Precolonial and Colonial Genealogies. Oxford: Berghahn Books.

GURVEN, M., AND K. HILL

2009   Why Do Men Hunt? A Reevaluation of "Man the Hunter" and the Sexual Division of Labor. Current Anthropology 50:51–74.

GURVEN, M., K. HILL, AND F. JAKUGI

2004   Why Do Foragers Share and Sharers Forage? Explorations of Social Dimensions of Foraging. Socioeconomic Aspects of Human Behavioral Ecology Research in Economic Anthropology 23:19–43.

GURVEN, M., K. HILL, AND H. KAPLAN

2002   From Forest to Reservation: Transitions in Food-Sharing Behavior among the Aché of Paraguay. Journal of Anthropological Research 58(1):93–120.

GURVEN, M., K. HILL, H. KAPLAN, A. HURTADO, AND R. LYLES

2000   Food Transfers among Hiwi Foragers of Venezuela: Tests of Reciprocity. Human Ecology 28(2):171–218.

GURVEN, M., AND C. VON RUEDEN

2006   Hunting, Social Status and Biological Fitness. Biodemography and Social Biology 53(1–2):81–99.

HADDON, A. C.

1890   The Ethnography of the Western Tribe of Torres Straits. Journal of the Anthropological Institute of Great Britain and Ireland 19:297–440.

HAMES, R.

1990   Sharing among the Yanomamö, Part I: The Effects of Risk. *In* Risk and Reciprocity in Tribal and Peasant Economies. E. Cashdan, ed. Pp. 89–106. Boulder, CO: Westview.

HAMES, R., AND W. VICKERS

1982   Optimal Diet Breadth Theory as a Model to Explain Variability in Amazonian Hunting. American Ethnologist 9:358–378.

HARAKO, R.

1976   The Mbuti as Hunters: A Study of Ecological Anthropology of the Mbuti Pygmies. Kyoto University African Studies 10:37–99.

HARDER, M., AND G. W. WENZEL

2012   Inuit Subsistence, Social Economy and Food Security in Clyde River, Nunavut. Arctic 65(3):305–318.

HARDING, R. S., AND G. TELEKI, EDS.

1981   Omnivorous Primates: Gathering and Hunting in Human Evolution. New
          York: Columbia University Press.

HARRIS, D. R.

1989   An Evolutionary Continuum of People-Plant Interactions. *In* Foraging and
          Farming: The Evolution of Plant Exploitation. D. R. Harris and G. C. Hill-
          man, eds. Pp. 11–26. London: Unwyn Hyman.

HARRIS, K. M., F. F. FURSTENBERG, AND J. K. MARMER

1998   Paternal Involvement with Adolescents in Intact Families: The Influence of
          Fathers over the Life Course. Demography 35(2):201–216.

HART, C. W. M., A. R. PILLING, AND J. C. GOODALE

1988   The Tiwi of North Australia. New York: Holt, Rinehart, and Winston.

HART, T. B., AND J. A. HART

1986   The Ecological Basis of Hunter-Gatherer Subsistence in African Rain For-
          ests: The Mbuti of Eastern Zaire. Human Ecology 14:29–55.

HAWKES, K.

1990   Why Do Men Hunt? Benefits for Risky Choices. *In* Risk and Uncertainty in
          Tribal and Peasant Economies. E. Cashdan, ed. Pp. 145–166. Boulder, CO:
          Westview Press.

1993   Why Hunter-Gatherers Work: An Ancient Version of the Problem of Public
          Goods. Current Anthropology 34(4):341–361.

2000   Big Game Hunting and the Evolution of Egalitarian Societies: Lessons from
          the Hadza. *In* Hierarchies in Action: Cui Bono? M. W. Diehl, ed. Pp. 59–83.
          Carbondale: Southern Illinois University Press.

HAWKES, K., AND R. BLIEGE BIRD

2002   Showing Off, Handicap Signaling, and the Evolution of Men's Work. Evolu-
          tionary Anthropology 11:58–67.

HAWKES, K., K. HILL, AND J. F. O'CONNELL

1982   Why Hunters Gather: Optimal Foraging and the Aché of Eastern Paraguay.
          American Ethnologist 9:379–398.

HAWKES, K., J. F. O'CONNELL, AND N. G. BLURTON JONES

2001a   Hadza Meat Sharing. Evolution and Human Behavior 22:113–142.

2001b   Hunting and Nuclear Families: Some Lessons from the Hadza about Men's
          Work. Current Anthropology 42(5):681–709.

HAWKES, K., J. F. O'CONNELL, AND J. E. COXWORTH

2010   Family Provisioning Is Not the Only Reason Men Hunt. Current Anthro-
          pology 51(2):259–264.

HEADLAND, T. N.

1987   The Wild Yam Question: How Well Could Independent Hunter-Gatherers Live in a Tropical Rainforest System? Human Ecology 15:463–491.

HEADLAND, T. N., AND R. C. BAILEY

1991   Have Hunter-Gatherers Ever Lived in Tropical Rain Forests Independently of Agriculture? Human Ecology 19:115–122.

HEADLAND, T. N., AND L. REID

1989   Revisionism in Ecological Anthropology. Current Anthropology 38(4):605–630.

HEINRICH, A.

1963   Eskimo-Type Kinship and Eskimo Kinship: An Evaluation and a Provisional Model for Presenting Data Pertaining to Inupiaq Kinship Systems. PhD dissertation, Department of Anthropology, University of Washington.

HENN, B. M., C. R. GIGNOUX, M. JOBIN, J. M. GRANKA, J. M. MACPHERSON, J. M. KIDD,
L. RODRÍGUEZ BOTIGUÉ, S. RAMACHANDRAN, L. HON, A. BRISBIN, A. A. LIN,
P. A. UNDERHILL, D. COMAS, K. K. KIDD, P. PARHAM, P. J. NORMAN,
C. D. BUSTAMANTE, J. L. MOUNTAIN, AND M. W. FELDMAN

2011   Hunter-Gatherer Genomic Diversity Suggests a Southern African Origin for Modern Humans. Proceedings of the National Academy of Sciences 108:5154–5162.

HENRICH, J., AND F. J. GIL-WHITE

2001   The Evolution of Prestige: Freely Conferred Deference as a Mechanism for Enhancing the Benefits of Cultural Transmission. Evolution and Human Behavior 22(3):165–196.

HEWLETT, B. S.

1988   Sexual Selection and Paternal Investment among Aka Pygmies. *In* Human Reproductive Behavior: A Darwinian Perspective. L. Betzig, M. Borgerhoff Mulder, and P. W. Turke, eds. Pp. 263–276. Cambridge: Cambridge University Press.

1990   Foragers and Rural Development. Ngotto: Republique Centrafricaine, Projet ECOFAC- Composante RCA, Ngotto Reserve.

1991   Intimate Fathers: The Nature and Context of Aka Pygmy Paternal Infant Care. Ann Arbor: University of Michigan Press.

HIATT, L. R.

1982   Traditional Attitudes to Land Resources. *In* Aboriginal Sites: Rites and Resource Development. R. Berndt, ed. Pp. 47–53. Perth: University of Western Australia Press.

1996   Arguments about Aborigines: Australia and the Evolution of Social Anthropology. Cambridge: Cambridge University Press.

HIERNAUX, J., AND D. B. HARTONO

1980   Physical Measurements of the Adult Hadza of Tanzania. Annals of Human
         Biology 7:339–346.

HILDEBRAND, E. A.

2003   Motives and Opportunities for Domestication: An Ethnoarchaeologi-
         cal Study in Southwest Ethiopia. Journal of Anthropological Archaeology
         22:358–378.

HILL, J.

1984   Prestige and Reproductive Success in Man. Ethology and Sociobiology
         5(2):77–95.

HILL, K., AND K. HAWKES

1983   Neotropical Hunting among the Aché of Eastern Paraguay. *In* Adaptive
         Responses of Native Amazonians. R. B. Hames and W. T. Vickers, eds.
         Pp. 139–188. New York: Academic Press.

HILL, K., AND A. M. HURTADO

1996   Aché Life History: The Ecology and Demography of a Foraging People. New
         York: Aldine de Gruyter.

HILL, K., B. M. WOOD, J. BAGGIO, A. M. HURTADO, AND R. T. BOYD

2014   Hunter-Gatherer Inter-band Interaction Rates: Implications for Cumulative
         Culture. Plos One 9(9):e102806.

HILTON, C. E., AND R. D. GREAVES

2004   Age, Sex, and Resource Transport in Venezuelan Foragers. *In* From Biped to
         Strider: The Emergence of Modern Human Walking, Running, and Resource
         Transport. J. Meldrum and C. E. Hilton, eds. Pp. 163–181. New York: Kluwer.

HITCHCOCK, R. K.

2001   "Hunting is our heritage": The Struggle for Hunting and Gathering Rights
         among the San of Southern Africa. *In* Parks, Property, and Power: Managing
         Hunting Practice and Identity within State Policy Regimes. D. G. Ander-
         son and K. Ikeya, eds. Pp. 139–156. Senri Ethnological Studies, 59. Osaka:
         National Museum of Ethnology.

2002   "We are the first people": Land, Natural Resources, and Identity in the Cen-
         tral Kalahari, Botswana. Journal of Southern African Studies 28(4):793–820.

HITCHCOCK, R. K., AND L. G. BARTRAM JR.

1998   Social Boundaries, Technical Systems, and the Use of Space and Technology
         in the Kalahari. *In* The Archaeology of Social Boundaries. M. T. Stark, ed.
         Pp. 12–49. Washington, DC: Smithsonian Institution Press.

HITCHCOCK, R. K., AND J. I. EBERT

1984   Foraging and Food Production among Kalahari Hunter/Gatherers. *In* From
         Hunters to Farmers: The Causes and Consequences of Food Production in

Africa. J. D. Clark and S. A. Brandt, eds. Pp. 328–348. Berkeley: University of California Press.

HITCHCOCK, R. K., AND R. MASILO

1995   Subsistence Hunting and Resource Rights in Botswana. Gaborone: Department of Wildlife and National Parks.

HITCHCOCK, R. K., M. SAPIGNOLI, AND W. BABCHUK

2011   What about Our Rights? Settlements, Subsistence, and Livelihood Security among Central Kalahari San and Bakgalagadi. International Journal of Human Rights 15(1):67–87.

HLADIK, A., S. BAHUCHET, C. DUCATILLION, AND C. M. HLADIK

1984   Les plantes à tubercules de la forêt dense d'Afrique Centrale. Revue d'Ecologie (Terre et Vie) 39:249–290.

HLADIK, A., AND E. DOUNIAS

1993   Wild Yams of the African Forest as Potential Food Resources. *In* Tropical Forests, People and Food: Biocultural Interactions and Applications to Development. A. H. Hladik, C. M. Hladik, O. F. Linares, H. Pagezy, A. Semple, and M. Hadley, eds. Pp. 163–176. Man and the Biosphere, 13. Paris: UNESCO.

HOFFMAN, C.

1986   The Punan: Hunters and Gatherers of Borneo. Ann Arbor, MI: UMI Research Press.

HOLDEN, C. J.

2002   Bantu Language Tree Reflects the Spread of Farming across Sub-Saharan Africa: A Maximum Parsimony Analysis. Proceedings of the Royal Society: Biological Sciences 269(1493):793–799.

HOLMBERG, A.

1950   Nomads of the Long Bow: The Sirionó of Eastern Bolivia. Institute of Social Anthropology, Publication 10. Washington, DC: Smithsonian Institution.

HONIGMANN, J., AND I. HONIGMANN

1965   Eskimo Townsmen: Ethnic Backgrounds and Modernization. Ottawa: Université St. Paul.

HOPCROFT, R. L.

2006   Sex, Status, and Reproductive Success in the Contemporary United States. Evolution and Human Behavior 27:104–120.

HOWELL, N.

1979   Demography of the Dobe !Kung. New York: Academic Press.

2000   Demography of the Dobe !Kung. 2nd edition. Hawthorne, NY: Aldine-DeGruyter.

2010   Life Histories of the Dobe !Kung: Food, Fatness and Well-Being over the Life-Span. Berkeley: University of California Press.

HUGHES, C. C.

1965   Under Four Flags: Recent Culture Change among the Eskimos. Current Anthropology 6(1):3–69.

HURTADO, A. M., AND K. HILL

1987   Early Dry Season Subsistence Ecology of Cuiva (Hiwi) Foragers of Venezuela. Human Ecology 15:163–187.

1990   Seasonality in a Foraging Society: Variation in Diet, Work Effort, Fertility, and Sexual Division of Labor among the Hiwi of Venezuela. Journal of Anthropological Research 46:293–346.

ICHIKAWA, M.

1983   An Examination of the Hunting-Dependent Life of the Mbuti Pygmies. African Study Monographs 4:55–76.

1991   The Impact of Commoditization on the Mbuti of Eastern Zaire. Senri Ethnological Studies 30:135–162.

2005   Food Sharing and Ownership among Central African Hunter-Gatherers: An Evolutionary Perspective. *In* Property and Equality: Ritualisation, Sharing, Egalitarianism, vol. 1. T. Widlok and W. Gossa Tadesse, eds. Pp. 151–164. New York: Berghan Books.

2012   Central African Forests as Hunter-Gatherers' Living Environment: An Approach to Historical Ecology. African Study Monographs, suppl., 43:3–14.

IKEYA, K.

1994   Hunting with Dogs among the San in the Central Kalahari. African Study Monographs 15(3):119–134.

1996   Road Construction and Handicraft Production in the Xade Area, Botswana. African Study Monographs, suppl., 22:67–84.

1999   The Historical Dynamics of the Socioeconomic Relationships between the Nomadic San and the Rural Kgalagadi. Botswana Notes and Records 31:19–32.

2001   Some Changes among the San under the Influence of Relocation Plan in Botswana. *In* Parks, Property, and Power: Managing Hunting Practice and Identity within State Policy Regimes. D. Anderson and K. Ikeya, eds. Pp. 183–198. Senri Ethnological Studies, 59. Osaka: National Museum of Ethnology.

IMAMURA-HAYAKI, K.

1996   Gathering Activity among the Central Kalahari San. African Study Monographs, suppl., 22:47–66.

INGOLD, T.

1999   On the Social Relations of the Hunter-Gatherer Band. *In* The Cambridge
        Encyclopaedia of Hunters and Gatherers. R. Lee and R. Daly, eds.
        Pp. 399–410. Cambridge: Cambridge University Press.

INGOLD, T., D. RICHES, AND J. WOODBURN, EDS.

1988   Hunters and Gatherers 1: History, Evolution and Social Change. Oxford:
        Berg.

IRONS, W.

1979   Cultural and Biological Success. *In* Evolutionary Biology and Human Social
        Behavior: An Anthropological Perspective. N. A. Chagnon and W. Irons, eds.
        Pp. 257–272. North Scituate, MA: Duxbury.

ISAAC, G.

1978   The Food Sharing Behavior of Protohuman Hominids. Scientific American
        238(4):90–108.

JENNESS, D.

1922   The Life of the Copper Eskimos. Report of the Canadian Arctic Expedition,
        1913–18, vol. 12. Ottawa: F. A. Acland.

JOCHIM, M. A.

1998   A Hunter-Gatherer Landscape: Southwest Germany in the Late Paleolithic
        and Mesolithic. New York: Plenum.

JOHNSTON, H.

1902   The Pygmies and Ape-Like Men of the Uganda Borderland. Pall Mall Maga-
        zine 26:173–184.

JOHNSTONE, K., AND A. EVANS

2012   Fertility and the Demography of Indigenous Australians: What Can the
        NATSISS 2008 Tell Us? *In* Survey Analysis for Indigenous Policy in Aus-
        tralia, vol. 32. Boyd Hunter and Nicholas Biddle, eds. Pp. 35–47. Canberra:
        ANU E-Press.

JONES, J. H., R. BLIEGE BIRD, AND D. W. BIRD

2013   To Kill a Kangaroo: Understanding the Decision to Pursue High-Risk/High-
        Gain Resources. Proceedings of the Royal Society B: Biological Sciences
        280(1767).

JONES, R.

1969   Fire-Stick Farming. Australian Natural History 16(7):224–228.

KAARE, B., AND J. WOODBURN

1999   Hadza. *In* The Cambridge Encyclopedia of Hunters and Gatherers. R. B. Lee
        and R. Daly, eds. Pp. 200–204. Cambridge: Cambridge University Press.

KADUNA, J. D.

1982   Water as a Constraint on Agricultural Development in the Semi-arid Areas
          of Tanzania. Water Supply and Management 6:417–430.

KAPLAN, H., AND K. HILL

1985   Hunting Ability and Reproductive Success among Male Aché Foragers: Pre-
          liminary Results. Current Anthropology 26(1):131–133.

1992   The Evolutionary Ecology of Food Acquisition. *In* Evolutionary Ecology and
          Human Behavior. E. A. Smith and B. Winterhalder, eds. Pp. 167–201. New
          York: Aldine de Gruyter.

KATZ, R.

1982   Boiling Energy: Community Healing among the Kalahari !Kung. Cambridge,
          MA: Harvard University Press.

KATZ, R., M. BIESELE, AND V. ST. DENNIS

1997   Healing Makes Our Hearts Happy. Rochester, VT: Inner Traditions.

KAYBERRY, P. M.

1939   Aboriginal Woman: Sacred and Profane. London: Routledge.

KEEN, I.

2006   Constraints on the Development of Enduring Inequalities in Late Holocene
          Australia. Current Anthropology 47(1):7–38.

KELLY, R. L.

2013   The Lifeways of Hunter-Gatherers: The Foraging Spectrum. Cambridge:
          Cambridge University Press.

KEMP, W. B.

1971   The Flow of Energy in a Hunting Society. Scientific American 224(3):104–115.

KENT, S., ED.

2002   Ethnicity, Hunter-Gatherers, and the "Other": Association or Assimilation in
          Africa. Washington, DC: Smithsonian Institution Press.

KERLE, J. A., J. N. FOULKES, R. G. KIMBER, AND D. PAPENFUS

1992   The Decline of the Brushtail Possum, *Trichosurus vulpecula* (Kerr 1798), in
          Arid Australia. Rangeland Journal 14(2):107–127.

KIEMA, K.

2010   Tears for My Land: A Social History of the Kua of the Central Kalahari
          Game Reserve, Tc'amnqo. Gaborone: Mmegi.

KIMBER, R.

1983   Black Lightning: Aborigines and Fire in Central Australia and the Western
          Desert. Archaeology in Oceania 18(1):38–45.

KINGDON, J.

1997   The Kingdon Field Guide to African Mammals. London: Academic Press.

KITANISHI, K.

1995   Seasonal Changes in the Subsistence Activities and Food Intake of Aka
        Hunter-Gatherers in Northeastern Congo. African Study Monographs
        16(2):73–118.

1998   Food Sharing among the Aka Hunter-Gatherers in Northeastern Congo.
        African Study Monographs, suppl., 25:3–32.

2003   Cultivation by Baka Hunter-Gatherers in the Tropical Rain Forest of Central
        Africa. African Study Monograph, suppl., 28:143–157.

2006   The Impacts of Cash and Commoditization on the Baka Hunter-Gatherer
        Society in Southeastern Cameroon. African Study Monographs, suppl.,
        33:121–142.

KJELLSTROM, R.

1973   Eskimo Marriage: An Account of Traditional Eskimo Courtship and Mar-
        riage. Nordiska museets handlinger, 80. Stockholm: Nordiska museets.

KLEIMAN, K.

1999   Hunter-Gatherer Participation in Rainforest Trade-Systems: A Comparative
        History of Forest vs Ecotone Societies in Gabon and Congo, c. 1000–1800
        AD. *In* Central African Hunter-Gatherers in a Mulitdisciplinary Perspective:
        Challenging Elusiveness. K. Biesbrouck, S. Elders, and G. Rossel, eds.
        Pp. 89–104. Leiden: University of Leiden Press.

KLEIN, R.

2009   The Human Career. 3rd edition. Chicago, IL: University of Chicago Press.

KNIGHT, J.

2003   Relocated Roadside: Preliminary Observations on the Forested Peoples of
        Gabon. African Study Monographs, suppl., 28:81–121.

KOELLE, S. W.

1854   Polyglotta Africana; or, A Comparative Vocabulary of Nearly Three Hundred
        Words and Phrases, in More than One Hundred Distinct African Languages.
        London: Church Missionary House.

KÖHLER, A.

2005   Money Makes the World Go Round? Commodity Sharing, Gifting and
        Exchange in the Baka (Pygmy) Economy. *In* Property and Equality:
        Encapsulation, Commercialisation, Discrimination, vol. 2. T. Widlok and
        W. Gossa Tadesse, eds. Pp. 32–55. New York: Berghan Books.

KRAMER, K. L.

2005   Maya Children: Helpers at the Farm. Cambridge, MA: Harvard University
        Press.

2008   Early Sexual Maturity among Pumé Foragers of Venezuela: Fitness

Implications of Teen Motherhood. American Journal of Physical Anthropology 136:338–350.

2011   The Evolution of Human Parental Care and Recruitment of Juvenile Help. Trends in Ecology and Evolution 26:533–540.

KRAMER, K. L., AND R. D. GREAVES

2007   Changing Patterns of Infant Mortality and Fertility among Pumé Foragers and Horticulturalists. American Anthropologist 109:713–726.

2010   Synchrony between Growth and Reproductive Patterns in Human Females: Early Investment in Growth among Pumé Foragers. American Journal of Physical Anthropology 141:235–244.

2011   Postmarital Residence and Bilateral Kin Associations among Hunter-Gatherers: Pumé Foragers Living in the Best of Both Worlds. Human Nature 22:41–63.

KRAMER, K. L., R. D. GREAVES, AND P. T. ELLISON

2009   Early Reproductive Maturity among Pumé Foragers: Implications of a Pooled Energy Model to Fast Life Histories. American Journal of Human Biology 21:430–437.

KRAMER, K. L., AND E. OTÁROLA-CASTILLO

2015   When Mothers Need Others: Life History Transitions Associated with the Evolution of Cooperative Breeding. Journal of Human Evolution 84:16–24.

KROEBER, A. L.

1939   Cultural and Natural Areas of Native America. Berkeley: University of California Press.

LADEN G., AND R. W. WRANGHAM

2005   The Rise of Hominids as an Adaptive Shift in Fallback Foods: Plant Underground Storage Organs (USOs) and Australopith Origins. Journal of Human Evolution 49:482–498.

LANCASTER, P. A., J. S. INGRAM, M. Y. LIM, AND D. G. COURSEY

1982   Traditional Cassava-Based Foods: Survey of Processing Techniques. Economic Botany 36:12–45.

LANGDON, S.

1984   Alaska Native Subsistence: Current Regulatory Regimes and Issues, vol. 19. Anchorage: Alaska Native Review Commission.

LATZ, P. K., AND J. GREEN

1995   Bushfires and Bushtucker: Aboriginal Plant Use in Central Australia. Alice Springs: IAD Press.

LAURANCE, W., B. M. CROES, L. TCHIGNOUMBA, S. LAHM, A. ALONSO, M. E. LEE,
P. CAMPBELL, AND C. ONDZEANOT

2006   Impacts of Roads and Hunting on Central African Rainforest Mammals.
        Conservation Biology 20(4):1251–1261.

LAYRISSE, M., Z. LAYRISSA, E. GARCIA, AND J. WILBERT

1961   Blood Antigen Groups of the Yaruro Indians. Southwestern Journal of
        Anthropology 17:198–204.

1964   Variaciones genéticas de grupos sanguíneos en 12 tribus de Caribes en Vene-
        zuela y Guayana Británica. Actas y Memorias del 25 Congeso Internacional
        de Americanistas 3:49–55.

LEACOCK, E.

1982a   Myths of Male Dominance. New York: Monthly Review Press.

1982b   Relations of Production in Band Society. *In* Politics and History in Band
        Societies. E. Leacock and R. Lee, eds. Pp. 159–170. Cambridge: Cambridge
        University Press.

LEACOCK, E., AND R. B. LEE, EDS.

1982   Politics and History in Band Societies. Cambridge: Cambridge University
        Press; and Paris: La Maison des Sciences de l'Homme.

LEE, R. B.

1968   What Hunters Do for a Living; or, How to Make Out on Scarce Resources. *In*
        Man the Hunter. Pp. 30–48. Chicago, IL: Aldine.

1969   Eating Christmas in the Kalahari. Natural History December:14–22, 60–63.

1979   The !Kung San: Men, Women and Work in a Foraging Society. Cambridge:
        Cambridge University Press.

1984   The Dobe! Kung. Orlando, FL: Holt, Rinehart, and Winston.

1990   Primitive Communism and the Origin of Social Inequality. *In* The Evolu-
        tion of Political Systems: Sociopolitics in Small-Scale Sedentary Societies.
        S. Upham, ed. Pp. 225–246. Cambridge: Cambridge University Press.

2002   Solitude or Servitude: Ju/'hoan Images of the Colonial Encounter. *In* Eth-
        nicity and Hunter-Gatherers: Association or Assimilation. S. Kent, ed.
        Pp. 178–196. Washington, DC: Smithsonian Institution Press.

2013a   The Dobe Ju/'hoansi. 4th edition. Belmont, CA: Cengage.

2013b   "In the bush the food is free": The Ju/'hoansi of Tsumkwe in the 21st
        Century. Paper presented at the School for Advanced Research Seminar
        "21st-Century Hunting and Gathering: Foraging on a Transnational Land-
        scape," Santa Fe, NM, May 5–9.

LEE, R. B., AND R. DALY, EDS.

1999   The Cambridge Encyclopaedia of Hunters and Gatherers. Cambridge: Cam-
           bridge University Press.

2005   Cambridge Encyclopedia of Hunters and Gatherers. Cambridge: Cambridge
           University Press.

LEE, R. B., AND I. DEVORE, EDS.

1968   Man the Hunter. Chicago: Aldine.

1976   Kalahari Hunter-Gatherers: Studies of the Kung San and Their Neighbors.
           Cambridge, MA: Harvard University Press.

LEE, R. B., AND M. GUENTHER

1993   Problems in Kalahari Historical Ethnography and the Tolerance of Error.
           History in Africa 20:185–235.

LEE, R. B., AND S. HURLICH

1982   From Foragers to Fighters: South Africa's Militarization of the Namibian
           San. *In* Politics and History in Band Societies. E. Leacock and R. B. Lee, eds.
           Pp. 327–346. Cambridge: Cambridge University Press; and Paris: La Maison
           des Sciences de l'Homme.

LEE, R. B., AND I. SUSSER

2008   Confounding Conventional Wisdom: The Ju/'hoansi and HIV/AIDS. *In*
           AIDS Culture and Africa. D. Feldman, ed. Pp. 45–60. Gainesville: University
           Press of Florida.

LEEDS, A.

1960   The Ideology of the Yaruro Indians in Relation to Socio-economic Organiza-
           tion. Antropológica 9:1–8.

1961   The Yaruro Incipient Tropical Forest Horticulture: Possibilities and Limits.
           In The Evolution of Horticultural Systems in Native South America: Causes
           and Consequences. J. Wilbert, ed. Pp. 13–46. Antropológica Supplement, 2.
           Caracas: Editorial Sucre.

1964   Some Problems of Yaruro Ethnohistory. Actas y Memorias del 25 Congreso
           International de Americanistas 2:157–175.

LEGENDRE, P., AND L. LEGENDRE

1998   Numerical Ecology. 2nd edition. New York: Elsevier.

LETNIC, M., C. R. DICKMAN, M. K. TISCHLER, B. TAMAYO, AND C. L. BEH

2004   The Responses of Small Mammals and Lizards to Post-fire Succession and
           Rainfall in Arid Australia. Journal of Arid Environments 59(1):85–114.

LEWIS, J.

2005   Whose Forest Is It Anyway? Mbendjele Yaka Pygmies, the Ndoki For-
           est and the Wider World. *In* Property and Equality: Encapsulation,

Commercialisation, Discrimination, vol. 2. T. Widlok and W. Gossa Tadesse, eds. Pp. 56–78. New York: Berghan Books.

LONNER, T.

1980   Subsistence As an Economic System in Alaska: Theoretical and Policy Implications. Technical Paper, 67. Anchorage: Alaska Department of Fish and Game, Division of Subsistence.

LOVEJOY, C. O.

1981   The Origins of Man. Science 211(4480):341–380.

LOW, B. S.

1990   Occupational Status, Landownership, and Reproductive Behavior in 19th-Century Sweden: Tuna Parish. American Anthropologist 92(2):457–468.

LUNDIE-JENKINS, G.

1993   Ecology of the Rufous Hare-Wallaby, *Lagorchestes hirsutus* Gould (Marsupialia: Macropodidae) in the Tanami Desert, Northern Territory, I: Patterns of Habitat Use. Wildlife Research 20(4):457–475.

LUNDIE-JENKINS, G., L. K. CORBETT, AND C. M. PHILLIPS

1993a   Ecology of the Rufous Hare-Wallaby, *Lagorchestes hirsutus* Gould (Marsupialia: Macropodidae) in the Tanami Desert, Northern Territory, III: Interactions with Introduced Mammal Species. Wildlife Research 20(4):495–511.

LUNDIE-JENKINS, G., C. M. PHILLIPS, AND P. J. JARMAN

1993b   Ecology of the Rufous Hare-Wallaby, *Lagorchestes hirsutus* Gould (Marsupialia: Macropodidae) in the Tanami Desert, Northern Territory, II: Diet and Feeding Strategy. Wildlife Research 20(4):477–493.

LUPO, K. D.

2011   A Dog Is for Hunting. *In* Ethnozooarchaeology: The Present and Past of Human-Animal Relationships. U. Albarella and A. Trentacos, eds. Pp. 4–12. Oxford: Oxbow Press.

2011–2012   Implications of Bofi and Aka Ethnoarchaeology in the Congo Basin for Understanding Late Holocene Technological Change. Before Farming 4:2.

LUPO, K. D., J. M. FANCHER, AND D. N. SCHMITT

2013   The Taphonomy of Resource Intensification: Implications of Resource Scarcity among Bofi and Aka Forest Foragers for the Zooarchaeological Record. Journal of Archaeological Method and Theory 20(3):420–447.

LUPO, K. D., J.-P. NDANGA, AND C. KIAHTIPES

2014   On Late Holocene Population Interactions in the Northwestern Congo Basin: When, How and Why Does the Ethnographic Pattern Begin? *In* Hunter-Gatherers of the Congo Basin: Cultures, Histories, and Biology of African Pygmies. Barry S. Hewlett, ed. Pp. 59–84. New Brunswick, NJ: Transaction.

LUPO, K. D., AND D. N. SCHMITT

2002   Upper Paleolithic Net Hunting, Small Mammal Procurement and Women's Work Effort: A View from the Ethnoarchaeological Record of the Congo Basin. Journal of Archaeological Method and Theory 9:147–180.

2004   Meat-Sharing and the Archaeological Record: A Preliminary Test of the Show-Off Hypothesis among Central African Bofi Foragers. *In* Hunters and Gatherers in Theory and Archaeology. G. Crothers, ed. Pp. 241–260. Center for Archaeological Investigations Occasional Paper, 31. Carbondale: Southern Illinois University.

2005   Small Prey Hunting Technology and Zooarchaeological Measures of Taxonomic Diversity and Abundance: Ethnoarchaeological Evidence from Central African Forest Foragers. Journal of Anthropological Archaeology 24:335–353.

MABULLA, A. Z. P.

2007   Hunting and Foraging in the Eyasi Basin, Northern Tanzani: Past, Present and Future Prospects. African Archaeology Review 24:15–33.

MACARTHUR, R. H.

1972   Geographical Ecology: Patterns in the Distribution of Species. Princeton, NJ: Princeton University Press.

MACARTHUR, R. H., AND E. PIANKA

1966   On Optimal Use of a Patchy Environment. American Naturalist 100:603–609.

MACE, R.

1996   Biased Parental Investment and Reproductive Success in Gabbra Pastoralists. Behavioral Ecology and Sociobiology 38(2):75–81.

MADDISON, S.

2008   Indigenous Autonomy Matters: What's Wrong with the Australian Government's "Intervention" in Aboriginal Communities. Australian Journal of Human Rights 14(1):41–60.

MAISELS, F., S. STRINBERG, S. BLAKE, J. HART, E. WILLIAMSON, R. ABA'A, AND G. ABITSI ET AL.

2013   Devasting Decline of Forest Elephants in Central Africa. PLOS One 8(3):e59469.

MALAISSE, F., AND G. PARENT

1985   Edible Wild Vegetable Products in the Zambezian Woodland Area: A Nutritional and Ecological Approach. Ecology of Food and Nutrition 18:43–82.

MANLY, B. F. J.

2006   Randomization, Bootstrap, and Monte Carlo Methods in Biology. 3rd edi-
        tion. Boca Raton, FL: Chapman & Hall/CRC.

MAREAN, C. W.

1997   Hunter-Gatherer Forging Strategies in Tropical Grasslands: Model Build-
        ing and Testing in the East African Middle and Later Stone Age. Journal of
        Anthropological Archaeology 16:189–225.

MARLOWE, F. W.

1999   Showoffs or Providers? The Parenting Effort of Hadza Men. Evolution and
        Human Behavior 20(6):391–404.

2002   Why the Hadza Are Still Hunter-Gatherers. *In* Ethnicity, Hunter-Gatherers,
        and the "Other": Association or Assimilation in Africa. S. Kent, ed.
        Pp. 247–275. Washington, DC: Smithsonian Institution Press.

2004   Marital Residence among Foragers. Current Anthropology 45:277–284.

2006   Central Place Provisioning: The Hadza as an Example. *In* Feeding Ecology
        in Apes and Other Primates. G. Hohman, M. Robbins, and C. Boesch, eds.
        Pp. 359–377. Cambridge: Cambridge University Press.

2010   The Hadza Hunter-Gatherers of Tanzania. Berkeley: University of California
        Press.

MARLOWE, F. W., AND J. C. BERBESQUE

2009   Tubers as Fallback Foods and Their Impact on Hadza Hunter-Gatherers.
        American Journal of Physical Anthropology 140:751–758.

MARSHALL, J.

1980   N!ai: The Story of A !Kung Woman [film]. Watertown, MA: Documentary
        Educational Resources.

2005   A Kalahari Family [film]. Cambridge, MA: Documentary Educational
        Resources.

MARSHALL, J., AND C. RITCHIE

1984   Death Blow to the Bushmen. Cultural Survival Quarterly 8(3):13–16.

MARSHALL, L.

1960   !Kung Bushman Bands. Africa 30:325–355.

1969   The Medicine Dance of the !Kung Bushmen. Africa 39:347–381.

1976   The !Kung of Nyae Nyae. Cambridge, MA: Harvard University Press.

1999   Nyae Nyae !Kung: Beliefs and Rites. Cambridge, MA: Peabody Museum
        Press.

MARTIN, D. F.

2001   Is Welfare Dependency "Welfare Poison"? An Assessment of Noel Pearson's
        Proposals for Aboriginal Welfare Reform. Center for Aboriginal Economic

Policy Research Discussion Paper, 213. Canberra: Australian National University.

MARUYAMA, J.

2003   The Impact of Resettlement on Livelihood and Social Relationships among the Central Kalahari San. African Study Monographs 14(4):223–245.

MASTERS, P.

1996   The Effects of Fire-Driven Succession on Reptiles in Spinifex Grasslands at Uluru National Park, Northern Territory. Wildlife Research 23(1):39–47.

MAUSS, M.

1924   The Gift. W. D. Halls, trans. New York: Norton.

1954   The Gift: Forms and Functions of Exchange in Archaic Societies. Glencoe, IL: Free Press.

MCCARTHY, F. D., AND M. MCARTHUR

1960   The Food Quest and the Time Factor in Aboriginal Economic Life. *In* Records of the American-Australian Scientific Expedition to Arnhem Land, vol. 2: Anthropology and Nutrition. C. P. Mountford, ed. Pp. 145–194. Melbourne: Melbourne University Press.

MCDOWELL, W.

1981   A Brief History of the Mangola Hadza. Ms. prepared for the Rift Valley Project. Ministry of Information and Culture, Dar es Salaam, Republic of Tanzania.

MCGREGOR, R.

1999   Wards, Words and Citizens: A. P. Elkin and Paul Hasluck on Assimilation. Oceania 69:243–259.

MCNIVEN, I. J., AND R. FELDMAN

2003   Ritually Orchestrated Seascapes: Hunting Magic and Dugong Bone Mounds in Torres Strait, Ne Australia. Cambridge Archaeological Journal 13(2):169–194.

MEGGITT, M. J.

1965   Desert People: A Study of the Walbiri Aborigines of Central Australia. Chicago, IL: University of Chicago Press.

MENARD, S.

2002   Applied Logistic Regression Analysis. 2nd edition. Thousand Oaks, CA: Sage.

MERCADER, J.

2002   Forest People: The Role of African Rainforests in Human Evolution and Dispersal. Evolutionary Anthropology 11:117–124.

MERCADER, J., M. GARCI-HERAS, AND I. GONZALEZ-ALVAREZ

2000a   Ceramic Tradition in the African Forest: Characterisation Analysis of

Ancient and Modern Pottery from Ituri, D. R. Congo. Journal of Archeological Science 27(2):163–182.

MERCADER, J., R. SALVADOR, AND P. GÓMEZ-RAMOS

2000b   Shared Technologies: Forager-Farmer Interaction and Ancient Iron Metallurgy in the Ituri Rainforest, Democratic Republic of Congo. Azania 35(1):107–122.

METZGER, D. J., AND R. V. MOREY

1983   Los Hiwi (Guahibo). *In* Los aborígenes de Venezuela, vol. 2. R. Lizarralde and H. Seijas, eds. Pp. 125–216. Caracas: Fundación La Salle de Ciencias Naturales.

MILLER, J. B., K. W. JAMES, AND P. M. A. MAGGIORE

1993   Tables of Composition of Australian Aboriginal Foods. Canberra: Aboriginal Studies Press.

MILNER-GULLAND, E. J., AND J. R. BEDDINGTON

1993   The Exploitation of Elephants for the Ivory Trade: An Historical Perspective. Proceedings of the Royal Society: Biological Sciences 252(1333):29–37.

MILTON, K.

1984   Protein and Carbohydrate Resources of the Maku Indians of Northwestern Amazonia. American Anthropologist 86:7–27.

MITRANI, P.

1988   Los Pumé (Yaruro). *In* Los aborígenes de Venezuela, vol. 3. J. Lizot, ed. Pp. 147–213. Caracas: Fundación La Salle de Ciencias Naturales.

MORGAN, C.

2015   Is It Intensification Yet? Current Archaeological Perspectives on the Evolution of Hunter-Gatherer Economies. Journal of Archaeological Research 23:163–213.

MORGAN, L. H.

1877   Ancient Society or Researchers in the Lines of Human Progress from Savagery through Barbarism to Civilization. London: Macmillan.

MORRISON, J.

2007   Caring for Country. *In* Coercive Reconciliation: Stabilize, Normalize, Exit Aboriginal Australia. J. Altman and M. Hinkson, eds. Pp. 249–261. North Carlton: Arena.

MOSONYI, E. E.

1975   El indígena venezolano en pos de su liberación definitiva. Caracas: Universidad Central de Venezuela, Facultad de Ciencias Económicas y Sociales, División de Publicaciónes.

MOSONYI, E. E., J. C. MOSONYI, AND J. R. GARCÍA

2000   Yaruro (Pume). *In* Manual de lenguas indígenas de Venezuela, vol. 2.

E. E. Mosonyi and J. C. Mosonyi, eds. Pp. 544–593. Serie Orígenes, 3. Caracas: Fundación Bigott.

MULLER, H.

1912   Ein Enkundungsgritt in das Kaukau-veld. Deutsches Kolonialblatt 25:530–541.

MYBURGH, P. J.

2014   The Bushman Winter Has Come: The True Story of the Last /Guikhwe Bushmen on the Great Sand Face. London: Penguin Global Books.

MYERS, F. R.

1982   Always Ask: Resource Use and Land Ownership among Pintubi Aborigines of the Australian Western Desert. *In* Resource Managers: North American and Australian Hunter-Gatherers. N. M. Williams and E. S. Hunn, eds. Pp. 173–195. Aaas Selected Symposia Series. Boulder, CO: Westview Press.

1986   Pintupi Country, Pintupi Self: Sentiment, Place and Politics among Western Desert Aborigines. Washington, DC: Smithsonian Institution.

1988   Critical Trends in the Study of Hunter-Gatherers. Annual Review of Anthropology 17:261–282.

1989   Burning the Truck and Holding the Country: Pintupi Forms of Property and Identity. *In* We Are Here: Politics of Aboriginal Land Tenure. Edwin N. Wilmsen, ed. Pp. 15–42. Berkeley: University of California Press.

2002   Painting Culture: The Making of an Aboriginal High Art. Durham, NC: Duke University Press.

NGASSE, G.

2003   Ngotto Forest, Central African Republic. *In* Sustainable Management of Tropical Forests in Central Africa: In Search of Excellence. I. Amsallem, M. L. Wilkie, P. Koné, and M. Ngandji, eds. Pp. 27–31. Rome: FAO.

NOË, R., AND P. HAMMERSTEIN

1994   Biological Markets: Supply and Demand Determine the Effect of Partner Choice in Cooperation. Behavioral Ecology and Sociobiology 35(1):1–11.

NOË, R., J. A. R. A. M. VAN HOOFF, AND P. HAMMERSTEIN

2001   Economics in Nature: Social Dilemmas, Mate Choice and Biological Markets. Cambridge: Cambridge University Press.

NOLIN, D. A.

2010   Food-Sharing Networks in Lamalera, Indonesia: Reciprocity, Kinship, and Distance. Human Nature 21:243–268.

2012   Food-Sharing Networks in Lamalera, Indonesia: Status, Sharing, and Signaling. Evolution and Human Behavior 33:334–345.

NOSS, A. J.

1995   Duikers, Cables and Nets: A Cultural Ecology of Hunting in a Central African Forest. PhD dissertation, Department of Geography and Center for African Studies, University of Florida.

1998   The Impacts of BaAka Net Hunting on Rainforest Wildlife. Biological Conservation 86:161–167.

NUNAVUT BUREAU OF STATISTICS

2013   Nunavut Population, July, 2004 to 2012. http://www.stats.gov.nu.ca/Publications/Popest/Population/Population%20estimates%20Report%20July%2012.pdf, accessed July 22, 2012.

NWMB (NUNAVUT WILDLIFE MANAGEMENT BOARD)

2004   The Nunavut Wildlife Harvest Study. Iqaluit: Nunavut Wildlife Management Board.

OBREGÓN MUÑOZ, H.

1981   La variabilidad de las lenguas indígenas venezolanas y algunos problemas de planificación lingüística. Antropológica 56:3–24.

OBST, E.

1912   Von Mkalama ins Land der Wakindiga. Mitteilungen der Geographischen Gesellschaft in Hamburg, 26, 1. Hamburg: Friederischsen.

O'CONNELL, J. F.

1987   Alyawara Site Structure and Its Archaeological Implications. American Antiquity 52:74–108.

1995   Ethnoarchaeology Needs a General Theory of Behavior. Journal of Archaeological Research 3:205–255.

O'CONNELL, J. F., AND K. HAWKES

1981   Alyawara Plant Use and Optimal Foraging Theory. *In* Hunter-Gatherer Foraging Strategies: Archaeological and Ethnographic Analyses. B. Winterhalder and E. Smith, eds. Pp. 99–125. Chicago, IL: University of Chicago Press.

1984   Food Choice and Foraging Sites among the Alyawara. Journal of Anthropological Research 40:504–535.

O'CONNELL, J. F., K. HAWKES, AND N. G. BLURTON JONES

1999   Grandmothering and the Evolution of *Homo erectus*. Journal of Human Evolution 36:461–485.

O'CONNELL, J. F., P. K. LATZ, AND P. BARNETT

1983   Traditional and Modern Plant Use among the Alyawara of Central Australia. Economic Botany 37(1):80–109.

OKIGBO, B. N.

1980   Nutritional Implications of Projects Giving High Priority to the Production of Staples of Low Nutritive Quality: The Case of Cassava (*Manihot esculenta*,

Crantz) in the Humid Tropics of West Africa. Food and Nutrition Bulletin, 2. Tokyo: United Nations University.

OOTA, H., B. PAKENDORF, G. WEISS, A. VON HAESELER, S. POOKAJORN,
W. SETTHEETHAM-ISHIDA, D. TIWAWECH, I. TAKAFUMI, AND M. STONEKING
2005   Recent Origin and Cultural Reversion of a Hunter-Gatherer Group. PLOS Biology 3:536–542.

OSAKI, M.
1984   The Social Influence of Change in Hunting Technique among the Central Kalahari San. African Study Monographs 5:49–62.

2001   Reconstructing the Recent History of the G/ui and G//ana Bushmen. African Study Monographs, suppl., 26:27–39.

O'SHEA, J.
1981   Coping with Scarcity: Exchange and Social Structure. *In* Economic Archaeology: Towards an Integration of Ecological and Social Approaches. A. Sheridan and G. Bailey, eds. Pp. 167–186. BAR International Series, 96. Oxford: B.A.R.

OSWALT, W. H.
1973   Habitat and Technology: The Evolution of Hunting. New York: Holt, Rinehart, and Winston.

OTÁROLA-CASTILLO, E.
2010   Differences between NISP and MNE in Cutmark Analysis of Highly Fragmented Faunal Assemblages. Journal of Archaeological Science 37:1–12.

OWENS, M., AND D. OWENS
1981   Preliminary Final Report on the Central Kalahari Predator Research Project. Report to the Department of Wildlife and National Parks, Gaborone.

1984   Cry of the Kalahari. Boston, MA: Houghton-Mifflin.

PANTER-BRICK, C., R. H. LAYTON, AND R. ROWLEY-CONWY
2001   Hunter-Gatherers: An Interdisciplinary Perspective. Cambridge: Cambridge University Press.

PARKER, C., R. BLIEGE BIRD, AND D. BIRD
N.d.   Beyond Firestick Farming: The Effects of Aboriginal Burning on Economically Important Plant Foods in Australia's Western Desert.

PASHA, E.
1888   Emin Pasha in Central Africa. G. Schweinfurth, F. Ratzel, R. W. Felkin, and G. Hautlaub, eds. and annotators. London: George Philip & Son.

PATIN, E., G. LAVAL, L. B. BARREIRO, A. SALAS, O. SEMINO, S. SANTACHIARA-
BENERECETTI, K. K. KIDD, J. R. KIDD, L. VAND DER VEEN, J.-M. HOMBERT,
A. GESSAIN, A. FROMENT, S. BAHUCHET, E. HEYER, AND L. QUINTANA-MURCI
2009   Inferring the Demographic History of African Farmers and Pygmy Hunter-
        Gatherers Using a Multilocus Resequencing Data Set. PLOS Genetics
        5(4):e1000448.

PERUSSE, D.
1993   Cultural and Reproductive Success in Industrial Societies: Testing the
        Relationship at the Proximate and Ultimate Levels. Behavioral and Brain Sci-
        ences 16:267–322.

PETERSON, J. T.
1978   The Ecology of Social Boundaries: Agta Foragers of the Philippines. Urbana:
        University of Illinois Press.

PETERSON, N.
1991a   Cash, Commoditisation and Authenticity: When Do Aboriginal People Stop
        Being Hunter-Gatherers? *In* Cash, Commoditisation and Changing Foragers.
        N. Peterson and T. Matsuyama, eds. Pp. 67–90. Senri Ethnological Studies,
        30. Osaka: National Museum of Ethnology.

1991b   Introduction: Cash, Commoditisation and Changing Foragers. *In* Cash,
        Commoditisation and Changing Foragers. N. Peterson and T. Matsuyama,
        eds. Pp. 1–16. Senri Ethnological Studies, 30. Osaka: National Museum of
        Ethnology.

1993   Demand Sharing: Reciprocity and the Pressure for Generosity among For-
        agers. American Anthropologist 95(4):860–874.

PETERSON, N., AND J. LONG
1986   Australian Territorial Organization: A Band Perspective. Sydney: University
        of Sydney.

PETRULLO, V.
1939   The Yaruros of the Capanaparo River, Venezuela. Anthropological Papers, 11.
        Bureau of American Ethnology Bulletin, 123. Pp. 161–290. Washington, DC:
        Smithsonian Institution.

PIANKA, E. R.
1995   Evolution of Body Size: Varanid Lizards as a Model System. American Natu-
        ralist 146(3):398–414.

PIANKA, E. R., AND S. E. GOODYEAR
2012   Lizard Responses to Wildfire in Arid Interior Australia: Long-Term Experi-
        mental Data and Commonalities with Other Studies. Austral Ecology
        37(1):1–11.

PICKETT, K. N., D. S. HIK, A. E. NEWSOME, AND R. P. PECH

2005   The Influence of Predation Risk on Foraging Behaviour of Brushtail Possums in Australian Woodlands. Wildlife Research 32(2):121–130.

PIKETTY, T.

2014   Capital in the Twenty-First Century. Cambridge, MA: Belknap Press.

PIPERNO, D. R., AND D. M. PEARSALL

1998   The Origins of Agriculture in the Lowland Neotropics. San Diego, CA: Academic Press.

POLANYI, K.

1944   The Great Transformation: The Political and Economic Origins of Our Time. Boston, MA: Beacon Press.

1957   The Economy as Instituted Process. *In* Trade and Market in the Early Empires: Economies in History and Theory. K. Polanyi, C. Arensberg, and H. Pearson, eds. Pp. 243–270. New York: Free Press.

POLITIS, G. G.

1996   Moving to Produce: Nukak Mobility and Settlement Patterns in Amazonia. World Archaeology 27:492–511.

2007   Nukak: Ethnoarchaeology of an Amazonian People. Walnut Creek, CA: Left Coast Press.

POLLAN, M.

2007   The Omnivore's Dilemma: A Natural History of Four Meals. New York: Penguin.

POOKAJORN, S.

1992   The Phi Tong Luang (Mlabri): A Hunter-Gatherer Group in Thailand. Bangkok: Odeon Store Printing House.

PRYOR, F.

1977   The Origins of Economy: A Comparative Study of Distribution in Primitive and Peasant Economies. New York: Academic Press.

PUTNAM, P. T.

1948   The Pygmies of the Ituri Forest. *In* A Reader in General Anthropology. C. S. Coon, ed. Pp. 322–342. New York: Holt.

PYKE, G. H., H. R. PULLIAM, AND E. L. CHARNOV

1977   Optimal Foraging: A Selective Review of Theory and Tests. Quarterly Review of Biology 52(2):137–154.

QUATREFAGES, A. DE

1895   The Pygmies. London: Macmillan.

QUINTAL, M.

2012   Inuit Women in the Northern Economy. Paper presented at the NIKAN
            Conference, Val d'Or, Quebec, November 1–3.

QUINTANA-MURCI, L., H. QUACH, C. HARMANT, F. LUCA, B. MASSONNET, E. PATIN,

L. SICA, P. MOUGUIAMA-DAOUDA, D. COMAS, S. TZUR, O. BALANOVSKY, K. K. KIDD,

J. R. KIDD, L. VAN DER VEEN, J.-M. HOMBERT, A. GESSAIN, P. VERDU, A. FROMENT,

S. BAHUCHET, E. HEYER, J. DAUSSET, A. SALAS, AND D. M. BEHAR

2008   Maternal Traces of Deep Common Ancestry and Asymmetric Gene Flow
            between Pygmy Hunter-Gatherers and Bantu-Speaking Farmers. Proceed-
            ings of the National Academy of Science 105(5):1596–1601.

RAI, N. K.

1990   Living in a Lean-To: Philippine Negrito Foragers in Transition. Anthro-
            pological Papers, 80. Ann Arbor: Museum of Anthropology, University of
            Michigan.

RAMBO, A. T.

1985   Primitive Polluters: Semang Impact on the Malaysian Rain Forest Ecosys-
            tem. Anthropological Papers, 76. Ann Arbor: Museum of Anthropology,
            University of Michigan.

RASMUSSEN, K.

1929   The Intellectual Life of the Iglulik Eskimos. Report of the Fifth Thule Expedi-
            tion, vol. 8, nos. 1–2. Copenhagen: Gyldendalske Boghandel.

R CORE TEAM

2013   R: A Language and Environment for Statistical Computing. Vienna: R Foun-
            dation for Statistical Computing.

RECHE, O.

1914   Die ethnographische Sammlung. *In* Das Abflusslose Rumpfschollenland im
            nordöstlichen Deutsch-Ostafrika. E. Obst, ed. Pp. 251–266. Mitteilungen der
            Geographischen Gesellschaft in Hamburg, 24. Hamburg: Friederischsen.

REPUBLIC OF BOTSWANA

1986   Wildlife Conservation Policy. Government Paper No. 1 of 1986. Gaborone:
            Government Printer.

1992   Wildlife Conservation and National Parks Act, 1992. Act No. 28 of 1992.
            Gaborone: Government Printer.

2002   Revised National Policy on Destitute Persons. Gaborone: Government
            Printer.

2014   Supplement C. Wildlife Conservation and National Parks (Prohibition of
            Hunting, Capturing, or Removal of Animals Order, 2014). Statutory Instru-
            ment No. 2 of 2014. Gaborone: Botswana Government Gazette.

RICHERSON, P. J., R. BOYD, AND R. BETTINGER

2001   Was Agriculture Impossible during the Pleistocene but Mandatory dur-
        ing the Holocene? A Climate Change Hypothesis. American Antiquity
        66:387–411.

RICHES, D.

1990   The Force of Tradition in Eskimology. *In* Localizing Strategies: Regional
        Traditions of Ethnographic Writing. R. Fardon, ed. Pp. 71–89. Edinborough:
        Scottish University Press.

RIVAL, L., AND D. MCKEY

2008   Domestication and Diversity in Manioc (*Manihot esculenta* Crantz
        ssp. *esculenta*, Euphorbiaceae). Current Anthropology 48:1119–1128.

ROBERTS, G.

1998   Competitive Altruism: Reciprocity to the Handicap Principle. Proceedings of
        the Royal Society of London Series B: Biological Sciences 265(1394):427–431.

ROBINSON, M. V.

1973   Change and Adjustment among the Bardi of Sunday Island, North-Western
        Australia. PhD dissertation, Department of Anthropology, University of
        Western Australia.

1979   Local Organization and Kinship in Northern Dampier Land. *In* Aborigines
        of the West: Their Past and Present. Ronald M. Berndt and Catherine H.
        Berndt, eds. Pp. 186–196. Nedlands: University of Western Australia.

ROSENBERG, H.

2003   Complaint Discourse, Aging and Caregiving among the !Kung San of
        Botswana. *In* The Cultural Context of Aging. J. Sokolovsky, ed. Pp. 19–41.
        New York: Bergin and Garvey.

ROTH, W. E.

1899   The Aborigines of Tasmania. Halifax: F. King and Sons.

ROUJA, P. M.

1998   Fishing for Culture: Toward an Aboriginal Theory of Marine Resource Use
        among the Bardi Aborigines of One Arm Point, Western Australia. PhD dis-
        sertation, Department of Anthropology, University of Durham.

ROWSE, T.

2002   Indigenous Futures: Choice and Development for Aboriginal and Islander
        Australia. Sydney: UNSW Press.

RUNGE, J.

2009   Remote Sensing–Based Forest Assessment: Recent Dynamics of Forest-
        Savanna Boundaries at N'Gottoe Forest, Central Africa. *In* Dynamics of For-
        est Ecosystems in Central Africa during the Holocene: Past-Present-Future.
        J. Runge, ed. Pp. 72–102. Boca Raton, FL: CRC Press.

RUSAK, E. M., J. DORTCH, K. HAYWARD, M. RENTON, M. BOER, AND P. GRIERSON

2011   The Role of Habitus in the Maintenance of Traditional Nonngar Plant Knowledge in Southwest Western Australia. Human Ecology 39:673–682.

RUSSELL, M.

1976   Slaves or Workers? Relations between Bushmen, Tswana and Boers in the Kalahari. Journal of Southern African Studies 2(2):178–197.

RUSSELL, M., AND M. RUSSELL

1979   Afrikaaners of the Kalahari: White Minority in a Black State. Cambridge: Cambridge University Press.

SAHLINS, M. D.

1959   The Social Life of Monkeys, Apes and Primitive Man. Human Biology 31(1):54–73.

1968   Notes on the Original Affluent Society. In Man the Hunter. R. B. Lee and I. DeVore, eds. Pp. 85–89. Chicago, IL: Aldine.

1972   Stone Age Economics. Chicago, IL: Aldine.

1974   Stone Age Economics. London: Tavistock.

1999   What Is Anthropological Enlightenment? Some Lessons of the Twentieth Century. Annual Review of Anthropology 28:i–xxiii.

SALZANO, F. M., AND S. M. CALLEGARI-JACQUES

1988   South American Indians: A Case Study in Evolution. Oxford: Clarendon Press.

SANDS, B.

1998   The Linguistic Relationship between Hadza and Khoisan. In Language, Identity, and Conceptualization. M. Schladt, ed. Pp. 265–283. Quellen zur Khoisan Forschung, 15. Koln: R. Köppe.

SAPIGNOLI, M.

2012   Local Power through Globalized Indigenous Identities: The San, the State, and the International Community. PhD dissertation, Department of Sociology, Essex University.

2015   Dispossession in the Age of Humanity: Human Rights, Citizenship, and Indigeneity in the Central Kalahari. Anthropological Forum: A Journal of Social Anthropology and Comparative Sociology.

SAPIGNOLI, M., AND R. K. HITCHCOCK

2013   Development and Dispossession: Impacts of Land Reform in Botswana. In Africa for Sale? Positioning the State, Land and Society in Foreign Large-Scale Land Acquisitions in Africa. S. Evers, C. Seagle, and F. Krijtenburg, eds. Pp. 131–159. Leiden: Brill Academic.

2014   Social Impact Assessment Anthropological Analysis of the Ghanzi Copper
            Mine Area, Western Botswana. Gaborone: Loci Environmental and SIAPAC.

SATO, H.
2001   The Potential of Edible Wild Yams and Yam-Like Plants as a Staple Food
            Resource in the African Tropical Rain Forest. African Study Monographs,
            suppl., 26:123–134.

SCELZA, B. A.
2009   The Grandmaternal Niche: Critical Caretaking among Martu Aborigines.
            American Journal of Human Biology 21(4):448–454.

2010   Fathers' Presence Speeds the Social and Reproductive Careers of Sons. Cur-
            rent Anthropology 51(2):295–303.

2012   Food Scarcity, Not Economic Constraint, Limits Consumption in a Rural
            Aboriginal Community. Australian Journal of Rural Health 20:108–112.

SCELZA, B. A., D. W. BIRD, AND R. BLIEGE BIRD
2014   Bush Tucker, Shop Tucker: Production, Consumption, and Diet at an
            Aboriginal Outstation. Ecology of Food and Nutrition 53(1):98–117.

SCELZA, B. A., AND R. BLIEGE BIRD
2008   Group Structure and Female Cooperative Networks in Australia's Western
            Desert. Human Nature 19(3):231–248.

SCHEBESTA, P.
1936   My Pygmy and Negro Hosts. London: Hutchinson.

SCHMITT, D. N., AND K. D. LUPO
2008   Do Faunal Remains Reflect Socioeconomic Status? An Ethnoarchaeological
            Study of Central African Farmers in the Northern Congo Basin. Journal of
            Anthropological Archeology 27:315–325.

SCHOENINGER, M. J., H. T. BUNN, S. S. MURRAY, AND J. A. MARLETT
2001   Composition of Tubers Used by the Hadza Foragers of Tanzania. Journal of
            Food Composition and Analysis 14:15–25.

SCHRIRE, C., ED.
1984   Past and Present in Hunter-Gatherer Studies. New York: Academic Press.

SCHWAB, R. G.
1995   The Calculus of Reciprocity: Principles and Implications of Aboriginal
            Sharing. CAEPR Discussion Paper, 100. Canberra: Centre for Aboriginal
            Economic Policy Research, Australian National University.

SCHWEINFURTH, G. A.
1874   The Heart of Africa: Three Years' Travels and Adventures in the Unexplored
            Regions of Central Africa from 1868 to 1871. E. Frewer, trans. Introduction
            by Winwood Reade. New York: Harper & Brothers.

SELEKA, T., H. SIPHAMBE, D. NTSEANA, N. MBERE, C. KERAPELETSWE, AND C. SHARP

2007   Social Safety Nets in Botswana: Administration, Targeting, and Sustain-
        ability. Gaborone: Lightbooks.

SHEA, J. J.

2011   *Homo sapiens* Is as *Homo sapiens* Was. Current Anthropology 52:1–35.

SHELLER, P.

1977   The People of the Central Kalahari Game Reserve: A Report on the Recon-
        naissance of the Reserve, July–September, 1976. Report to the Ministry of
        Local Government and Lands, Gaborone.

SHENK, M. K., AND B. A. SCELZA

2012   Paternal Investment and Status-Related Child Outcomes: Timing of Father's
        Death Affects Offspring Success. Journal of Biosocial Science 44(5):549–569.

SHOSTAK, M.

1976   Glass Beadwork of the !Kung of Northwestern Botswana. Botswana Notes
        and Records 8:175–179.

SILBERBAUER, G. B.

1965a   Bushman Survey Report. Gaberone: Bechuanaland Government Press.

1965b   Report to the Government of Bechuanaland on the Bushman Survey. Gabo-
        rone: Bechuanaland Government.

1972   The G/wi Bushmen. *In* Hunters and Gatherers Today. M. G. Bicchieri, ed.
        Pp. 271–326. New York: Holt, Rinehart, and Winston.

1981a   Hunter and Habitat in the Central Kalahari Desert. New York: Cambridge
        University Press.

1981b   Hunter/Gatherers of the Central Kalahari. *In* Omnivorous Primates: Gather-
        ing and Hunting in Human Evolution. R. S. O. Harding and G. Teleki, eds.
        Pp. 455–498. New York: Columbia University Press.

2012   Why the Central Kalahari Game Reserve? Botswana Notes and Records
        44:201–203.

SMITH, B. D.

2001   Low-Level Food Production. Journal of Archaeological Science 9:1–43.

SMITH, E. A.

1985   Inuit Foraging Groups: Some Simple Models Incorporating Conflicts of
        Interest, Relatedness and Central-Place Sharing. Ethology and Sociobiology
        6:27–47.

1991   Inujjuamiut Foraging Strategies: Evolutionary Ecology of an Arctic Hunting
        Economy. New York: Aldine de Gruyter.

1993   Comment on "Why Hunters Work" by Kristen Hawkes. Current Anthro-
        pology 34:356.

2004   Why Do Good Hunters Have Higher Reproductive Success? Human Nature
           15(4):343–364.

2013   Agency and Adaptation: New Directions in Evolutionary Anthropology.
           Annual Review of Anthropology 42:103–120.

SMITH, E. A., AND R. L. BLIEGE BIRD
2000   Turtle Hunting and Tombstone Opening: Public Generosity as Costly Signal-
           ing. Evolution and Human Behavior 21(4):245–261.

2005   Costly Signaling and Cooperative Behavior. *In* Moral Sentiments and
           Material Interests: On the Foundations of Cooperation in Economic Life.
           H. Gintis, S. Bowles, R. Boyd, and E. Fehr, eds. Pp. 115–148. Cambridge, MA:
           MIT Press.

SMITH, E. A., R. BLIEGE BIRD, AND D. W. BIRD
2003   The Benefits of Costly Signaling: Meriam Turtle Hunters. Behavioral Ecology
           14(1):116–126.

SMITH, E. A., AND B. WINTERHALDER, EDS.
1992   Evolutionary Ecology and Human Behavior. New York: Aldine de Gruyter.

SMITH, G. T., AND S. R. MORTON
1990   Responses by Scorpions to Fire-Initiated Succession in Arid Australian
           Spinifex Grasslands. Journal of Arachnology 18(2):241–244.

SMITH, M. A., A. N. WILLIAMS, C. S. M. TURNEY, AND M. L. CUPPER
2008   Human-Environment Interactions in Australian Drylands: Exploratory
           Time-Series Analysis of Archaeological Records. Holocene 18(3):389.

SMITH, MIKE
2013   The Archaeology of Australia's Deserts. Cambridge: Cambridge University
           Press.

SMITH, MOYA
1983   Joules from Pools: Social and Techno-economic Aspects of Bardi Stone Fish
           Traps. *In* Archaeology at Anzaas. M. Smith, ed. Pp. 29–45. Perth: Western
           Australian Museum.

1984   Bardi Relationships with the Sea. Anthropological Forum 5(3):443–447.

1987   Dots on the Map: Sites and Seasonality, the Bardi Example. Australian
           Archaeology 25:40–52.

SMITH, MOYA, AND A. C. KALOTAS
1985   Bardi Plants: An Annotated List of Plants and Their Use by the Bardi
           Aborigines of Dampierland, in North-Western Australia. Records of the
           West Australian Museum 12(3):317–359.

SMYTH, R. B.

1878   The Aborigines of Victoria: Notes Relating to the Habits of the Natives of Other Parts of Australia and Tasmania, vol. 1. London: Trübner.

SOENGAS, B.

2009   Preliminary Ethnographic Research on the Bakoya in Gabon. African Study Monograph 30(4):187–208.

SOLWAY, J., AND R. LEE

1990   Foragers, Genuine or Spurious? Situating the Kalahari San in History. Current Anthropology 31(2):109–146.

SPINAGE, C. A.

1991   History and Evolution of the Fauna Conservation Laws of Botswana. Gaborone: Botswana Society.

2012   African Ecology. Berlin: Springer.

STANNER, W. E. H.

1965   Aboriginal Territorial Organization: Estate, Range, Domain and Regime. Oceania 36(1):1–26.

STEARMAN, A. M.

1989   Yuquí: Forest Nomads in a Changing World. New York: Holt, Rinehart, and Winston.

STEPHENS, D. W., AND J. R. KREBS

1986   Foraging Theory. Princeton, NJ: Princeton University Press.

STERGIOS DOE, B.

1993   La etnobotánica del arbol "chiga" (*Campisandra*, Leguminaceae, Caesalpinaceae) en la región llanera de la cuenca de del medio río Orinoco en el suroeste de Venezuela. Biollania 9:71–90.

STEVENS, J. R., AND I. C. GILBY

2004   A Conceptual Framework for Nonkin Food Sharing: Timing and Currency Benefits. Animal Behavior 67:603–614.

STEVENS, J. R., AND D. W. STEPHENS

2002   Food Sharing: A Model of Manipulation by Harassment. Behavioral Ecology 13:393–400.

STEWARD, JULIAN

1936   The Economic and Social Basis of Primitive Bands. *In* Essays in Anthropology Presented to A. L. Kroeber in Celebration of His Sixtieth Birthday, June 11, 1936. R. H. Lowie, ed. Berkeley: University of California Press.

1938   Basin Plateau Aboriginal Sociopolitical Groups. Salt Lake City: University of Utah Press.

STILES, D.

1991   Tubers and Tenrecs: The Mikea of Southwestern Madagascar. Ethnology
            30:251–263.

STINER, M. C.

2001   Thirty Years on the "Broad Spectrum Revolution" and Paleolithic Demogra-
            phy. Proceedings of the National Academy of Sciences 98:6993–6996.

STOFFLE, R.

2005   Places That Count: Traditional Cultural Properties in Cultural Resource
            Management; Tribal Cultural Resource Management: The Full Circle to
            Stewardship. American Anthropologist 107:138–140.

SULLIVAN, P.

2010   The Aboriginal Community Sector and the Effective Delivery of Services:
            Acknowledging the Role of Indigenous Sector Organizations. DKCRC
            Working Paper, 73. Alice Springs: Desert Knowledge Cooperative Research
            Centre.

SUN, N. Y.

1889   The Smallest People in the World. Current Opinion 2:15–16.

SUSSER, I.

2009   AIDS, Sex and Culture: Global Politics and Survival in Southern Africa.
            Malden, MA: Wiley-Blackwell.

SUTTLES, W., ED.

1990   Handbook of the North American Indians, vol. 7: Northwest Coast. Wash-
            ington, DC: Smithsonian Press.

SUTTON, J. E. G.

1986   The Irrigation and Manuring of the Engaruka Field System. Azania 21:27–51.

1990   Sonjo and Engaruka: Further Signs of Continuity. Azania 25:91–93.

TAKADA, A.

2005   Early Vocal Communication and Social Institution: Appellation and Infant
            Verse Addressing among the Central Kalahari San. Crossroads of Language,
            Interaction, and Culture 6:80–108.

TANAKA, J.

1980   The San, Hunter-Gatherers of the Kalahari. A Study in Ecological Anthro-
            pology. Tokyo: University of Tokyo Press.

1987   The Recent Changes in the Life and Society of the Central Kalahari San.
            African Study Monographs 7:37–51.

2014   The Bushmen: A Half-Century Chronicle of Transformations in Hunter-
            Gatherer Life and Ecology. Balwyn: Trans Pacific Press.

TANAKA, J., AND K. SUGAWARA

1999 The /Gui and G//ana of Botswana. *In* The Cambridge Encyclopedia of Hunters and Gatherers. R. Lee and R. Daly, eds. Pp. 195–199. Cambridge: Cambridge University Press.

2010 An Encyclopedia of /Gui and//Gana Culture and Society. Kyoto: Laboratory of Cultural Anthropology, School of Human and Environmental Studies, Kyoto University.

TANNO, T.

1976 The Mbuti Net-Hunters in the Ituri Forest, Eastern Zaire: Their Hunting Activities and Band Composition. Kyoto University African Studies 10:101–135.

TANZANIA POPULATION AND HOUSING CENSUS

1978 Dar es Salaam: National Bureau of Statistics.

TAYLOR, J.

2006 Indigenous People in the West Kimberley Labour Market. CAEPR Working Paper, 35. Canberra: Centre for Aboriginal Economic Policy Research, Australian National University.

2008 Indigenous Labour Supply Constraints in the West Kimberley. CAEPR Working Paper, 39. Canberra: Centre for Aboriginal Economic Policy Research, Australian National University.

TAYLOR, N.

2011 The Origins of Hunting and Gathering in the Congo Basin: A Perspective on the Middle Stone Age Lupemban Industry. Before Farming 1:article 6. http://www.waspress.co.uk/journals/beforefarming/index/issue.php#20114, accessed June 2012.

TERASHIMA, H.

1983 Mota and Other Hunting Activities of the Mbuti Archers: A Socio-ecological Study of Subsistence Technology. African Study Monographs 3:71–85.

TERRA, G. J. A.

1964 The Significance of Leafy Vegetables, Especially of Cassava, in Tropical Nutrition. Tropical and Geographical Medicine 2:97–108.

TESTART, A.

1982 The Significance of Food Storage among Hunter-Gatherers: Residence Patterns, Population Densities, and Social Inequalities. Current Anthropology 23:523–537.

THOMAS, D. H.

2008 Native American Landscapes of St. Catherines Island, Georgia, vol. 1: The Theoretical Framework. Anthropological Papers, 88. New York: American Museum of Natural History.

THOMAS, D. S. G., AND P. A. SHAW

2010   The Kalahari Environment. Cambridge: Cambridge University Press.

THOMAS, E. M.

1959   The Harmless People. New York: Alfred A. Knopf.

2006   The Old Way: A Story of the First People. New York: Farrar, Straus, Giroux.

THOMSON, D. F.

1934   The Dugong Hunters of Cape York. Journal of the Royal Anthropological
         Institute of Great Britain and Ireland 64:237–263.

TISHKOFF, S. A., M. K. GONDER, B. M. HENN, H. MORTENSEN, N. FERNANDOPULLE,
C. GIGNOUX, G. LEMA, T. B. NYAMBO, P. A. UNDERHILL, U. RAMAKRISHNAN,
F. A. REED, AND J. L. MOUNTAIN

2007   History of Click-Speaking Populations of Africa Inferred from mtDNA
         and Y Chromosome Genetic Variation. Molecular Biology and Evolution
         24(10):2180–2195.

TISHKOFF, S. A., F. A. REED, F. R. FRIEDLAENDER, C. EHRET, A. RANCIARO,
A. FROMENT, J. B. HIRBO, A. A. AWOMOYI, J.-M. BODO, O. DOUMBO, M. IBRAHIM,
A. T. JUMA, M. J. KOTZE, G. LEMA, J. H. MOORE, H. MORTSENSEN, T. B. NYAMBO,
S. A. OMAR, K. POWELL, G. S. PRETORIUS, M. W. SMITH, M. A. THERE, C. WAMBEBE,
J. L. WEBER, AND S. M. WILLIAMS

2009   The Genetic Structure and History of Africans and African Americans.
         Science 324(5930):1035–1044.

TITMUSS, R. M.

1973   The Gift Relationship: From Human Blood to Social Policy. Harmonds-
         worth: Penguin.

TLOU, T., AND A. CAMPBELL

1997   History of Botswana. 2nd edition. Gaborone: Macmillan Botswana.

TOBIAS, P.

1956   On the Survival of the Bushmen, with an Estimate of the Problem Facing
         Anthropologists. Africa 26(2):175–186.

1957   Bushmen of the Kalahari. Man 47:33–40.

TONKINSON, M., AND R. TONKINSON

2010   The Cultural Dynamics of Adaptation in Remote Aboriginal Communities:
         Policy, Values and the State's Unmet Expectations. Anthropologica 52:67–75.

TONKINSON, R.

1974   The Jigalong Mob: Aboriginal Victors of the Desert Crusade. Menlo Park,
         CA: Cummings.

1988   Ideology and Domination in Aboriginal Australia: A Western Desert Test
         Case. *In* Hunters and Gatherers, vol. 2: Property, Power, and Ideology.
         T. Ingold, D. Riches, and J. Woodburn, eds. Pp. 150–164. New York: Berg.

1990 The Changing Status of Aboriginal Women: "Free Agents" at Jigalong. *In* Going It Alone: Prospectus for Aboriginal Autonomy. R. Tonkinson and M. Howard, eds. Pp. 125–147. Canberra: Aboriginal Studies Press.

1993 The Mardu Aborigines: Living the Dream in the Australian Desert. 2nd edition. New York: Holt, Rinehart, and Winston.

2007 From Dust to Ashes: The Challenges of Difference. Ethnos 72:509–534.

TUCKER, B.
2006 A Future Discounting Explanation for the Persistence of a Mixed Foraging-Horticulture Strategy among the Mikea of Madagascar. *In* Behavioral Ecology and the Transition to Agriculture. D. J. Kennett and B. Winterhalder, eds. Pp. 22–40. Berkeley: University of California Press.

TUCKER, B., M. TSIMITAMBY, F. HUMBER, S. BENBOW, AND T. IIDA
2010 Foraging for Development: A Comparison of Food Insecurity, Production, and Risk among Farmers, Forest Foragers, and Marine Foragers in Southwestern Madagascar. Human Organization 69:375–386.

TUCKER, B., AND A. G. YOUNG
2005 Growing Up Mikea: Children's Time Allocation and Tuber Foraging in Southwestern Madagascar. *In* Hunter-Gatherer Childhoods: Evolutionary Developments and Cultural Perspectives. B. S. Hewitt, ed. Pp. 147–171. New Brunswick, NJ: Aldine Transaction.

TURKE, P. W., AND L. L. BETZIG
1985 Those Who Can Do: Wealth, Status, and Reproductive Success on Ifaluk. Ethology and Sociobiology 6(2):79–87.

TURNBULL, C. M.
1965 Wayward Servants: The Two Worlds of the African Pygmies. New York: American Museum of Natural History.

VALIENTE-NOAILLES, C.
1993 The Kua: Life and Soul of the Central Kalahari Bushmen. Amsterdam: A. A. Balkema.

VALLEE, F.
1962 Kabloona and Eskimo in the Central Keewatin. NCRC-62–2. Ottawa: Department of Northern Affairs and National Resources.

VALLEE, F., D. SMITH, AND J. COOPER
1984 Contemporary Canadian Inuit. *In* Handbook of North American Indians, vol. 5: Arctic. D. Damas, ed. Pp. 662–675. Washington, DC: Smithsonian Institution.

VENABLES, W. N., AND B. D. RIPLEY
2002 Modern Applied Statistics with S. New York: Springer.

VERDU, P., F. AUSTERLITZ, A. ESTOUP, R. VITALIS, AND M. GEORGES ET AL.
2009   Origins and Genetic Diversity of Pygmy Hunter-Gatherers from Western
          Central Africa. Current Biology 19:312–318.

VETH, P. M., AND F. J. WALSH
1988   The Concept of "Staple" Plant Foods in the Western Desert Region of West-
          ern Australia. Australian Aboriginal Studies 2:19–25.

VINCENT, A. S.
1985   Plant Foods in Savanna Environments: A Preliminary Report of Tubers
          Eaten by the Hadza of Northern Tanzania. World Archaeology 17:131–148.

VOLAND, E.
1990   Differential Reproductive Success within the Krummhörn Population
          (Germany, 18th and 19th Centuries). Behavioral Ecology and Sociobiology
          26(1):65–72.

VON RUEDEN, C., M. GURVEN, AND H. KAPLAN
2008   The Multiple Dimensions of Male Social Status in an Amazonian Society.
          Evolution and Human Behavior 29(6):402–415.

2011   Why Do Men Seek Status? Fitness Payoffs to Dominance and Prestige. Pro-
          ceedings of the Royal Society B 278(1715):2223–2232.

WALSH, F.
1987   Patterns of Plant Use by Martujarra Aborigines. MS thesis, Department of
          Botany, University of Western Australia.

1990   An Ecological Study of the Traditional Aboriginal Use of "Country": Martu
          in the Great and Little Sandy Deserts, Western Australia. *In* Australian
          Ecosystems: 200 Years of Utilization, Degradation and Reconstruction.
          D. A. Saunders, A. J. M. Hopkins, and R. A. How, eds. Pp. 23–37. Proceedings
          of the Ecological Society of Australia, 16. Norton: Surrey Beatty and Sons.

2008   To Hunt and to Hold: Martu Aboriginal People's Uses and Knowledge of
          Their Country, with Implications for Co-management in Karlamilyi (Rudall
          River) National Park and the Great Sandy Desert, Western Australia. PhD
          dissertation, Department of Anthropology, School of Social and Cultural
          Studies, and Department of Ecology, School of Plant Biology, University of
          Western Australia.

WARD, R. E.
1999   Messengers of Love. Kearney, NE: Morris.

WATERS, M., N. ROSE, AND P. TODD
2009   The Economics of Polar Bear Trophy Hunting in Canada. Yarmouth Port,
          MS: International Fund for Animal Welfare; and Washington, DC: Humane
          Society International.

WENZEL, G. W.

1986   Subsistence, Cash and the Mixed Economy: Adaptation among Baffin Inuit. Discussion Paper Solicited by the Department of Economic Development and Tourism, Government of the Northwest Territories.

1991   Animal Rights, Human Rights: Ecology, Economy, and Ideology in the Canadian Arctic. Toronto: University of Toronto Press.

2000   Sharing, Money, and Modern Inuit Subsistence: Obligation and Reciprocity at Clyde River, Nunavut. *In* The Social Economy of Sharing: Resource Allocation and Modern Hunter-Gatherers. G. W. Wenzel, G. Hovelsrud-Broda, and N. Kishigami, eds. Pp. 61–85. Senri Ethnological Series, 53. Osaka: National Museum of Ethnology.

2001   "Nunamiut" or "Kabloonamiut": Which "Identity" Best Fits Inuit (And Does It Matter)? Études/Inuit/Studies 25(1–2):37–52.

2008a   Clyde Inuit Settlement and Community: From before Boas to Centralization. Arctic Anthropology 45(1):1–21.

2008b   Sometimes Hunting Can Seem Like Business: Polar Bear Sport Hunting in Nunavut. Edmonton: CCI Press.

2009   Inuit Settlement in the Clyde Area, Baffin Island, during "Contact–Exploration" Times (ca. 1820–1895). Études/Inuit/Studies 32(2):73–84.

WENZEL, G. W., J. DOLAN, AND C. BROWN

2010   A (Raw) Diachronic Look at Food Security in the Qikiqtaaluk Region of Nunavut. Paper presented at the 17th Inuit Studies Conference, Val d'Or.

WENZEL, G. W., G. HOVELSRUD-BRODA, AND N. KISHIGAMI

2000   Introduction: Social Economy of Modern Hunter-Gatherers; Traditional Subsistence, New Resources. *In* The Social Economy of Sharing: Resource Allocation and Modern Hunter-Gatherers. G. W. Wenzel, G. Hovelsrud-Broda, and N. Kishigami, eds. Pp. 1–6. Senri Ethnological Series, 53. Osaka: National Museum of Ethnology.

WENZEL, G. W., AND L.-A. WHITE

2000   Chaos and Irrationality: Money and Inuit Subsistence Practice. Paper presented at the 4th International Congress of Arctic Social Scientists, Quebec City.

WERNER, A.

1890   The African Pygmies. Popular Science Monthly 37:658–671.

WESTERBERG, L.-O., K. HOLMGREN, L. BÖRJESON, N. T. HÅKANSSON, V. LAULUMAA, M. RYNER, AND H. ÖBERG

2010   The Development of the Ancient Irrigation System at Engaruka, Northern Tanzania: Physical and Societal factors. Geographical Journal 175(4):304–318.

WESTERN AUSTRALIAN DEPARTMENT OF COMMERCE

2013   Fuelwatch Historical Prices. West Perth: Western Australian Department of
        Commerce.

WHITE, F.

1983   The Vegetation of Africa. Paris: UNESCO.

WHITE, L. A.

1959   The Evolution of Culture. New York: McGraw-Hill.

WIESSNER, P. W.

1982   Risk, Reciprocity and Social Influence in !Kung San Economics. *In* Politics
        and History in Band Societies. E. Leacock and R. B. Lee, eds. Pp. 61–84.
        Cambridge/Paris: Cambridge University Press/La Maison des Sciences de
        l'Homme.

1996   Leveling the Hunter: Constraints on the Status Quest in Foraging Societies.
        In Food and the Status Quest: An Interdisciplinary Perspective. P. Wiessner
        and W. Schiefenhovel, eds. Pp. 171–192. Providence, RI: Berghahn.

2002   Hunting, Healing, and Hxaro Exchange: A Long-Term Perspective on
        !Kung (Ju/'Hoansi) Large-Game Hunting. Evolution and Human Behavior
        23(6):407–436.

2003   Owners of the Future? Calories, Cash, Casualties, and Self-Sufficiency in
        the Nyae Nyae Area between 1996 and 2003. Visual Anthropology Review
        19(1–2):149–159.

2009   The Power of One? Big Men Revisited. *In* The Evolution of Leadership.
        K. J. Vaughn, J. W. Eerkens, and J. Kantner, eds. Pp. 195–222. Santa Fe, NM:
        SAR Press.

2014   Embers of Society: Firelight Talk among the Ju/'hoansi Bushmen. Proceed-
        ings of the National Academy of Sciences 111:14027–14035.

WILKIE, D. S., E. SHAW, E. ROTHBERG, G. MORELLI, AND P. AUZEL

2000   Roads, Development, and Conservation in the Congo Basin. Conservation
        Biology 14:1614–1622.

WILKIE, D. S., J. G. SIDLE, AND G. C. BOUNDZANGA

1992   Mechanized Logging, Market Hunting, and a Bank Loan in Congo. Conser-
        vation Biology 6:570–580.

WILKIE, D. S., M. STARKEY, K. ABERNATHY, E. N. EFFA, AND P. TELFER ET AL.

2005   Role of Prices and Wealth in Consumer Demand for Bushmeat in Gabon,
        Central Africa. Conservation Biology 19:268–274.

WILLS, W. H.

1995   Archaic Foraging and the Beginning of Food Production in the Ameri-
        can Southwest. *In* Last Hunters–First Farmers: New Perspectives in the

Prehistoric Transition to Agriculture. T. D. Price and A. B. Gebauer, eds. Pp. 215–242. Santa Fe, NM: SAR Press.

WILMSEN, E. N.

1983   The Ecology of Illusion: Anthropological Foraging in the Kalahari. Reviews in Anthropology 10:9–20.

1989   Land Filled with Flies: A Political Economy of the Kalahari. Chicago, IL: University of Chicago Press.

1997   The Kalahari Ethnographies (1896–1898) of Siegfried Passarge: Nineteenth-Century Khoisan- and Bantu-Speaking Peoples. Cologne: Rudiger Koppe Verlag.

WILSON, W. M., AND D. F. DUFOUR

2006   Ethnobotanical Evidence for Cultivar Selection among Tukanoans: Manioc (*Manihot esculenta* Crantz) in the Northwest Amazon. Culture and Agriculture 28:122–130.

WILTERMUTH, S. S., AND C. HEATH

2009   Synchrony and Cooperation. Psychological Science 20:1–5.

WILY, E.

1979   Official Policy towards San (Bushmen) Hunter-Gatherers in Modern Botswana: 1966–1978. Gaborone: National Institute of Development and Cultural Research.

WINTERHALDER, B., AND D. J. KENNETT

2006   Behavioral Ecology and the Transition from Hunting and Gathering to Agriculture. *In* Behavioral Ecology and the Transition to Agriculture. D. J. Kennett and B. Winterhalder, eds. Pp. 1–21. Berkeley: University of California Press.

2009   Four Neglected Concepts with a Role to Play in Explaining the Origins of Agriculture. Current Anthropology 50:645–648.

WINTERHALDER, B., AND E. A. SMITH

1992   Evolutionary Ecology and the Social Sciences. *In* Evolutionary Ecology and Human Behavior. E. A. Smith and B. Winterhalder, eds. Pp. 3–23. New York: Aldine de Gruyter.

2000   Analyzing Adaptive Strategies: Human Behavioral Ecology at 25. Evolutionary Anthropology 9:51–72.

WINTERHALDER, B., AND E. A. SMITH, EDS.

1981   Hunter-Gatherer Foraging Strategies: Ethnographic and Archaeological Analyses. Chicago, IL: University of Chicago Press.

WOOD, B. M., AND F. W. MARLOWE

2013   Household and Kin Provisioning by Hadza Men. Human Nature 24(3):208–317.

WOODBURN, J. C.

1968a   An Introduction to Hadza Ecology. *In* Man the Hunter. R. B. Lee and
         I. DeVore, eds. Pp. 49–55. Chicago, IL: Aldine.

1968b   Stability and Flexibility in Hadza Residential Groupings. *In* Man the Hunter.
         R. B. Lee and I. DeVore, eds. Pp. 103–110. Chicago, IL: Aldine.

1970   Hunters and Gatherers: The Material Culture of the Nomadic Hadza. Lon-
         don: British Museum.

1979   Minimal Politics: The Political Organization of the Hadza of North Tanzania.
         In Politics and Leadership: A Comparative Perspective. W. S. P. Cohen, ed.
         Pp. 244–266. Oxford: Clarendon Press.

1982   Egalitarian Societies. Man, n.s., 17(3):431–451.

1988   African Hunter-Gatherer Social Organisation: Is It Best Understood as a
         Product of Encapsulation? *In* Hunters and Gatherers: History, Evolution and
         Social Change, vol. 1. T. Ingold, D. Riches, and J. Woodburn, eds. Pp. 31–64.
         Oxford: Berg.

1997   Indigenous Discrimination: The Ideological Basis for Local Discrimina-
         tion against Hunter-Gatherer Minorities in Sub-Saharan Africa. Ethnic and
         Racial Studies 20(2):345–361.

1998   "Sharing is not a form of exchange": An Analysis of Property-Sharing in
         Immediate-Return Hunter-Gatherer Societies. *In* Property Relations: Renew-
         ing Anthropological Tradition. C. M. Hann, ed. Pp. 48–63. Cambridge: Cam-
         bridge University Press.

WORKMAN, J. L.

2009   Heart of Dryness: How the Last Bushmen Can Help Us Endure the Coming
         Age of Permanent Drought. New York: Walker.

WORMS, E. A.

1950   [Restricted Name of Mythical Being], the Creator: A Myth of the Bad (West
         Kimberley). Anthropos 45:641–658.

1952   [Restricted Name of Mythical Being] and His Relation to Other Culture
         Heroes. Anthropos 47:539–560.

WORMS, E. A., AND H. NEVERMANN

1986   Australian Aboriginal Religions. Kensington: Spectrum Publications for
         Nelen Yubu Missiological Unit.

YASUOKA, H.

2006a   Long-Term Foraging Expeditions (*Molongo*) among Baka Hunter-Gatherers
         in the Northwestern Congo Basin, with Special Reference to the "Wild Yam
         Question." Human Ecology 34:275–296.

2006b   The Sustainability of Duiker (*Cephalophus* spp.) Hunting for the Baka Hunter-Gatherers in Southeastern Cameroon. African Study Monographs, suppl., 33:95–120.

2009a   Concentrated Distribution of Wild Yam Patches: Historical Ecology and the Subsistence of African Rainforest Hunter-Gatherers. Human Ecology 37:577–587.

2009b   The Variety of Forest Vegetations in Southeastern Cameroon, with Special Reference to the Availability of Wild Yams for the Forest Hunter-Gatherers. African Study Monographs 30:89–119.

YELLEN, J. E.

1977   Archaeological Approaches to the Present: Models for Reconstructing the Past. New York: Academic Press.

ZAHAVI, A.

1977   The Cost of Honesty (Further Remarks on the Handicap Principle). Journal of Theoretical Biology 67(3):603–605.

ZEDER, M. A., AND B. D. SMITH

2009   A Conversation on Agricultural Origins: Talking Past Each Other in a Crowded Room. Current Anthropology 50:681–691.

ZENT, E. L., AND S. ZENT

2007   Los Jodï (Hotï). *In* Salud indígena en Venezuela, vol. 1. G. Freire and A. Tillet, eds. Pp. 77–130. Caracas: Ministerio del Poder Popular para la Salud, Editorial Arte.

2008   Los Jodï. *In* Los Aborígenes de Venezuela. M. A. Perera, ed. Pp. 499–570. Caracas: Ediciones IVIC, Monte Avila Editores, ICAS, Fundacíon La Salle.

Participants in the School for Advanced Research advanced seminar "21st-Century Hunting and Gathering: Foraging on a Transnational Landscape" co-chaired by Brian F. Codding and Karen L. Kramer, May 5–9, 2013. *Standing, from left*: Karen Lupo, James E. Coxworth, Rebecca Bliege Bird, Russell Greaves, George W. Wenzel, Nicholas Blurton Jones, and Karen L. Kramer. *Sitting, from left*: Richard B. Lee, Brian F. Codding, and Robert K. Hitchcock. Photograph by Jason S. Ordaz.

DOUGLAS W. BIRD
Department of Anthropology, Pennsylvania State University

REBECCA BLIEGE BIRD
Department of Anthropology, Pennsylvania State University

NICHOLAS BLURTON JONES
Department of Anthropology, University of California, Los Angeles

BRIAN F. CODDING
Department of Anthropology, University of Utah

JAMES E. COXWORTH
Department of Anthropology, University of Utah

RUSSELL D. GREAVES
Peabody Museum of Archaeology and Ethnology, Harvard University

K. HITCHCOCK
Department of Anthropology, University of New Mexico

KAREN L. KRAMER
Department of Anthropology, University of Utah

RICHARD B. LEE
Department of Anthropology, University of Toronto

KAREN D. LUPO
Department of Anthropology, Southern Methodist University

MARIA SAPIGNOLI
Department of Law and Anthropology, Max Planck Institute for
    Social Anthropology

GEORGE W. WENZEL
Department of Geography, McGill University

DAVID W. ZEANAH
Department of Anthropology, Sacramento State University

Additional Appendix Contributors

ADAM H. BOYETTE
Thompson Writing Project, Duke University

KIRK ENDICOT
Department of Anthropology, Dartmouth College

MAXIMILIEN GUEZE
Institut de Ciència i Tecnologia Ambientals, Universitat Autònoma
    de Barcelona

THOMAS N. HEADLAND
Department of Anthropology, SIL International

BARRY S. HEWLETT
Department of Anthropology, Washington State University Vancouver

KIM HILL
School of Human Evolution and Social Change, Arizona State University

THOMAS S. KRAFT
Department of Biological Sciences, Dartmouth College

LUCENTEZZA NAPITUPULU
Faculty of Economics, University of Indonesia–Depok

DAVE N. SCHMITT
SWCA Environmental Consultants

IVAN TACEY
Département d'Anthropologie, Université Lumière

BRAM TUCKER
Department of Anthropology, University of Georgia

VIVEK VENKATARAMAN
Department of Anthropology, Dartmouth College

POLLY WIESSNER
Department of Anthropology, University of Utah

BRIAN M. WOOD
Department of Anthropology, Yale University

Page numbers in italic text indicate illustrations.